SECURITY IN THE MIDDLE EAST

About the Book and Editors

This book examines the deep-seated problems in the Middle East and their impact on the United States and its allies. Exploring the disruptive effects of the double-edged sword of nationalism and modernization, the contributors discuss the full range of Western security interests in the region. Case studies of key countries emphasize the prospect for peaceful political, economic, and cultural change. The authors analyze the ramifications of the Arab-Israeli conflict and the threats posed by Soviet penetration. Arguing that confusion and contradiction mark U.S. policy in the Middle East, the book concludes that U.S. strategists should focus not on curing the region's internal problems but on coping with them without sacrificing long-term goals for quick fixes.

SAMUEL F. WELLS, JR., is associate director of the Woodrow Wilson International Center for Scholars. MARK A. BRUZONSKY is a political consultant in Washington, D.C.

Published in cooperation with

THE WILSON CENTER

SECURITY IN THE MIDDLE EAST

Regional Change and Great Power Strategies

EDITED BY

Samuel F. Wells, Jr., and Mark A. Bruzonsky

Westview Press / Boulder and London

Published in 1987 in the United States of America by Westview Press, Inc.; Frederick A. Praeger, Publisher; 5500 Central Avenue, Boulder, Colorado 80301

Library of Congress Cataloging-in-Publication Data
Security in the Middle East.
  Papers from Core Seminar meetings sponsored by
the International Security Studies Program of the
Woodrow Wilson International Center for Scholars,
1981–1983.
  Includes index.
  1. Near East—Politics and government—1945- .
2. Near East—Strategic aspects. I. Wells, Samuel F.
II. Bruzonsky, Mark A. III. Woodrow Wilson International
Center for Scholars. International Security Studies
Program. IV. Series.
DS63.1.S426 1987   327′.0956   86-28091
ISBN 0-8133-0121-1
ISBN 0-8133-0122-X (pbk)

Composition for this book originated with conversion of the editors' word-processor disks.

Printed and bound in the United States of America

6   5   4   3   2

Contents

Preface

This book originated in a core seminar on "Security in the Middle East and the Gulf" sponsored by the International Security Studies Program of the Woodrow Wilson International Center for Scholars in Washington, D.C. This series of fifteen meetings, held over two years in 1981–1983, was attended by a top-level group of scholars, policymakers, journalists, and businesspeople from the Middle East, Europe, and the United States. They directed their reactions and criticisms to a diverse series of papers, and much of the insight in the chapters in this book comes from the exchange of views in those meetings.

The route from the Core Seminar meetings to this book was not simple or direct. The war in Lebanon and the crises that it produced for Israel and its neighbors, the Palestine Liberation Organization, and the United States and its allies that participated in the Lebanese peacekeeping force caused more than one revision of many chapters and the replacement of some contributions by others. The book still reflects the original goal: to present a diverse range of quality analyses on the important problems of the Middle East for the Western industrial democracies and Japan.

The opinions and interpretations appearing in these chapters represent the views of the authors only; they do not reflect the positions of the Wilson Center or in many cases of the other authors or the editors. We hope that those who read this volume will find adequately represented the range of views expressed in debates on the Middle East and enough evidence to allow them to search further for information about the strengths and weaknesses of various positions.

This entire project is indebted to the generosity of the organizations that funded it. We are especially grateful to the trustees of the Robert Wood Johnson, Jr., Charitable Trust for their generous and enthusiastic support of this project throughout its evolution. We are also most appreciative of the support provided by Thomas Klutznick and the Urban Investment and Development Company of Chicago, which allowed us to bring additional important participants to the series from the Middle East.

The editors and the authors would like to acknowledge the invaluable assistance of numerous staff members at the Wilson Center. These include Robert Pollard, Scott Davis, Myra S. McKitrick, Robert Litwak, and Kathryn Babayan. Helen Loerke edited and typed the entire manuscript with care and good humor; Kuross Samii provided valuable insight and assistance in substantive revisions; Jane Mutnick valiantly assisted in the proofreading and correction process; and Susan Ballard served tirelessly and efficiently as the manuscript coordinator for the book.

We remain responsible for errors that appear in the final version despite our efforts to remain true to the contributors' texts.

Samuel F. Wells, Jr.
Mark A. Bruzonsky

Introduction

Samuel F. Wells, Jr.,
and Mark A. Bruzonsky

The course of Middle Eastern politics, although at times seemingly full of untamed and unpredictable twists and turns, still contains enduring themes and characteristics susceptible to incisive scholarly analysis and policy prescription. But to make these themes understandable a scholar requires both dispassionate courage to confront the uncomfortable historical evidence and awareness of contemporary issues reflecting the anguish and the frenzy of Middle Eastern societies, their internal political dynamics, and their often confrontational relationship with the West, particularly with the United States. This approach, although difficult to develop, is necessary for a correct reading of the angry division often separating the Middle Eastern countries from each other and from the major powers.

The single most pervasive and increasingly important theme of Middle Eastern politics is the role of nationalism. During the early modern era, the emergence of national consciousness among Arabs, Persians, and Turks shattered the delusion of the supremacy of a common religion over cultural peculiarities and later paved the way for the birth of modern nation states capable of managing parochial loyalties and allowing a measure of control over the disillusioned Islamic communities. At the opening of the sixteenth century, the Persians turned Islam—the ideology of the Arab conquerors of Iran and the symbol of legitimacy of Ottoman rulers—against the idea of an ecumenical Islamic community by adopting the Shi'i creed as the official religion and thus declaring their independence from the Islamic empire. The Arabs, on the other hand, gradually succeeded in making the Arabic language and loosely related cultural traditions the tools by which to thwart vestiges of Turkish domination. After the dismantlement of the Ottoman Empire, nationalism released a potent mass of ambitions and initiatives that created the type of turbulent politics still characteristic of the region.

Although the exact dates of the appearance of nationalism on the world stage and its emergence in the Middle East remain contested issues, scholars

1

generally agree that the modern concept of nationalism—a phenomenon of mass politics shaping nation states—is the byproduct of the European struggle for emancipation and equality. According to this view, the French Revolution marked the beginning of the nationalist era and provided operative ideas that were later exported as the European sphere of domination expanded.[1] What subsequently became known as the period of European imperialism witnessed the transfusion of Western ideas and institutions into alien cultures either by direct control, such as that of Great Britain over India, or by proxy, such as that transmitted by the Western-educated elite of emerging societies. Whatever the method, a profound irony accompanied the experience. As one of the leading specialists on Western imperialism noted: "In transmitting to the rest of the world what it has evolved for itself, the West loosed the same forces as those which had engineered its own transformation."[2]

For the Middle East, the confrontation with the West was inspired as much by the infusion of Western ideology as by the bitter memory of European physical encroachment in the region. Many European nations, led by France, Britain, and Russia, had exerted their influence at various times and in various parts of the Middle East. The most enduring intervention stemmed from the Anglo-Russian imperial rivalry that began in the second half of the eighteenth century and evolved into a fixture of Middle Eastern politics by the end of the nineteenth century. During this period, while the British pursued imperial interests in India, Iran, and Afghanistan and around the Gulf, the Russians in their wars with Iran managed to annex large territories, including Georgia, Baku, Daghestan, Erivan, and Nukhichevan. In fact, countries such as Iran and Afghanistan were allowed to retain a precarious independence because, as a specialist on the region declared, "Iran and Afghanistan occupied a geographical belt at which the dynamics of Russian expansion and British expansion met. Neither Britain nor Russia could have gained and solidified control there without risking a major war."[3]

The result of subsequent European encroachment in the Middle East was no less dramatic. When carving out and controlling their respective domains, the European powers often imposed arbitrary borders, divided communities, and collaborated with local rulers to create new countries. Whereas the French shaped the division of power among the religious factions in Lebanon, the British helped to set up the modern states of Jordan, Iraq, Saudi Arabia, and Kuwait and to effect the mandate over Palestine that finally led to the establishment of the state of Israel. Such European activities, accompanied by continual and often daily intrusion in the politics of that region, left a legacy of distrust that invariably shaped the political consciousness of Middle Eastern societies and later emerged as an inseparable part of their political culture. Against this background, it is understandable why the eruption of nationalism in the Muslim Middle East almost inevitably carried an anticolonial and anti-European component.

As they moved out of their obscurity and complacency, societies of the Middle East began to view nationalism as the most reliable instrument by which to confront not only foreign powers but also their own incompetent and corrupt rulers. Consequently, centuries-old ethnic, tribal, linguistic, and religious loyalties and identifications began to compete with the newly defined state nationalism. The subordination of parochial loyalties to an abstract notion of the common good of the state was not without its perils; yet no matter how painful the adjustment, diverse groups viewed it as useful because it promised a new point on which to focus their feelings of indignity and injured pride. In a political sense, nationalism served as a medium through which to express an accumulated anger toward the existing order. To the extent that foreign powers were perceived as responsible for this order, they became the targets of an ambivalent, and at times incoherent, admixture of rage and self-assertion.

But the anticolonial or the anti-European component of nationalism in the Middle East should not be equated with either an indiscriminate xenophobia or with the emergence of anti-U.S. sentiments in that region.[4] To invoke the term *xenophobia* (hatred and fear of foreigners) to describe the political culture of Middle Eastern societies is not only incorrect but tends to remove the historical responsibility of foreign powers that exploited the internal divisions and the mediocre leadership of those countries. As the experiences of many emerging nations indicate, the search for legal as well as economic independence placed them at odds with the colonialism of the past and with the policy they subsequently viewed as modern imperialism. Nevertheless, as a recent work demonstrated, "while some of the emerging nations may harbor Anglophobia, Russophobia, Francophobia, anti-Americanism, or any combination of the above, they certainly do not suffer from a case of undifferentiated and indiscriminate xenophobia."[5]

The evidence of history does not support the familiar contention that the confrontation between Middle Eastern societies and European powers developed from a mysterious anti-Western sentiment, which, by definition, implicates the United States. Throughout the nineteenth and much of the twentieth centuries, the United States was viewed by the people of the Middle East as a new force that could redress global injustice. The traditional U.S. anticolonial posture, coupled with the tendency of the country's leaders to express foreign policy through a set of moral principles, had sent a message of hope to subjugated peoples around the world. The nobility of expressed U.S. ideals and the craving for hope had carved a savior image for the United States and had prompted the countries of the Middle East to invite American involvement to counter the pressure of European power politics.[6]

That the United States generally chose to ignore such invitations during the nineteenth and early twentieth centuries reflected its isolationist approach, which stemmed from geographical detachment and a sense of self-sufficiency and relative security. The prevailing mood in the United States was perhaps best expressed by Henry Adams in 1906: "The Secretary of State exists only to recognize the existence of a world which Congress would rather ignore."[7]

But despite America's distance and disinterestedness, some individuals such as Alfred Thayer Mahan and Theodore Roosevelt possessed political horizons large enough to comprehend that the changing international environment would create new economic and security concerns for the United States. As early as 1902, Captain Alfred Thayer Mahan showed unusual foresight in stating that, "The question of the Persian Gulf, and of South Persia in connection with it, though not yet immediately urgent, is clearly visible upon the horizon of the distant future."[8] With regard to the security requirements of the area, Mahan wrote: "Unhappily, the powers that border the Persian Gulf, Persia itself, Turkey, and some minor Arabian communities, are unable to give either the commercial or the military security that the situation will require."[9]

The fulfillment of Mahan's prophecy notwithstanding, his generation could not anticipate in 1902 that the two forthcoming global wars would dramatically transform the U.S. role in the world. They could not foresee that these conflicts would inextricably involve the United States in the affairs of the Old World, that a Communist revolution would sweep Russia, that the traditional Anglo-Russian imperial rivalry in the Middle East would be replaced by a Soviet-U.S. struggle for power, and that what Mahan called "minor Arabian communities" would evolve into modern nation states often pitted against each other, against other Muslim states, and against a Jewish state created in Palestine. All these developments awaited U.S. policymakers in the post–World War II era.

An Expanded U.S. Role

Active U.S. government involvement in the Middle East began as a result of World War II. American troops were sent to Iran to establish the Persian Gulf Command in 1943, making Iran the principal southern supply route to help Russia's war effort against the Axis forces. As the war drew to an end, the United States began to envision its role as an impartial guarantor of the new international order. But the ensuing rivalry with the Soviet Union persuaded American leaders to take an even more active world role. They responded to the Soviet challenge by expanding the reach, commitments, and global responsibilities of the United States. This reaction set the stage for gradual yet accelerating U.S. involvement in the politics of the Middle East.

The northern tier—Iran, Turkey, Greece—became an early battleground of the cold war.[10] In President Harry S Truman's words, "The first crisis came in 1945 and 1946, when the Soviet Union refused to honor its agreement to remove its troops from Iran. . . . So we took our stand. We made it clear to the Soviet Union that we expected them to honor their agreement and the Soviet troops were withdrawn."[11] Truman's stand against Stalin in 1946 and the application of containment to Greece and Turkey in the Truman Doctrine of 1947 became the operating axiom of U.S. foreign policy everywhere.

With the establishment of Israel in 1948 and the development of American petroleum interests in Saudi Arabia, the Middle East assumed an important role in U.S. strategic planning, second only to the commitment to defend Western Europe. By the early 1950s, Washington's concern with the Middle East was fully reflected in statements such as the recommendation in a National Security Council (NSC) study that "the United States should make its interests in the area of the Middle East and South Asia more explicit." The authors of the document also asserted that "it should be recognized that diminished British power will require the United States to assume an increasing responsibility in the area."[12]

Without fully appreciating the magnitude of the task, American leaders accepted not only the responsibility of protecting the Middle East against Soviet aggression but also the obligation to help develop solutions to problems created by years of European imperialism. Further complicating the situation was the fact that U.S. proclamations concerning the Middle East reasserted the Wilsonian objectives of self-determination and liberation from the social ills of the Old World. The projection of this image of the future, while enhancing the prestige of the United States, overlooked the frequent conflict between American ideals and perceived self-interest and produced exalted but unrealistic expectations.[13] Hopes of this type prompted Mohammed Musaddiq of Iran to ignore Anglo-American cultural affinities and seek U.S. assistance against the British.[14] Similar expectations encouraged Gamal Abdel Nasser of Egypt and other Arab nationalists to request U.S. aid in the struggle against Israel. The failure of American policies to achieve the goals set forth in pledges and rhetoric helped to sow seeds of discontent with the United States and fostered a critical and unflattering perception of America's role in the Middle East.

Despite disappointment at the perceived American failure to play a more noble role, most nationalist groups in the Middle East still sought assistance from the United States to drag their crippled societies into the twentieth century. If the United States could not be the expected savior, it might yet be the purveyor of progress, reasoned the nationalists who succeeded Musaddiq and Nasser. This approach was in line with the general behavior of Third World societies as described by Rupert Emerson:

> If the first reaction of the peoples on whom the West imposed itself was generally a xenophobic defense of the existing order, the next phase was likely to be a swing in the direction of an uncritical self-humiliation and acceptance of alien superiority. The third phase, in the fashion of Hegelian dialect, was a nationalist synthesis in which there was an assertion or reassertion of a community with pride in itself and in its past but still looking, at least as far as its leaders were concerned, in the direction of Westernization and modernization. Those leaders were, almost without exception, men who had achieved substantial acquaintance with the West.[15]

Although this description contains a core of truth, it is far too optimistic in projecting a nationalist synthesis that could blend modernization and cultural peculiarities of the Third World nations. At least in the case of the Muslim Middle East, there has never been any sustained indication of such synthesis. The experience in Iran proved the contrary, and the verdict on the rest of the region must await the test of time. Iran's current experiment in rejecting the established international system and attempting to travel to a distant past will have as much to say about the eventual outcome as do the efforts of other Middle Eastern countries to abandon traditions and seek modernity and acceptance from the outside world.

"Undoubtedly the most disruptive force in the Middle East and especially in the Gulf region is modernization," writes Shahram Chubin in Chapter 13. "Constituting a multiple challenge that requires often contradictory responses, it is intrinsically destabilizing and immune to fine-tuning. The simultaneity of its demands and the disorientation it wreaks politically, socially, economically, culturally, and psychologically are nowhere identical and never entirely predictable."[16] The development needs, which invite the influence of the encircling civilization, are indispensable to and, ironically, also inimical to the survival of the Middle Eastern régimes. The complexities of modernization, coupled with the ambivalence of local nationalism, could indeed lead to frustration and failure for both the superpowers and their clients. As demonstrated by the U.S. experience in Iran, even for countries with the best of intentions, rapid modernization encouraged by an outside power can interact with nationalist sentiments to produce a range of undesirable consequences beyond the control of the participants.

In attempting to promote modernization in the Middle East, while preventing any expansion of Soviet influence, U.S. strategists have pursued a variety of options to bridge the gap between vastly expanded national interests and finite power to protect them. Since World War II, these options have included (1) the Truman Doctrine, (2) the Eisenhower-Dulles policy of promoting regional security treaties, (3) John F. Kennedy's push for economic and political reforms, (4) the Nixon-Kissinger reliance on regional powers, (5) Jimmy Carter's promise of human rights, and (6) Ronald Reagan's reliance on the threat of force to stabilize the Middle East. The common thread that binds these options together is the ever-present concern with the Soviet threat. All these options are in fact strategies of containment intended to limit Soviet aggression. Because the United States also sought to support the interests of its friends and allies in the Middle East, it has applied these declared policies spasmodically and at best incompletely.

Among the factors that exacerbate the problem are the confusion and contradiction that exist among American interests in the Middle East. Indeed, within the policymaking establishment, the definition of American interests has been the subject of intense debate. Too often conducted in an atmosphere lacking both calmness and clarity, these debates have revealed an inability to establish priorities among conflicting foreign policy interests and a refusal to coordinate international commitments and domestic political needs. Against this tradition, the definition of American interests put forward at the start of the Reagan administration by Richard Burt, director of the

State Department's Bureau of Politico-Military Affairs, was unusually clear. Before a House subcommittee meeting on March 23, 1981, Burt identified four basic interests:

- Demonstrate the ability to counter the influence of the Soviets and their allies.
- Ensure continued Western access to the oil of the Gulf in adequate quantities and at a reasonable price.
- Ensure the continued existence and strength of U.S. friends in the region.
- Continue to work toward peace between Israel and its neighbors.

Burt also explained that the administration viewed the Middle East, including the Gulf region, "as part of a larger politico-strategic theater, the region bounded by Turkey, Pakistan, and the Horn of Africa." The principal obstacle toward peace in the region, he suggested, lay in the insecurity of Middle Eastern countries. "Only when local states feel confident of U.S. reliability and secure against Soviet threats," Burt concluded, "will they be willing to take the necessary risks for peace."[17]

To achieve this goal, the Reagan administration sought to establish a strategic consensus with certain countries of the region including Pakistan, Turkey, Saudi Arabia, Egypt, and Israel. Although this strategy allowed the Reagan administration to place U.S. commitments in the region in the context of East-West conflict, it ignored the fact that intensified pressure for alignment increases the insecurity of local states plagued by internal divisions and mindful of being perceived as pawns in U.S.-Soviet power play. Robert G. Neumann, former U.S. ambassador to Afghanistan, Morocco, and Saudi Arabia who was dismissed from the last post by Secretary of State Alexander Haig, addressed the issue with uncommon candor: "The trouble with a strategic conception as a guide for policies is that you look at a region as a piece of territory and you forget there are people living on that territory, and if those people do not share your perception, what good is it?"[18]

The most serious divergence between U.S. and Arab policies is the nature of U.S. support for Israel. Arab nations view the United States as an accomplice in the shifts of Israeli policies—from wanting certain security advantages on the West Bank, to accepting a few settlements in the occupied territories, and, finally, to claiming the territories as part of historic Israel. Even less comforting to Arab states is the perception that the Israeli lobby in Washington can persuade the U.S. Congress to grant massive military and economic aid to Israel, at times in amounts that exceed those requested by the government in Jerusalem. Beyond occasional references to the demands of domestic politics, U.S. policymakers have never seriously addressed this fundamental contradiction in Washington's policy for the region.[19]

Whatever the logic of American policy toward Israel, the negative attitudes created in the Arab world militate against building a coalition of moderate

Arab states responsive to U.S. interests. To Arab countries, America's unqualified support for Israel affords opportunity for local elements to destabilize pro-Western régimes and allows the Soviets to justify their intrusions into the region under the pretext of helping the Arabs against Israel.

A related concern is the fate of the Palestinians. Although not the most salient issue for any Arab country, the Palestinian problem serves as a test of American willingness to be responsive to Arab needs. Unfortunately, the pattern of recent American involvement in this question—initiating peace plans and then ignoring them, as in the case of the Camp David accords—has reduced America's capacity to function as a catalyst for peace and stability. Because the United States is the only nation capable of influencing Israeli policies, the reduction of America's credibility can only prolong the vicious circle of violence in the Middle East. For the Palestinians, the latest humiliation of the PLO in the aftermath of the Israeli invasion of Lebanon only increases the feeling of impotence and helplessness that has often erupted in terrorist acts. For many Arabs the Reagan administration's close ties with Israel through the war in Lebanon and more recently in the covert supply of arms to Iran make official U.S. pronouncements supporting the Arab-Israeli peace process appear increasingly hollow.

No less unsettling is the growing divergence between U.S. and European perceptions. Differences in outlook between Western Europe and the United States go beyond the East-West conflict and evolve from a web of factors including the Arab-Israeli conflict, interpretation of energy policy, and concern with the internal developments of Middle Eastern countries. Whereas U.S. administrations have tended to view the supply of petroleum, the Arab-Israeli problem, and the Iran-Iraq war as separate issues, the Europeans have been inclined to see links among them and even to argue that the resolution of one problem would help reduce the danger posed by others.

That the Atlantic Alliance does not have a common policy toward the Middle East is also reflected in the competition for commerce and the share of petrodollars invested in the financial institutions of the West. For Great Britain, which became self-sufficient in oil in 1981, the issue remains access to Middle East markets for its exports. Both Labour and Conservative governments in the United Kingdom have followed a remarkably uniform policy in this regard. Unlike the British, the German government—both Social Democrats and Christian Democrats—although seeking trade with Middle East countries, have avoided direct involvement such as sending peacekeeping troops to Lebanon. The picture for France, however, is somewhat different. Having strongly supported Israel until the early 1960s, the French government then began to favor Arab countries and establish friendly ties with oil-producing nations. But in recent years, François Mitterrand appears to have found a delicate balance among France's competing interests by showing willingness to cooperate with Israel, trying to keep the Arabs happy by selling them massive French armaments and buying oil in return, and protecting Western interests by sending troops to Lebanon in cooperation with the United States and Italy.

Generally speaking, the Europeans as well as the Japanese have failed to respond decisively or uniformly with regard to the Middle East. When threatened with the possibility of oil shortage, they tried to strike separate deals with oil producers. These moves were made both in the aftermath of the Arab oil embargo of 1973 and during the 1979–1980 oil crisis caused by the Iranian revolution. The same pattern of separate but indecisive response was displayed on the occasion of the Soviet invasion of Afghanistan. Such behavior by the Europeans and the Japanese is largely explained by their views that U.S. policy in the Middle East is too closely linked to the interests of Israel, is molded in classical cold war terms, and thus is inadequate to protect their interests.

Without dismissing the importance of containment or discounting its success in limiting Soviet advances, we should point out that, unlike the late 1940s, competitive power projection against the Soviet Union is no longer sufficient to protect the interests of the United States and its allies in the Middle East. This new situation dates from the Soviet achievement of nuclear parity in 1970 and acquires additional dimensions after 1973 when the rise in the price of petroleum elevated the purchasing power of many Middle Eastern countries and enabled them to develop significant indigenous military capabilities. Yet the consequences of such military power in the Middle East, and for that matter in the Third World, need not be regarded as a zero-sum loss for the United States. On the contrary, as Robert Paarlberg recently argued: "As indigenous Third World capabilities continue to grow, the projection of Soviet power will also meet frustrations. Moreover, the capacity of the Soviet Union to adjust to Third World change may prove to be less than that of the U.S. If this is the case, then the U.S. should welcome the growth of indigenous Third World capabilities with greater strategic self-confidence."[20]

On balance, the long-term interests of the United States and its allies in the Middle East are threatened at least as much by Soviet penetration of that region as they are by the local rulers who often do not represent much beyond their own personal and class interests and who often present the United States as an accomplice in their oppressive internal policies. The origins of the Islamic revolution in Iran reveal a clear recent manifestation of this danger to future U.S. involvement in this region. Iran is also a prime example of a case in which, in the absence of a legitimate government, neither the promise of superpower intervention nor access to modern armament could abate the power of social and ideological dynamics. These very same forces, although not always clearly visible, are present in other parts of the Middle East and are capable of changing the political map of that region. The crucial task of American strategists lies not so much in finding a cure for the internal problems of the Middle East as in seeking to cope with them in ways that will not sacrifice long-term interests for short-term, marginal gains.

Furthermore, the Arab-Israeli conflict has entered an ominous phase. Behind all the discussion of the wisdom of the U.S. and Israel cooperating to sell arms to Iran, a major arms race is taking place and preparations for war are increasing between Israel and Syria. The siege of Beirut in 1982 and more recently the Iran-Iraq war have shown the tremendous destructive power of modern artillery shells and missiles against residential areas as well as the massive injuries inflicted by chemical weapons. The potential is increasing for a major war in the Middle East that could involve the United States and the Soviet Union.[21] The need for a serious and carefully prepared American initiative to resolve the Arab-Israeli conflict has never been greater.

Finally, the fundamental factors explaining the expansion of U.S. security interests in the Middle East are so rooted in the American ethos and so dependent on elemental international developments that they seem like forces of nature that can only be accommodated, not controlled. Given this situation, the dangers of insolvency that arise from the imbalance between interests and power can only be reduced, as suggested by former Ambassador Philip Habib, if the United States places itself on the side of justice, stability, and peace.[22] Above all, designing an appropriate American response to the needs of Middle Eastern societies would be the closest thing to a workable grand strategy. Although the needs of those societies may appear shrouded in mystery, they still bear a marked resemblance to those observed by a U.S. statesman during a visit to that region in 1942: "They need more education. They need more public health work. They need more modern industry, and they need more of the social dignity and self-confidence which come from freedom and self-rule."[23] A major sustained U.S. effort to help Middle East societies develop and mature, coupled with renewed efforts to achieve Arab-Israeli peace, would go a long way toward bringing lasting security to the region.

Notes

1. For analysis of the role of European ideas in influencing nationalist movements, see Rupert Emerson, *From Empire to Nation: The Rise to Self-Assertion of Asian and African Peoples* (Boston: Beacon Press, 1960); also Richard Cottam, *Nationalism in Iran* (Pittsburgh: University of Pittsburgh Press, 1964).

2. Emerson, *From Empire to Nation*, p. 17.

3. Cottam, *Nationalism in Iran*, p. 158.

4. These themes are addressed in the work of Kuross A. Samii, "Involvement by Invitation: The American Experience in Iran" (Ph.D. dissertation, School of Advanced International Studies, Johns Hopkins University, 1984).

5. *Ibid.*, p. 45.

6. This was particularly true of the Persian monarchs during the nineteenth century, *ibid.*, p. 55.

7. Henry Adams, as cited by Eric F. Goldman in *The Crucial Decade and After: America, 1945–1960* (New York: Knopf, 1960), p. 124.

8. Alfred Thayer Mahan, "The Persian Gulf and International Relations," *National Review* 40 (September 1902), p. 37.

9. *Ibid.*, p. 32.

10. For a review of American policies, see Bruce Robellet Kuniholm, *The Origins of the Cold War in the Near East: Great Power Conflict and Diplomacy in Iran, Turkey, and Greece* (Princeton, N.J.: Princeton University Press, 1980).

11. President Truman's Farewell Address, January 15, 1953, *Department of State Bulletin* 28 (January 26, 1953), p. 127.

12. National Security Council, 141, June 19, 1953, Record Group 273, National Archives, Washington, D.C.

13. For scholarly analysis of this theme, see Robert E. Osgood, *Ideals and Self-Interest in America's Foreign Relations* (Chicago: University of Chicago Press, 1953).

14. Samii, "Involvement by Invitation," pp. 213–220.

15. Emerson, *From Empire to Nation*, pp. 10–11.

16. Shahram Chubin, "Soviet Policy in the Middle East," see Chapter 13 of this book.

17. Reported in *The Middle East*, fifth edition (Washington, D.C.: Congressional Quarterly, 1981), pp. 6–7.

18. *Ibid.*

19. For a description of the influence of the Jewish and Israeli lobbies, refer to Paul Findley, *They Dare To Speak Out: People and Institutions Confront Israel's Lobby* (Westport, Conn.: Lawrence Hill, 1985).

20. Robert L. Paarlberg, "A More Capable Third World: Consequences for U.S. Security Policy," paper presented at the Wilson Center, June 19, 1985.

21. Among numerous reports on these events and their implications, see Stephen Green, "Going 'MAD' in the Middle East," *The Nation* 243 (September 27, 1986), p. 1.

22. Speech by Philip Habib, delivered at American Enterprise Institute, Washington, D.C., November 15, 1984.

23. Statement by Wendell L. Willkie, cited by Kurt Grunwald and Joachim Ronall, *Industrialization in the Middle East* (New York: Council for Middle Eastern Affairs Press, 1960), p. 5.

PART ONE

Stability and Change
Within the Region

1

Syria

John F. Devlin

To assess Syria in the late 1980s is to seek answers to some very fundamental questions about a country that recently celebrated its fortieth birthday. Is the country settling down to institutionalize the changes that revolutionary developments have fostered over the past quarter century? Or, are antirégime forces developing strength sufficient to halt Syria's revolution or markedly alter its course? How do opinion leaders and policymakers see themselves and their state—as members of a particular community, as citizens of the Syrian Republic, as belonging to a larger "geographic" Syria, as advocates of Pan-Arabism?

These questions are posed against a background of lengthy continuity of administration and policy. Hafiz al-Asad has led Syria since November 1970; the Baath party regionalists have dominated it since 1966; the party has controlled since 1963. All three terms represent record tenures in modern Syrian history. The years of Baath dominance are the culmination of a process initiated when Syria emerged from French mandate into full independence in 1946.

A change in the governance of Syria would have complex implications for domestic politics and for the country's external relations. So would a drawn-out struggle for power. So would the continuation of Asad's régime. Because Syria is a pivotal state, able to affect events outside its borders, developments respecting it will affect U.S. policies and interests in the area.

Régime and System

Hafiz al-Asad's régime and the governmental system of the Syrian Arab Republic are not identical, but they have become very closely intertwined. Not only is Asad's approach a product of the Baathist ideology as it spread in the 1940s and 1950s within the Arab world, but he and his associates, past and current, have reshaped that ideology. Syria of the 1970s and early 1980s has been a very different country from the one that made "the Syrian coup d'état" a byword in Arab politics of the 1950s. Of the factors that brought about the changes, five are most significant:

1. Transformation of the Baath party from one in which Arab unity was a primary goal to one dominated by regionalists whose political terrain is essentially Syria and its immediate neighbors. This transformation stemmed from the failure of Syria's experiment in unity with Egypt (the United Arab Republic of 1958–1961) and the consequent discrediting of the party's founders.

2. Destruction of the political and economic primacy of the city-based, Sunni Muslim families.

3. Emergence at the top of the power structure of party militants from small towns and villages; a disproportionate number came from the Alawi and Druze minorities, although the Sunni majority (70 per cent of the population) was well represented.

4. Control of the Baath party in Syria by military officers, a circumstance that dates from the February 23, 1966, coup that ousted the party's founders.

5. A preponderance of Alawis in the key military and security posts.

It would be a mistake to view Syria as a country in which every post of importance is filled by a soldier, in uniform or out, and an Alawi at that. The situation is much more complex. There is no question that Asad's position rests on his control of the armed forces and their support for him. Nor is there any question that Alawis are a key element in those forces. But the country is administered by a combination of civilian bureaucracy, party structure, and associated mass or people's organizations. These apparatuses broadly reflect the ethnic makeup of the country. In addition to the president and the prime minister, important members of the government, such as Vice President Abd al-Halim Khaddam,[1] Defense Minister Mustafa Talas, and Interior Minister Nasir al-Din Nasir, are members of the regional command of the party. (In Baath parlance, each Arab state is a region; the whole Arab world is the nation.) The majority of the members of that body are neither military nor Alawi;[2] the same is true for the cabinet. In the thirteen provinces, important local officials are also members of the provincial (branch) commands of the party. All play parts in running the country.

Syria is a one-party state. Although three left-of-center political groups are associated with it in a National Progressive front, the Baath party dominates all aspects of government. Hafiz al-Asad controls the party. The system is cumbersome and bureaucratic; sometimes the lines of authority duplicate or conflict. However, many Syrians are involved in the political process, and they have a large stake in the system. The local party secretary in a town, for example, can use party, government bureaucracy, or other channels to get services for constituents.[3] The choice of channel may be dictated or influenced by the secretary's own profession and/or family connections and by circumstances. In matters relating to agriculture, for example, the Peasants' Union has the top position. This union dominates agricultural policy, and, in practice if not in theory, the Ministry of Agriculture and Agricultural Reform is subordinate to it.[4] Other domestic ministries have the stronger hand in their areas of concern.

During the 1960s and 1970s, Syrians built a contemporary, centralized form of administration, with industry, communications, education, and most other spheres of activity directed from the capital. Damascus—where all the party, administrative, and mass organizations are headquartered—has outclassed its centuries-old rival city, Aleppo, and has reduced it to the status of a provincial capital. In all this modernity, family and patron-client relationships remain important and indeed are vital to the business of ruling. However, the day-to-day tasks required for the functioning of an increasingly complex economy are falling more and more into the hands of technicians who have education and abilities suited to their professional responsibilities.

During the same period Syria's leaders transformed the country's economy. As in most developing nations, the change is very apparent in the relative positions of the rural and urban populations. Thirty per cent of Syria's 2.5 million people lived in urban areas in 1940; about half of the present population of nine million lives there today. Agriculture accounted for 40 per cent of gross domestic product (GDP) in the early 1950s, but its share has declined to a little more than 15 per cent today. Agriculture is, however, the stronghold of the private sector in a socialist state. When Hafiz al-Asad took power in 1970, he stopped a trend toward collectivized agriculture that his more doctrinaire predecessors had fostered. The few remaining state farms are primarily agricultural research stations; four-fifths of the land under cultivation is either privately owned or leased by individuals from the state.

The agricultural sector is not without problems. Efforts to expand the area under irrigation, for example, are hampered by cost and increasing soil salinity. Basic crops remain at the mercy of the weather, with grain production showing differences of over a million tons from one year to the next (e.g., from 0.6 million in 1973 to 1.6 million in 1974). But the rural half of the population has benefited from two decades of development not only through direct agricultural improvements but also through such amenities as schools, electrification, and roads. Syrian farmers are today much more dependent upon the state, which tells them what to plant and sets prices for their crops, but they live far better than they did only twenty years ago. The rural population is an asset to the régime, which represents their interests more than any previous government has. Big city pashas do not run their affairs; people from their own countryside do.

In the first five Five Year Plans since 1960, Syria worked to create an infrastructure and build factories that would permit it to become more independent of foreign sources for manufactured goods. Rather poorly endowed with natural resources, and a small country to boot, there has never been any chance that Syria could become self-sufficient. Although each plan has fallen well short of target, much has been accomplished. Syria has built major irrigation and electric power projects, and the country manufactures a variety of consumer goods from underwear to television sets. In its industrial and especially in its service sectors, it is providing employment for a significant portion of the growing work force—the result of a better than 3 per cent a year population growth rate.

Although Syria experienced inflation well into double digits during the second half of the 1970s, it has also managed to keep its economy growing. This development is partly the result of substantial financial aid provided by oil-rich Arab states according to decisions of the Arab summit conferences of 1974 (Rabat) and 1978 (Baghdad). Donors have held up payments at times for political reasons, and by 1983 Syria was receiving less than half the annual $1.8 billion agreed to at the Baghdad summit. But the sums have kept Syria's balance of payments deficits within bounds, and in 1984 Syria continued to produce more oil than it consumed. This condition may soon be reversed, however, because the economic growth requires more oil each year. Late in the 1980s, unless some new fields are found and put into production, Syria will become a net oil importer. The nation will also be consuming all the electricity it can produce from hydropower; hence it is already studying the use of thermal power plants.

The large military establishment that Syria maintains is a burden on the economy. Budgeted expenditures for national security have grown steadily from about $2 billion in 1980 toward $3 billion in the mid-1980s, over half the ordinary budget.[5] Since 1982 a Syrian military build-up has continued with Syrian leaders publicly acknowledging that their goal is strategic parity with Israel. The military services tie up a substantial percentage of the labor force, about 12 per cent in the mid-1970s. The percentage was less in the early 1980s, as the persons in armed forces for several years stabilized at about 225,000, whereas the population and work force continued to grow. In economic terms, the military establishment takes much from and contributes little to the state's economic well-being. But in this regard, Syria is no different than many countries; security must come first.

Elements of Opposition

The changes in Syria since 1960 have not occurred without strain. Many people have embraced the new ways; others resent the loss of power or privilege, bridle at being governed by members of a rural community who occupied the lowest rank in Syrian society only a generation ago, or are angry at the secularism of the Baath. The frequently reported troubles of the régime need to be viewed against this background.

One cause of antipathy, although not a principal cause of violence, is simply the régime's time in office. The longevity of the Baath, of the regionalists, and of Asad himself is unprecedented in modern Syria's short history. Among the consequences of having the same people in office for an extended period are insufficient new blood in many positions, bureaucratic rigidity, and corruption (on a scale large enough to have generated an anticorruption campaign in 1977 and to still be a problem).

A second cause of antipathy is the dominance of the Alawis. For many Syrians, and especially for those from the cities with their long tradition of cultural, political, and economic superiority, being governed by people of provincial origin and low social rank is offensive. This feeling, of course, adds to the "outs versus ins" attitude present in virtually any political situation. Allied to the social aspect is a religious one. For many Sunni Muslims, Alawis are heretics because their belief in a triple manifestation of the Deity goes beyond acceptable Islamic belief. Alawis say that they are good Shi'i Muslims and that the Ottoman state considered them so. Asad has been careful to appear at Muslim religious ceremonies appropriate to the head of state. Nevertheless, differences over religion lie at the heart of the current violence directed at the régime.[6]

Acts of violence against the régime began to occur more frequently in the early 1970s. The numbers of assassinations of individual Alawis, attempts on political figures, and random acts of terror grew to serious proportions in 1976–1977. The government attributed these to Iraqi instigation. Although the activity died down in 1978 with the improvement of Iraqi-Syrian relations—an indication that there had been external involvement—it did not disappear, and antirégime violence with a clear sectarian twist continued and grew. Responsibility for many killings has been claimed by groups professing Islamic orthodoxy, the Muslim Brothers and the Islamic Front. The former began armed opposition to the Asad régime in 1976; the latter, which came to life in 1980, appears to consist of the Muslim Brothers and a small number of other Sunni Muslims.[7]

In the first part of 1980, Syrian cities, especially Aleppo, saw a sharp rise in antirégime violence. The government responded with vigor, moved in troops (chiefly the special security units commanded by Asad's brother Rifaat), and, with a use of force unprecedented in independent Syria up to that time, crushed open manifestations of discontent and restored order. Many lives were lost and strongholds of opposition destroyed. Damascus remained calm through these events.

The régime stepped up its efforts to break the power of the Muslim Brothers and the front. Its methods have been very severe; in security roundups, people having no connection with terrorism have been arrested, mistreated, or killed. This approach has succeeded in limiting antirégime violence but has not wiped it out. Several major government installations, including a Ministry of Defense building, were damaged by car bombs in 1981.

The most severe episode of antirégime violence took place in Hamah in February 1982. Although the affair was triggered by government security forces searching for arms, the insurgents were well armed and fought from prepared positions. Government forces fought back with tanks and artillery, destroying much of the old city. Antigovernment spokesmen claimed 20,000 were killed; more neutral observers put the figure at around 5,000. Even that number indicates intense fighting.[8] There has been no repetition of that sort of hostility, and attacks on government buildings and officials virtually ceased during the next few years. The renewed attacks during 1985 and 1986 have been limited in number.

It should not be surprising that there is strife between ethnic groups in Syria. Baath philosophy is nonsectarian: It holds that sect should not determine a person's status or role in society, contrary to the centuries-old custom in the area. Minorities understandably took up this tenet; it gave them a route to power. Once in power, they also followed the time-honored custom of promoting the fortunes of and deriving support from relatives and clients. The predominance that the Alawis achieved in this way threw the former politico-social system out of balance. What we are seeing now is a struggle among Syrians to shape both their political and cultural future.

Among the several aspects to that struggle is the issue of President Asad's longevity in office; another is the prolongation of the current situation in which Alawis hold positions in number and importance out of proportion to their numbers in the country; a third is the solidity of the socialist system developed by the Baathists. As to the first issue, time is against Asad. As the person in charge of Syria—he is regularly identified in the official press as president, commander-in-chief, and secretary general of the Baath party—responsibility for the country's problems lies at his door. He is a target for those who want his job and for those who want to change the whole course of Syria's future. He could be assassinated and nearly was in June 1980. His illness at the end of 1983 and his reduced work capacity have caused members of his entourage to maneuver themselves into advantageous positions for devolution of power or a succession struggle. A cabal in the military could move against him. Such a move would have to be intra-Baath, as the armed forces are heavily politicized and the Baath is the dominant ideology. (Only the Baath is allowed to conduct political activity in the armed forces, which have a party structure similar to that of its civilian counterpart.) Such a cabal could be inspired by a variety of reasons—a military setback in Lebanon at the hands of the Israelis, a desire on the part of senior officers to refurbish the régime's image—and could protect the positions of cabal members by getting rid of certain people in Asad's entourage or by attempting to make the régime appear less obviously Alawi. If that were a motive, Alawi officers from outside Asad's clan could collaborate with Sunnis.

It does not appear likely that members of Syria's Alawi minority will occupy a predominant position indefinitely. The rest of the population will continue to resist such a trend. But those already in office will strongly oppose attempts to relegate Alawis to their home province. For Syrians to move their country to a situation in which sect and family status are largely subordinate to the socially egalitarian Baath philosophy will not be easy or quick. Vested interests and attitudes formed over centuries rarely change fundamentally over decades.

Some Syrians, such as members of the Islamic front, wish to overturn the régime and all that it stands for. But even though it can draw support from persons disenchanted with the régime for other reasons—from Aleppines who resent being relegated to the status of residents of a mere provincial capital instead of a rival to Damascus or from the once dominant city families—the religious-based opposition appears to lack a large enough following. It is centered in the cities, especially Aleppo, Homs, and Hamah, which are traditional centers of mosque-based militancy, and has not apparently made many converts from the countryside. Whatever their religious sensibilities, rural people have done well under Baath rule. Furthermore, popular involvement in the running of Syria through membership in the party, the people's organizations affiliated with it, and the civil administration has thus far prevented the development of viable opposition to Asad's government.

If Asad were to be assassinated, removed by coup, or die, the Baath system would stay. The change of leadership could be as smooth as the one when he took over in 1970. Then the top layer of the party was removed, a party congress approved the proceedings, and Syria moved on. Or the change could be tumultuous if factions fight for control. The country, however, will remain in the control of the militarized Baath. Neither a return to laissez-faire economics nor a fundamentalist religious triumph is likely.

Regional Affairs

Location and history have combined to give Syria a prominent place in contemporary Middle Eastern affairs. These factors also contribute to a problem of Syrian identity. Several causes have inspired Syrians' political loyalty: the Arab world, Greater Syria, and the country within its present boundaries. All these have played a role in addition to those of long-standing sect and family ties.

If Syrians did not actually invent Pan-Arab nationalism, they certainly were foremost among those who successfully propagated this ideology. Damascus, for that reason, has been termed "the beating heart of Arabism," and it is no accident that the first and by far the most successful party devoted to Pan-Arabism, the Baath, was created in Syria. For many Syrians the short rule of Faisal following World War I should have been the first step toward an independent state encompassing all Arabs. Although such aspirations continue, they are largely sublimated to more pragmatic concerns.

The formation of the United Arab Republic in 1958 seemed at the time to be a major step toward the Pan-Arab goal. Created out of a combination of forces—Pan-Arab psychology, the hope for a solution to Syrian domestic political problems, and Egyptian President Nasser's prestige—the republic failed in three and a half years, mostly as a result of what Syrians perceived as Egyptian control of all important decisionmaking posts. The failure drove Pan-Arabists out of office in Syria. And although Damascus has three times started down the road of political unification with one or more Arab states—the Federation of Arab Republics (1971), the abortive start of a link with Iraq (1979), and the proclamation of union with Libya (1980)—each attempt had a primary purpose other than unity. The federation served as a cover for Egypt and Syria to plan the 1973 war; the short-lived rapprochement with Iraq stemmed from opposition to the Camp David accords; that with Libya was a price of Qaddafi's financial aid, which may well have been less than the Syrians expected.

Its location, its Arab nationalist past, and its potential influence in regional politics have made the modern Republic of Syria a target of other Arab states' ambitions or a cause of concern to them. The late King Abdullah of Jordan wished to dominate a state uniting Syria and Jordan; his grandson, Husayn, would like a government in Damascus more compatible with his interests than is that of Hafiz al-Asad. It is too early to say if the rapprochement between Husayn and Asad during the first half of 1986 signals a basic realignment within the Arab political world or an accommodation of far lesser significance. To Iraqis, Syria has the potential to block access to the Mediterranean; though Iraqi oil pipelines have long crossed Syria, they have been closed for political reasons several times. Consequently, Iraq has sought, more often than not fruitlessly, to promote the existence of a pro-Baghdad administration in Damascus. Especially since the rival Baath régime took power in Iraq in 1968, relations have been poor. Each régime considers itself the legitimate successor of the original Baath. The effort at unity in 1979 was doomed because neither Asad nor Saddam Husayn would accept a subordinate role. But in 1985 and early 1986, and with the help of King Husayn, some kind of improvement in relations between Syria and Iraq was at least being discussed.

For much of the post–World War II period, Egypt has also been concerned with keeping Syria on its side. Two high points mark these efforts—the United Arab Republic of 1958–1961 and Syrian-Egyptian collaboration in the October War of 1973. Those were times when Egypt exerted leadership among the Arab states. But the two states have since parted company. Egypt is no longer claiming first place; other Arab states are seeking leading roles. The result is a high level of inter-Arab strife, which affects Syria's efforts to influence events in its immediate neighborhood. In the past, Syrian regional power has largely depended on relations with Egypt. Although Egyptian and Syrian interests often did not harmonize, on the occasions that they did, in 1958–1961 and 1973–1975, Damascus had good leverage over its neighbors. When Syrian-Egyptian relations are bad, as they have been since 1977, Syria finds that controlling its neighbors is virtually impossible.

The neighborhood constitutes basically what was known in the past as Greater Syria. Prior to World War I, the name Syria applied to the region from the Taurus mountains and the Gulf of Alexandretta to southern Palestine, and between the desert and the Mediterranean Sea. This area was divided and subdivided by the victorious allied powers, France and Britain. Family and business ties throughout this area were and are strong; so is a sense of common political interest. The Syrian Social National party once considered this area to be the heartland of a separate state. Syrian people have resented the divisions, especially the addition by France in 1920 of largely Muslim areas to the Maronite heartland (the autonomous Sanjak of Mount Lebanon of late Ottoman days) to make a larger Lebanon. Indeed, Syria has strong interest in these neighboring areas. Therefore, it is not an aberration that Syrian troops are in Lebanon, that in the past they have invaded Jordan, and that they fought in Palestine in 1948.

With respect to Greater Syria, Damascus's desires are fairly simple. It wants to be in a position to be able to lead, or at least influence, its immediate neighbors—Jordan, the Palestine Liberation Organization (PLO), Lebanon and the factions therein—rather than be forced to follow their initiatives in matters of serious concern to Syria.[9] If these actors appear to be forcing Syria's hand beyond tolerable limits, Damascus is prepared to act. It sent forces into Lebanon in 1976, for example, to prevent the Palestinians and their Lebanese allies from inflicting very serious, perhaps fatal, harm on the Maronites' position. The reason was not so much solicitude for the Maronites as to avoid giving Israel a reason for moving deep into Lebanon to help its Maronite allies, a move that would force Syria to respond. Asad then turned to support the Palestinians when the Maronites too openly asserted their desire for a separate state, threatening to tear the precarious republic apart and setting a poor example for Syria's own multireligious state.

Lebanon—A Political Swamp

When Asad sent Syrian forces into Lebanon in mid-1976, his régime was in a very strong position: It had yet to face serious domestic challenge, the economy was in fairly good condition, and major development projects such as the Euphrates Dam had begun to contribute to the country's well-being. Although several Arab states opposed the Syrian move and expressed their displeasure by suspending payments that they had agreed to make to Syria as a confrontation state, in only a few months Damascus found its intervention approved by most Arab states. Under an Arab League agreement, engineered by the Saudis, the Syrian forces were designated Arab Deterrent Forces. Token units from other states joined them. Syria's southern neighbor, Jordan—having an interest in keeping a tight control over the Palestinians—supported the Syrian move.

By 1978, Syrian troops were fighting the Maronite militias; Israeli forces occupied a large part of southern Lebanon for some weeks until replaced by the United Nations International Force in Lebanon (UNIFIL). Israel turned over a strip along the border to Major Saad Haddad, a Christian officer who controlled the area by an Israeli-armed, -trained, and -paid militia. Israel continued to give support to militias in the Maronite heartland, which could provide potential military advantage in the event of hostilities with Syria. Asad's forces controlled the Bekaa Valley, the highway over the mountains to Beirut, and other strategic areas. And Damascus, with allies primarily among the Muslim components of the Lebanese body politic, appeared to have developed a tacit understanding with Israel that neither would encroach on the other's domain or permit its protégés to do so.

Yet the Syrian political position in Lebanon remained poor. Although Syria continued to seek a way to promote the rebuilding of a Lebanese state, it lacked the power to achieve such a result. Too many other actors either did not want to see the reemergence of a Lebanese state or did not want such a state to be subject to Syrian influence.

The fragility of Lebanon's situation and the hazards for Syria in that country were graphically illustrated in the events of spring and summer 1981. The Maronite Phalangists sent militia forces into the Christian, but non-Maronite, town of Zahle. Zahle is located in an area outside the Maronite heartland. This move represented an attempt to encroach on territory under direct Syrian protection; it may also have been an attempt to push the Maronite area of control a bit closer to Major Haddad's enclave in the south. Syrian efforts to drive the militia out of the town and to control its access roads resulted in serious fighting. Israel, in an unprecedented move, used its air force to shoot down two Syrian helicopters involved in the military operations in the area. Syria responded by moving in surface-to-air missiles. The involvement of a skilled U.S. diplomat and several weeks of maneuvering were necessary to restore the Zahle situation to the status quo ante. The end of hostilities came only after an intense Israeli air raid on Beirut led to a broader cease-fire, ostensibly between Israel and Lebanon, in fact between Israel and the PLO.

The situation in Lebanon did not improve. The Begin administration in Israel, following the ideas of Defense Minister Ariel Sharon, conceived a plan to destroy the military capability and political organization of the PLO. Seizing on the pretext of the attempted assassination of an Israeli diplomat in Europe, Israel launched reprisal air raids on PLO installations in Lebanon and drew the anticipated artillery response; Israeli forces invaded Lebanon.[10] The course of the war and its aftermath are well known. As for Syria, its air force lost heavily, and its ground forces were pushed back. For a year, Damascus seemed to have lost most of its capacity to influence the course of events in Lebanon.[11]

With the effective elimination of the PLO as a factor in Lebanese domestic politics, the factions that had fought the civil war since 1975 came to the fore. The Shia and Druze demanded greater shares of political power for their communities, and new leaders in these communities challenged the traditional bosses. Syria backed these factions against the central government, whose orientation was old guard and Maronite. Only after the withdrawal of European and U.S. troops and after President Amin al-Gemayel spent three days in Damascus in April 1984 was the Lebanese government restructured to include representatives of the major warring factions. Syrian influence in Lebanon was on the rise.

The future of Lebanon, and Syria's role therein, is inextricably linked with the Palestinian problem. No configuration in Lebanon—whether a thin federal layer covering several autonomous components or a revision of the former system—has any chance of working until some arrangement is made for the several hundred thousand Palestinians in Lebanon. Likewise, no West Bank solution can be viable without participation of Palestinians and their leaders, both local and in exile. Ignored, they can play the spoilers' game. In effect, Syrian acquiescence is a sine qua non for any arrangement in Lebanon and the West Bank to have a chance of lasting. Syria, too, could be a spoiler.[12]

Syria's own interests include recovery of the territory lost to Israel in 1967. The régime appears to believe that the only way to retrieve the Golan Heights is with the backing of a broad Arab solidarity grouping directed at Israel.[13] At the same time, Damascus has an interest in seeing a solution to this decades-old conflict that would permit the Palestinians to run their own state. From the perspective of the presidential palace in Damascus, such a state should be dominated by Damascus. Although the form of domination would differ from the tight controls that Syria has kept on the Palestinians for many years, Damascus's purpose would be the same—to have the capacity to take the initiative in the area it regards as its proper sphere of influence. Jordan also wants a role in such a state. King Husayn and President Asad do not see eye to eye on the modalities. In the mid-1970s, they were close to tacit agreement on the issue of the Palestinians. Given the turning wheel of Arab politics, in the future they could agree again as the recent cautious rapprochement suggests.

Damascus showed its muscle in the southern part of its sphere of influence in fall 1980. Jordan, on good terms with Syria in the mid-1970s, began to pull away from the relationship as the decade ended. Especially after Saddam Husayn took the lead in marshaling opposition to the Egyptian-Israeli treaty, King Husayn moved to associate Jordan closely with Iraq. Baghdad spent sizable amounts of money on agricultural and transportation projects in Jordan. Asad, harassed by antirégime elements supported by Iraq (except for the brief unity discussions of 1978-1979), saw Jordan's move away from close ties with Syria as harmful. He accused King Husayn of harboring and supporting the religious elements that were striking at Syria and called on him to desist. In fact, the Jordanians appear to have been guilty of turning a blind eye to the activities of Asad's opponents rather than sponsoring them. But Asad reacted strongly by moving several divisions to the Jordanian border.[14]

The Syrian-Jordanian affair was a standoff. Jordan stood up to Syria; the Saudis mediated. At the same time, Damascus showed the PLO and the rest of the Arab world that the Palestinian organizations functioned at Syrian sufferance. It boycotted the Arab summit in Amman and forced the PLO not to attend as well. Syria was less successful after the defeat of its forces by the Israelis in 1982. It abetted a revolt by some Fatah military commanders, which weakened Yasir Arafat's position and worked against the Palestine National Council meeting that was eventually held in Amman during 1984. PLO leaders—those aligned with Yasir Arafat or others—cannot ignore Syria as they try to restore their fortunes in Arab capitals far from Palestine.

Limited Role in the Arab World

Syria's relations with other Arab states are a function of those states' attitudes toward Damascus's desire to be the dominant power among its immediate neighbors. However, under the Baathists, Syria has not striven for a leading role in the wider Arab world. On the contrary, other Arab states have sought a role in the area that Syria considers its sphere of influence, especially Lebanon. More often than not, this approach has led to conflict with Syria.

In 1973, Egypt and Syria collaborated in war against Israel. Since the late President Sadat entered into a second disengagement agreement with Israel late in 1975, relations between Cairo and Damascus have been poor, and they worsened drastically after the Camp David accords and Sadat's trip to Jerusalem. In 1977, Syria helped to found the Steadfastness and Confrontation front, which grouped Libya, Algeria, the PLO, and South Yemen in opposition to Israel. Sadat customarily used contemptuous and insulting language about Asad and the Baath and lent support to groups in Lebanon that would normally have looked to Damascus. That each of the two leaders was under attack by domestic Islamic forces for essentially the same reason—their policies of separating religion from government— did nothing to diminish their mutual animosity.

Syria's relations with Iraq have become even more strained. They began to deteriorate in July 1979 when Saddam Husayn implied that Syria was behind a movement against him, and they became even worse when Iraq opened a major offensive against Iran in September 1980. From the beginning of hostilities, Syria gave verbal support to Iran, later extending some military supplies and forging economic ties. The reasons are varied: historical Baghdad-Damascus rivalry, competition for Baath leadership, annoyance at Iraq's wooing Jordan away from close ties with Syria, minimization of the chances for friction with Iran over Damascus's dealings with Lebanese Shia, and— for the Alawi element—perhaps some sympathy for coreligionists (Alawis identify themselves as followers of the Twelfth Imam, as do Iranian Shia). Both Syria and Iraq extended political and material support to opposition elements in the other state. Syria went so far as to stop Iraqi oil shipments across its territory in April 1982, and has resisted efforts by such diverse mediators as the Saudis and the Soviets to allow oil to flow again. Even though there are hints that Syrian-Iranian ties may be loosening, relations with Iraq have not improved.[15]

With the oil-rich states of the Arabian peninsula and the Gulf, Syria's relations are fair to good. Syria has come to rely heavily on their financial assistance, paid to it as a confrontation state, which was pegged at $1.8 billion a year in 1979. (Iraq was among the contributors and made payments as late as mid-1980 despite poor mutual relations.) These same states, especially Saudi Arabia, paid for the Arab Deterrent (Syrian) Forces in Lebanon, which meant political support for Syria's aims in Lebanon—chiefly preventing partition, opposing Israel, and, until summer 1982, helping the Palestinian forces. Saudi Arabia has long been important to Syria; ties date from the 1940s and 1950s. The Saudis have been instrumental in solving problems involving Syria, such as arranging for the Arab Deterrent Forces in 1976, mediating between Damascus and Amman in 1980, and facilitating a return to the status quo in Lebanon in summer 1981. Syria gives sober consideration to what Saudi Arabia thinks when undertaking any policy change but is by no means an obedient client. Moreover, as Saudi money dwindles so does Saudi influence.

Syria's other prime source of money, Colonel Muammar al-Qaddafi of Libya, figures very differently in Damascus's calculations. Qaddafi holds positions that are nearly identical to Asad's on Egypt and that are close to Asad's on the Palestinians, and he has paid substantial sums for essentially verbal support for himself and some of his ideas. He is serious about Arab unity and about—to be charitable—a unique form of Islamic revitalization. Although Asad is not concerned with either, words and gestures from Damascus have kept Qaddafi from supporting Islamic militants in Syria and from gravely complicating Syria's situation in Lebanon. The unity between the two countries that Qaddafi announced in September 1980 is still in the planning stage.[16]

The treaty of friendship and cooperation between Syria and the Soviet Union on October 8, 1980, represented success for Moscow after much effort. For years Damascus had resisted Soviet urging to improve their relationship. Asad agreed in 1980 because of his country's near isolation in the Arab world, the limited assistance he could expect from other Arab states in the event of hostilities with Israel, and the considerable domestic security difficulties confronting Syria. Asad may have concluded that a formal tie with the USSR would bolster his strength, if not his reputation, with his own citizens.

The USSR already had a strong position in Syria. Its navy used Syrian ports for anchorage, rest and recuperation, and minor repairs. It had no actual military bases or on-shore combat formations. The Communist party of Syria has a formal position in the system, with two cabinet members and representation on the executive board of the National Popular front, but it has little real power. A steady stream of delegations exchanges visits with Communist and fraternal parties. From the Soviet point of view, these represent an important but supplementary element of contact between the two states and are encouraged to increase Syrian exposure to Communist ways.

Before the Israeli invasion of Lebanon, there was little evidence that the 1980 treaty had produced any qualitative change in Syrian-Soviet relations. Syrian units have participated in a small-scale military exercise, providing the defending forces for an amphibious landing. Damascus's boycott of the Arab summit meeting and its mobilization of troops on Jordan's border in autumn 1980 were consistent with past behavior. The formal treaty relationship may have emboldened Syria in its confrontation with Israel over Lebanon in spring 1981, but again Syrian moves were in harmony with prior behavior.

The Soviet presence in Syria began to change after Israeli forces inflicted severe losses on Syrian air force and armored units in Lebanon in June 1982. Moscow sent a very senior military team to assess the Syrian needs and quickly provided massive shipments of new armaments, including MIG-

23 and MIG-25 fighters, M-72 tanks, SA-5 antiaircraft missiles, and SS-21 short-range surface-to-surface missiles that can hit Israeli population centers. Early in 1984 some 7,000 Soviet military advisers and technicians were in Syria, and Soviet crews manned the SA-5 and SS-21 batteries. Yet despite its provision of large numbers of modern weapons and the presence of a significant military force, the Soviet Union has not changed its role in Syria. Virtually no specialist on the region regards Syria as an instrument of Soviet policy, and President Asad appears firmly in control of his nation's policies at home and in the region.[17]

Outside domestic and regional concerns, Syria has been supportive of Soviet actions and policies. It was conspicuous in not denouncing the Soviet invasion of Afghanistan when most other Muslim states did. It has established close relations with the Ethiopian régime, a policy in sharp contrast to its long-term support for the Eritrean Liberation front and to the claim in the masthead map of the party paper, *Al-Baath*, that Eritrea is part of the Arab world.

Several factors limit the effectiveness of the USSR in influencing Syria. One is a streak of independent-mindedness: Syrians have frequently chosen to march to their own drum, even when it put them at odds with their fellow Arabs. Another is Syria's strong and unpleasant memory of having been under foreign rule. A third is its appreciation for the economic, technical, and cultural wares of the West.

Despite the quarter century of Soviet and East European aid, Syria's economy remains oriented to the West. Although the country is socialist, 40 per cent of the gross domestic product is in the private sector. Trade with the Council of Mutual Economic Assistance (COMECON) countries has been steadily losing ground to that with the West; the Communist countries accounted for only 17 per cent of the whole in 1979, but the proportion has begun to rise as hard currency availability has lessened. Syria even bought Soviet commercial aircraft in 1983, a sharp change from its established preference for Boeing products. European firms are heavily involved in Syria's development program.[18]

The United States provides two necessities for Syria. One is an alternative to the USSR. The existence of such an alternative is a useful reminder to Moscow that Damascus has another option if it feels that the Soviets are pushing it too hard. And the alternative is real; the Soviets only have to review the history of their relations with Egypt. The second is support in the Arab-Israeli area. The Syrian régime believes that it can get what it wants from Israel only through the agency of a strong united front of Arab states. It also judges that only the United States can exercise the necessary suasion to get Israel to agree to satisfactory terms on Lebanon, the Palestinians, and its own territory. For these reasons, Syria, though it may distance itself from Washington, will not irrevocably break off dealing with it.

Conclusion

In the later part of the 1980s Syria will continue to be disturbed internally as forces try to stop the revolution and unseat the Baath. Although a drastic change is highly unlikely, challenges to the present leadership are in prospect and antipathy to Alawi dominance is endemic. In consequence, Syria is likely to be unstable and not in a position to influence its immediate surroundings as it would wish.

Within Syria, changes in leadership are to be expected by the late 1980s or soon thereafter, a process stimulated by Asad's bout of ill health. The Baath system and military control of the government will both continue to be cardinal features of Syrian political life.

Major hostilities with Israel, initiated by Syria, are highly unlikely. Syria will feel compelled to keep forces in Lebanon indefinitely; they will constitute a political and economic drain on the country and will carry high risk of unintended escalation of incidents.

Despite the Israeli preference for Lebanon and the U.S. choice of Jordan, Syria is the logical state to follow Egypt in settling with Israel. By most indicators, Syria is a more powerful state than Jordan; it needs to improve its relations with Israel to be able to disengage from Lebanon; both Syria and Israel have an interest in a PLO tamed or hedged in by the restrictions of a political settlement.

The United States will face an untidy situation with respect to Syria and its immediate neighbors as the Syrians work out for themselves how their country should progress and as the neighbors counter Damascus's efforts to extend its influence. But as events in Lebanon have demonstrated both the United States and Israel should take Syria more seriously into their plans for any regional settlement.

Notes

1. Khaddam, foreign minister from November 1970 until appointed vice president in March 1984, continues to be the principal figure in the conduct of Syria's external affairs.

2. Of the 20 living members of the 21-person regional command chosen at a party congress in January 1980, 14 are Sunni Muslim, 3 are Alawis, 2 are Christians, and 1 is a Druze. See, for example, Nikolaos van Dam, *The Struggle for Power in Syria*, second edition (London: Croom Helm, 1981), p. 122, n. 38.

3. Raymond A. Hinnebusch, "Party and Peasant in Syria: Rural Politics and Social Change in a Mobilizational Regime," paper presented at the 1975 Convention of the Middle East Studies Association, Louisville, Ky., November 19–22, 1975, pp. 58–59. This study has also been published by the American University in Cairo, *Cairo Papers in Social Science* 3, no. 1 (1979).

4. Robert Springborg, "Baathism in Practice: Agriculture, Politics, and Political Culture in Syria and Iraq," *Middle Eastern Studies* 17 (April 1981), p. 201.

5. International Institute for Strategic Studies, *The Military Balance 1983–1984* (London, 1983), p. 62.

6. Hanna Batatu, "Some Observations on the Social Roots of Syria's Ruling, Military Group and the Causes for its Dominance," *Middle East Journal* 35 (summer 1981), pp. 335ff.

7. Umar Abd-Allah, *The Islamic Struggle in Syria* (Berkeley, Calif.: Mizan Press, 1983), chaps. 3 and 4; also my review of it in *Middle East Insight* 3 (1983), p. 43.

8. John F. Devlin, "Syria: Clash of Values," *Middle East Insight* 2 (May 1982), p. 31.

9. Thirty to forty years ago, Syrians hoped to prevent the establishment of a Zionist state in Palestine. The Republic of Syria has, by accepting UN Resolution 242, acknowledged the existence of Israel within (in Damascus's interpretation) its June 5, 1967, boundaries. See Hafiz al-Asad speech, Radio Damascus, March 8, 1972, in *Foreign Broadcast Information Service* (FBIS), March 9, 1972.

10. Ze'ev Schiff and Ehud Ya'ari, *Israel's Lebanon War* (New York: Simon and Schuster, 1984), chap. 3 and pp. 97–101.

11. Ze'ev Schiff, "Lebanon: Motivations and Interests in Israel's Policy," *Middle East Journal* 38 (spring 1984), pp. 224–225.

12. Rashid Khalidi, "The Palestinians in Lebanon: Social Repercussions of Israel's Invasion," *ibid.*, p. 266.

13. Extension on December 14, 1981, of "the law, jurisdiction, and administration" of Israel to the Golan does not change Syrian desires in regard to it. The action merely makes Syrian desires more difficult to achieve.

14. This was the third time in ten years that Damascus felt a need to menace Jordan; the earlier occasions were in 1970 and 1973. *New York Times*, November 25, 1980; *Washington Post*, December 9, 1980.

15. *New York Times*, May 17, 1984, citing *Al-Nahar* (Beirut) to the effect that most of the 1,000 Iranian revolutionary guards in Lebanon had been asked to leave by Syria.

16. Actual amounts for the Libyan financial support are not available, but they appear to be much less than those sometimes reported. For example, Libya did not pay anywhere near the one-half billion dollars reported to be Syria's price for uniting in 1980.

17. *New York Times*, October 16, 1983, February 14 and March 18, 1984; *International Herald Tribune*, July 23, 1984.

18. Economist Intelligence Unit, *Quarterly Report for Syria and Jordan*, no. 2, 1983.

2

Lebanon

Augustus Richard Norton

Lebanon—today wrecked and wretched—was once considered a prototype to be emulated by developing states. Respectable studies of just a decade ago cannot be read today without a shake of the head and a sense of how pathetic the plight of this small Mediterranean country has been. For example, David R. and Audrey C. Smock, two Western scholars, contended that "the Lebanese approach, while not wholly adequate and not exportable in toto, has much to offer other states confronting serious problems of religious, ethnic, and racial conflict."[1] Lebanese scholars themselves were often blissfully unaware of the inherent fragility of the Lebanese system and of the explosions to come. Elie Salem, scholar and later foreign minister, marveled at the flexibility of the Lebanese system: "Lebanon is a country where one's first impressions are often proved wrong; it has been described as 'precarious,' 'improbable,' and as a 'mosaic,' but the flexibility of its system, the experience and shrewdness of its leaders, and the stability of its institutions have surprised all observers."[2]

If those writing before the bloodletting began often failed to anticipate even the broad outlines of what was to come, subsequent observers have hardly distinguished themselves with incisive analyses. In short, the carnage on the Lebanese battlefield has obscured the real story in Lebanon: social and political change. Even before the onset of civil war in 1975, momentous changes were under way—changes that would upset the traditional distribution of political privilege and greatly complicate any attempt to write surcease to the decade of violence. Blinded by the dust of battles and skirmishes, observers scarcely noticed the changes transforming the Lebanese body politic. Although journalists, diplomats, and academics churned out reams of articles, dispatches, reports, and monographs, the very conditions that have hidden change have also served to discourage incisive, probing analysis.

In fact, knowledge of this strife-torn country is strangely constricted in both time and space. Armed conflict is hardly a hospitable laboratory for the discovery of sociological verities, so for the past decade it was always easier to accept crude, often distorted descriptive templates. The favored template froze the Lebanese situation in an early 1975 time warp, and few commentators stopped to ask whether the truths of 1975 remained accurate in 1979 or 1982; fewer still considered whether the truths were even applicable in 1975.[3] Instead the conflict was blithely reported as one between Christians and Muslims or between the Right and the Left (a dichotomy that was often no more than a synonym for Christians versus Muslims).

Neither the Muslim nor the Christian side has been as homogeneous or monolithic as is sometimes thought. When the fighting began in spring 1975, a loosely integrated coalition of Maronite Christian militias was arrayed against an admixture of Palestinian guerrillas (or fedayeen), Greek Orthodox, Shi'i and Sunni Muslims, and Druze. On either side, alliances often proved to be transient. Moreover, a large number of Muslims (Sunnis in particular) and Christians (including the Armenian community) studiously avoided any involvement in the fighting.

The impermanence of political alliances is well illustrated by the relatively short-lived relationship between the Palestinian Resistance and the Shi'i Muslims. By the end of the 1970s, the Lebanese, including erstwhile allies of the fedayeen, were approaching unanimity in their opposition to the presence of alien military forces—whether Syrian, Palestinian or Israeli—in their country. The economically underprivileged and politically under-represented Shi'i Muslims, once considered the natural allies of the Palestinians, were fighting pitched battles against the fedayeen in large part because they had simply tired of being caught in the Israeli-PLO crossfire. Few commentators noticed this important shift in alliance preference.

Furthermore, Western understanding of Lebanon is defined by the city of Beirut. Reports—whether scholarly, journalistic, or diplomatic—were formulated from the vantage point of the capital because no other city in Lebanon offered the conveniences of Beirut: telexes, restaurants, hotels, shops, and sources. Journalists, often unprepared for the complexities of Lebanon, found that the requisite number of column inches could easily be written from their relatively pleasant Beirut base. Moreover, a journalist has little incentive to pursue a story that is unlikely to appear in print, and few editors encouraged their reporters to grapple with Lebanon in all its complexity.

The few who strove to transcend the mundane regimen encountered many pitfalls. Since 1975, Lebanon has been divided into a patchwork of fiefdoms and security zones controlled by militias, armies, and gangs.[4] Not only was it necessary to navigate a series of checkpoints operated by temperamental militiamen, but upon arrival at a destination it was hazardous to travel without escorts, liaison officers, or authorized spokesmen. So even the adventurous and conscientious handful who left the familiar comforts of Beirut usually did little more than get a feel for the situation. Rare indeed was the journalist who would attempt to escape from this constrictive environment. As a result reports from the hinterlands were seldom more revealing than those written in Beirut. To a large degree, the journalists' reportorial myopia only reflected the attitudes of the sophisticated Beiruti, who all too often could have cared less about events occurring in a backwater like the south. Moreover, for many journalists the story in Lebanon was not Lebanon but the Palestinian resistance. Lebanon was merely the stage upon which the Palestinian drama was played. Although a large number of stories were filed with a Beirut dateline, many did not deal with Lebanon at all.

Diplomats, especially U.S. diplomats, had even less freedom of movement than their cohorts in the press corps. Legitimate security threats resulted in severe restrictions on the movement of diplomatic personnel. For example, in 1980 U.S. embassy personnel were not permitted to travel south of Damur without the express permission of the ambassador. In such circumstances, diplomats became increasingly dependent upon friendly sources, who often had their own desiderata and agendas. Given the risks, it hardly comes as a surprise that many diplomats found the confines of Beirut, with its network of contacts and abundance of creature comforts, an acceptable domain. (Of course, a few exceptional diplomats recognized the cost of isolation and made every effort to move beyond the diplomatic circuit.) Because much of the reporting, whether by the press or diplomats, was produced by a three-way synergism of journalist-diplomat-official spokesman, it is easy to understand how truths took on a life of their own.

Academics are a rather different case. For the past decade, Lebanon has not offered a hospitable research environment. Scholars intrigued by the politics of Lebanon often found it safer to study from afar rather than risk cherished myths by actually visiting the country. A few Lebanese scholars did produce useful and informative books on the 1975–1976 period, and Walid Khalidi (a Palestinian scholar) has offered an elegant essay on the civil war and its aftermath, but by and large the scholarly cupboard is surprisingly bare.[5] By comparison, the work of the best journalists makes the scholarly offering seem especially small.[6] When interest in Lebanon was revived because of the 1982 war, scholars discovered "new" facts that were sometimes new only to themselves. Nor were the academic woods empty of opportunists. One scholar wrote a book about Israel's 1982 invasion based on 21 days of field research and the friendly assistance of Israel Defense Forces (IDF) information officers.

Admittedly, research opportunities for Westerners in Lebanon have been limited in recent years. The country has always been a locus for conspirators, agents, and flamboyant bon vivants, but the onset of conflict multiplied the characters as well as the conspiracies (whether real or imagined). With ample evidence of duplicity all around them, many Lebanese believed there was good reason not to take people for what they purported to be. Scholars researching political questions had an enormous gulf of suspicion to bridge, and innocuous questions would often be treated with reticence. Whether the community of interest was the Maronite, Shi'i, or Palestinian, scholars often needed many months to get answers to very basic and seemingly benign questions relating to demographics or social and political programs. Thus, many of the best Middle East scholars simply turned their attention elsewhere rather than enmesh themselves in such a hostile research environment.

The Evolution of Confessional Politics

We usually date the Lebanese state from 1943, when the unwritten National Pact (Mithaq al-Watani) established the current distribution of political office by confession (religious affiliation) on the basis of the population figures revealed by a problematic 1932 census. (As a reflection of the 1932 figures, the Maronites were accorded the office of the presidency, the Sunnis the office of prime minister, and the Shia the position of parliamentary speaker.) In point of fact, the modalities of the political system were well established long before 1943. For example, in 1841 Bashir III organized a confessional council of ten members (three Maronites, three Druze, one Greek Catholic, one Greek Orthodox, one Shi'i and one Sunni) who represented the country's divergent primordial identities.[7]

In 1860, after Maronite peasants rose up against their Druze landlords, as many as 11,000 Maronites were killed over a period of several weeks. After the 1860 massacres and under pressure from the British, Russians, French, and Austrians—each of which had its own Lebanese confessional client—the Règlement Organique of 1861 was acceded to by the Ottomans, the ostensible imperial power. The Règlement Organique provided for the establishment of a representative council to consist of two representatives of each major confessional community. The latter system was revised in 1864 to give greater numerical representation to the Maronites, Druze, and Greek Orthodox, but here again, confessional diversity was recognized. Although the ratios changed from time to time, the formula remained.

By the beginning of the French mandate in 1920, the dynamics of Lebanese politics were already well established. Patterns of identity, based on shared religion, geographic propinquity, and unique external ties, produced a political system in which vertically organized confessional segments were led by *zu'ama* (traditional political bosses) who interacted with one another at the leadership level, while sectarian exclusivity was preserved at less exalted levels. Political competition was intra- rather than inter-confessional. This characteristic was formalized in the modern electoral system which, through its mixed list system, put a premium on candidates' willingness to accommodate the interests of voters from confessions other than their own. (Nearly all electoral districts consist of voters from two or more confessional groups. Each qualified voter is entitled to vote for one candidate for each parliamentary seat, even for those seats allocated to confessions other than his or her own.) Thus, the Lebanese were in the midst of a political milieu in which politics and sectarianism were inextricably linked. Escaping from a confessional identity was no easy matter, even in matters of the heart; by prohibiting civil marriage, even wedlock became politicized.

Demographic Shifts

Unfortunately, Lebanon's confessional political system proved to be exceedingly fragile and unresponsive to demands spawned by demographic, social, economic, and political changes. A decisive determinant of the system's fragility was the redrawing of Lebanon's boundaries by the French in 1920. Although intended to enhance the state's viability, the expansion in 1920 from Mount Lebanon to Le Grand Liban (Greater Lebanon) doubled the state's territory, but it also greatly complicated its political future. The enlargement of the state added the Shi'i Muslims of the south and the Bekaa Valley, the Greek Orthodox, Armenians, and Sunnis of the coastal cities, and the Greek Catholics of the Bekaa Valley. The expansion of the confessional puzzle ensured that no community would dominate. As the relative power of each communal group was reduced, the value of internal alliances (such as between the Greek Catholics and the Maronites; and the Sunnis and the Greek Orthodox) increased, and the appeal of relationships with external powers grew.

When we examine the political history of the past century and a half, we find that, until Lebanon achieved independence in 1943, there were periodic readjustments both in the ratios of confessional representation and in the allocation of specific offices. However, since the promulgation of the National Pact in 1943, there have been only modest adjustments, despite the fact that confessional birthrate differentials have significantly changed Lebanon's demographic profile. Not surprisingly, those population segments enjoying higher socioeconomic status, such as urban-dwelling Maronites and the Sunni Muslims, have experienced diminishing birthrates, whereas those on the bottom rung, especially the Shia, have experienced very high rates. (Joseph Chamie calculated that the respective rates of natural increase are as follows: Shia, 3.8 per cent; Sunnis, 2.8 per cent; Catholics, including Maronites, 2.0 per cent; Druze, 2.0 per cent; and Orthodox, 1.7 per cent.[8])

Variations in migratory patterns have also worked against the Christian community as a whole and in favor of the Shi'i Muslims in particular. In other words, Christian Lebanese were more likely to settle outside the country (particularly in Western Europe and the Americas), whereas the Shi'i Muslim migrants were more likely to return to Lebanon after a few years in the Gulf region or West Africa.

Precise demographic data are impossible to obtain in the present circumstances, but the skillful manipulation of limited data by demographers certainly indicates that the Christians have long since ceased to enjoy the previous 6:5 population advantage over the Muslims.[9] Indeed, although the 1932 census purportedly indicated that the Shia were only the third largest community, following the Maronites and the Sunnis, they now are indisputably the largest, constituting 30 per cent (or more) of the country's population. Taken together, the Muslims (Shi'i, Sunni, and Druze) probably represent 60 per cent of Lebanon's population. All the preceding demographic shifts have occurred without corresponding changes in the distribution of political power. Indeed, if the distribution logic that prevailed in 1943 were to be reapplied in 1984, the resultant shifts of political power would be dramatic. The current 99-seat Chamber of Deputies, elected in 1972, includes seats for 19 Shi'is and 30 Maronites. Yet recent population estimates would justify 29 or 30 seats for the Shi'a and only 19 or 20 for the Maronite community.

Another important demographic factor has been the influx of Palestinian refugees to Lebanon. Perhaps as many as 100,000 Palestinian civilians moved to Lebanon between 1948 and 1967. However, many of these Palestinians are sociologically similar to the Lebanese in terms of patterns of employment, residence, and personal relationships. Even though there are significant exceptions, it is still fair to assert that many of the early refugees think of themselves as Lebanese and are accepted by their Lebanese cohorts as such. (One of the most important leaders of the Shi'i community in south Lebanon was part of the first wave of refugees.) Although the earliest influx of Palestinians was in large part assimilated, the second wave of refugees that began in 1967 (after the June War) proved harder to absorb and therefore more destabilizing for an already fragile Lebanon. More militant as a result of the 1967 humiliation by Israel and the 1970 defeat at the hands of the Jordanian army, and better led, the second influx—which included many Palestinian fighters—severely strained the limited Lebanese political system. By the beginning of the 1970s, the Lebanese found themselves faced with a human infusion that equaled 10 per cent or more of the country's population and that could not be easily absorbed or controlled. Furthermore, since most of the Palestinians were Muslims, they were viewed by many Maronite Christians as a dangerous threat to Maronite supremacy in Lebanon.

Economic Conditions

Prior to 1975, many economic development specialists considered Lebanon to have a model developing economy. Lebanon had a thriving private sector, and the government did not intervene significantly in the free market. By the end of 1974, Lebanon was poised for rapid expansion, but the bright prospects dimmed with the outbreak of civil war in 1975. An easing of political tension in 1977 allowed a surprisingly strong recovery, and by 1980 real gross national product (GNP) had increased 73 per cent from its 1976 low.[10] This recovery slowed following the June 1982 Israeli invasion of Lebanon.

In spite of the political turmoil since 1975 and the effects of the 1982 Israeli invasion, Lebanon's economy remained surprisingly resilient until mid-1983. In 1983, exports fell by half, and net income from services dropped 40 per cent.[11] The two sectors most adversely affected by the post-1975 deterioration in Lebanon's political and security situation are agriculture and industry—which represent respectively 8 per cent and 15 per cent of Lebanon's GNP.[12] Agriculture has traditionally been a weak sector in Lebanon, but after the Israeli invasion this sector has been plagued by physical destruction (of irrigation networks, orchards, storage facilities) as well as by indirect damage (shifts of population, loss of fertile land and of livestock).[13] Industry has suffered similarly from physical destruction and disinvestment. Recent estimates indicate that industrial plants function at 10 to 40 per cent of their capacity as a result of widespread destruction of capital and equipment goods. In some cases, entire industrial zones (such as Jiyeh, south of Beirut) were destroyed during combat.[14]

One observer identified the service sector as one of the paradoxes of the Lebanese economy. Although during the past ten years the country's physical infrastructure has been ravaged, there has been a large increase in the banking sector. From June 1976 to June 1982, private deposits increased by more than 600 per cent. This "improvement" was a product of Lebanon's decay: Remittances from Lebanese who had fled to work abroad accounted for a large share of this increase. By 1981, these remittances accounted for 45 per cent of Lebanon's national income.[15]

The increased flow of capital into Lebanon was not without its price. Surplus capital gave rise to inflation and a decrease in the standard of living, as demonstrated by the depreciation of the minimum wage. In nominal value, the minimum wage increased from 225 Lebanese pounds in 1974 to 925 pounds in 1982; however, in constant 1974 pounds, this represented only 223 pounds.[16] Following the 1983 economic and political crisis, foreign transfers fell from 150 million Lebanese pounds/month to 65 million Lebanese pounds/month. As the economic crisis deepened in 1984 and continued into 1985 and 1986, the long-term effects of excess capital manifested themselves in the form of runaway inflation, foreign exchange crises, and increase in public deficit.

Few components of the Lebanese economy—including those which were traditionally the strongest—escaped the negative effects of the 1983 crisis. According to the Banque du Liban (central bank), for example, gold and foreign exchange reserves fell from 12,474 million Lebanese pounds at the end of 1982 to 9,260 million Lebanese pounds at the end of 1984. The exchange rate during the same period fell from 5.49 pounds/US$1 to 8.89 pounds/US$1. By March 1985, the pound had plummeted to almost 18 pounds/US$1 and hovered around 17 pounds/US$1 at the end of 1985.[17] (By November 1986 the pound had crashed to 58 pounds/US$1.) A troubling consequence of the economic crisis is the development of a balance of payments deficit. This balance, which had almost perenially experienced a surplus, registered a deficit of $933 million in 1983 and $1,353 million in 1984.[18] Even more worrying, the figures for government revenue and expenditure in 1984 showed a real deficit of about $1,120 million—three times the budgeted deficit and almost as much as total budgeted expenditure. Officials identified the dismal performance of customs (which usually represent 40 per cent of government revenues) as a major contributor to this deficit. Revenues for 1984 from customs were nearly 65 per cent less than the 1983 total, and actual revenues in 1985 are believed to have been only a fraction of the budgeted figure of 11,017 million Lebanese pounds. This disparity in income resulted largely from refusal to turn revenues over to the government, increased smuggling, and the existence of illegal ports.

Some observers assert that, should civility, if not tranquility, be restored to Lebanon, the economy could rebound. This assessment is based on an appreciation of the inherent qualities of Lebanon: well-educated, capable, and innovative people, an economy based on services (which have been less affected than other sectors by physical destruction), a strong tradition of private sector initiative, a free market environment, and, finally, Lebanon's geographic location and strong international ties, especially with the United States and Europe.[19]

Dimensions of Political Change

More than a decade of internal conflict, invasion, and civil disorder have intensified the socioeconomic forces that were changing Lebanon even before the civil war began in 1975. Carnage may have stolen the headlines, but the real story in Lebanon is the social and political change associated with modernization. Vast numbers of Lebanese, who in the past were politically mute, have now found their political voice and are no longer content to accept a political system that ignores their demands.

The ranks of the politicized have swollen, and the contours of politics in Lebanon have changed radically. Devoid of strong central political institutions, Lebanese politics have long been the domain of a coterie of political bosses known as *zu'ama*. Drawn from a few dozen families (26 families have held 35 per cent of all parliamentary seats), each *za'im* represented a clientele that traded its acquiescent political loyalty for the *za'im's* stock-in-trade political favors. Power was passed from father to son as a political inheritance. Surnames like Gemayel, Chamoun, Salam, Asad, Jumblatt, Franjiya, and Solh appeared again and again on ministry portfolios. But the conflict in Lebanon and the accelerating social and economic changes that preceded and accompanied it have rendered the *zu'ama* increasingly irrelevant in contemporary Lebanon. In a seemingly self-reinforcing process, the *zu'ama* proved incapable of meeting the burgeoning needs and demands of their clients, which in turn led to further political instability. Since the Israeli invasion of 1982, one of the more fascinating spectator sports has been watching an anachronistic political guard scramble to recover its control of fiefdoms now controlled, at least in part, by a new generation of leaders—often people with obscure family names. Of course, the *zu'ama* have not lost all political significance, but the breadth of their influence—particularly in the Shi'i and Maronite communities—has been considerably narrowed.

As a result of increases in literacy, internal and external migration, exposure to the media, and occupational shifts away from agriculture and toward the services sector, even Lebanese dwelling in villages have transcended the isolation and malleability that we often glibly associate with nonurban populations. Although Lebanese wax poetic about their pristine villages, such places are now only social history.

Even before the fighting began in 1975, a wide variety of political organizations competed for the growing pool of prospective recruits. Many of the most successful political movements appealed to the confessional (religious) identity that every Lebanese acquires at birth. The success of recruitment based on primordial sentiments is hardly surprising. We have already noted that the Lebanese find it difficult to escape from their hyphenated identities as Sunni-Lebanese, Greek Orthodox–Lebanese, and so on. From the citizen's identity card specifying confession to the allocation of political rewards according to confessional formulae, it is impossible for a person to simply be a Lebanese.[20] However, the salience of such groups as the Lebanese Forces (Maronite), Harakat Amal (Shi'i), and the Progressive Socialist party (Druze) should not be allowed to mask a fundamental underlying factor: a profound broadening of the politically relevant population. This factor complicates relations not only between communal groups but within them as well.

The contenders for power have included political unknowns like Fadi Frem, and his coreligionists Elie Hobeika and Samir Jaejae, all political rivals within the Maronite community, as well as Nabih Berri, the leader of the Shi'i Amal movement. In temperament, social origin, and wealth these men are antithetical to the *zu'ama* they seek to supplant.

The predominately Maronite Lebanese Forces were created in 1976 by Bashir al-Gemayel, the scion of the founder of the Kata'ib (or Phalange) party, Pierre al-Gemayel. Although Bashir was certainly not a political unknown, the organization he created was largely made up of lower and lower middle-class Maronites from Beirut's eastern suburbs who, in most cases, rejected the politics of the old guard (including the Kata'ib party). Lewis Snider noted that the Lebanese Forces were not just a militia but a political ethos that rejected old style politics as practiced by the Christian and Muslim establishment. Simply put, the Lebanese Forces reject the rule of Lebanon by a cartel of elites.[21] Since the assassination of Bashir in September 1982, the leadership has fallen to a group of young activists who are as staunch in their desire to retain a share of political power as they are committed to the protection of their community's Maronite identity.

Perhaps the most remarkable political transformation has occurred in the long-ignored Shi'i community, which has recently been especially vocal in demanding its rights.[22] The most important Shi'i organization has been the Amal movement, the creation of a charismatic and pragmatic religious leader, Imam Musa al-Sadr, who purposefully and successfully challenged the authority of the established political bosses. Al-Sadr disappeared (he seems to have been murdered) during an enigmatic visit to Libya in 1978. His disappearance, the powerful exemplar of the Islamic Revolution in Iran, and the punishing blows sustained by the Shi'a in the south have combined to invigorate the community with a sense of self that has long been absent.

Amal is today led by Nabih Berri. Berri, a lawyer, was born in Sierra Leone of a trader family from south Lebanon. Berri's name often evokes the contempt of *zu'ama*, who deride his dearth of the traditional requisites for elite status. Nevertheless, Nabih Berri now speaks for a majority of the Shia, although he is under increasing challenge from the pro-Iranian Hizballah (Party of God) which juxtaposes a call for Islamic rule in Lebanon to Amal's reformist stance. The Amal movement demands the abolition of a political system that allocates political privileges by sectarian criteria, while it has proved itself an adept player in the very system it derides; in contrast Hizballah's solution is based upon the exemplar of the Islamic Revolution in Iran. Although Amal retains the upper hand, it is quite clear that the intense intra-communal competition will continue.[23]

Putting Lebanon Back Together

Viewing Lebanon from afar, we can easily reel off prescriptive mottoes. The reestablishment of civility in Lebanon undeniably demands a reconciliation of contending views about the nature of the state and the allocation of political privileges within the state. Certainly the restraint or, even better, the withdrawal of foreign forces (whether Palestinian, Syrian, or Israeli) seems a precondition for allowing the Lebanese to resurrect legality and restore a measure of peace to their war-torn country. Clearly, the initiation of a program of economic reconstruction would at least offer the promise of redress for the pressing needs of many impoverished Lebanese and, at the same time, undercut the demagoguery that so often feeds on misery and hopelessness. Yet what makes the problems facing Lebanon so formidable and intractable is the fact that the country faces an array of dilemmas. When considered in isolation from one another, each dilemma poses serious challenges, but what makes the task of rebuilding so gargantuan is that the dilemmas are not isolated. They feed on one another, thus enmeshing Lebanon in a sticky web of interconnected problems.

Dilemma Number One: Reconciliation

If each sect in Lebanon were socially and politically unified, intersectarian reconciliation would be a much less difficult problem. The survival imperatives of intrasectarian politics often preclude necessary compromises. Many political leaders, whether their motives are sublime or ignoble, face serious competitive challenges from within their own sects. These challenges severely restrict and harden their negotiating positions, often to the extent of politically disabling those prone to compromise. The problem, then, is not just to accommodate the demands of contending communities but to determine who effectively represents each community or segment.

The dilemma is shown dramatically in the case of President Amin al-Gemayel's relations with the Shi'i community. Gemayel, elected to the presidency in September 1982 after the assassination of his brother Bashir (who was president-elect), has lacked a firm and broad constituency in his own Maronite community. Faced with the obvious need to stand above confessional politics and lead Lebanon back to civility, Amin al-Gemayel chose instead to attempt to satiate his many Maronite detractors by working to preserve the political privileges of his sect. Although he did attempt, unsuccessfully, to reach a rapprochement with the Druze leader, Walid Jumblatt, Gemayel chose not to deal with the Shi'i leader, Nabih Berri. Instead he opted to turn to Kamel al-Asad, the Shi'i speaker of the Chamber of Deputies. However, the speaker's once considerable hold on the Shi'i community has weakened to the point of disappearance, and for most Shia, Kamel al-Asad epitomizes the faults and corruption of Lebanese politics. Not unexpectedly, the president's actions did little more than feed the growing impression that he sought above all else to avoid any accommodation toward the emerging social forces (outside of his own community). The joint Shi'i-Druze takeover of West Beirut on February 6, 1984, demonstrated the president's strategic misjudgment.

Dilemma Number Two: Time Has Opened New Wounds

Anyone who visited Lebanon immediately after the Israeli invasion of 1982 can testify to the extraordinary ebullience and hope that the invasion produced. For many years, the Lebanese had been waiting for the "last battle," and the invasion seemed to signal just that. The increasingly unpopular, even detested PLO had been cut down to size in Lebanon, and the all-powerful United States had finally decided to solve Lebanese problems once and for all. To be sure, the problems were recognized to be considerable, but with Washington's energy focused on a solution, there seemed little to worry about. If the optimism of the Lebanese seemed unbounded, so did the ecstasy of the United States as it savored the strategic opportunity that had been dropped in its lap.

This is not the place for a retrospective analysis of the U.S. failure in Lebanon, but suffice it to note that during a crucial and opportune period in fall 1982 new fighting and further bloodshed broke out. By the end of 1982, the Syrian forces in Lebanon had caught their breath and were being reequipped by the Soviet Union; the Israelis had settled into the occupation of south Lebanon; the PLO, increasingly under Syrian pressure, was consolidating its positions in the Bekaa Valley and north Lebanon; new fighting had erupted in the Shouf region southeast of Beirut between the Maronite Lebanese Forces and Druze militias, with both sides enjoying a degree of assistance and encouragement from Israel; and the southern suburbs of Beirut, densely populated by Shia, were increasingly bearing the brunt of widespread arrests, acts of intimidation, and armed attacks by government security forces that sometimes seemed to be acting in league with Maronite militia. If the United States (and its European allies) indeed had an opportunity to foster a Lebanese renewal, there is good reason to believe that the opportunity expired by early 1983. In retrospect, it is hard to claim that a speedy Israeli and Syrian withdrawal would have led to a worse situation than we have witnessed. Whatever the prospects may have been, the lesson is transparent. Opportunities are not permanent, at least not in Lebanon, and if not quickly grasped, they disappear. The situation in Lebanon does not and will not stand still. Blink, and it changes, becoming ever more dangerous with each new iteration.

Perhaps the most poignant development of the postinvasion period has been the degree to which moderation has been discredited. Moderate, hopeful politicians have little save empty hands to show for their pains. In the Shi'i community, growing frustration and anger have helped to enliven politics at the extremes. The centrist politicians of the Amal movement openly expressed their fear that they would lose control of their constituents, as radical movements such as the Hizballah (widely believed to have played a role in the terrorist attacks on the Americans and the French) capitalized on the climate of despair. In such an environment, the dynamics of survival are clear: The moderates either temper their moderation or risk being pushed aside. In all of Lebanon's communities, time has hardened positions and fostered a resurgence of sectarian identities.

Dilemma Number Three:
Insecurity Enhances the Value of External Alliances

Meddling by foreign powers has been a hallmark of Lebanon's history. In nineteenth-century Lebanon, confessional insecurity served to justify and foster ties with external powers. If Lebanese politics today seem less like domestic politics and more like international balance of power politics, it is largely because of the shifting alliance patterns between Lebanon's power brokers and external allies. Syria, for instance, has in recent years been aligned with significant factions among the PLO, Druze, Shia, Sunnis, and even the Maronites.

As in most international alliances, the benefits of alliance accrue to both parties, and astute Lebanese politicians, such as the Druze leader Walid Jumblatt, have masterfully played off one external power after another. Following Israel's withdrawal from the Shouf in 1983, it became clear that Jumblatt was enjoying the support of the Israelis as well as the Syrians. Thus, it is not always clear who is manipulating whom.

The ready availability of external support clearly diminishes the attraction of intersectarian compromise and increases the appeal of going it alone. As one community becomes identified with the interests of an external power, it often becomes a hostage to the ebb and flow of regional politics. For example, though the Shi'i Amal movement has maintained friendly relations with Damascus, the movement attempted to keep its distance from Syria in the postinvasion period. When opposition politicians sponsored by Syria created a front in opposition to President Gemayel in 1983, Amal declined to join. However, as the promise of the U.S. role in Lebanon soured and the Israeli occupation of the south (which is the spiritual and population center for the Shia) wore on, Amal's leaders found they had little choice but to move closer to Syria. In doing so, they antagonized the Israelis, who perceived them as Syrian surrogates, thereby further diminishing the prospects for a tacit deal that would have enabled Israel to begin withdrawing from the south prior to February 16, 1985.

There seems to be little hope of escaping this complex dialectic unless one external power is willing to play the role of the honest broker and is permitted to do so without interference from other outside actors. Many Lebanese had hoped that the United States could play such an enlightened role, but it was not to be. The enmity separating Israel and Syria seems sufficient to ensure that Syria will be thwarted in any attempt to effectively dominate all Lebanon, just as Israel was thwarted in its attempt to recreate Lebanon in the vision of the Lebanese Forces. In sum, the play of regional politics in Lebanon is likely to promote the continued disintegration of the state rather than its reunification.

If there is a common ground of agreement on Lebanon, it is that attempts to put the country back together by resorting to an obsolete blueprint are doomed to failure. Beyond that consensus, there are yawning disagreements. Politics in Lebanon are played as a zero-sum game and the stakes are survival. If some are to gain in political power, then others must lose, and they will not do so willingly. Although most Lebanese yearn for peace, the prospects for continued social and political fragmentation remain high.

Notes

1. David R. and Audrey C. Smock, *The Politics of Pluralism: A Comparative Study of Lebanon and Ghana* (New York: Elsevier, 1975), p. ix.

2. Elie Adib Salem, *Modernization Without Revolution: Lebanon's Experience* (Bloomington, Ind.: Indiana University Press, 1973), p. xiii.

3. For a notable exception, see Iliya Harik, *Lebanon: Anatomy of Conflict* (Hanover, N.H.: American Universities Field Staff Reports, no. 49, 1981).

4. See A. R. Norton, "Lebanon's Shifting Political Landscape," *New Leader*, March 8, 1982, pp. 8-9.

5. Walid Khalidi, *Conflict and Violence in Lebanon: Confrontation in the Middle East* (Cambridge: Center for International Affairs, Harvard University, 1979); Marius Deeb, *The Lebanese Civil War* (New York: Praeger, 1980); and Kamal S. Salibi, *Crossroads to Civil War: Lebanon 1959-1976* (Delmar, N.Y.: Caravan, 1976).

6. John Kifner and Thomas Friedman of the *New York Times*, Trudy Rubin, John Cooley, and Robin Wright of the *Christian Science Monitor*, Jonathan Randal and David Ottoway of the *Washington Post*, and David Ignatius of the *Wall Street Journal* have all set very high standards in their reporting.

7. This period is brilliantly treated by William R. Polk in *The Opening of South Lebanon, 1788-1840: A Study of the Impact of the West on the Middle East* (Cambridge: Harvard University Press, 1963).

8. Joseph Chamie, *Religion and Fertility: Arab Christian-Muslim Differentials* (Cambridge, England: Cambridge University Press, 1981), p. 85.

9. *Ibid.*, and *al-Safir*, April 18, 1984, for population estimates.

10. John D. Law and Richard B. Parker, *The Reconstruction of Lebanon*, a report prepared for the U.S. Businessmen's Commission on the Reconstruction of Lebanon, February 29, 1984.

11. Nora Boustany, "As Economic Miracle Crumbles, Lebanese Face Harder Times," *Washington Post*, February 23, 1985.

12. *Atlaseco 1984*, Paris: RTL.

13. *The Reconstruction of Lebanon*.

14. Albert Dagher, "La grande détresse de l'économie libanaise: Essor de speculation, effondrement de la production," *Le Monde Diplomatique*, January 1985.

15. David Ignatius, "How to Rebuild Lebanon," *Foreign Affairs* 6 (summer 1983), p. 1152.

16. Dagher, "La grande détresse."

17. *Middle East Economic Digest*, December 21, 1985.

18. *Ibid.*, March 29, 1985.

19. *Ibid.*, January 11, 1985.

20. It is significant that the major policy statement delivered by Prime Minister Rashid Karami on May 31, 1984, calls for the abolition of religious specification on identity cards: an important symbolic and practical step toward the abolishment of sectarianism.

21. Lewis W. Snider, "The Lebanese Forces: Their Origins and Role in Lebanon's Politics," *Middle East Journal*, no. 38 (winter 1984), pp. 1–33, see p. 3.

60922. See A. R. Norton, "Harakat Amal," in *Religion and Politics* (Political Anthropology III) (New Brunswick, N.J.: Transaction Books, 1984), pp. 105–131. On the general issue of political and social change in Lebanon, see Ronald McLaurin and Paul Jureidini, "Social Change and Political Change in Lebanon" (unpublished); and Jureidini, McLaurin, Norton et al., *The Emergence of a New Lebanon* (New York: Praeger, 1984).

23. See A. R. Norton, "Shi'ism and Social Protest in Lebanon," in Juan Cole and Nikki Keddie, eds., *Shi'ism and Social Protest* (New Haven, Conn.: Yale University Press, 1985), pp. 156–178.

3

Israel

Bernard Reich

Israel remains a central actor in the Middle East despite its small size and population and its political isolation in the region. Notwithstanding its estrangement from much of the third world, with which it shares numerous characteristics, it has become an increasingly important actor in the politics of the Middle East and in U.S. foreign policy, partly because of the continuing Arab-Israeli conflict. Israel's rapid development and achievements in the scientific and social areas have received much attention, and Israel has been the region's most politically and socially innovative state. It has melded immigrants from more than 70 countries into a uniquely Israeli population. Although almost devoid of natural resources, it has developed a thriving economy and its citizens have achieved a high standard of living.

Israel faces a number of crucial issues in the coming years, many of which were highlighted by the Knesset (parliament) elections of 1984. Domestically, there is the question of political succession and leadership as Israel moves from the generation of the founders to a new generation of political leaders lacking the special aura of involvement in the creation of the state.

The proportional representation system, the resultant multiplicity of parties, and the wide divergence of views held by Israelis have produced substantial splintering within parliament. Although the ability of 15 political parties to secure seats in the Knesset in 1984 is an implementation of the democratic process, it raises questions about the continuing ability of Israel's political leaders to form a viable government, especially a government strong enough to make difficult decisions on major foreign policy and domestic questions. A series of demographic issues, centering on the Oriental question, continue to affect the character of the state. Israel's economic "miracle" has been obscured by triple-digit inflation that apparently reached a 400 per cent annual level during the 1984 election campaign and reminded the electorate of more deep-seated economic problems. Tension between secular and religious Jews has been on the rise. The Arab-Israeli conflict, particularly the future of the occupied territories and of the Palestinians, and the

45

relationship with the United States continue to be central issues for the nation's future foreign and security policy.

Political Dynamics and the 1984 Election

The July 1984 Knesset election marked a crucial milestone in Israel's history. It reminded observers that Israel is a functioning democracy but also that it faces substantial problems in its continued efforts to survive as a Jewish state in the Middle East. In its search for solutions to these problems, Israel's body politic was far from united in 1984. Both the campaign debate and the election results reflected the divisions within the population.

The resignation of Prime Minister Menachem Begin in September 1983 marked the end of an era—that both of Menachem Begin and of the founders of the state (David Ben-Gurion, Moshe Sharett, Levi Eshkol, Golda Meir). Since then, a new phase of leadership by more conventional individuals has begun—a phase of politics without charisma (although not all the founders possessed personal charisma; certainly Sharett and Eshkol were suspect in that regard). The 1984 campaign also lacked a sense of vibrancy that could generate interest in the election process and in the issues facing Israel.

Begin's refusal to emerge from his self-imposed retirement brought to an end the period of father figures. It was thus left to Yitzhak Shamir (Likud) and Shimon Peres (Labor Alignment) to lead the lackluster politicians who vied for the voters' approval. The results, in part, reflected their inability to entice the noncommitted voter to full participation. Neither party could generate dynamism, and both were characterized as colorless. Labor was unable to capitalize on Likud's misfortunes, including the retirement and seclusion of Begin, the Lebanese quagmire, and the economic problems (reflected in the oft-quoted figure of 400 per cent inflation). Shamir proved able to retain much of Likud's electoral support, thus avoiding what many thought (and the polls earlier predicted) would be a Labor victory by a substantial margin.

Since independence, stability has characterized the government of Israel, owing in large measure to the broad agreement concerning the basic ethos of the state. Yet during the nearly forty years of independence, the nation has had more than twenty governments, and no party has ever achieved a parliamentary majority. The proportional representation system has been a major factor in ensuring that multiple parties are represented in parliament. Although such a system can be justified as a true reflection of the diversity of political perspectives in Israel, it has led to the need for coalition governments, which has had a great effect on the policies and evolution of the state. Decisions concerning government positions and policies are reached after compromise among the parties making up the coalition. Even the smallest parties can affect the government's ability to remain in power— as was seen in 1984 when Tami (with only three of 120 seats in the Knesset) chose to withdraw its support from the coalition, thereby forcing early elections.

The ability of numerous groups to create viable election lists (by paying a small deposit and securing a small number of signatures on an election petition) and to secure the minimal 1 per cent of the vote needed to share in the distribution of seats in the Knesset suggests that Israel's parliament will continue to see numerous parties representing diverse political views or the ambitions of a particular individual. The result is that coalition formation and the establishment of a government are complicated. But it also suggests the vulnerability of the system to the caprice of small parties reflecting a minute portion of the vote but able to exact concessions for their parliamentary support because they are able to force the government from office or determine which of the larger parties will govern. This structure, coupled with the current lack of forceful leaders, tends to produce indecisive governments. Nevertheless, the National Unity Government formed by Labor and Likud in October 1984 proved more durable than most analysts expected.

Fifteen of the 26 political parties that contested the 1984 election secured the necessary 1 per cent of the valid votes cast to obtain a seat in parliament. The two major blocs were relatively close: The Labor Alignment secured 724,074 votes (44 seats), and the Likud secured 661,302 votes (41 seats). The remaining parliamentary seats were not distributed in any clear pattern that would facilitate the forming of a new government. Following the prescribed procedure, President Chaim Herzog consulted with the leaders of the parties and eventually designated Labor's Shimon Peres as the member of the Knesset who should try to form a government. This decision followed the maneuvering of the two major parties to induce the smaller parties to join with them to form a coalition with a majority in parliament. It reflected the president's assessment, probably tempered by his own long-time membership in the Labor party, that Peres had a better chance of forming a government given the complicated configuration of the party structure in the newly elected Knesset. Herzog sought to promote the idea of a national unity government as the most appropriate and efficacious means of governing Israel in the ensuing period. His views (and those of many others) were conditioned by the perspective that either major party would have difficulty forming a government on any but a narrow, and therefore fragile, coalition base involving numerous small parties each pursuing its own program. Such a government would find it extremely difficult, if not impossible, to make important decisions on crucial issues such as the economy, the presence in Lebanon, and the peace process.

The election had a number of other important results, including the success, after failure in previous elections, of Rabbi Meir Kahane and his Kach party in gaining nearly 26,000 votes and a parliamentary seat. Kahane had campaigned on a theme of "making Israel Jewish again" by seeking the expulsion of the Arabs from Israel as well as from the West Bank and Gaza. Initially, the party was banned from participation in the election by the central elections committee, but its ruling was reversed by the supreme court—a move which gained the party additional publicity and probably facilitated its effort to secure a Knesset seat. Since the 1984 elections support for Kahane has continued to grow, so much so that it is predicted that he may gain as many as two or three additional seats when new elections are called.

Kahane's success seems to reflect a small but perceptible shift to the right in the electorate as a whole. The Labor Alignment and its closest parliamentary allies secured about the same number of seats in 1984 as they had held in the outgoing parliament, whereas Likud appeared to lose some of its support. However, Tehiya gained seats, and Kach's victory resulted from a move to the Right of enough voters to gain the minimum percentage required for a seat. The soldiers' vote, which is counted separately, also seemed to move to the Right in supporting candidates. According to estimates, as many as 50 per cent of the soldiers' votes went to Likud and Tehiya, a substantial increase over the 1981 results. At the same time the vote of the Oriental Jewish community seemed instrumental in Kahane's victory, in the move to the Right of the soldiers' vote and in the securing of the four seats gained by the Sephardi Torah Guardians, apparently at the expense of the more European-dominated establishment Agudat Israel (which lost half of its seats). In general, ever since Begin's victory in 1977, the Oriental vote has been associated with Likud and its allies to the Right.

Basically the results of the 1984 election were inconclusive even though Shimon Peres and Yitzhak Shamir were able to form a unique National Unity government in which they agreed to trade jobs after two years— Peres to become foreign minister and Shamir to become prime minister. The government that resulted from the 1984 election reflected that Israelis are divided on many of the key issues facing the country in the foreign policy, political, economic, social, or religious arenas and between those who supported Likud and those who supported Labor. Furthermore a host of smaller parties with their own particular agendas and conceptions will continue to play a disproportionate role in Israel's future.

The Oriental Issue

In 1948, Israel's Jewish population of some 650,000 was overwhelmingly of Ashkenazi origin. The massive immigration to Israel of Jews from Oriental communities and their higher birthrate have changed the demographic nature of the state: Israel today has an Oriental majority among its 3.6 million Jews.

Geographically and demographically Israel is an Oriental country, but its culture, society, and political system are Western in nature and orientation. The early Zionists laid the foundations for an essentially European culture in Palestine—with its concepts, ideals, and ideologies—and subsequent immigration accelerated the trend. The Western immigrants created and developed the Yishuv structure of land settlement, institutions, trade unions, political parties, and educational system, with its attendant assumptions and premises, in preparation for a Western-oriented Jewish national state. Future immigrants had to adapt to a society that had formed these institutions. Zionism was initiated by European Jews as a response to European anti-Semitism, and the membership and leadership of the World Zionist Organization were overwhelmingly European; its programs were almost entirely European oriented. The overwhelming majority of Jewish immigrants to Palestine (more than 85 per cent) were European.

After the Holocaust, the focus of attention shifted as the creation of Israel and the first Arab-Israeli war generated impossible conditions for the Jews in the countries of the Middle East and North Africa. Whole communities were transported to Israel. Massive Oriental immigration thus created a situation in which a large portion of the population has societal and cultural traditions (customs, practices, and attitudes) akin to the Arab populations among whom they lived for generations but different from those of their Western coreligionists. The religious tradition of the entire Jewish population is an asset as it provides a common core of values and ideals, but there are major differences in outlook, frames of reference, levels of aspiration, and other social and cultural components.

Israel's communal problem is one of ethnic-cultural cleavages within the Jewish community that have existed since the communities came into contact during the Palestine mandate. At the outset, the communities had limited contact, in part because of segregated housing and because of different forms of employment, educational patterns, and level of involvement in politics and public affairs. The socioeconomic gap continues to be manifest in a number of inequalities. But changes are occurring and members of Israel's Oriental community have risen to high rank in the military, serve in large numbers in the Knesset, and are ministers in the cabinet. Yitzhak Navon served as president and David Levy is today one of the aspiring leaders of the Likud. There has also been increasing social intercourse between the two communities, and improvements in housing and education have helped to reduce the gap between Israel's predominantly Ashkenazi upper class and its less privileged Oriental majority.

Israel's Oriental Jewish community has reacted in numerous ways to its perceived unequal treatment in the system. During much of the first three decades of independence, the Oriental population was politically quiescent and its actions low key. There were petitions, protests, demonstrations, and strikes, but such weak efforts were only partially sucessful in creating interest groups and political movements to focus attention on the core issues. In more recent years as concerns have grown, Oriental political manifestations have increased. The Oriental population has emerged as a political force with increased support for Likud. Menachem Begin seemed to be an authority figure to whom the Oriental population could relate as it sought to manifest its resentment of the treatment it had received under the Labor establishment, which had run Israel during the mandate and since independence. First in 1977 and then in the 1981 parliamentary election, Likud proved to be immensely popular among the country's Oriental Jewish voters. In 1981 Likud succeeded in securing the overwhelming portion (probably 70 per cent) of Oriental ballots, although the Oriental voters, who were generally of lower socioeconomic strata, should have had an affinity for the programs championed by the Labor Alignment. A similar phenomenon was replicated in the 1984 election.

The Oriental Jewish community of Israel seems to have found a political home with the Likud and appears to support the party almost reflexively. Why it votes that way remains unclear, but a number of factors seem to be involved. There is an appeal in Likud's nationalist and traditionalist approach to political and religious matters and in a strong anti-Arab sentiment in foreign and security policies. At the same time, the Oriental community (as indeed most Israelis) has had a significant increase in the standard of living and in private consumption. The Likud is thus often equated with prosperity, whereas the Labor governments are associated with years of deprivation. These perceptions are powerful generators of votes, and the Oriental Jewish community has become an increasingly significant political factor given its growing proportion of the population and its growing political awareness and participation.

Religion in the Jewish State

The UN Partition Plan for Palestine of November 1947 provided for the establishment of a Jewish state, and when that state became independent in May 1948, it regarded itself as both Jewish and secular. Israel's Declaration of Independence recalls the spiritual and religious connection of the Jewish people to the land of Israel but also guarantees its citizens freedom of religion and conscience. Since independence, Israel has had to come to terms with the concept of its Jewishness and the definition of who is a Jew. It has also had to address the meaning of a Jewish state and the roles to be played by religious forces and movements in the state. Israel has not resolved these questions, and the conflict between the secular and religious perspectives on these and related matters has been a continuing characteristic of the country. Indeed, in recent years tensions between secular and religious Jews have resulted in open fighting which some have described as near civil war.

Israel is a Jewish state, but it permits its various religious communities substantial autonomy in a system derived from the Ottoman *millet* structure, as continued with modifications under the British mandate. The contentious religious issues are centered within the Jewish community and focus on the authority and power of the Orthodox religious authorities and their desire to mold the system in their preferred image. To a significant degree this issue has been summed up under the rubric of the question of who is a Jew; but the problem is actually the extent to which the Orthodox religious authorities can impose their will on the system and on Israelis who have different perspectives of the role religion should play in the Jewish state.

The question of who is a Jew has been at the center of the religion-state controversy and has theological, political, and ideological overtones with specific practical dimensions. Secular and religious authorities and ordinary citizens have faced the question for purposes of immigration, marriage, divorce, inheritance, and conversion and for registering with appropriate authorities. During Israel's early years when a special effort was made to encourage immigration, Prime Minister David Ben-Gurion used a broad, liberal interpretation of the concept. The Orthodox religious leadership sought to restrict Jewish identification and ensure its conformity with Orthodox doctrine as determined by traditional Orthodox authorities. A compromise to obviate clashes took the form of the so-called status quo agreement that retained the situation as it had existed upon independence. The Orthodox community has sought to expand its perspective, and periodically the matter has engendered substantial public attention and discussion.[1]

Political maneuvering on religious issues increased during the Begin years owing to his own proclivity and the importance of Agudat Israel and the National Religious party for the narrow Begin-led coalitions of 1977 and 1981. The religious factor became more prominent following the 1981 elections when the religious parties became even more indispensable for the formation of a government, thereby gaining for themselves substantial power. Agudat Israel and the National Religious party insisted on substantial concessions from Begin and Likud prior to joining and supporting the coalition. The result was a lengthy coalition agreement that focused on important changes in the role of religion in Israel and on the question of who is a Jew. Israel has yet to resolve these matters, and they threaten to strain relations not only between the various factions within Israel but also between Israel and some of its Jewish supporters abroad. At times major strains have been created between the Orthodox Jewish community in Israel and the large Conservative and Reform Jewish movements in the United States.

Economic Problems

Israel's economy has undergone substantial change, and the economic well-being of its people has significantly improved since independence. Israel remains something of an economic "miracle" despite the pre-independence prophecies that its troubled economy could not long endure. Israel—virtually bereft of natural resources and faced with substantial burdens of absorption imposed by massive immigration and of defense imposed by Arab hostility, which has led to six wars and an Arab boycott—has achieved a relatively prosperous economic level in the 1980s. The country's standard of living is comparable to that in such Western European countries as Italy and Great Britain. Its life expectancy levels are among the highest in the world; it has maintained a high level of social services for its population; its GNP has made dramatic progress since the 1950s. These achievements are matched by similar statistics in other sectors.

The lack of substantial natural resources has been a problem, but it has been offset by the unusually valuable asset Israel has in its human resources. Massive immigration created problems for the Jewish state in its early years, but it also endowed Israel with skilled workers and professionals. Israel has developed its own highly regarded educational and scientific establishment, illiteracy is virtually nonexistent, and its population is one of the most highly educated in the world. It is in the forefront of scientific accomplishment in fields such as energy technology and medical-scientific research. Israel's only significant domestic energy source is solar power; it has no coal or hydroelectric power and possesses very little oil. The lack of domestic energy resources makes its economy particularly sensitive to international oil developments and its economic policies vulnerable to price increases. This energy dependence was exacerbated when Israel relinquished Sinai and offshore oil fields to Egypt as required by the Egypt-Israel Peace Treaty and was thereafter forced to purchase large quantities of oil on the world market. Since 1979, its balance of payments deficits largely have been the result of dependence on imported oil.

Israel has lacked the capital necessary for its economy to function efficiently and has had to import capital as well as raw materials. Since 1948, Israel has relied on foreign capital inflows for its capital formation to finance its growing economy and current expenditures; it has borrowed to finance capital equipment and current consumption. External sources have included loans, grants, contributions, outside investments, U.S. government aid, the sale of Israel bonds, German reparations and restitutions payments, and Jewish donations.[2]

These sources and methods of raising capital have permitted Israel to pursue a policy of rapid economic and demographic expansion. Between 1950 and 1972 it maintained a real output rate of nearly 10 per cent per year and its output per worker more than tripled. The rapid increase in economic output has been accompanied by significant increases in the standard of living; per capita income reached $5,500 in 1984. Concomitantly inflation has become a feature of the economy—double digit since the early 1970s and triple digit in more recent years. At the time of the July 1984 election, it was estimated at a 400 per cent annual rate. Israel's population has been insulated from the adverse effects normally associated with inflation and related economic pressures through the mechanism of linkage or indexing; virtually all aspects of financial life in Israel are linked to the domestic consumer price index so that the wages and assets of most individuals rise to keep pace with prices. This approach protects individuals from the worst effects of inflation but also makes them less willing to make the sacrifices necessary to help control inflation.

Israel's economy is greatly affected by the conflict with the Arabs, reflected in its extraordinarily high levels of defense expenditure. Defense expenditures and foreign debt service, much of which is for previous defense-related expenditures, account for more than 60 per cent of the current state budget. Large portions of the GNP have been utilized by the government sector, and private demand has been substantial. The result has been high inflation, large deficits in the current account, and constant devaluations of the Israeli shekel (formerly the lira or pound). The pattern of imports exceeding exports has had an adverse effect on Israel's foreign debt position.

In recent years Israelis have become more aware of economic issues and more concerned about the failure of the government to deal effectively with them, though there have been improvements in recent years. Prior to 1985 there seemed to be little confidence that the government could deal with the economic problems. But since the average Israeli was well insulated from the effects of poor economic policies and management, inflation and trade deficits and related themes were subjects for academic discussion, not everyday concerns of the population. The labor union movement was instrumental in helping to ensure that the average worker maintained a high standard of living, and indexation protected the average Israeli from the ravages of inflation with regard to both wages and savings.

In fall 1983 when Yigal Cohen-Orgad replaced Yoram Aridor as Israel's finance minister, austerity measures were introduced that included policies to strengthen the balance of payments and to cut imports. Cohen-Orgad sought to cut private and public consumption and indexation as well as subsidies on a variety of consumer items while including new revenue measures. Although these policies sought to move Israel in the right direction, the question remains whether Israel can reverse the negative economic trends (inflation and stagnation) of the late 1970s and early 1980s given the required burdens of defense and related sectors of the economy. Although improvements were made during 1985 and 1986, Israel's economic problems remain serious and very difficult.

The Quest for Peace and Security

Israel's preeminent concern is with national survival and security because of its conflict with its Arab neighbors and its geostrategic situation. During its first 34 years, it fought six wars with the Arab states and the Palestine Liberation Organization (PLO) and still remains at war (technically, if not actually) with all but Egypt. It spends on a continuing basis a major portion of its budget and GNP on defense and defense-related items and has a sizable standing army and mobilizable reserve force that involves virtually all of its citizens. Its military power is substantial but not unlimited, constrained by its own demography and economy as well as by international factors. Its military is civilian controlled, and retired officers play an important, though limited, role in politics. Virtually all aspects of foreign policy are dominated by Israel's policy that focuses on the survival and security of the state and, hence, on the Arab world. Nevertheless, and as a component of that concern, Israel continues to seek positive relations with as many states as possible. The pursuit of peace through negotiations with the Arab states, the assurance of security in a region of hostility through an effective defense capability, and the attainment of international support continue to be the central and dominating elements in Israel's political life and in its foreign and security policy. At the outset Israel also held a strongly positive view of the United Nations, but because of that body's increasingly large anti-Israel majority and its support for the Palestinian and Arab perspectives, Israel does not regard the United Nations as a helpful factor in the quest for peace and security.

The unremitting hostility of the Arab world (with the exception of Egypt since the peace treaty of 1979) tends to color and affect all other aspects of Israeli life. Six wars and countless skirmishes and terrorist attacks, as well as the Holocaust and Arab hostility during the mandate period, have all left their mark on Israel's national psyche and perceptions. The Arab threat is not seen as an aberration of history but as its latest manifestation. This historical-psychological perspective is supplemented by Israel's geographical and political isolation and the lack of an alliance structure that commits a state formally to come to its defense or provide support in the event of war. Israel's diplomatic relationships have declined since the June 1967 war and it has been increasingly condemned in the United Nations and other international forums in recent years. But in recent years the United States has stepped in with greater amounts of military and economic aid as well as a strategic partnership that has perplexed the Arab world.

Israel judges the basic threat to be confined to the Arab world and, in a narrower military sense, to the confrontation Arab states and the PLO. Although it has been concerned about Soviet actions and potential roles, neither the Soviet Union nor others have been at the center of security planning or conceptions, since a potential Soviet threat is regarded as a concern of the West, not a matter for Israel to deal with on its own. Nevertheless, the 1981 United States–Israel Memorandum of Understanding on Strategic Cooperation focused on "the threat to peace and security of the region caused by the Soviet Union or Soviet-controlled forces from outside the region introduced into the region."

Israel's response to the perceived threat has taken the form of an effective military capability and a carefully constructed military doctrine.[3] The Israel Defense Forces (IDF) is an impressive military establishment, especially in relation to Israel's population, size, and resources. From the beginning and even before the founding of the state, the IDF (and Haganah before independence) sought to achieve the essential military strength and to acquire the wherewithal to meet the identified threat and provide for the defense of the state. This policy has fostered a continuous effort to secure military equipment and to have the necessary quantity and quality of materiel to ensure the country's defense. A significant portion of GNP and budget has been allocated to defense and defense-related expenditures and the development of a substantial defense production capability.

Despite the creation of an impressive military establishment with much of the latest and most sophisticated military equipment, the IDF has limited its capacity to act primarily in response to specific threats from the Arab world. It is constrained by the limited natural resource base and the small population of the state. Israel does not possess the raw materials necessary for its military industry nor those that might generate financial resources or political leverage abroad. It has projected its power into Jordan and, in battle, has struck in Egypt, Syria, and Lebanon and in Iraq in 1981 to eliminate a perceived nuclear threat. The invasion of Lebanon in 1982 was a major military assault with lasting ramifications in many areas. But, except for the July 1976 raid on Entebbe, Uganda, to secure the release of hostages and the strike against the PLO near Tunis in 1985, it has not employed force beyond its own limited geographic area. In recent years this approach has been more the result of political decision than of inherent limits in forces or equipment.

Israel's military assistance efforts have involved limited training of foreign personnel (primarily in Israel), and some advisers have served abroad, mostly in connection with specific and limited tasks including some military sales. Other than the sale of Israeli-produced military equipment and the transfer to third parties of some materiel acquired from other powers, including Soviet military and ancillary equipment captured from the Arab states, Israel's ability to influence worldwide military or security developments is limited. It has not been able to help finance other states' military acquisitions; it has not supported terrorist or similar operations abroad; it has not had long-range military action or shows of force or other symbolic uses of power beyond its immediate area. But there are substantial rumors concerning Israel's support of various minority groups in neighboring states (such as the Kurds in Iraq and the southern Sudanese) and beyond, in part to reduce those states' ability to join in the Arab effort against Israel and in part to make a point concerning survival of beleaguered minorities. It has been active in counterterrorism in Europe and elsewhere, sometimes in ways that have troubled even allies, and the Pollard spy case in 1986 called into question the nature and scope of Israeli espionage activities, even against the United States.

Arms acquisition has involved purchases from foreign sources and domestic production. Israel has benefited from access to modern and sophisticated equipment of virtually all types (including those which Israel cannot produce), but this has increased its debt and dependence. At the same time Israel has increasingly sought to produce and co-produce (and sometimes develop) equipment as a means of guaranteeing supply, reducing defense costs and external debt, and earning foreign exchange through sales. An indigenous military industry has been an element of security planning since independence, and considerable resources have been invested in it with uneven results; the basic shortcoming has been natural and financial resources. Israel has overcome many of these obstacles and produces a wide range of high quality, advanced weapons and related defense items and is an exporter ranking only after the major powers.[4]

Paralleling its security efforts is Israel's involvement in the political process to achieve peace. In the early years after independence, Israel tended to be optimistic about achieving peace, and it expected that the armistice agreements of 1949 could be converted into peace accords. However, there were no negotiations that would lead to formal peace treaties with the Arab states. Israel then became convinced of the implacable hostility of the Arab states and became preoccupied with survival and security, factors that played a role in the 1956 war. No significant moves toward peace with the Arab states that significantly modified the content of the issues central to the dispute occurred in period prior to the June 1967 war.

The victory and occupation of Arab territory in Sinai, the West Bank, the Gaza Strip, and the Golan Heights generated discussion within Israel concerning appropriate policies. Between 1949 and 1967, Israel was prepared for peace with the Arab states on the basis of the 1949 armistice lines, with minor modifications, but after the events of May and June 1967 many argued for change in the security situation. Religious and ideological/historical claims to territory complemented that view. In the initial flush of victory, Israel hoped that the extent of the Arab defeat might generate a willingness to come to terms to achieve a full settlement of the dispute. But there was no responsive chord from the Arab world, which at its August/September 1967 Khartoum summit reiterated that the Arab states continued to adhere to the principles of "no peace with Israel, no recognition of Israel, no negotiations with it, and adherence to the rights of the Palestinian people in their country." The various efforts made to move toward a settlement were ultimately unsuccessful, and the 1969–1970 war of attrition and the 1973 October War marked the fourth and fifth rounds of conflict between Israel and the Arabs.

The termination of hostilities in 1973 facilitated a new approach to peace. The Kissinger shuttles (1974 and 1975) and the Sadat initiative (1977) ultimately yielded concrete results, most significantly the Treaty of Peace between Egypt and Israel in 1979. Their successes were not followed by additional achievements of consequence despite the war in Lebanon and the Israel-Lebanon agreement of May 1983, which was later abrogated by Lebanon under Syrian pressure.

Israel's polity has long identified its positions on the central issues of the conflict, and although Israelis differ over some areas, they exhibit remarkable unanimity of perspective—a national consensus—toward the main policy lines.

The central theme is Israel's desire for real peace within borders that will allow the country to defend itself. Fulfillment of this desire requires normalization of relations with the Arab states. The borders would be determined in the negotiation process, which would identify the extent of Israel's withdrawal from occupied territories. However, Israel would not withdraw to the armistice lines that existed prior to the June 1967 war: Modification of those armistice lines would be essential, and the extent of withdrawal remains a major point of contention among various groups. Likud focuses on retaining the West Bank and Gaza Strip (Judea and Samaria), whereas Labor has advocated territorial compromise for that sector. Israel extended its law and jurisdiction to the Golan Heights in December

1981. Jerusalem is not considered occupied territory—it is the united capital of Israel for nearly all Israelis—and discussions concerning its status are limited to the disposition of the holy places and to the accommodation of the religious sensibilities of other faiths. This perspective is reflected in "Basic Law: Jerusalem, Capital of Israel," adopted by the Knesset in July 1980, which says, "Jerusalem united in its entirety is the capital of Israel" and "the Holy Places shall be protected."

The Palestinians evoke a more complex perspective. For most Israelis Palestinian terrorists are a security issue to be dealt with by the appropriate security forces whereas Palestinian refugees are a humanitarian issue to be treated within the context of the appropriate UN resolutions and with due consideration for the Jewish refugees who fled Arab lands and immigrated to Israel. The political future of the Palestinians increasingly has been recognized as a complex problem that must be resolved, but Israel opposes the creation of an independent Palestinian state, and, although it remains opposed to dealing with the PLO and other terrorist organizations, it has committed itself to negotiation with Palestinians in the search for a solution.

Although these elements of the national consensus have remained consistent over time, they were modified after 1977 when the Labor government was replaced by a Likud coalition under Menachem Begin. The most significant alteration was the extensive effort made to increase the number of Israeli settlements and settlers in the occupied territories, especially in the West Bank. Between 1967 and 1977 the Labor governments sought to limit settlements to those that would serve a security function and sought to avoid conflict between the settlers and the local Arab population. There were exceptions, however, and some settlements were established for a combination of ideological, religious, traditional, and historical reasons. The Begin governments deviated from this policy in that settlements in Judea and Samaria were no longer even said to be restricted to those that are primarily security oriented. According to Likud doctrine, Judea and Samaria are considered integral parts of Eretz Israel, and settlement there is viewed as a natural and inalienable Jewish right. Accordingly, Labor remains prepared for territorial compromise in the West Bank and Gaza, whereas Likud believes that the West Bank should not be relinquished.

Prior to its establishment, and especially since 1948, Israel has continued to recognize that peace and cooperation with the neighboring Arab states is vital for the survival and development of the Jewish state over an extended period, and this approach has remained a cornerstone of its public policy. Following the failure to convert the armistice agreements of 1949 into peace treaties, Israel directed its foreign policy attention beyond the circle of neighboring states and the Middle East to the broader international community. The effort to establish friendly relations with the states of the developing world and Europe, as well as with the superpowers, was conceived as having a positive effect cn the Arab-Israeli conflict, in addition to its strictly bilateral political and economic advantages. The bilateral relationships were also viewed as mechanisms to ensure Israel's deterrent strength through national armed power and through increased international support for its position.

Israel has seen Europe and the developing world (especially Africa and Latin America) as important components of its overall policy. It has sought to maintain positive relations with Europe based on the commonality of the Judeo-Christian heritage and the memories of the Holocaust. Israel's approach to the developing world has focused on its ability to provide technical assistance in the development process. Despite substantial effort in those sectors, the centrality of the Arab-Israeli conflict has enlarged the role of the superpowers. Initially there was some hope that perhaps Israel could remain nonaligned in the East-West struggle. But that aspiration was not attained, and Israel moved increasingly toward a preferred alignment with the Western camp and especially the United States. The West provided Israel with the political and moral support and arms and economic assistance essential for its survival and defense; at the same time the Soviet Union increasingly identified itself with the Arab cause. France, Germany, and England became important in the 1950s and 1960s, and the U.S.-Israel relationship grew (although it had not yet achieved the level attained after June 1967). The relationship with the United States became the most significant because of U.S. political and moral support, because of extensive economic and technical assistance, and because of the arms aid and central position of the United States in the effort to achieve an Arab-Israeli peace. The U.S. Jewish community also helped to create and maintain a special link between Israel and the United States.

Israel's special but complex relationship with the United States, revolving around a broadly conceived ideological factor and based on substantial positive perception and sentiment evident in public opinion and official statements and manifest in political-diplomatic support and military and economic assistance, has not been enshrined in a legally binding commitment joining the two states in a formal alliance or requiring the United States to take up arms automatically on its behalf.[5] Nevertheless, it has been assumed that the United States would come to Israel's assistance should it be gravely threatened.

Undergirding the relationship is a general agreement on broad policy goals. The two states maintain a remarkable degree of parallelism and congruence on such objectives as the need to prevent major war, both within the region and between the superpowers, the need to resolve the Arab-Israeli conflict without allowing the creation of a Palestinian state, and the need to maintain Israel's existence and security and to help provide for its economic well-being. U.S.-Israeli noncongruence of policy on specific issues has derived from various differences of perspective. After the June 1967 war the two countries differed as to technique as well as specific issues such as the appropriate form of response to Arab terrorism, the value of great power efforts in the resolution of the Arab-Israeli conflict, and required military supplies. They also clashed on the status of Jerusalem, the extent of Israeli withdrawal from occupied territories, the increase in Israeli settlements there, and the role of the Palestinians (and the PLO) in the quest for Arab-Israeli peace. As the dialogue has increasingly focused on details, rather than broad areas of agreement, there have been disturbances in the relationship. There have also been differences over Israel's war in Lebanon, the Jonathan Pollard spy scandal, and Israel's Lavi jet aircraft project. Nevertheless, these and similar issues have had limited and generally short-term effects.

The United States is today an indispensable, if not fully dependable, consistent, wholehearted, or unwavering, ally. It provides Israel, through government or private channels, with economic, technical, military, political, diplomatic, and moral support. It is seen as the ultimate protector against the Soviet Union, and it is the primary source of Israel's sophisticated military hardware. Furthermore, the United States remains central to the Arab-Israeli peace process. Nevertheless, agreements on broad goals and discord on specifics will probably characterize the future relationship between Israel and the United States.

Conclusion

The 1984 Knesset elections highlighted the issues facing Israel and the views of Israelis concerning them. It remains unlikely that any single party will emerge in Israel with sufficient backing to form a government on its own. The division of the Israeli polity reflected in the election of 15 parties to parliament belies the consensus of these otherwise divergent groups on many issues. Nevertheless, the National Unity Government was successful in withdrawing Israeli forces from Lebanon—which, by reducing the level of casualties and removing Lebanon from the forefront of daily concerns, alleviated much malaise—and in reducing inflation to low double-digit levels. These achievements were accompanied by a relatively smooth rotation of the government in the fall of 1986 that brought Yitzhak Shamir back to the position of prime minister and moved Shimon Peres to the Foreign Ministry. Despite the shift in positions and in responsibility, Peres continued to promote the idea of an international conference as a means to achieve peace. Various efforts, public and private, seemed to yield some agreements on procedure and to generate some optimism concerning progress in the peace process, although the Israeli public remained sharply divided on many of the central issues in conflict and on what negotiating posture should be assumed in the event of a reinvigorated peace process. The maneuvering in the spring of 1987 suggested an immobility in Israel in regard to the peace process in the absence of an (unlikely) dramatic initiative from an Arab leader that would catalyze the effort and force major soul searching and decision making in the Israeli body politic.

Whatever the result of the next elections, which must occur in 1988 or sooner, the new government will face issues similar to those before the present one: peace with the Arabs, including some progress in resolving the Palestinian issue, economic problems manifest in the need to control inflation and devaluation of the shekel, the divergence between the European and Oriental communities, the continued controversy over the role of religion, and maintenance of the special relationship with the United States and of a strong international posture. Outsiders should neither exaggerate their enormity nor underestimate Israel's ability to respond to them. The nature of Israel's response will be determined by its political dynamics, and the resultant policies will determine Israel's future position in the region and beyond.

Notes

1. Alongside the split between the religious and secular approaches to the problems of religion in the Jewish state are differences within the Orthodox religious community, manifest in part by the large number of religiously based parties contesting the 1984 election and the fact that a number of them were offshoots of existing religious parties. Numerous factions, each with its own leadership and agendas, compete to secure loyalty, votes, program goals, and political patronage.

2. Bernard Reich, *Israel: Land of Tradition and Conflict* (Boulder, Colo.: Westview Press; London, Croom Helm, 1985), especially chap. 3, "The Economy."

3. For elaboration see Bernard Reich, "Israel," in Edward A. Kolodziej and Robert E. Harkavy, eds., *Security Policies of Developing Countries* (Lexington, Mass., and Toronto: Lexington Books, Heath and Co., 1982), pp. 203–225.

4. Given the importance and centrality of the security issue, the Israeli Defense Forces (IDF) might be seen as a critical political actor. The IDF is virtually unique in the Middle East in that it does not, as an entity, play a role in politics, despite its size, budget, importance, and centrality in the Israeli system. Although individual officers, soldiers, and senior commanders have played important roles, they have done so as individuals when not on active service and without the backing of the military institution. The IDF functions in the role of the traditional army—defending the state—in an apolitical fashion. It has not been seen as a threat to the régime, and there has never been consideration of a military coup. Military personnel have played a key role in political life only after their retirement from active duty. Contributing to its limited role is the citizen nature of the IDF, so different from its counterparts in states of the nondeveloped world.

5. Israel is not now, nor has it ever been, allied by treaty to any other state, and no state is formally committed to come to its defense in the event of attack. There is no formal mutual security pact and no Soviet-style treaty of friendship and cooperation. It has joined in implicit or quasi alliances, first with France and then with the United States and, in the instance of the Suez War of 1956, with England and France. These relationships have been useful, but all have been viewed as limited. Israel's multifaceted relationship with the United States is a major exception to its international go-it-alone posture. See Bernard Reich, *The United States and Israel: Influence in the Special Relationship* (New York: Praeger, 1984), especially chap. 5.

4

Egypt

Ali E. Hillal Dessouki

In the 1970s, Egypt restructured its foreign policy orientation, to reflect a trade-off between economic and political objectives as perceived by Egypt's primary decisionmaker, President Anwar al-Sadat. Foreign policy restructuring entails a major alteration or breakup in the orientation of an actor in favor of establishing a new set of commitments and alliances. It is more than a change in tactics or instruments of policy implementation; it also goes beyond the fluctuations and oscillations of foreign policy behavior of developing countries. It involves a basic reconsideration of an actor's perceptions of the global or regional system and of the country's role within that framework. Indicators of the restructuring of foreign policy orientation include patterns of diplomatic, commercial, security, and cultural relations between the country and the outside world.[1]

In the 1970s, Sadat managed to change the name of Egypt (from the United Arab Republic to the Arab Republic of Egypt), its flag, and its national anthem. Economically, Egypt moved away from Nasser's Arab socialism and toward liberalization of the economy and encouragement of private capital. Egypt's one-party political system, which had existed since 1953, was gradually replaced by a form of controlled political pluralism. At the regional level, the country changed its alliances in 1971–1973 and forged a close relation with pro-Western, conservative oil-producing states, particularly Saudi Arabia. As a result of Sadat's visit to Jerusalem in November 1977, Egypt was expelled from all Arab and Islamic councils. At the global level, Egypt moved from an essentially pro-Soviet position that included the granting of naval and air facilities to a virtual strategic alliance with the United States.

This chapter examines the sources, dynamics, and contradictions of Egypt's restructuring of its foreign policy orientation. The analysis underlines issues such as the role of domestic economic factors in foreign policy change, the perception of foreign policy as a resource mobilization activity, the strain resulting from the divergence between role conceptions developed in the 1950s and 1960s and the new environment with which Egypt had to deal, and the dilemma of maintaining a balance between increasing reliance on foreign aid and assistance and protection of the country's independence.[2]

Comparative studies of foreign policy restructuring or alliance switching show that change occurs for various reasons: security considerations, perceptions of gross external dependency and asymmetrical vulnerabilities, ideological disputes, and nationalism. In Egypt's case, three crucial variables must be considered.[3] The first concerns relations between the superpowers. When breaking with one superpower, a small country must take into account the timing. The alternate superpower has to be both able and willing to assume the relationship formerly held by the opposing superpower. Thus, alliance switching is more easily accomplished in a cold war situation or at least in a situation involving strong competition between the superpowers.

A second variable is the personality traits of the leaders. This variable is particularly important in third world countries characterized by low political institutionalization. We should not, however, overstate the importance of personal attributes; leaders do not act in a vacuum, and they are not entirely free to indulge their biases and idiosyncrasies. On the contrary, structural conditions—global, regional, and domestic—determine the environment in which individual leaders must operate. Domestic conditions, including the internal balance of political groups and the degree of political stability or instability, are particularly important for their impact on foreign policy.

The third variable is the nature of any close relationship or alliance involving unequal states in the global stratification system. For a while, a small state may feel profound gratitude for the military and economic help from a superpower, but soon it may also resent the dependent relationship. The breakup of this patron-client relationship is to a certain extent predictable. The necessary conditions form a pattern: sufficient motivation (feeling of dependence), the existence of an alternative (the other superpower), and perception of potential benefits from a breakup.

Geography

Some authors treat the geography of Egypt as an independent variable, postulating a sort of geographic determinism. In a three-volume book of more than 2,500 pages, the eminent Egyptian geographer Gamal Hamdan viewed the history of Egypt as an interaction between the Nile and the desert and drew from this depiction a number of conclusions about Egypt's national interest and policy.[4] The problem with this perspective is its static bias—its assumption of certain unchanging geographic effects of foreign policy. From the perspective of this study, the effects of geography depend upon the interaction between geographic factors and a particular elite or leader's perception of their significance.

Egypt, a land of broad cultural and social homogeneity, is a distinct geographical and historical entity. Its geographical data are simple but extremely significant. The country occupies the northeastern corner of

Africa with an extension across the Gulf of Suez into the Sinai Peninsula in Asia. It is bordered by the Mediterranean Sea to the north, the Sudan to the south, the Red Sea to the east, and Libya to the west. Egypt consists of three regions: (1) the Nile Valley and Nile Delta (a little less than 4 per cent of the total area), which extend from the Sudan northward to the Mediterranean; (2) the eastern desert and the eastern gate to Egypt—the Sinai Peninsula (28 per cent), which extends from the Nile Valley to the Red Sea east of the Suez Canal; and (3) the western desert (68 per cent), which stretches from the Nile Valley westward to Libya. Briefly stated, Egypt is a line of water and verdure that runs between two deserts and widens near the Mediterranean Sea.

Egypt's geographic position made it an easy country to control and to rule. Two main features of the Egyptian society and polity are centralized rule and the absence of long-standing regional allegiances. Dependence on the Nile for irrigation called for central administration and enabled the government to extend its authority to the distant parts of the land. Because the territory is mostly desert, 96 per cent of Egyptians live on less than 4 per cent of the total area of their country.

Egypt's geographic position lends itself to two different perceptions and, therefore, to two different foreign policy objectives. Some view the relative physical isolation of the valley as the most important factor in Egypt's situation: It sets the country apart from its neighbors. In the twentieth century, this perception gave rise to tendencies toward isolationism, Swiss-type neutrality, and the advocacy of an "Egypt first" policy. Others see Egypt's geographic position primarily as a bridgehead, a linking point, a crossroads between Africa and Asia and between the eastern and western parts of the Arab world. Adherents of this school advocate an active foreign policy in the Arab world and Africa. Egypt's eastern, Arab policy is justified in terms of Arab nationalism and security, whereas its southern, African policy rests on the need to protect the Nile waters, the lifeline of Egypt. Nasser embraced the activist view throughout most of his rule, but Sadat gradually emphasized Egyptian patriotism and the urgency of concentrating on Egypt's domestic economic problems. In the war of words that followed the Camp David accords in 1978, Sadat openly accused Arab leaders of being dwarfs, uncivilized and unfit to understand the complexities of the modern world. Because of its wars with Israel, Egypt had become the poorest Arab state, Sadat frequently reminded the Egyptians.

Population and Social Structure

Egypt's population is characterized by social cohesiveness and, since the 1950s, by a baby boom. Historically, Egypt is one of the oldest continuously settled communities in the world. Egyptians long ago acquired the sense of being one people. All Egyptians speak Arabic, with the exception of the Nubians (less than 1 per cent) and an insignificant number of isolated Berber-speaking groups in the western desert. More than 90 per cent of

the people are Muslims, and Islam is the state religion. The indigenous
Copts form the largest of the other religious groups. Estimates of their
numbers vary between 2.3 and 4 million. The Copts speak Arabic, and
hardly any racial or ethnic differences exist between them and the Muslims.
In 1986, the population of Egypt reached almost 50 million and was
increasing by more than one million every year. The population growth
rate between 1966 and 1976 was about 65,000 persons each month, or 2,141
every day and one every 41 seconds.[5]

A direct consequence of the population explosion is the youthfulness
of Egypt's population. Almost one-half of Egyptians are under twenty years
of age; two-thirds are under thirty. Another consequence is the high
dependency ratio, or the large number of dependents supported by working
adults, a situation that put severe constraints on the economy in the 1970s.
The government is increasingly incapable of meeting the demands for food,
education, and work opportunities. A third consequence is the migration
of some three million Egyptians in search of work to other Arab countries,
particularly the oil-producing states.

In contrast to the situation in most developing countries, the population
of Egypt shows a high degree of social and national integration. Both Nasser
and Sadat spoke proudly of Egypt's national unity. There are no fundamental
minority cleavages to constrain foreign policy makers and limit their options.
The one major area of anxiety is the Copts' concern about the implementation
of Islamic law in Egypt and the status of Copts in an Islamic state. Sadat
used to contrast Egypt's deep-seated unity with the sectarian, familial, and
communal fragmentation of other Arab countries. According to Sadat, this
unity allowed Egypt to pursue a purposeful foreign policy and to make
hard decisions impossible for most Arab countries because of their domestic
fragmentation. The population of Egypt constitutes a relatively large human
resource pool. It allowed the government to mobilize an army of about one
million in 1973. Two million Egyptians working abroad provide another
positive resource: Their remittances reached over $3 billion in 1985 and
constituted the single largest source of Egypt's foreign exchange.

Notwithstanding these positive aspects, population growth has had an
adverse impact and has limited Egypt's developmental efforts. The population
explosion has aggravated unemployment problems, increased the dependency
ratio, augmented rural migration to urban centers, and led to the diversion
of resources from investment to consumption needs.[6] Egypt is a prime
example of structural imbalance between population and material resources.
Population is increasing at a rate far beyond the growth in arable cropped
land and far beyond educational and industrial development. The per capita
cropped area declined from 0.73 feddans per person in 1882 to 0.33 feddans
per person in 1970 (a feddan equals 0.42 ha or 1.04 acres). Thus, although
the cropped area almost doubled during this period, population growth
absorbed and surpassed the increase. Since the 1970s Egypt has used its
limited hard currency to import foodstuffs, and in 1985 it imported over
half its food. This made the country more dependent on the outside world

and more vulnerable to the fluctuations of world food market prices. The extent and consequences of food dependency are likely to be major policy concerns in Egypt for years to come.

Economic Capability

In the 1970s, economic factors played a crucial role in the determination of Egypt's foreign policy objectives. By 1980, inflation was running at nearly 30 per cent a year, debts reached a total of $17 billion, and the GNP per capita was $580. Sadat's decision to visit Israel was largely motivated by economic considerations: the reduction of defense expenditures (37 per cent of the GNP in 1977), the encouragement of foreign private capital, and the need for more U.S. aid. Even before this step, Sadat's Arab policy and his forging of a Cairo-Riyadh alliance had also been predicated on expected economic gains.

Since World War II, Egypt's balance of payments deficit has had to be filled from other sources. From 1948 to 1958 it was filled from existing Egyptian reserves; from 1958 to 1964 Egypt received foreign aid from Eastern and Western sources; from 1965 to 1971 the USSR shouldered most of the deficit; from 1971 to 1977 the aid was Arab money; and since 1978 it has been U.S. money. In 1981 Egypt received $2.2 billion in Western aid, of which half came from the United States. The aid has continued into the mid-1980s with nearly $2.5 billion in combined military and economic aid from the U.S. alone in 1984.[7] In the 1970s Egyptian debts increased by a yearly average of 28 per cent, compared with the 13 per cent in the 1960s.

Thus, Egyptian foreign policy has faced the important task of mobilizing external resources to ease the growing population-resources gap. Because of its important strategic-political position and role, Egypt has successfully managed to find aid to bail the country out, but its success is tragic in that it proves the failure of Egypt's developmental plans.

The Egyptian record in the 1970s demonstrates the tensions resulting from a limited resource base, the pursuit of an activist foreign policy, and increasing economic troubles at home. Economic difficulties contributed to the evolution of a more inward-looking and less activist foreign policy. The failure of the government's development efforts to meet the needs of the country's population resulted in growing numbers of shantytowns and the potential for political instability. This failure led the Egyptian leadership increasingly to seek external help to resolve the country's difficult economic situation. The era of revolutionary zeal and enthusiasm (1955–1965), during which Egypt and a number of other third world states had ascended in international politics, was gradually replaced by one characterized by more sober behavior in the 1970s. In Egypt, ideological and political considerations were overshadowed by more immediate economic concerns, and as John Waterbury (political scientist) wrote, "the primacy of economics has become undisputed in Egypt of 1975."[8] Thus, the balance between external and domestic concerns was greatly affected by Egypt's poor economic performance in the face of an ever expanding population.

In 1974, Sadat inaugurated Al-Infitah, an open door economic policy (ODEP), to lure foreign investment into Egypt. He justified the Infitah on the following grounds: (1) the failure of Nasser's socialist experience; (2) the availability of Arab capital from the oil-producing countries; and (3) the international context of détente. From an economic standpoint, the two essential purposes of ODEP were to attract export-oriented foreign enterprises by the establishment of dutyfree zones and to attract foreign capital through a liberal investment policy. However, the ultimate goal of the policy was to set the stage for the development of the Egyptian economy through joint ventures and projects bringing together Egyptian labor, Arab capital, and Western technology and management expertise.[9]

Any analysis of policymaking processes in developing countries divorced from their foreign environment can only lead to erroneous and misleading conclusions. Given their low degree of political institutionalization, their high level of political and social instability, the general structure of their international economic relations, and most important, their dependence upon the outside world for almost everything from food to armaments, developing countries are highly susceptible to external influences.

External factors have greatly influenced the choices and priorities of Egyptian officials. Indeed, their role may be ingrained in the logic of any open door policy. When a ruling elite decides to pursue a development strategy based on foreign aid and capital, it follows that all necessary steps will be taken to attract and reassure its creditors. And the more dependent it is on others, the more vulnerable a country becomes to their pressures, especially in developing countries whose leadership fails to produce coherent development strategies. In the case of Egypt, the initial vagueness of ODEP's goals and the lack of consensus on its content among the ruling elite allowed external factors to play a more crucial role.

The World Bank, the International Monetary Fund (IMF), private financial institutions, and the oil-producing Arab states have all played a role in influencing Egypt's economic policy.[10] For two years (1975 and 1976) international financial institutions and Arab and Western creditors pressured Egypt to make its economy more acceptable and accessible to the world capitalist market by curbing subsidies and devaluing the Egyptian pound. For two years Egyptian officials resisted, mainly because the subsidies and the currency supports allowed the lower middle and lower classes to maintain an already low standard of living. By fall of 1976, oil-producing Arab states joined the United States and the IMF in pressing Egypt for additional fundamental changes. They refused to give Egypt more than a limited amount of money until the government agreed to the reforms proposed by the IMF. Egypt's requests for loans from the IMF and United States banks were delayed in the face of a $1.25 billion deficit for the second half of 1976. Western countries provided short-term loans to finance their exports to Egypt, but the big money needed to meet debt obligations and the balance of payment deficit was not forthcoming.

In January 1977, the government announced price increases for a number of basic commodities such as rice, sugar, gas, cigarettes, and household cooking gas. Almost immediately, violent demonstrations erupted in major cities, leaving an official death toll of about 70. An estimated 800 people were injured, and 1,270 were arrested. Economic decisions were suspended, a curfew was imposed, and the army was called in to maintain law and order. The January 1977 riots underlined the political explosiveness of the subsidy issue. Immediately after the riots, the United States and the oil-producing Arab states came to the rescue. Again in fall 1984 increased food prices sparked riots and the government subsequently decided to rescind the decision.[11]

Both of these events illustrate the impact of economic factors and their influence on foreign policy. First, Egypt's limited resources put a constraint on its government's ability to pursue an activist foreign policy and encouraged it to reach a modus vivendi with conservative rich Arab states; second, the economic troubles made Egypt more dependent on foreign aid and therefore more vulnerable to external influence.

Military Capability

In the 1970s, Egypt's arms arsenal was considerably weakened by three developments: (1) the failure of the Soviet Union to resupply the army adequately after the war of 1973 and the eventual severance of the Soviet military link in 1976; (2) the time needed to shift procurement needs from the Soviet Union to the West and to forge a new link with the United States; and (3) the economic costs of massive rearmament. From 1967 to 1975, according to official estimates, Egypt spent $25 billion for military purposes, matched by an equal amount in war-related losses. During the same period, Egypt received less than $900 million from Arab states.[12]

Of particular interest in this regard is the experience of the Arab military armaments organization (AMIO), founded in 1975 as a joint venture by Egypt, Saudi Arabia, the United Arab Emirates, and Qatar. AMIO was endowed with more than $1.4 billion in an effort to combine oil money with Egypt's skilled labor force. By 1978 the groundwork was laid for the establishment of a basic Arab defense industry located mainly in Egypt. Contacts were initiated with American Motors Corporation to assemble jeeps, with the Ryan Teledyne Corporation to produce high-altitude Drones (pilotless planes equipped with light and infrared sensors), and with Lockheed Aircraft Industries to build C-130 military transports.[13] Contacts were also made with Westland of Britain to construct 50 Lynx helicopters and the Swingfire antitank missile.[14] This project was reduced by half in May 1979 in protest over the Egyptian-Israeli treaty, and the other three Arab partners decided to terminate the venture as of July 1, 1979. Egypt rejected the decision and instead transformed AMIO into a fully Egyptian enterprise. In 1983 Egypt assembled the new French Alpha jets. Increasingly, Egyptian arms deals are made on the basis of coproduction, with an Egyptian role in assembly and parts production.[15]

The relative erosion of Egyptian military power put a constraint on the use of the military instrument in conducting foreign policy. However, the military role did not vanish altogether: Egypt still has one of the best trained and most highly skilled armies in the region, and Egyptian armed forces number well over 300,000, makir.g Egypt's military the largest in the Arab world and Africa. Since the late 1970s, Egypt has embraced an ambitious program for the modernization of its armed forces, ordering more than $6 billion worth of equipment and defense services from the United States and more than $1 billion from Britain and France. U.S. military aid to Egypt has remained steady in recent years at around $1.3 billion a year.[16] Thus, Egyptian decisionmakers still emphasize the readiness of their country to help other Arab states militarily. For instance, Egypt played a crucial role in supporting Iraqi military efforts against Iran by providing arms, ammunition, and logistical aid, and a number of Arab and African armies are already using weapons manufactured in Egypt. Sales of arms and ammunition in 1983 reached $1 billion, and Egypt emerged as a major third world arms exporter.

Political Structure

From 1952 to 1970, the basic characteristics of the political régime in Egypt were absence of political competitiveness, centralization of power, emphasis on mobilization rather than participation, supremacy of the executive over the legislative branch, and repression of political dissent. A clear imbalance existed between politics and administration; output institutions (bureaucracy, policy, and army) far outgrew input institutions (interest groups and political organizations). Whenever possible, the government attempted to penetrate and dominate intermediary associations and groups such as trade unions, professional associations, religious institutions, and universities, bringing them under its legal and financial control. The political system gave its leaders, Nasser and Sadat, an almost free hand in the conduct of foreign policy. The leader was not accountable to a free press, opposition parties, or an independent strong parliament. The régime controlled both the mass media and the legislature and could mobilize their support for its objectives.

In the 1970s, two important processes took place: increasing civilianization of the ruling elite and the development of a constrained political pluralism. Sadat followed a policy of professionalizing the army, disengaging it from current political affairs, and placing more reliance on civilians in high posts. For the first time since 1952, civilians assumed the post of vice president (Mahmoud Fawzi) and prime minister (Aziz Sidky, Fawzi, Abdel-Aziz Hegazi, and Mustafa Khalil). In the realm of foreign policy, Ismail Fahmy, a career diplomat, became the minister of foreign affairs for five years, 1973–1977, until his resignation in protest over Sadat's Jerusalem visit. In 1977, Boutros Ghali, a professor of political science at Cairo University, became the state minister for foreign affairs.

The second development was the gradual democratization of the political structure, leading in 1976–1977 to the establishment of a controlled multiparty system. The democratization process was inspired in part by foreign policy considerations: Sadat's rapprochement with the United States and his desire to project the image of a stable, democratic Egypt. In 1985, opposition political parties included the new Wafd party led by Fuad Serageldin; the Labor Socialists party (LSP), led by Ibrahim Shukry; the National Progressive Unionist party (NPUP), led by Khaled Mohie al-Din; the Liberal Socialist party, led by Mustafa Kamel Murad; and the Umma party, led by Ahmed al-Sabahi. The opposition has a weak parliamentary following (57 seats out of 549), but it exercises far greater influence through its newspapers and publications. Foreign policy was a major bone of contention between the régime and the opposition. The LSP and the NPUP attacked Sadat's pro-Western policy, Egypt's increasing dependency on the United States, Sadat's policy toward Israel, and the break with Arab countries. Until its closure by the government in September 1981, the Moslem Brotherhood's journal, the monthly *Al-Da'wa* (The Call), also voiced most of these concerns, and its writers condemned governmental policies.

The government could have viewed these criticisms as a justification for stiffening its negotiating position toward Israel. Sadat, however, perceived them as signs of vulnerability, weakness, and the erosion of his personal stature, an interpretation that led to political polarization and the confrontation of September-October 1981, the arrest of 1,963 persons in September, and Sadat's assassination in October.

Foreign Policy Orientation

President Sadat assumed office in October 1970 under circumstances that obliged him to emphasize continuity with his predecessor's policies. Nasser's sudden death as a hero restrained Sadat's freedom to change Nasser's domestic and foreign policies. In a meeting of parliament on November 19, 1970, he presented a ten-point program for national action that included "working for Arab unity, playing a role in the nonaligned movement and in the Third World revolutionary movement."[17] In an essay entitled "Where Egypt Stands," published in *Foreign Affairs* in 1972, Sadat reiterated the basic tenets of Nasser's foreign policy: nonalignment and Arab unity.[18] Sadat lived in Nasser's shadow until 1973, when he acquired legitimacy in his own right through success in the October War. The new legitimacy allowed him to pursue domestic and foreign policies different from Nasser's.

Egyptian general foreign policy objectives in the 1970s, as articulated and acted upon by Sadat, were as follows: (1) the restoration, preferably by negotiation, of Egyptian territories occupied by Israel since 1967 (as a consequence, when Sadat's February 1971 peace plan failed, the only option left was war); (2) the termination of the war with Israel, as the economic costs had become increasingly unbearable; (3) the improvement of relations with Washington, as the United States was the only country that could influence Israel; (4) the rejuvenation and modernization of the economy through the import of modern Western technology and private capital; and finally (5) the modification of Egypt's global and regional policies to pursue these objectives more effectively.

Sadat's decision to seek better relations with the United States was influenced by his mistrust of and hostility toward the Soviets and by the belief that the United States would help solve Egypt's pressing economic problems. Sadat was a pragmatist, a realist with little attachment to grand theories and ideologies. He was essentially anti-Communist and anti-Soviet. East-West détente gave him the chance of a lifetime. Sadat saw détente and explained it to the Egyptians as the alliance between the two superpowers and their agreement on international issues. The Arabic word used to describe détente, *wifaq*, is actually the equivalent of entente.

In 1971 and 1972, Sadat viewed the delay in Soviet arms deliveries as a pressure on Egypt. He clearly saw in it an agreement between the two superpowers to prevent a new major war in the area and interpreted the inclusion in the U.S.-Soviet communiqué of May 1972 of the expression "military relaxation" in reference to the Middle East as justification for his suspicions. It follows that Sadat saw no difference between the United States and the Soviet Union insofar as their position toward the Middle East was concerned. This interpretation made the shift from one superpower to another less difficult.

Sadat's attitude toward the Soviet Union was primarily one of mistrust and hostility. In his speeches on the Soviet Union one detects feelings of humiliation, frustration, and violated dignity. Sadat spoke of the many promises given and never fulfilled, the many messages from Cairo unanswered. He once described the Soviets as "crude and tasteless people."[19] By the late 1970s, Sadat became a publicly avowed anti-Soviet; he cautioned the United States against underestimating the Soviet threat and pointed out that U.S. influence in the region was on the wane.[20] Sadat volunteered the services of the Egyptian army and territory to combat the Soviet threat. In the late 1970s, Egyptian officials spoke of the Soviet encirclement of the Middle East through surrogate states with the objective of destabilizing and overthrowing moderate pro-Western Arab régimes, particularly that in Egypt. In September 1981, Egypt's minister of defense stated: "Egypt is now in a very critical situation because of the threat surrounding it on the West and from the South."[21]

Sadat's strategy concerning the United States was designed to achieve three objectives: (1) to outbid Israel and secure U.S. support in the peace negotiations; (2) to obtain U.S. military and economic aid at an increasing rate; and (3) to assure pro-Western Arab governments that their opposition to Egypt's relationship with Israel would lead nowhere and that Egypt remained the centerpiece in U.S. strategy in the region.

As early as November 1973, in his first meeting with Henry Kissinger, Sadat talked about common strategy between Egypt and the United States to remove Soviet influence from the Middle East. He expanded his strategic vision to encompass a local triangular hegemony in the Middle East, an axis of the three predominant anti-Communist powers: Egypt, Saudi Arabia, and Iran.[22]

Sadat believed in the importance of close economic and strategic links with Western countries, particularly with the United States. Anti-imperialism, Afro-Asia solidarity, and similar cliches were out of date and no longer useful to Egypt. Sadat was attracted to the American way of life, the consumer society, and the capitalist path of development. Politically, the United States held "the key to peace" in the area, "99% of the cards of the game," he frequently stated. This was because the United States was the only country that could exert influence on Israel. Sadat's view of the superpowers was reinforced by his desire to cement his relations with oil-rich conservative Arab countries which he perceived as a vital source of economic aid.

Contrary to Nasser, who saw the Arab world as Egypt's natural sphere of influence and leadership and as the main arena for an active foreign policy, Sadat saw Egypt's leadership position as a structural property, not a behavioral attribute, as a property that could not be challenged or taken away. Consequently, he did not feel the need to pursue an activist Arab policy to maintain this leadership. For instance, as early as 1974–1975 Egypt dismantled its apparatus of influence in Lebanon, which had included financial support to friendly political groups, subsidies for newspapers, strong intelligence presence, and close contacts with local politicians. In Sadat's mind, the costs of that leadership style overshadowed its dividends.

As generally argued, leadership is a two-way process, involving influence as well as responsibility. The credibility of a regional power depends on its ability to support friendly states. Thus, the resources of a state and its readiness to translate them into effective instruments of foreign policy are major factors in the determination of regional leadership. For Sadat, the ultimate constraint was the unavailability of resources to pursue an active Arab foreign policy and to compete with countries with immense financial resources such as Saudi Arabia and Iraq. This view was reinforced by his desire in the early 1970s to develop a broad Arab consensus against Israel in preparation for the war. Consequently, Egypt followed a policy of coexistence with other Arab régimes, primarily those that had oil wealth and happened to be conservative. He was ready to praise and court the Saudis in public, and by 1973 the Cairo-Riyadh axis became paramount in inter-Arab politics.[23] Moreover, he was ready to develop closer relations with the Shah of Iran and to find a role for Iran in the region.

Sadat emphasized the need for greater Arab cooperation and solidarity. What was important, he kept saying, was not legal and constitutional formulae but the ability of the Arabs to coordinate and act jointly and effectively. According to Sadat, Arab states must recognize the differences existing between them and the fact that there could be no total or permanent convergence between their interests. He attacked his critics as ignorant dwarfs and stooges of foreign powers (namely of the USSR) motivated by malice and locked into the same rotten mentality that had existed for thirty years.[24]

The Decisionmaking Process

Under Nasser and Sadat, foreign policy was the *domaine privé* of the president and his close associates. Although the two leaders differed in their styles and orientations, both centralized and personalized the foreign policymaking process, limiting the role of institutions. The influence of different individuals upon the process depended not on their position in the cabinet or the bureaucracy but rather on their personal relations and access to the president. Thus, for instance, when the responsibilities of Ismail Fahmy, minister of foreign affairs from 1973 to 1977, were increased, it reflected Sadat's confidence in Fahmy and not a change in the functions of the ministry as an institution.

Although this picture is essentially accurate, the dynamics of the decisionmaking process are more complex. Presidents and kings, however authoritarian and unaccountable, do not make decisions in a vacuum but rather in a specific institutional context. The context affects the behavior of individuals, the formulation of options, and the way choices are made. Compared with other developing countries, Egypt is an organizationally developed and intellectually diversified society. Consequently, the leader, notwithstanding his immense power, has to assume the various roles of arbiter, mediator, and lobbyist at one time or another.

Egypt's foreign policy decisionmaking process comes closest to the "leader-staff group" or the "presidential center" type.[25] This type of process involves an authoritative decisionmaker who can act alone, with little or no consultation with other people or institutions except for a small group of subordinate advisers. These advisers are appointed by the leader and have no autonomous power base.

The leader-staff type of decisionmaking results in a highly personalized diplomacy. It is also characterized by the ability to respond quickly and to adopt nontraditional behavior. On July 8, 1972, upon the receipt of an unsatisfactory message from the Soviet Union, Sadat immediately informed the Soviet ambassador of his decision to dismiss Soviet advisers. He announced the decision ten days later. To understand leader-staff policymaking, we must take a closer look at the leader, President Sadat.

President Sadat (1918–1981) had a colorful and controversial political background before the revolution of 1952. He graduated from military college in 1939, mixed with different political groups, and in the 1940s was engaged in several intrigues against the government and the British. He was sacked from the army and then worked as a journalist and a truck driver and at several petty jobs. After 1952 he held a number of prestigious titles, including vice president and speaker of the parliament, but his power was more nominal than real. All through this period, however, he was able to watch Nasser decide and act, and this valuable experience was useful to him when he assumed the presidency in October 1970.

Sadat's political style was characterized by initiative, surprise moves, unexpectedness, and shock treatments; he described it as one of "electric shocks." He surprised his own associates as well as his opponents. For example, Mustafa Khalil, the prime minister, was taken by complete surprise when President Jimmy Carter, after his private meeting with Sadat at Cairo Airport in March 1979, announced that Sadat had agreed to Israeli terms on the peace treaty. Similarly, contradicting a statement Boutros Ghali, state minister for foreign affairs, made in May 1979—that Egyptian-Israeli borders would not be open before the official date for the normalization of relations— Sadat promised Begin a week later that borders would open once the Sinai capital, al-Arich, had been handed over to Egypt.[26]

Another feature of Sadat's style was personalization. He spoke of *my* people, *my* army, *my* initiative, *my* foreign policy, and he viewed relations between states as a function of the relations between their leaders. In many speeches he referred to other leaders as personal friends; the list included Carter, Faisal, Ford, d'Estaing, and a host of others.[27] In his analysis of Egyptian-Soviet relations, he emphasized the personal mistreatment he had been subjected to. Finally, Sadat related that when he was considering the visit to Jerusalem, his primary concern centered on Begin: "Was he a strong man, was he capable of making hard decisions?" In another instance he said that he studied Begin's personality and character as a boxer would those of an adversary.[28]

Sadat had the ability to attract the media and use it to further his objectives. He managed, perhaps to a degree unmatched by any third world leader, to remain a center of Western media attraction. Major Western newspapers and radio and television stations established permanent offices in Cairo or enlarged existing ones. Sadat was conscious of the importance of the media and kept himself surrounded by its representatives. To succeed Sadat had to say what would be interesting and attractive to them. The role of the media was crucial in the few days preceding his visit to Jerusalem. Indeed, the media, particularly television, played an important role in promoting the visit. In November and December 1977, Sadat met 1,500 media representatives and appeared on the covers of some 143 magazines.[29]

To sum up, Sadat was a man of constant action; "I prefer action to reaction," he stated once in 1975.[30] One of his favorite expressions in relation to the peace negotiations was the necessity of "keeping the momentum" and "the process going on." He was a master of adaptation and survival, ready to change strategy quickly in the course of his political maneuvers. For some, Sadat represented the perfect diplomat, the professional politician—a fox whose political skills enabled him to manipulate conditions for his own objectives. Others saw him as an unprincipled person who sought international recognition and fame and was ready to say or do whatever would keep the media interested.

Egyptian-Soviet Relations

For a long time, Egypt was the cornerstone of Soviet Arab and Middle Eastern policy, and Egyptian-Soviet relations were thought of as a model of cooperation between the Soviet Union and a non-Communist third world country. Ironically, since 1967 Soviet influence and prestige have correlated adversely with the fortunes of Egypt. The 1967 defeat greatly enhanced the Soviet presence, and the success of 1973 contributed to its waning. In the post-1973 era, relations were primarily characterized by mutual mistrust and hostility. Disagreement between the two countries covered a broad range of issues: political-diplomatic (renewed relations with the United States as a means of resolving the Arab-Israeli conflict); military (armament, compensation for weapons lost in the war, and Egypt's decision in 1975 to diversify its sources of supply); and economic (rescheduling the debt).[31]

Sadat's relations with the Soviet Union were strained most of the time. In May 1971, he removed from office the group that was perceived as pro-Moscow. The Soviets were so worried that they rushed a high-level delegation, headed by Podgornyi, to sign a friendship and cooperation treaty with Egypt. Sadat found the timing inappropriate because the treaty would appear to be a reaction of the purge of "Soviet friends." He suggested postponing it until the celebrations of July two months later, but the Soviets insisted. The treaty was signed on May 27, 1971, less than two weeks after the purge of this group.

On July 19, a Communist coup in Sudan was crushed with Egyptian help. Against Soviet advice to recognize the new régime, Sadat ordered the Egyptian air force to transport back to Khartoum a Sudanese paratroop brigade that was stationed in Egypt. The brigade was instrumental in the countercoup of July 22–23.[32] The Soviet Union also obviously mistrusted Sadat's intentions and his attempts to build bridges with Saudi Arabia and the United States. Military, economic, and political issues were bones of contention between the two countries.

Political-Diplomatic Relations

As early as November 1973, Sadat appeared ready to put the U.S. option into effect. He saw the limited help that the Soviet Union could provide in a peaceful resolution of the Arab-Israeli conflict. The Soviets officially cochaired the Geneva conference held in December with the United States, but Heikal (political writer) reported that "they were relegated to the role of spectators."[33]

The Soviets felt uneasy about the developing Egyptian-U.S. relations. They did not like Kissinger's monopoly, with Egyptian consent, of the negotiation process, which resulted in the first disengagement agreement between Egyptian and Israeli forces on January 20, 1974. Diplomatic relations between Egypt and the United States were resumed in March, followed by

Richard Nixon's visit in June. The Soviet Union expressed grave concern, and Egypt's foreign minister, Ismail Fahmy, was dispatched to Moscow to discuss Soviet-Egyptian relations.

The culmination of these events was on March 14, 1976, when Sadat, in a speech to the parliament, unilaterally abrogated the Soviet-Egyptian treaty of 1971. He gave five reasons for his action: (1) the Soviet Union showed no desire for peace in the Middle East; (2) the Soviet Union opposed Egypt's new economic policy; (3) the Soviet Union refused to reschedule Egypt's debts and demanded interest on military debts; (4) the Soviet Union not only refused to overhaul Egyptian aircraft and provide spare parts—a clear violation of Article 8 of the treaty—it also forbade other countries (India) to do so; and finally (5) the Soviet Union had a hand in Ali Sabri's plot to overthrow Sadat.

According to Sadat, it was also a matter of upholding Egyptian independence and sovereignty. In the same speech he said, "The Soviets thought at one time that they had Egypt in their pocket, and the world has come to think of the Soviet Union as our guardian. I wanted to tell the Russians that the will of Egypt was entirely Egyptian; I wanted to tell the whole world that we are always our own master. Whoever wished to talk to us would come over and do it, rather than approach the Soviet Union."[34]

Egyptian-Soviet relations suffered another setback in August 1976 when the Soviet Union supported Libya in its dispute with Egypt. In July 1977, three Soviet technicians were reportedly killed during an Egyptian bombing raid on a Libyan radar station. This action resulted in condemnation from Moscow and Egyptian countercharges of Soviet involvement in Libya. In December 1977, in the aftermath of Sadat's visit to Israel, the Soviet consulates in Alexandria, Port Said, and Aswan were closed. Egyptian-Soviet relations came to almost a complete halt. The Soviet Union opposed Egypt's policy toward Israel on the basis that it would not lead to a comprehensive peace in the area. Sadat escalated his anti-Soviet and anti-Communist remarks; he also criticized the U.S. "Vietnam complex" and asked for a more active U.S. role.

In September 1981, the Soviet embassy in Cairo was accused of being involved in harmful spying activities, and the Soviet ambassador and a number of diplomats were asked to leave the country.

Military Relations

The military dimension of the Egyptian-Soviet rift is complex. It includes problems of arms supplies, economic costs of the weapons, and interpersonal conflicts between Egyptian and Soviet officers. The Soviets were reluctant to respond to Egyptian demands for arms. Lt. General Saad al-Shazly, chief of staff of Egyptian forces (1971–1973), wrote: "As a monopoly supplier the Soviets could and did control their release of arms to us: the weapons, the amounts, and their dates of delivery."[35] Throughout 1971 and 1972, few arms reached Egypt. Gradually a reconciliation was effected, and by the beginning of April 1973, Sadat was able to declare: "The Russians are providing us now with everything that's possible for them to supply and I am quite satisfied."[36]

In the aftermath of October 1973, the problem surfaced again. Egypt requested Soviet compensation for the arms lost in the war, just as the United States had compensated Israel and the Soviet Union had done for Syria. For months to follow Egypt's requests met with rejection. In June 1975, Sadat declared that if the Soviet Union continued to ignore Egypt's demands and took no notice of its economic situation, he would have to do something about it. In particular, Sadat was critical of the Soviet massive armament of Libya, whose relations with Egypt were deteriorating. He perceived this as an avenue of Soviet penetration in the area and a potential threat to Egypt.

Another dimension of the military rift was the result of interpersonal conflicts between Egyptian and Soviet officers before 1972, which left a legacy throughout the 1970s. Shazly, who worked closely with senior Soviet officers, said: "The Russians have many qualities, but concern for human feelings is not among them. They are brusque, harsh, frequently arrogant and usually unwilling to believe that anyone has anything to teach them."[37]

Soviet facilities in Egypt presented another touchy issue for the Egyptian military. The Soviets had exclusive control over a number of airfields that provided air cover for the Soviet fleet. Soviet ships obtained facilities in several ports—Alexandria, Port Said, and Al-Salloum.[38] From 1974 to 1976, Sadat continually reminded his people of the Soviet legacy in Egypt. He played on the sentiments of the military by reminding them that Soviet bases were a breach of Egyptian sovereignty, and commentators emphasized the theme of liberating Egypt from Soviet influence and domination.

A third dimension of military relations was financial. Although the famous 1955 arms deal was largely a barter agreement, hard currency was increasingly the required medium of payment for Soviet weapons and personnel. In a December 1971 interview, Sadat told Arnaud de Borchgrave of *Newsweek* that "all the Soviet officers and men [are] paid in hard currency, not Egyptian money. We are paying through the nose for the maintenance of these Soviet SAM crews in Egypt."[39] By 1972, Shazly reported that the Soviet Union "was demanding payment in full and hard currency" for all new equipment.[40] Sadat was to cite this frequently in his speeches to show that the Soviets were not the true friends they claimed to be.

Economic Relations

In December 1975, Egypt's nonmilitary debt to the Soviet Union was $4 billion; its military debt totaled $7 billion. Despite repeated requests, the Soviet Union refused to reschedule the debt, and on December 14, 1975, Sadat announced that Egypt would not sign the trade protocol with the Soviet Union for 1976. When Egypt was ready to sign in January 1976, the Soviets postponed the signing. The protocol was finally signed on April 28, 1976, but at $640 million, it provided for $160 million less in trade than the figure negotiated the previous December.[41] In August 1977, Sadat suspended cotton exports to the Soviet Union and two months later announced that debt repayments would be suspended for ten years beginning January 1978.

Economic and trade relations decreased during this period. Economic aid agreements with Egypt declined from $1 billion in 1955–1964 to $440 million in 1965–1975, and then to zero in 1975–1979.[42] Trade relations also declined after the cotton embargo and Egypt's refusal to maintain the large trade surplus used to service its debt. The Soviet share of Egyptian exports fell from 50 per cent in 1970–1975 to less than 15 per cent in 1975. Egyptian imports from the Soviet Union also dropped from about 25 per cent of Egypt's total imports to around 10 per cent. Soviet exports to Egypt dwindled from 301 million rubles in 1974 (about $4 million) to 200 million rubles in 1976, to 148 million in 1978, and to 127 million in 1979. Soviet imports from Egypt decreased as well, from 427 million rubles in 1974, to 331 million in 1976, and to 198 million in 1978 and 1979.[43] By 1979, a few Soviet technicians and a limited volume of trade were the remnants of a once flourishing relationship. In the political crisis of September 1981, when the Soviet embassy in Cairo was accused of helping some Communist elements and indulging in spying activities, most of those technicians were ordered to leave the country.

Egyptian-U.S. Relations

In the 1970s, the United States made a dramatic return to Egypt and the Arab world. U.S. diplomacy could contain, outmaneuver, and sometimes expel Soviet influence from the area. Even with radical Arab states such as Algeria, Iraq, or Syria, the United States maintained flourishing commercial and economic relations. The big success story, however, is that of U.S.-Egyptian relations. In 1970, there were no diplomatic relations between the two countries; they were resumed in March 1974. Within four to five years, Egypt developed special relations with the United States. Since 1978, the United States has become a partner in Egyptian-Israeli relations, the major supplier of arms, and the primary donor of economic assistance to Egypt.

Political-Diplomatic Relations

In the first three years of Sadat's rule, 1970–1973, the United States continued its policy of total support to Israel. The Israeli occupation of Arab territories seized in 1967 seemed stable, and the Arab states appeared incapable of launching a new war. The United States, on the other hand, was busy ending its Vietnam involvement, opening new inroads to China, and inaugurating a decade of détente.

In February 1971, Sadat proposed opening the Suez Canal and signing a peace treaty with Israel, but nothing much came from this proposal. The expulsion of Soviet advisers from Egypt in July 1972 provided a new opportunity for the United States. It seems that Egyptian-U.S. contacts were initiated at that time. Heikal reported that talks were conducted through two channels, the diplomatic channel of foreign ministries and also a quiet one suggested by Nixon—the U.S. Central Intelligence Agency (CIA).[44] In addition, a third avenue was provided by Saudi Arabia, whose dignitaries communicated messages between Washington and Cairo. All efforts, however, including National Security Adviser Hafez Ismail's visit to the United States in 1973, led nowhere. The war of 1973 was necessary to finally bring the seriousness of the situation to Washington's attention. It became clear that Egypt and the Arabs could act and take the initiative; they could coordinate an attack and harm Israel. The use of oil as a weapon showed that U.S. interests in the area could be threatened.

Through his famous shuttle diplomacy, Kissinger monopolized the indirect negotiation process after the war, resulting in the first disengagement agreements between Egypt, Syria, and Israel in 1974. The oil embargo was lifted, and in June 1975, the Suez Canal was opened. Egypt signed the second Sinai agreement in September 1975, a step that created a rift in the Arab world because of the failure of Israel to make a similar agreement with Syria.

In 1977–1978, Sadat became more emphatic about the importance of the U.S. role. The United States was not just a mediator but a full partner in the peace process. Thus, Sadat concentrated on American public opinion: He spent endless hours with media people, senators and representatives, and leaders of the Jewish community. And he did make an impact on them. One is tempted to argue that the target of his visit to Jerusalem was not only the Israelis but equally the American people. He made the visit in front of television cameras, and well-established news stars such as Walter Cronkite and Barbara Walters accompanied him. The visit was a media event, an exercise in television diplomacy, and Sadat captured the imagination of millions in the West. He definitely improved the image of Egypt and its leadership, but his more subtle objective—political disengagement between Israel and the United States—did not materialize and strong U.S. pressure on Israel was not forthcoming. U.S.-Egyptian relations were closely related to the negotiations with Israel. Carter's decision to take an active role in 1978 resulted in the signing of the Camp David framework and the Egyptian-Israeli treaty in 1979. The treaty opened the door for much closer economic and military relations. This basic approach survived Sadat's assassination into the years of Hosni Mubarak's presidency. One should also note that the vital U.S. role in regaining for Egypt the lands occupied by Israel generated the continuing public support for Sadat's diplomatic reorientation and has sustained it.

Military Relations

Military cooperation between the two countries has taken various forms: arms supplies, transfer of military technology, provision of military facilities, and joint training and maneuvers. In 1975, Sadat emphasized the need to diversify Egypt's sources of arms. Egypt acquired some British and French jet fighters, helicopters, and air-to-surface missiles, and U.S. arms came slowly and gradually. In 1975, after the signature of the second disengagement agreement, Egypt bought six C-130 transport airplanes. In summer 1977, 14 additional C-130s were provided. Military relations developed at an unprecedented rate after the visit to Jerusalem. The cost of arms sales from the United States to Egypt jumped from $68.4 million in 1976 to $937.3 million in 1978.[45] In 1979, Egypt was offered further U.S. military credits, making the United States Egypt's major arms supplier. During 1980–1984, the United States sold Egypt nearly $6 billion in military equipment; only Saudi Arabia and the U.K. bought more.[46]

Military relations between Egypt and the United States also included the licensing and coproduction of arms. After the collapse of AMIO in October 1979, Egypt and the United States agreed to cooperate in the manufacturing and assembling of armored vehicles and electronic equipment. As another form of cooperation, Egypt offered the United States temporary limited access to airfields near Cairo (Cairo West) and in Ras Banas on the Red Sea. Though separated from the Gulf by Saudi Arabia, Ras Banas is still a strategic point in relation to the Suez Canal and the Mediterranean. It is all the more important as more oil is shipped through Saudi Arabia by pipeline and up to the Red Sea, through the Suez Canal to the Mediterranean.[47]

The United States hoped to convince Sadat to sign an agreement making the Ras Banas base available to the U.S. Army. Secretary of State Alexander Haig discussed this possibility during his visit to the region in April 1981 but with no success. Egypt resisted the idea of signing a formal agreement with the United States guaranteeing access to military facilities.[48] Sadat's formal position was that Egypt would make the facilities available to the United States in response to a request by any member of the Arab League. This commitment was reiterated by President Mubarak.

The United States and Egypt also collaborated in joint training and maneuvers. On January 1, 1980, two U.S. AWACS (airborne warning and control system) planes flew to Qena Air Base in upper Egypt with 250 air force personnel to "practice contingencies such as directing fighter bombers to targets."[49] It was acknowledged that the exercise was aimed in part as a response to events in Iran and Afghanistan. Another objective was to test the capability of the planes to use the Qena base.[50] In July, five C-141s and 28 C-5s airlifted equipment, supplies, and some U.S. Air Force personnel to Cairo West. Also in July a squadron of 12 F-4E Phantom fighter bombers landed in Cairo West after a nonstop 13-hour flight. The squadron spent three months in operation Proud Phantom, which involved air combat exercises with the Egyptian air force.

In November 1980, U.S. rapid deployment forces—including approximately 1,400 troops and eight A-7 tactical ground-support planes—participated in a two-week exercise in Egypt. The exercises, called Bright Star, gave the rapid deployment forces their first taste of duty in Middle Eastern deserts and brought to attention a number of problems in both operations and equipment.[51] Similar exercises were conducted in 1981, 1983, 1984, and

1986. Although some strains have developed since 1984, military relations remain very strong between the U.S. and Egypt.

Economic Relations

In the last three decades, Egypt has been a major recipient of foreign aid in the third world. Thirty-seven per cent of total investments in development and 36 per cent of total imports between 1952 and 1975 were financed by foreign aid. As for the United States, between 1946 and 1984, U.S. economic aid totaled $10.5 billion, over 90 per cent of which was given in the late 1970s and early 1980s.[52] The increase in economic aid coincided with the shift in Egypt's domestic and foreign policies. The political underpinnings of the aid were articulated in a 1981 AID (Agency for International Development) document as follows: "Our high level of aid to Egypt is premised on the belief that President Sadat's peace initiatives are crucial to that objective and that these efforts will be supported and enhanced by a vigorous and growing economy."[53]

The aid covers a broad range of needs: food, infrastructure improvement, the upgrading of social services, technical assistance, agricultural and industrial projects, and loans to help Egypt's balance of payments. This last item, called general economic support, is the largest single item of aid. From 1975 to 1980, it amounted to $3.2 billion, or 47 per cent of total U.S. aid to Egypt, and included commodity-import programs and payment for PL 480 food-for-peace shipments. Similar amounts of aid have continued into the mid-1980s. Payments for food are another major item. Wheat and flour deliveries amounted to nearly $1.22 billion between 1975 and 1980, about 20 per cent of the total aid. Food aid allowed Egypt to keep wheat prices low and maintain its massive food subsidy program. It also released government resources for other activities. Another major item (about $1.05 billion in 1975–1980) covered infrastructure projects—power, communications, urban water and sewage, and transportation. A third item, commodity deliveries, amounted to $1.7 billion in the 1975–1980 period. This money was spent to import U.S.-made machinery, spare parts, buses, tractors, and raw materials for industry.

U.S.-Egyptian relations have thus changed drastically since 1973, from no diplomatic relations to very close political and military relations. The new pattern of relations does have its problems and contradictions. In the early 1980s, Egyptians grew wary of the increasing dependence of their country on the United States and the decline of Egypt's image as a nonaligned country. In addition, U.S. Middle East policies coupled with Israeli actions and attitudes have further irritated Egyptian-American relations.

The Arab World

In the 1970s, Egypt's Arab policy had been primarily motivated by two immediate objectives: the need for a good Arab consensus to reach a comprehensive solution of the Arab-Israeli conflict and the need to generate massive economic and financial aid. Egyptian tactics and positions have changed over time in pursuing these two objectives.

In the early 1970s, Sadat ridiculed the distinction between revolutionary and conservative Arab states; the real criterion should be a country's position toward the Arab effort against Israel. "Egypt measures each Arab country by its relation and orientation to the Palestinian resistance," Sadat stated on October 15, 1972. He started to build a broad Arab front by reconciling differences between Arab régimes, advocating nonintervention in each other's internal affairs, and emphasizing the need for Arab solidarity. To achieve this, Sadat paid many visits to various Arab countries; he was the first Egyptian head of state ever to visit Iraq or Kuwait.

Sadat demonstrated his ability for swift action; in most cases he could outbid and outmaneuver his critics. The ups and downs of Egypt's relations with other Arab countries must be seen in the context of its search for an end to the Arab-Israel conflict. Thus, for instance, the first public rift between Egypt and Syria centered around Egypt's second disengagement treaty and its acceptance of Kissinger's step-by-step approach. The major developments, however, took place after Sadat's visit to Israel in November 1977.

The decision to visit Israel was motivated by a number of factors: Sadat's frustration with Arab disunity, the feeling that Syria was not enthusiastic about an early resumption of the Geneva conference, increasing economic problems at home (the January food riots), and U.S. impatience with the push and pull of Arab politics. The reactions of Arab states to the visit differed markedly. Morocco, Sudan, Somalia, and Oman supported the move; Algeria, Libya, Syria, Iraq, South Yemen, and the PLO condemned it in a meeting they held in Tripoli in December 1977. Sadat responded by severing diplomatic relations with the five Arab states. In the middle, Saudi Arabia, Jordan, and the Gulf states were neutral, giving Sadat the benefit of the doubt.

The Camp David accords (1978) and the ensuing Egyptian-Israeli treaty (1979) were met by almost universal Arab rejection. In an Arab summit meeting in Baghdad, Arab states decided to break off diplomatic relations with Cairo, suspend Egypt's membership in the League of Arab States, transfer the headquarters of the league from Cairo to Tunis, and boycott any Egyptian company that would do business with Israel.

A number of Arab countries had special relations with Egypt. Chief among them was Saudi Arabia. (As mentioned earlier, in the early 1970s there was a close alliance between the two countries.) Egypt needed Saudi Arabian financial help, and Faisal needed Sadat to sustain stability in the Arab East. He expected Sadat to tarnish Nasser's revolutionary model of development, cut Egypt's close relations with the Soviet Union, and restrain radicals in Syria, Iraq, and the PLO. One story relates that President Richard Nixon urged Saudi Arabia in mid-June 1972 to pressure Egypt to get rid of the Soviet presence as a precondition to an active U.S. role.[54] Relations between the two countries were not affected by the visit to Israel. Indeed,

Saudi Arabia agreed to represent Egyptian interests in Iraq, Syria, and South Yemen after the severing of diplomatic relations. Later Saudi Arabia went along with other Arab countries, breaking off diplomatic relations with Egypt and refusing to pay for the 50 U.S.-made F-5E fighter jets ordered earlier by Egypt.

Sadat accused Saudi Arabia of leading an anti-Egyptian campaign and using its financial clout to isolate Egypt in concert with Libya and Iraq. He ridiculed the Fahd-Saddam axis and advised the Saudi rulers to pay more attention to their growing domestic problems as manifested in the attack on the Grand Mosque of Mecca in November 1979.[55]

The Mubarak Era

Mohamed Hosni Mubarak assumed the presidency of Egypt in October 1981 at a difficult time. Serious problems stemmed from the assassination of Sadat, open armed clashes between members of militant Islamic groups and police in upper Egypt, and delicate relations with Israel prior to the completion of withdrawal from Sinai. The early months of his presidency brought a revolution of rising expectations, which Mubarak shrewdly deflated by talking about Egypt's economic problems and admitting that they were greater than he had previously thought.

Indeed, Mubarak's political shrewdness surprised most Egyptians and foreign observers alike. He released political prisoners, reinstated the Coptic Pope Shunuda III in his position, and displayed a high degree of tolerance for criticism and different points of view. He consulted with opposition leaders and listened to a wide range of political judgments. Personally, he maintains a low profile and projects an image of dedication and seriousness. He usually acts with an admirable spontaneity as a man of the people. In a country used to seeing its president make pronouncements and policies on the spot, Mubarak made an impression in early 1982 when, in a public meeting, he deferred questions to the appropriate ministers to answer, commenting himself only afterward. He called for and convened a series of conferences to discuss economic reform, population explosions, and enhancing exports. Yet as Egypt's basic problems have continued to worsen, popular dissatisfaction with Mubarak began to grow in the mid-1980s.

In contrast to Sadat—who made effective use of Vice President Mubarak by allowing him to convey important messages and act as mediator in inter-Arab disputes—Mubarak by late 1987 had not named a vice president, although he offered the post to Defense Minister Abdul Halim Abu Ghazala, the person thought to be next in line for the Egyptian presidency. Abu Ghazala preferred to keep his military post.

With regard to the role of Ministry of Foreign Affairs, the picture is somewhat different. During Sadat's presidency, the foreign minister acted mainly as a presidential adviser. He did not attend all the president's meetings with foreign officials. In November 1973 and January 1974, Kissinger primarily conferred with Sadat alone. Messages were exchanged directly between the president and other countries without the knowledge of the ministry, and Egyptian ambassadors to Arab capitals were not informed about the many visits Ashraf Marwan made to these countries in the early 1970s.[56] But under Mubarak, the role of the ministry has significantly increased. For the first time the president made a point of meeting all new Egyptian ambassadors before they assumed their jobs, and also for the first time, heads of departments in the ministry were sent as presidential envoys.

Initially Mubarak's guiding slogan in domestic affairs was the Great Awakening with which he has tried to inspire the Egyptian people. Several observers question the success of Mubark's attempt to build democracy and indicate that he will be increasingly obliged to rely on the army to maintain order. The army was employed in this capacity in February 1986 when it intervened to quell riots by security police conscripts in South Cairo. Acting on rumors that the conscription period for security policy was to be increased from three years to four years, 17,000 police conscripts out of a countrywide total of 282,000 were involved in the riots. By the time calm was restored, more than one hundred people had been killed and two thousand police conscripts arrested. Although the army was able quickly to restore a semblance of order, this calm cannot mask the tensions building up in Egyptian society.[57]

Mubarak's vision of Egypt seems to include both continuity and change. He emphasizes the thrust of Sadat's basic domestic policies but does not shy away from considering or proposing changes for better results. Although Gamal Abdel Nasser and Anwar al-Sadat had an appeal to the masses as "dream merchants of Arab glory," Mubarak is a stolid technocrat who does not hesitate about speaking of harsh realities. The appeal of this relatively untried technique remains uncertain.[58] In the realm of foreign policy, Mubarak has attempted to rehabilitate the country's position in Arab, African, Islamic, and nonaligned councils without introducing a sudden or major shift in its foreign policy orientation.

On the one hand, Mubarak has emphasized the continuity of Sadat's basic policies: peace with Israel and special relations with the United States. On the other hand, he has stressed Egypt's nonaligned position. Mubarak attended the 1983 nonaligned summit meeting in New Delhi and has allowed the Egyptian press to criticize U.S. policy on a great number of issues involving its support of Israel. Vehement anti-Soviet attacks are no longer pronounced in Cairo, and relations with the Soviet Union have moved gradually to normalcy. A cultural and educational agreement between the two countries was signed in April 1983, and a trade protocol, the first since 1976, was signed the following month.

Regionally, Mubarak condemned the Israeli invasion of Lebanon in 1982 and withdrew the Egyptian ambassador from Tel Aviv after the refugee camp massacre. He also refused to visit Jerusalem because its new status as the capital of Israel is still a subject of negotiations. Egypt has terminated its war of words with other Arab states, increased its military support to Iraq, and coordinated its policies with Jordan. By July 1983, Mubarak had exchanged political notes with most Arab heads of state, and Cairo had developed close relations with Amman and Baghdad, as well as with Arafat's part of the fractured PLO. Oman, Somalia, and Sudan had maintained cordial relations with Egypt all along, although after the ouster of Jasfar Numeri in Khartoum there have been strains in Egypt's relations with the Sudan.

In 1984–1985, these trends of Egyptian diplomacy resulted in a number of gains. In January 1984, the summit meeting of the Islamic conference organization, held in Casablanca, invited Egypt to resume its membership in the organization. Also in January, Egypt assumed its seat in the UN security council as a representative of Africa. On September 25, Jordan decided to restore full diplomatic relations with Egypt—a decision that opened the way for cooperation between the two countries in economic, transportation, and military affairs. The two armies conducted common maneuvers in 1985. In November 1986 Djibouti resumed diplomatic relations as well.

Egypt argues that its contractual commitments according to the Camp David agreements do not prevent it from shouldering its Arab responsibilities. Thus, Egypt continued to help Iraq militarily. Mubarak visited Jordan and Morocco in 1984 and Iraq in 1985. In June 1985 the vice president of Iraq visited Egypt, and a number of bilateral agreements were signed.

Egypt severed diplomatic relations with El Salvador and Costa Rica after they transferred their embassies to Jerusalem. It supported the UN call for an international conference for peace in the Middle East. As a result, a "cold peace" continued with Israel.

In the words of Boutros B. Ghali, minister of state for foreign affairs, "the year 1984 was a year characterized by a feeling of bitterness and hopelessness due to the continued Israeli policy aiming in general at perpetuating its control over the occupied territories and its inhabitants."[59] Little improvement occurred in 1985, but the following year saw limited progress. The Mubarak-Peres summit in Alexandria September 10-11, 1986, resulted in agreement on the composition of the Taba arbitration team, and on September 23, 1986, Egypt elevated its chargé d'affaires in Tel Aviv to the status of ambassador.

On the African level, Egypt continued to mend its fences. In 1984, Mubarak visited Zaire, Kenya, Tanzania, and Somalia, and Cairo received the presidents of Mali, Central Africa Republic, Guinea, Angola, and Chad. Of particular interest in Egypt's African relations is the idea of tripartite cooperation, bringing together Egyptian expertise and foreign capital in the delivery of development assistance to African countries.

Egypt has already cooperated with Japan and the European Economic Community in this regard. In July 1985, Mubarak presided over Egypt's delegation to the Organization of African Unity (OAU) summit meeting in Ethiopia, where he held important meetings with the presidents of Algeria, Sudan, and Ethiopia. Among the nonaligned states, in 1984 Mubarak visited Yugoslavia, and Egypt assumed the presidency of the group of 77.

On the global level, Egypt's special relations with the United States remained almost intact. Despite the existence of areas of contention, such as the conditions of American use of the military facility in Ras Banas, the issue of repayment of military debts, and the Achille Lauro controversy in October 1985, the United States remained the primary source of economic and military assistance to Egypt. In 1984 Mubarak visited the United States, France, and West Germany, and he received President Mitterrand. Egypt is keen on its European links, possibly because of their long existence and the diversity they add to its Western relations. When a number of mine explosions took place in the Red Sea, threatening international navigation in the Suez Canal, Egypt invited the United States, the United Kingdom, France, and Italy to help in clearing the waterway. On the other side, Egyptian relations with the Soviet Union continued to improve slowly. On July 7, 1984, Cairo and Moscow announced their decision to send back ambassadors to resume their duties and Egypt supported the Soviet peace plan in the Middle East. During the year, Egypt received the prime ministers of Yugoslavia and Romania, as well as various ministers of East Germany, Yugoslavia, Albania, and Hungary.

Conclusion

In the 1970s, Egypt was not the only state in Africa and the Middle East whose foreign policy changed fundamentally. Somalia and Sudan underwent similar major shifts in the same direction. Ethiopia moved in the opposite direction, from being a Western strategic asset to having close relations with the Soviet Union. Revolutionary Iran broke links with the United States, and in the early 1980s, both foreign and domestic policies were still in turmoil in Iran.

In the case of Egypt, the crucial factors in restructuring foreign policy orientation seem to have been increased economic troubles and anticipated economic gains through change; the existence of the United States as an alternative ally as a result of the U.S.-Soviet competition in the Middle East; leadership orientation; and finally, the dialectics of big state/small state relations.

Under Mubarak, the thrust of Egypt's foreign policy seems to be one of equilibrium, stability, and incremental change. In the five years of his presidency, he has not made drastic or sensational decisions similar to those of his predecessors Nasser and Sadat. He seems to be trying to achieve different objectives at the same time, e.g., maintaining special relations with the United States while enhancing Egypt's role as a nonaligned country. Yet Egypt's nonalignment is constrained by its increasing economic dependency on the United States for food. Similarly Egypt's attempt to reinstate its role in the Arab world is constrained by the American support of Israel.

Skillful diplomacy is likely to be capable of pursuing different, even contradictory, objectives for a while. But when these objectives are related to global alliances and links with the superpowers, the space for maneuverability is likely to be limited. How long Mubarak will be able to maintain his foreign policy balancing act and which direction Egypt will eventually take remain open questions.

Notes

1. On the concept of foreign policy restructuring, see K. J. Holsti, *Why Nations Realign: Foreign Policy Restructuring in the Post-War World* (London: Allen and Unwin, 1982).

2. This issue was discussed in Franklin Weinstein, *Indonesian Foreign Policy and the Dilemma of Dependence* (Ithaca, N.Y.: Cornell University Press, 1976).

3. Ali E. Hillal Dessouki, *Egypt and the Great Powers 1973–1981* (Tokyo: Institute for Developing Economies, 1983).

4. Gamal Hamdan, *The Character of Egypt*, 2 vols. (Cairo: Maktabat Alam Al-Kutub, 1980 and 1982) (in Arabic).

5. *Al-Ahram Al-Iktisadi* (The Economist), May 1, 1977, pp. 8–9.

6. Robert Mabro and Samir Radwan, *The Industrialization of Egypt* (Oxford: Clarendon Press, 1976), p. 32.

7. *The Middle East*, sixth edition (Washington, D.C.: Congressional Quarterly, 1986), p. 74

8. John Waterbury, "Egypt: The Wages of Dependency," in A. L. Udovitch, ed., *The Middle East: Oil, Politics and Hope* (Lexington, Mass.: Lexington Books, 1976), p. 293.

9. Ali E. Hillal Dessouki, "The Politics of Income Distribution in Egypt," in Gouda Abdel Khalek and Robert Tignor, eds., *The Political Economy of Income Distribution in Egypt* (New York: Holmes and Meier, 1982), pp. 55–87.

10. Ali E. Hillal Dessouki, "Policy-Making in Egypt: A Case Study of the Open Door Economic Policy," *Social Problems* 28, 4 (1981), pp. 410–416.

11. *The Middle East*, sixth edition (Washington, D.C.: Congressional Quarterly, 1986), p. 145.

12. Interview with Egypt's minister of planning, *New York Times*, April 9, 1975.

13. *Christian Science Monitor*, February 8, 1978.

14. *Arabia and the Gulf*, September 18, 1978, p. 10.

15. Jim Paul, "The Egyptian Arms Industry," *MERIP Reports* 112 (February 1983), pp. 26–28.

16. *The Middle East*, sixth edition (Washington, D.C.: Congressional Quarterly, 1986), p. 74.

17. *Africa Diary* 10, p. 5262.

18. Anwar Sadat, "Where Egypt Stands," *Foreign Affairs* 51, 1 (1972), pp. 144–153.

19. *Time*, January 2, 1978, p. 19.

20. Interview with Joseph Kraft in the *Los Angeles Times*, April 14, 1980.

21. Interview with Field Marshal Abu Gazala in *Armed Forces Journal International*, September 1981, p. 49.

22. Edward Sheehan, *The Arabs, Israelis and Kissinger: A Secret History of American Diplomacy in the Middle East* (New York: Reader's Digest Press, 1976), p. 89.

23. On Egyptian-Saudi relations, see Ali E. Hillal Dessouki, "The New Arab Political Order: Implications for the 1980s," in Malcolm H. Kerr and El Sayed

Yassin, eds., *Rich and Poor States in the Middle East: Egypt and the New Arab Order* (Boulder, Colo.: Westview Press, 1982), pp. 330–336.

24. See Sadat's interviews (in Arabic) in the weekly *October*, no. 59, December 11, 1977; no. 70, February 26, 1978; no. 72, March 12, 1978; no. 74, March 26, 1978.

25. Charles Hermann, "Decision Structure and Process Influences on Foreign Policy," in Murice A. East, S. Salmore, and C. Hermann, eds., *Why Nations Act* (Beverly Hills, Calif.: Sage Publications, 1978), pp. 69–102.

26. *Middle East Reporter* 20, 531 (May 30, 1979), p. 11.

27. *October*, no. 59, December 11, 1977.

28. *Ibid.*

29. *October*, no. 60, December 18, 1977; and *Al-Ahram*, December 10, 1977, and November 21, 1978.

30. *Time*, June 9, 1975, p. 28.

31. For a general survey of Soviet-Egyptian relations, see Karen Dawisha, *Soviet Foreign Policy Towards Egypt* (New York: St. Martin's Press, 1979), pp. 54–82.

32. Jon D. Glassman, *Arms for the Arabs: The Soviet Union and War in the Middle East* (Baltimore, Md.: Johns Hopkins University Press, 1975), p. 90.

33. Mohamed H. Heikal, *The Sphinx and the Commissar* (New York: Harper and Row, 1978), p. 219.

34. Speech on July 22, 1972, printed in *Al-Ahram*, July 23, 1972.

35. Saad al-Shazly, *The Crossing of the Suez* (San Francisco: American Mideast Research, 1980), p. 49.

36. *Newsweek*, April 9, 1973, p. 46.

37. Shazly, *The Crossing of the Suez*, p. 50.

38. Ammon Sella, *Soviet Political and Military Conduct in the Middle East* (London: Macmillan, 1981), p. 31.

39. *Newsweek*, December 13, 1971, p. 43.

40. Shazly, *The Crossing of the Suez*, p. 76.

41. K. Dawisha, *Soviet Foreign Policy Towards Egypt*, p. 76.

42. *Communist Aid Activities in Non-Communist Less Developed Countries, 1979* (Washington, D.C.: Foreign National Center, 1980), p. 7.

43. Alan H. Smith, "The Influence of Trade on Soviet Relations with the Middle East," in A. Dawisha and Karen Dawisha, eds., *The Soviet Union and the Middle East* (London: Heinemann Educational Books, 1982), pp. 110–111.

44. Mohamed H. Heikal, *The Road to Ramadan* (Glasgow: William Collins, 1975), p. 202.

45. Ibrahim Karawan, "Egypt and the Western Alliance: The Politics of Westomania," in Steven L. Speigel, ed., *The Middle East and the Western Alliance* (London: Allen and Unwin, 1982), pp. 174–175.

46. *The Middle East*, sixth edition (Washington, D.C.: Congressional Quarterly, 1986), p. 71.

47. Christopher Madison, "U.S. Reducing Act in the Middle East," *National Journal* 28 (November 1981), p. 2107.

48. *Newsweek*, March 23, 1981, p. 35.

49. Joe Stork, "The Carter Doctrine and U.S. Bases in the Middle East," *MERIP Reports* 90 (1980), p. 8.

50. *Wall Street Journal*, January 9, 1980, and the *Washington Post*, January 9, 1980.

51. *Newsweek*, December 29, 1980, p. 23.

52. *The Middle East*, sixth edition (Washington, D.C.: Congressional Quarterly, 1986), p. 74.

53. Quoted in Saad Eddin Ibrahim, "Superpowers in the Arab World," *Washington Quarterly* 4, no. 3 (Summer 1981), pp. 88–89.

54. *New York Times*, July 24, 1972.

55. See Sadat's speeches and interviews in the daily *Al-Ahram* of August 6, 13, 22, and 24, and October 2 and 11, 1979. See also *October*, September 23 and 30, 1979.

56. Hamid Al-Taheri, *Five Years of Politics* (Cairo: Publisher not identified, 1982), pp. 21–23 (in Arabic).

57. David Butler, "Egypt: Mubarak's Debt to the Army," *Middle East Economic Digest*, March 8, 1986.

58. John Kifner, "The Egyptian Economy Has No Place to Turn," *New York Times*, July 6, 1986.

59. Boutros B. Ghali, *Egyptian Diplomacy 1984–85* (Cairo: State Information Service, 1985), p. 12.

5

Saudi Arabia

Adeed I. Dawisha

Almost a decade has passed since some five hundred Muslim fanatics forcibly took control of Mecca's grand mosque in November 1979, and riots and demonstrations erupted among the Shi'i population of Saudi Arabia's eastern province. At that time, Western analysts became convinced that the demise of the House of Saud was not just inevitable; it was imminent. Although still dealing with the shock of the shah's downfall in Iran, some Western observers had concluded that Saudi Arabia was next in line to become a victim of the seemingly inevitable political and social disintegration. But just as Western analysts had inflated the shah's strength, they also exaggerated the weakness of the House of Saud.

This is not to suggest that domestic problems have been nonexistent in Saudi Arabia; rather it is proposed that the nature of such problems has been misunderstood in the West. For example, although the Shi'i civil disturbances in 1979 and 1980 showed the community's heightened militancy, the revolutionary potential of the Shi'i activists remained very limited. Constituting no more than 10 per cent of the Saudi population, the Shia had been lagging behind in both economic and social standings. In fact, the Shi'i people have recently begun to accrue the benefits of Saudi Arabia's economic boom. And it seems that the gradual removal of their grievances has reduced their susceptibility to revolt and diminished their destabilizing influence. Also the middle classes, and particularly the emerging technocratic elite, have always resented the excesses of the royal family. Although these classes have sometimes voiced their discontent, they have learned from history that their economic, social, and political interests would not be served by a revolutionary situation that might replace the House of Saud with a Khomeini, a Qaddafi, or a South Yemeni–type Marxist leader.

Impact of Modernization

Much more potent a concern is the impact of the rapid modernization process on the country's traditional attitudes and way of life. There have been heated debates within the royal family over the value and implications of "dragging Saudi Arabia into the twentieth century." Many members of the ruling elite, especially the older ones, want the process stopped, even reversed. Indeed, there have been intermittent reports that the government was planning to lower capital expenditure, slow down growth, decrease urban development, switch investment from the industrial to the agricultural sector, tighten rampant consumerism, and reassess modern education. None of these measures seems to have been fully implemented since, despite the influence of the conservative princes, the royal family is fully aware that turning the clock back can be much more dangerous than confronting an uncertain future.

The modernization process, having been abruptly and massively accelerated in the 1970s, cannot be reversed, or even stopped, without serious consequences for the régime. The House of Saud, therefore, has to perform a delicate balancing act between continuing the modernization process and endeavoring to maintain and even strengthen traditional values. In pursuing this goal, the then Minister of Planning Hisham Nazer stated in 1978 that the institution of family was the "arsenal of Islam which will defend the Saudis against the corruptions of the modern world."[1] Four years later, Nazer enthusiastically declared that the kingdom is succeeding in "importing technology without ideology."[2] The Saudi régime is likely to encourage further strict adherence to traditional values, particularly religion, through the regulation and supervision of the country's judicial and educational systems, while continuing the process of economic development. Both the third five-year plan (1980–1985) and the fourth five-year plan (1985–1990) reaffirmed that the top priority of economic development was to maintain the religious and moral values of Islam, adding that the role of al-Sharia' (the Islamic law) should be strengthened and that the defense of religion should be ensured.

Hoping to be protected by the institutions of religion and family, the Saudi régime, for example, went ahead with the third five-year plan with a projected budgeted spending of $268 billion. This level of expenditure clearly refuted speculation that the Saudis were planning a sharp cutback in government spending. Nevertheless, it confirmed that the small Saudi population could not sustain the wide-ranging industrial and agricultural growth envisaged by the Saudi rulers and that further expansion in the economy would exacerbate the existing problem of immigrant workers.

At present, estimates indicate a workforce of two million, of whom some 70 per cent are foreigners. The largest and most problematic group is the 600,000 Yemenis who have been excluded almost completely from the considerable state benefits available to Saudi nationals and who are treated by the Saudis with contempt as second-class, even third-class citizens. This group, which includes many radical Shia, represents a potentially destabilizing agent for the régime. In addition to the Yemenis, there are some 260,000 Pakistanis, 200,000 Egyptians, and about 150,000 Lebanese and Palestinians. These are internal problems facing the Saudi régime, but the West should neither exaggerate the enormity of these problems nor underestimate the ability of the House of Saud to overcome them. For instance, as a result of the drop in oil prices in the mid-1980s, many of these immigrant workers have returned to their original countries with hardly a murmur of public dissent.

International Influence

Given the interdependence of domestic and foreign policy, particularly in the politics of the Middle East, the Saudi régime has tended to use foreign achievements to bolster the internal credibility of the régime. Thus, throughout the 1970s and 1980s the Saudis became more active not only in their traditional pursuit of strengthening conservative and anti-Communist forces abroad but also in their drive to attain a higher profile in regional and international affairs. From this the House of Saud hopes to accrue the dual benefits of decreasing external threats to the régime and increasing the domestic prestige of the House of Saud. During the 1980s, therefore, Saudi Arabia has vigorously participated in Gulf, Middle Eastern, and international affairs.

Saudi Arabia has been able to exercise regional and international influence through its foreign aid programs. The country's massive financial resources in the 1970s and early 1980s, which have considerably outweighed the economy's absorptive capacity, have allowed Saudi Arabia to accumulate huge financial reserves (estimated to exceed $100 billion in 1985, which constitutes more than one-third of the financial reserves of all IMF countries), which in turn have been used to further Saudi foreign policy objectives. Estimates indicate that the kingdom's disbursed aid in 1984 totaled $3.3 billion.[3] This figure is second only to the amount allocated by the United States. As a percentage of gross domestic product (GDP), Saudi Arabia's aid is by far the largest in the world. It must be noted that the bulk of Saudi aid has gone to Muslim and third world countries, but some has been directed to the Western countries and the international monetary system.

In extending foreign aid, the Saudis have consistently used their influence to combat destabilizing agents and ideas in their own area and in the wider international arena, particularly to help status quo governments repel Soviet and Communist influences. For example, the Saudis granted considerable aid (estimated at about $3 billion by 1979) to the Omani Sultan Qabus during his struggle against the Marxist rebellion (backed by the Soviet-supported South Yemeni régime) in the Dhofar region.[4] Similar tactics have been used successfully with Somalia, and the Saudis have been major donors to the North Yemenis to strengthen their anti-Communist resolve and to the Afghan rebels in their war against the Soviet invaders. The Saudis have also been aiding the Eritrean rebellion against the Soviet-backed Ethiopian government. Moreover, financial assistance has gone to such distant countries as South Korea, Taiwan, and Zaire simply because of their virulent anti-communism. Saudi aid has also been used to encourage Muslim states to reestablish and/or reinforce Islamic norms and values in their political and social systems.

In brief, Saudi Arabia has poured considerable sums of money into the Asian Islamic states of Pakistan, Bangladesh, Malaysia, and Indonesia and African Muslim states of Nigeria, Uganda, Mali, Niger, Cameroon, Gabon, Senegal, and, until recently, Chad. In total, about fifty states have been the recipients of Saudi assistance. From all indications, even with the dramatic drop in oil prices it appears that Saudi authorities are likely to continue the level of foreign aid in the coming years for the purpose of maintaining, and if possible augmenting, Saudi influence and prestige in the international system.

Saudi Limitations

Several factors, however, limit Saudi Arabia's capabilities. The population is small, numbering about 6.5 million. With the cultural restrictions on women, half of the population is underutilized, leading to national shortages of human resources. These shortcomings have adversely affected the military capability of the country and constrained foreign policy. To deal with these problems, the Saudis have been using foreign nationals not only for technical assistance but also for labor resources. Koreans maintain the naval facilities in the eastern province, and Pakistanis and Taiwanis work in the Royal Saudi Air Force. Moreover, Americans constitute the technological backbone of the Saudi armed forces.

Aware of their internal weakness, the Saudis have been endeavoring to improve their military capability, and they now boast the world's highest per capita defense expenditure of approximately $4,000. In the 1984-1985 Saudi budget, spending on defense represented 30.7 per cent of the total and by far the largest single slice.[5] However, the bulk of this expenditure represents infrastructural costs, including the construction of buildings, roads, ports, airstrips, and housing. Some of the expensive items include the military construction projects at King Khalid Military City on the Iraqi border, Tabuk in the northwest near Israel, and Khamis Mushayt in the southwest near Yemen, as well as extrememly expensive military academies, naval facilities, and support systems for the kingdom's F-5E, F-15, and Tornado fighters.

In spite of these increases in defense expenditure, Saudi Arabia is and will remain a second-rate military power for the foreseeable future. More important, lacking the military might to complement its financial power, Saudi Arabia has not been, and will not be, able to manipulate intra-Arab politics in accordance with its own values and attitudes.

Saudi Arabia, therefore, cannot independently achieve its foreign policy goals in the area but must always seek alliances with other states and governments. In this regard, the Camp David agreement created a problem, because it directly led to the breakup of the powerful pro-Western alliance between Saudi Arabia and Egypt. However, this axis seems to have been replaced recently by an emerging entente among Saudi Arabia, Jordan, and Iraq. The irony is that in the early and mid-1970s Iraq—ruled by the Pan-Arab socialist and revolutionary Baath party—was actively engaged in a hostile campaign against the "feudalist and imperialist puppets of Saudi Arabia." But the emergence of the ayatollahs' rule in Iran and its disruptive potential within the majority Shi'i population in Iraq dampened the revolutionary inclinations of the Iraqi rulers.

Immediately after the departure of the shah in January 1979, and given increasing problems on its eastern frontier, the Baghdad government became aware of the necessity to stabilize the situation on its southern border. The Iraqis dispatched Izzat Ibrahim al-Douri, an important leader, to Riyadh to discuss "common security interests." The Saudis, naturally welcoming what appeared to be a radical shift in Iraq's policy orientations and in any case seeking a new partner to replace Egypt, were bound to respond positively. Moreover, the royal family would have liked to see a diminution of the ayatollahs' influence in the Gulf, particularly in view of its potential impact on the Shi'i community in Saudi Arabia.

The Shia constitute only a small portion of the Saudi population and as such can hardly be expected to emulate the feat of their coreligionists in Iran. Nevertheless, they live almost exclusively in the oil-producing eastern province and make up a majority of Saudis working in oil production. The capacity of the Shi'i community, therefore, to inflict great damage on the Saudi economy is a real threat of which the Saudi rulers are very much aware. They cannot forget that, during the Mecca siege, Ayatollah Khomeini urged Saudi oil field workers to revolt. Indeed, on February 1, 1980—the anniversary of Khomeini's triumphant return to Iran from exile—a major riot in the eastern city of Qatif led to the near demolition of two banks, the burning of over fifty buses and cars and the local electricity office, and the death of at least four people.[6] Since then, however, the socioeconomic conditions of the Shia have improved considerably, and their revolutionary potential has consequently declined.

Impact of Islamic Revolution

On a more general level, the Saudis feared the transnational implications of the Islamic revolution in Iran, particularly as the present Iranian régime made public on more than one occasion its irredentist ambitions in the Gulf, and various ayatollahs repeatedly declared their intention to export the Islamic revolution to other parts of the region. As part of this effort, the Iranians broadcast regularly across the Gulf through a clandestine station (believed to be situated in the Iranian holy city of Qum) called The Voice of the Islamic Revolution in Saudi Arabia. In an interview, Crown Prince Fahd bin Abd al-Aziz intimated that although he saw no reason for a conflict between Shi'i and Sunni Muslims, the situation would change if the Iranians were to try "to impose their Shi'i belief upon the other Moslem countries in the area."[7]

The Islamic government in Iran has responded by trying to destabilize the House of Saud on a number of fronts. The ayatollahs have used Iranian pilgrims to demonstrate their support for Khomeini vociferously, and at times violently, in the holy places. The Iranians have also tried to draw Saudi Arabia into the Iraq-Iran war. In 1984, the Iranian air force attacked tankers traveling in Saudi waters and then engaged units of the Saudi air force in an aerial battle. This time, however, the Iranians lost the battle, and Iran's flexing of its military muscle stopped abruptly. On the propaganda side, however, Tehran continues to attack Saudi Arabia's "shameful dependence on the United States," particularly the seeming contempt with which the Western superpower deals with its Gulf client. When the United States—after public debates that were singularly humiliating to the Saudi rulers—agreed to an arms package with the Saudis that was less than 10 per cent of the original Saudi request, Radio Tehran's Arabic service responded with obvious glee. To Iran's propagandists, these sales were

> an insult to Saudi Arabia. . . . Any independent country which possesses a genuine political will cannot accept such humiliating conditions, especially when the Zionist entity is party to these conditions. Perhaps it is logical to ask: Do the Saudis have an opinion on what the Reagan administration says about them? This is just a question, the practical answer to which we will undoubtedly find in upcoming events.[8]

Given its growing apprehension of Khomeini's Iran and its desire to stabilize political relations in the Arabian Peninsula, and given its need for a strong alliance within the Arab world, Saudi Arabia has been trying vigorously to foster and strengthen the burgeoning relationship with Iraq, as evidenced by its support for Iraq during the Gulf war.

On the diplomatic level, Saudi Arabia has been a consistent supporter of Iraq's case in its war with Iran. Not wishing to antagonize the Iranians, Saudi backing has been low key; yet it has been forthright and consistent. More important, since 1982 Saudi Arabia has donated a major portion of the Gulf's annual $10 billion aid to help Iraq in its war effort. And when the war began to tilt Iran's way, the Saudis, under the auspices of the Organization of the Islamic Conference, tried vigorously to use diplomatic efforts to end the war. However, though the Iraqis were willing to compromise, the Iranians, invigorated by their military successes, thwarted all mediation efforts.

The threat from the unpredictable and messianic Iranian régime, therefore, remains, heightened in early 1986 by the Iranian occupation of the southern Iraq port town of Fao. So does the threat from the Marxist régime of South Yemen. In explaining the decision in 1979 to withdraw the Saudi contingent from the Arab peace-keeping force in Lebanon, Foreign Minister Prince Saud al-Faisal told the Lebanese prime minister: "Just as you are burdened with your problems in the south, we also have a southern problem at the Saudi-Yemeni border."[9] A major Saudi worry is that the two Yemens will merge. This would present a formidable challenge to Saudi Arabia, since the more dynamic and better organized Marxist leadership of South Yemen would undoubtedly emerge as the dominant political authority. Saudi anxieties had been heightened perceptibly in 1979 when South Yemen signed a 20-year friendship and cooperation treaty with the Soviet Union, paving the way for almost unlimited Soviet penetration. The Saudis subsequently have become very suspicious of Aden's real intentions, especially since over 5,000 Soviet, East German, Czechoslovak, and Cuban advisers are believed to be in South Yemen endeavoring to improve the capability of the country's 25,000-person armed forces.

Impact of Arab-Israeli Conflict

On the broader yet equally destabilizing issues of the Arab-Israeli conflict, the Palestinian problem, and the continuing retention by Israel of East Jerusalem, Saudi Arabia can act only in unison with the majority opinion of the Arab world. These issues transcend inter-Arab disagreements and discords and almost constitute the standard by which the merits and faults of the various Arab leaders are judged. Saudi Arabia is in a particularly delicate position, not only because of its inability to act as independently as Egypt but also because of its status as the guardian of Islam—a status that forms a crucial legitimizing agent for the régime. Jerusalem ranks as one of the three holiest cities in Islam (the other two being Mecca and Medina in Saudi Arabia), and as such, the Riyadh government cannot afford to be seen by Arabs and Muslims alike as abandoning the struggle to restore the revered Islamic shrine to Arab sovereignty. Consequently, Saudi Arabia has to confine itself within the general parameters imposed by the broader Arab orientation. Saudi Arabia's position has been clearly and officially enunciated in the following terms:

> The attitude of the kingdom of Saudi Arabia toward the Middle East problem and the issue of Palestine is firm, clear and known. It derives from the *Arabs' unanimous attitude* that the issue of Palestine is the core of the Middle East problem, and that a just and comprehensive solution cannot be achieved unless Israel withdraws from all the Arab territories occupied in 1967, including, first and foremost, Holy Jerusalem, to which Arab sovereignty must be restored. No solution of the Palestinian issue can achieve peace unless it is based on recognition of the Palestinian people's legitimate rights to return and to self-determination, including the setting up of an independent state on their territory. In all this, Saudi Arabia pursues a *unanimous Arab attitude, to which it is committed and which it supports.*[10] (Emphasis added.)

The U.S. Connection

On a global level, the American connection remains and in all probability will continue to be a crucial concern of Saudi policymaking. In the economic domain, the Saudis have endeavored to create a situation of interdependence between the two countries. Saudi Arabia's imports from the United States amount to over a quarter of all the kingdom's imports, and some 75 to 85 per cent of its accumulated financial surpluses is held in dollars. Moreover, about $60 billion of the kingdom's foreign assets are believed to be in U.S. government securities and those of American banking and financial institutions. Strategically, the Saudi rulers persist in perceiving the United States as the guarantor of the Saudi régime. They are well aware that the prospect of radical elements overthrowing the ruling family, and thereby controlling the volume and supplies of oil to the United States and the Western world, is almost as unacceptable to Washington as it is to Riyadh.

The Saudi rulers tend to equate U.S. policy toward their country with the American attitude toward the royal family. Inevitably, therefore, to the Saudis U.S. sale of military equipment to the kingdom has tended to have a political rather than a strategic rationale. Within this context, the Saudis have endeavored to extract American commitments in the form of military hardware, as well as of the necessary personnel and technical expertise needed to operate and service the equipment. Thus, one analyst suggested that the sale of weapons systems to Saudi Arabia has made the kingdom "so dependent on long-range U.S. follow-on training and support that such arms programs nearly approximate a treaty."[11]

Despite the military link, the perceived American support for Israeli policies naturally has made the Saudi rulers reluctant to demonstrate publicly unequivocal support for U.S. policy. The Saudis have been further alienated from American policy when Congress, after a particularly hostile onslaught against Riyadh in 1986,[12] allowed less than 10 per cent of an original $3 billion Saudi arms request to go through. That congressional debate was a symptom of the increasing tendency in the mid-1980s to associate Arabs with terrorism, and of the growing power and assertiveness of Israel's friends in Washington. The result was a seeming U.S. inability to differentiate between its friends and enemies in the Arab world. In this political and psychological milieu, the Saudis were bound to be torn between their mounting frustration with American policy and their continuing dependence on the American strategic connection. This dilemma has yet to be resolved, but in the meantime the Saudi rulers continue to be pro-American but anti–Camp David and anti–direct negotiations with Israel outside Arab consensus, hoping for a change in United States policy that would extricate them from their predicament.

Given the importance of the United States to Saudi security, and given Saudi Arabia's intense fear and mistrust of international communism, there exists very little possibility that the House of Saud would ever seek rapprochement with the Soviet Union. Saudi hostility to the Soviet Union intensified after the invasion of Afghanistan, both because the latter is an Islamic state and because the Soviet threat is felt to have become too close for comfort. Accordingly, Saudi Arabia was the first country to announce a boycott of the Moscow Olympics in summer 1980, and Prince Saud al-Faisal, the kingdom's foreign minister, must take much of the credit for the firmness of the declaration issued by the Islamabad meeting of Muslim foreign ministers. Saudi aid to the Afghan Mujahedin during 1985-1986 amounted to more than $500 million.[13] Moreover, countries that are recipients of Saudi aid are told that continuation of Saudi assistance will be dependent on strict adherence to the Saudi line. The Saudis have voiced their suspicion that Soviet ambitions might stretch beyond Afghanistan to the oil riches of the Gulf, and they consider that in such an eventuality words like *independent action, nonalignment,* and *indigenous defense* become meaningless. Nevertheless, Saudi Arabia's rulers are hoping that the "cardinal importance of this area to the West" is not lost on the Kremlin.[14] Yet the House of Saud is well aware that, in the final analysis, the country must depend on American and Western resolve and power to counteract potential Soviet threat.

Economic Considerations

Saudi Arabia has been concerned about the health of the Western economic system, which has been manifested throughout the 1970s and early 1980s in the kingdom's moderating influence within the Organization of Petroleum Exporting Countries (OPEC). For example, Saudi Arabia continued during the late 1970s to keep its production level artificially high at 9.5 million barrels per day in an effort to balance the cutbacks in production by Iran, Libya, Algeria, and Kuwait, even though this amount exceeded its economy's absorptive capacity. This was done to satisfy the seemingly insatiable Western, and particulary American, appetite for energy. During the Iran-Iraq war, Saudi Arabia was reported to have increased its daily output to 10.4 million barrels per day.

The problem that the Saudis encountered during the first two years of the Iranian revolution was that, although they produced almost a third of OPEC's oil and about a fifth of the non-Communist world output, the massive Iranian cutbacks tended to negate the kingdom's earlier tactics of increasing production and stabilizing prices. An anomalous situation was consequently created during 1979–1981 whereby Saudi oil was selling at approximately $8 to $10 less than spot-market prices and $7 less than the price demanded by Iran for the same quality crude. This policy was accompanied by consistent Saudi refusal to cut production, a policy which by the end of 1981 was beginning to create massive oil surpluses in the West. Even Saudi Arabia's friends became concerned about the kingdom's oil policy. In July 1981, President Saddam Husayn of Iraq leveled "brotherly yet serious criticisms against some Arab brothers whose policies had led to the creation of great surpluses in the oil market."[15] Saudi Arabia persisted with its policy until the other more hawkish OPEC members were finally coerced in November 1981 to accept Saudi Arabia's stand on price unification, which was set at $34 per barrel.

The picture had changed dramatically by 1985–1986. For a start the price of oil had slumped to around $12/barrel, and Saudi production had plummeted to 2.3 million barrels/day by August 1985.[16] The change was the result of rising non-OPEC oil production, world recession, energy conservation and substitution in consuming countries, and the absence of a long-term price policy in OPEC. Although the kingdom boosted production to around 4.5 million barrels/day in 1986, it could not avoid the adverse effects on its economy. For the first time since the 1960s, the kingdom recorded a budget deficit in 1983–1984, and subsequently, government expenditure was cut steadily. In 1985–1986, spending was 30 per cent lower than in 1981–1982. Even so, the budget deficit remained considerable because of the falling oil production.[17] Problems, which Saudi Arabia was able to buy off in the past, now had to be confronted with vigor and strong leadership.

The Need for Strong Leadership

To solve these problems effectively, the Saudis need, first and foremost, strong and determined leadership from a clearly identifiable source of authority, which would command the allegiance not only of the Saudi population but also of the other members of the royal family. Only through uncontested leadership of the late Kings Abd al-Aziz and Faisal were stability and progress maintained in Saudi Arabia. Conversely, the greatest fears for the kingdom's possible disintegration occurred during the weak and indecisive reign of King Saud. In all three cases, a direct and positive relationship seemed to exist between the loyalty of the people to the House of Saud and the perceived ability of the king to ensure the obedience of the royal princes to his wishes and dictates. This relationship is hardly surprising given the patriarchal nature of Saudi society, in which the extended family constitutes the basic social unit.

When the dual leadership of King Khalid and Prince Fahd emerged after the assassination of King Faisal in April 1975, it was assumed that the crown prince would hold the reins of power, whereas the king, old and not in good health, would be accorded ceremonial functions. After an uncertain start, however, Khalid began to become increasingly involved in the kingdom's domestic and foreign policy, thus gradually encroaching on Fahd's power to the extent that the crown prince no longer could be described as the central and effective decisionmaker. This gradual diminution of Fahd's authority related not only to the king's increasing involvement in policymaking but also to certain personal weaknesses in Fahd's leadership, particularly within the royal family. Too often he was irresolute when a firmer hand was needed, particularly in his dealings with his own son Muhammad. Various business deals with which Prince Muhammad's name had been linked attracted widespread and bitter criticisms because he allegedly received huge commissions by abusing his power. In the face of mounting allegations of corruption, Fahd failed to act decisively and quickly to quell the commercial activities of his son and other members of the royal family. On the contrary, he explained in an interview that he was unable "to prevent those outside the framework of government from practicing free trade."[18] After becoming king in 1982 Fahd tried to reestablish within the royal family the binding moral authority so characteristic of the strong rule of the late kings Abd al-Aziz and Faisal. But there was no dramatic change, and the country, as well as the ruling family, continued to lack strong and authoritative leadership. This does not bode well for the future.

In the meantime, the moral authority of the present leadership, as well as the position of the House of Saud generally, would be enhanced by greater sensitivity from the United States and the Western world to Saudi Arabia's delicate political situation in the area. The Saudi régime needs American support. Yet, as has been argued, Saudi Arabia's Arab and Islamic status makes it difficult for the country to identify fully and publicly with American policies, particularly those relating to the Palestinian issue. Until this basic contradiction in the Saudi situation is resolved, the United States needs to exercise far greater discretion in its policies in the area generally and toward Saudi Arabia specifically. Abrasive diplomatic pressure as applied by successive American administrations to move the kingdom on the road of direct negotiations with Israel only provokes resentment. The use or threat of military operations in the region simply creates a perception among the people of the area that there is little difference between the two superpowers in attitudes or behavior. Moreover, the Reagan administration, Congress, and the media could try to show more appreciation for Saudi Arabia's vigorous and persistent efforts to serve American and Western interests within the third world generally.

The Palestinian issue is a major obstacle that will impede the Saudi pursuit of stability and full entente with the United States. The United States has to understand that, unlike Egypt, Saudi Arabia cannot follow a course of action on the Palestinian problem independent of the Arab and Muslim worlds. Unwavering American support for Israel embarrasses the Saudi régime and undermines its credibility among its own people and the Arab world at large.

The Palestinian problem will remain a determinant that ultimately will factor in Saudi-U.S. relations. The House of Saud, desiring security and the stability of the kingdom, is torn between strengthening its ties with the United States and complying with Arab hostility to the American position regarding the Arab-Israeli conflict. The Saudi leadership emphasized its moderation and pragmatism by presenting a constructive alternative to the Camp David agreement in the Fahd plan, which was adopted by the summit of Arab heads of state in Fez in 1982. If the United States wants to preserve Saudi stability and strengthen its own ties with the existing régime, Washington needs to begin the search for a new comprehensive peace formula that would not only bring about a solution acceptable to all parties of the conflict but would also go a long way toward resolving the contradictions of Saudi Arabia's own situation, thus creating the environment for the final consolidation of the Saudi-U.S. partnership.

Notes

1. *New York Times*, March 15, 1978.

2. *Al-Mostaqbal* (Paris), February 6, 1982, p. 53.

3. *Saudi Arabia, MEED Special Report*, May 1986, p. 20.

4. Adeed Dawisha, *Saudi Arabia's Search for Security, Adelphi Paper 158* (London: The International Institute for Strategic Studies, 1979), p. 20.

5. *The Middle East*, sixth edition (Washington, D.C.: Congressional Quarterly, 1986), p. 160.

6. *The Times*, March 12, 1980.

7. *Sunday Times*, February 3, 1980.

8. *FBIS*, vol. 8, June 18, 1980, p. 13.

9. *Al-Hawadith* (Beirut), April 13, 1979.

10. British Broadcasting Corporation, *Summary of World Broadcasts, Part 4, The Middle East*, ME/6431/A/3, May 29, 1980.

11. *International Herald Tribune*, February 27, 1980, p. 85.

12. See *Congressional Record*, June 5, 1986, pp. S 6794–S 6817.

13. *Washington Post*, June 20, 1986.

14. This seemed to be the feeling held by Crown Prince Fahd as articulated in an interview with Frank Giles in the *Sunday Times*, February 3, 1980.

15. President Saddam Hussein, *Sha'bana wa Tariq al-Huriya* (Our People and the Road of Freedom) (Baghdad: Dar al-Huriya, 1981), pp. 36–37.

16. See Ghassan Salameh, "Hangover Time in the Gulf," *Middle East Report* (March-April 1986), p. 40.

17. *Saudi Arabia, MEED Special Report*, May 1986, p. 6.

18. *Financial Times*, January 11, 1980.

6

Iraq

Christine Moss Helms

Iraq's potential to play a leadership role in the Middle East and the orientation of its present foreign policy are affected by many historical factors. Iraq's governing elites have always believed that their country had great potential for economic development and political influence relative to other areas of the Middle East. In earlier centuries this potential came from Iraq's renewable water resources and its strategic location; in this century it comes from another resource—oil. Yet geopolitical constraints have tempered these hopes and will continue to shape the strategies of the nation's current leadership.

Despite the fact that the West has had little contact with Iraq since the revolution of 1958 and that the Iran-Iraq war begun in 1980 holds serious and unknown consequences, there is nevertheless much that can be understood about Iraqi political life. The first sections of this chapter look at Iraq's assets, expectations they have produced, and inherent constraints on their development. Subsequent sections discuss the way these resources have caused Iraqi governments after the revolution, particularly that of the Baath party since it took control in 1968, to redefine their strategic concerns and the regional role of the state. The origins of the Iran-Iraq war are better understood within such an analysis. The concluding section focuses on the fundamental determinants all future Iraqi governments must face in establishing priorities for domestic and foreign policy.

Resource Potential

When the Baath party took over the Iraqi government in 1968, it inherited the economic and political problems that characterize many third world countries. The Baathists were a young, educated elite, more accustomed to

---

Reprinted, by permission, from Christine M. Helms, *Iraq: Eastern Flank of the Arab World* (Washington, D.C.: The Brookings Institution, 1984). Copyright: The Brookings Institution, 1984.

managing the clandestine affairs of their party, whose activities had been either forbidden or curtailed by former governments, than to functioning as government bureaucrats. Nevertheless, they were quick to recognize Iraq's human and material wealth and their potential for establishing the country as a prominent regional power in the years ahead. Among the most compelling reasons for this potential are Iraq's oil reserves and the financial revenues they produce, the possibility to diversify Iraq's economic base, and the coupling of Iraq's strategic position with its historical role in the region.

The nation's oil resources have the most observable impact. Iraq's proven reserves—50 billion barrels with an additional 46 billion of estimated reserves—rank second only to those of Saudi Arabia in the Middle East. Prior to the initiation of hostilities with Iran, Iraqi production—approximately 3.5 million barrels per day out of a total capacity of 4 million barrels per day—was 11 per cent of the OPEC total for 1979 or about 5 per cent of world production. Because production levels have been linked to ambitious Baath plans for social and economic development, Iraq is one of the few Arab oil states that gradually increased both productive capacity and production during the 1970s.[1]

Iraq simultaneously experienced a continual rise in oil revenues from $5.7 billion in 1974 to approximately $21 billion in 1979. Oil revenues for 1980 already totaled some $25 billion before the outbreak of war in September. Despite increasing government expenditures, Iraq's current account surplus rose from $3 billion in 1977 to an estimated $20 billion in 1980, and its foreign exchange reserves from $6.7 billion in 1977 to around $35 billion in 1980 prior to the war. At that time, Iraq had a major portion of its foreign assets in countries belonging to the Organization for Economic Cooperation and Development (OECD); and Western financial analysts, praising the country's careful and balanced investment policies, predicted that Iraq would continue to make even longer term investments and expand its banking facilities.

These revenues have important implications for the Baathist government, which has felt a growing sense of responsibility to foreign countries. By the mid-1970s, Iraq had considerably expanded its role within OPEC, the Organization of Arab Petroleum Exporting Countries (OAPEC), the Arab League, and the nonaligned movement, and an ambitious foreign aid program further improved its image among third world and other Middle East countries. Jordan, for example, received over $200 million from Iraq in 1979, more than it got from either the United States or Saudi Arabia; and many Jordanian businesspeople and farmers began to profit from increased levels of trade in the early years of the Iran-Iraq war.

The second reason for Iraq's importance is its unique potential for development. Arab oil producers such as Saudi Arabia or the Gulf shaikhdoms are characterized by sparse populations, arid climates, and few resources other than oil. Iraq, however, has numerous assets. It has a larger population and thus a greater capacity to absorb oil revenues. It has a heritage of more diverse economic, political, and military institutions and expertise, a well-developed middle class, and strong socioeconomic links between the rural and urban communities. Most important, Iraq has renewable water supplies, offering the possibility of an expanded economic base in both agriculture and industry. The only other Arab countries that have social and geographical assets similar to Iraq—Egypt and Syria—lack its vast oil resources.

Iraq's physical location provides yet another reason for the country's importance. Bordering two states—Saudi Arabia and Turkey—presently identified with Western interests and in proximity to the Soviet frontier, Iraq occupies an area of strategic concern to both superpowers. Regionally, Iraq is perceived to have a pivotal position between Israel to the west and the Gulf to the east, where it literally forms the eastern flank of the Arab world.

Factors Constraining Development

The utilization of these assets is constrained, however, because unique geographic and historical factors in Iraq have a critical influence on the interaction between rural and urban society, the legitimacy of a central government, and the territorial aspirations of ruling elites relative to regional political forces. These factors have produced a number of recurring themes in Iraqi political life. Iraqis themselves continue to view domestic affairs and major foreign policy issues, such as the Iran-Iraq conflict, regional alliance patterns, and the vulnerability of their resources, within the context of these themes. Six themes have been and remain pertinent to Iraqi politics.

1. Modern Iraq, like its ancient counterparts, has had to develop extensive and complicated networks of trade with Europe, North Africa, and India in order to obtain basic raw materials, such as stone, metal ore, and timber. Except in the northeast mountain region of Iraq, the absence of stone, for example, has hindered road construction and is one reason why many regions of southern Iraq, have not been easily accessible during the wet seasons of winter and spring. This single factor has had an important impact on the military conduct of the Iran-Iraq war.

2. Geography and the availability of water have exerted powerful influences on social structure, economic organization, and political jurisdiction in Iraq. The unique régimes of the Tigris and Euphrates rivers, the arid plains of the south, and the mountainous region of the north set fundamental conditions that have affected patterns of settlement and human interchange so much that different regional economies within the state have resulted.

3. These regional economies correspond to divisions that continue to pervade the social fabric of Iraq. Centuries of ethnic, tribal, geographic, linguistic, class, and religious forms of identification now compete with newly defined state nationalism and political ideologies to affect Iraq's domestic and foreign affairs. Although 75 per cent of Iraq's people speak Arabic, the remaining quarter speak Kurdish, Turkish, or Farsi. Islam is the religion of 90 to 95 per cent of the population, but there are smaller groups of Christians, Jews, Yazidis, Sabeans, and Shabaks. Shia Muslims constitute an

estimated 50 to 55 per cent of Iraq's total population and Sunni Muslims about 40 per cent. Although most of the people are Arabs, some 18 to 20 per cent are Kurds who are predominantly Sunni. There are also smaller groups of Turkomans, Armenians, Assyrians, and Persians. Groups such as the Kurds and the Shia are not distributed throughout Iraq but remain geographically concentrated. This pluralism opens a Pandora's box of questions about Iraqi nationalism because emotive symbols associated with these groups can easily become powerful political tools. The processes of modernization have further complicated political identity by fluctuations in the growth and distribution of populations, improvement in communications systems, and exploitation of new resources. These changes have altered the interaction between groups, enhancing stability or intensifying divisions as social groups compete for participation in economic and political processes.

4. Yet another theme in Iraqi political life is that ever since the second millennium B.C., many leaders in Mesopotamia have shared a common aspiration—the political union of the northern and southern sectors of the Tigris-Euphrates basin that meet at a geographic and climatic zone of transition north of Baghdad. The success and failure of these attempts at union constitute the history of ancient Iraq and remain a focal point in modern Iraqi politics.

5. The territory included within the present state of Iraq has been a frontier in the sense that Mesopotamia's unique features and location have attracted a succession of invading powers. These forces have contributed to the cultural diversity now found in Iraq and, some argue, continue to shape the regional perspective shared by many Iraqis. External influence is further heightened by Iraq's position on the eastern flank of the Arab world adjoining two large non-Arab countries, the modern states of Iran and Turkey, with which Iraq shares related population groups.

6. The creation by foreign powers of the modern Iraqi state, whose borders remained undefined until 1926, has only intensified the interaction among geographical, historical, and political factors. In foreign affairs, for example, the boundaries delineated between Syria and Iraq created as yet unresolved problems over the jurisdiction of the water resources of the Euphrates. Domestically, there remains continuing tension between the state as a political authority, utilizing its control within a certain internationally prescribed territorial unit, and the nation, as distinguished in the case of Iraq by smaller autonomous and competing social units such as the Kurds. Unlike Egypt, which has had an established national identity for centuries, the Iraqi nation is a still evolving entity.

The imposition by the British in 1921 of the Hashemite monarchy in Iraq, which they hoped would be perceived as a legitimate political authority because of the family's esteemed Islamic heritage, can be seen as the first deliberate attempt to foster nascent state patriotism in this century. Subsequent governments, all secular and antimonarchic, have continued to confront the problems of establishing the legitimacy of a central government. This approach has meant that they have had to seek a broader base of political legitimacy, whether by force or by more subtle political and economic rationales. Since the early 1920s, Iraqi authorities have endeavored to eliminate centrifugal tendencies, thereby centralizing government control, through a variety of political tools: settlement of powerful tribal shaikhs in urban areas, land reform measures, and relocation within or expulsion from the country of segments of the population.

Irrespective of the political ideologies of Iraqi governments or their base of political support, all of these themes play a major role in Iraqi perceptions of the state's strategic interests. They have assumed, however, different priorities through time.

The State Redefines Its Strategic Concerns

The issues that culminated in the revolution of 1958 represent a pivotal point in Iraqi perceptions of domestic and foreign policy. Prior to that date both the leadership and the population of Iraq were oriented toward the so-called Fertile Crescent region and toward the West. As late as 1955, Iraq's government had joined an American-sponsored security treaty known as the Baghdad Pact in the face of strong opposition by Arab nationalists who criticized it as a pro-Western, hence anti-Arab alliance. The association of the West with what Iraqis perceived as wrongs committed against the country by the pro-Western Hashemites not only led to an almost immediate cessation of former policies by the new government but also had a profound impact on Iraqi political thought in the post-1958 period. Anti-Western attitudes became heightened when, just as Great Britain prepared to withdraw from the Gulf, the United States became more openly associated with its conservative and hereditary régimes.

Iraq's foreign interests by the 1960s had shifted firmly toward the southeast, the Gulf region, because of one very tangible reason—the country's oil resources. Governments in Baghdad desired greater control over the exploitation and marketing of oil, which even in the early 1960s contributed nearly 40 per cent of the gross national product (GNP), and took steps to that end. Authorities imposed additional charges on oil shipments in 1961 and expropriated all the primarily Western-owned Iraq Petroleum Company's unexploited concessions. The expansion of port and oil facilities in southern Iraq and Iraq's reiteration of its historical claims to Kuwait also may be understood within the context of these geopolitical concerns.

Another factor that contributed to Iraq's shift in interests from the West toward the Gulf was the coupling of two events during the latter half of the 1960s. The first was a split in 1966 in the national leadership of the Baath party, which had been headquartered in Syria; the second was a reassertion in 1968 of Baath control of the Iraqi government, which had been primarily dominated by military factions since the revolution of 1958. In consequence of regional and political differences, autonomous national Baath commands in Syria and Iraq gradually began to pursue interests in what would become their respective and independent spheres of influence, Syria in the west and Iraq in the east.

During the 1970s, the Baathists continued to be concerned with Iraq's potential to play a regional role in Arab affairs, particularly in those concerning the Gulf. Foreign policy, however, remained subsidiary to four pressing domestic concerns that preoccupied the ruling Baath elite until the start of the Iran-Iraq war in 1980: the internal consolidation of the party, the acquisition by party members of bureaucratic skills, the preeminent establishment of the party's legitimacy within the Iraqi state through extensions of the party apparatus, and a greater degree of cooperation among the country's numerous particularistic groups.

These goals were gradually translated into concrete achievements, including the consolidation of civilian rather than military control over the Baath and government bureaucracies, the establishment of the Kurdish Autonomous Region in 1970, the promulgation of a National Action Charter in 1971, which allowed opposition movements to participate in the political process as long as they stayed within proscriptive guidelines, the establishment of the National Assembly in 1980, the formation of ministries that focused on the needs of interest groups such as youth and women, and development programs such as a literacy campaign. Oil production levels were increased as revenues were utilized to expand the agricultural and industrial sectors and broaden existing social programs. Kurdish areas in the north and Shi'i areas in the south became major beneficiaries of these policies.

Iraq's foreign policy during this period primarily responded to rather than initiated events. Official statements, characterized by radical ideological rhetoric, ironically differed from substantive activity that more often than not was moderate and pragmatic. Examples of this pragmatism include:

- caution in the Jordanian crisis in 1970;
- restraint in the October 1973 Arab-Israeli war;
- increased production and export levels of oil throughout the 1970s;
- qualified support, sometimes repression, of Palestinian groups;
- settlement of outstanding disputes with Iran in the mid-1970s;
- attempt to ameliorate the crisis between the two Yemens in 1979;
- foreign aid program to third world countries;
- restrained diplomatic reaction at the United Nations to Israel's bombing of Iraq's nuclear reactor in 1981;
- continued support for the restoration of peace to Lebanon;
- reformulation of the concept of pan-Arab unity in 1982;
- announcement regarding Israel's right to security in 1982;
- support for an arrangement to withdraw all foreign forces from Lebanon in May 1983.

With regard to the superpowers, Iraqi Baathists refined the ideology of positive neutralism, elucidating their own nonaligned posture which opposed both American and Soviet involvement in Iraqi and Middle Eastern affairs. Notably, Iraq became one of the first countries in the world to condemn harshly the Soviet invasion of Afghanistan, Soviet support of Ethiopia against Somalia, and repeated Soviet attempts to subvert Middle Eastern governments through local Communist parties.

Relations with Iran

As early as the accession of the Baathists to power in 1968, Iran and the Shah's ambitions became major determinants in the formulation of Iraqi policies toward the Gulf and Arab states, the United States and Israel, and the Soviet Union, and even in the shaping of Iraqi domestic affairs. Two geopolitical concerns then relevant to Iraqis were to become no less so under Ayatollah Khomeini than they had been under the Shah.

One revolved around the anticipated expansion and utilization of Iraq's oil wealth, an essential component of the ambitious social and economic development projects of the Baath. Many Iraqi actions, beginning with those of the military governments of the 1960s, can be viewed as indicators of Iraq's sense of the vulnerability of the oil industry. During the 1970s, this concern led to a series of actions including the nationalization of Iraq's northern oil fields in 1972, the implementation of plans in 1975 and 1976 for construction of a strategic reversible pipeline between Haditha (near the Syrian border) and the Gulf and of a pipeline through Turkey that deflected Iraqi dependence on the Syrian pipeline, and the construction of additional oil facilities in the south around Basra. Iraqi claims, somewhat diminished in scope, were renewed to the Kuwaiti islands of Warba and Bubiyan which dominate the estuary of the Iraqi port of Umm Qasr.

Among all the other states of the region, Iran posed the most direct threat to the Iraqi oil industry for social, logistical, and political reasons. In the northern Kurdish region, which produced at that time almost 65 per cent of the country's total annual oil production, Iraq was vulnerable to internal political unrest fomented by outside powers and to direct bombing in wartime. Urban areas and economic facilities in the south, through which one-half to two-thirds of all Iraqi oil was shipped, were susceptible to foreign agitation, to direct attack, and to blockade. In fact, the majority of Iraq's urbanized areas, whether considered numerically or by population size, lay east of or along the Tigris River. Additionally, the marshes of Misan province provided an ideal locale for smuggling arms or other support from Iran to political opposition movements inside Iraq.

Another geopolitical concern of Iraq in the late 1960s came from the Iraqi Baath leadership's growing sense of political isolation from the con-servative and hereditary régimes in the Gulf. Even before the Baathists took control, it can be argued that Iraq was geographically, socially, and economically distinct from other Arab Gulf states. This distinction, in fact, was the precise reason that the Gulf states gave for excluding Iraq from the Gulf Cooperation Council.

Iranian actions during the early years of the new Baathist government did not dispel Iraqi fears. Among the Shah's activities were:

- claims to Bahrain, initiated by his father in 1937 and not renounced until 1969;
- subsequent abrogation of the treaty regarding the Shatt al-Arab waterway in April 1969;
- attempts to form a cooperative relationship with Iraq's southern neighbor of Saudi Arabia during 1969 and 1970, which coincided with American military assistance to Saudi Arabia in 1970;
- alleged involvement in a conspiracy to overthrow the Baathist régime in Baghdad in 1970;
- military occupation of three strategic islands in the Strait of Hormuz in 1971;
- active economic and military assistance to Kurdish rebels in northern Iraq beginning in 1972 and not ending until 1975;
- support of Iranian intelligence (SAVAK) activities in Iraq;
- continued economic, political, and military links with Israel.

Iraqi concerns became even more trenchant after Iran became a major recipient of American military sales and the de facto guardian of the Gulf. American military equipment to Iran began to flow in significant quantities after 1955, and between 1973–1974 and 1976–1977 Iran received more than one-third of all American military sales. Between 1972 and 1976 these sales amounted to $10.6 billion.

Propelled by its political ideology and the Iranian threat, the Baath government in Baghdad responded by boycotting Iranian goods, stressing the strategic importance of Kuwait in any future Iran-Iraq conflict, and lending succor to nationalist movements in Baluchistan and Khuzistan in Iran. After Iran abrogated the treaty concerning the Shatt al-Arab in 1969 and annexed the three Gulf islands in 1971, Iraq expelled at first 20,000 and then some 70,000 Shia of Iranian origin. The Iraqi government claimed that these people were illegal aliens who had come for pilgrimage in al-Najaf and Karbala and then settled permanently. Because it was difficult to maintain control of pilgrims, they could avoid naturalization, obligatory service in the armed forces, and payment of taxes. They were also considered a potential security risk because of the pro-Iranian Shi'i underground groups in Iraq. Iraq also aided the revolutionary Dhofar Liberation front in Oman, whereas the Shah assisted the Omani sultan.

Superpower involvement further polarized the Iranian and Iraqi régimes by the early 1970s, propelling the conflict onto a new plateau of intransigence. Certainly the ideological rhetoric of the Baath did nothing to bridge a gap that had been heightened by late 1972 with the United States' two pillar policy. This policy relied on two regional allies in the Middle East—Iran and to a lesser extent Saudi Arabia—to act as political stabilizers for U.S. interests. Pressed beyond capacity by the country's rivalry with Iran, by the fledgling nature of Iraqi bureaucratic expertise, by the need to establish its legitimacy among disparate interest groups, and by the anticipated nationalization of Iraq's oil industry, the Baghdad government sent a delegation to Moscow in July 1970 to seek weapons. Then in April 1972, Iraq signed a 15-year treaty of friendship with the Soviet Union.

The conflict between Iraq and Iran erupted into open hostilities in 1974 in the Kurdish region as the shah, with American help, supported Kurdish insurgents on both sides of the border. The human and economic costs were high in Iraq. From a purely legalistic perspective, the issues susceptible to a negotiated settlement between Iran and Iraq clustered into three discernible groups: those concerning the Shatt al-Arab, those involving the central sector of the Iran-Iraq border, and those dealing with Iraq's Kurds in the north. These issues had plagued all previous Iraqi governments, including the Hashemites. Houari Boumedienne, the president of Algeria, intervened in the midst of this conflict and negotiated the Algiers Declaration of March 6, 1975. The declaration was designed to settle disputed land borders, territorial waters and river borders, and internal security issues. It revolved around one major exchange: In return for Iraq's acceptance of the southern border with Iran as the *thalweg* (or midpoint of the navigational channel) rather than the east bank of the Shatt al-Arab, both agreed to the principle of noninterference in the internal affairs of the other country. Thus Iran agreed to cease its aid to the Kurdish guerrillas.

The immediate advantage to Iraq of what became known as the Algiers Treaty was that it presented more diverse and sorely needed policy options. In foreign affairs, Baath leaders would not soon forget that the Soviet Union had abruptly stopped its arms shipments to Iraq during the Kurdish troubles despite the friendship treaty and that the Soviet Union continued to support the interests of the Iraqi Communist party, a long-time rival of the Baathists. Nor could Iraq forget that America had played a role in the costly Kurdish dispute. Consequently, Iraq almost immediately began to pursue nonalignment in its economic and political life. In September 1975, less than six months after negotiation of the Algiers Treaty, Saddam Husayn, then the right-hand man and soon to be the successor of Iraqi President Ahmad Hasan al-Bakr, went to Paris to seek closer economic ties and to investigate the possibility of purchasing advanced weaponry. By 1978, countries belonging to the Organization for Economic Cooperation and Development (OECD), primarily France, West Germany, and Italy, accounted for some 75 per cent of Iraq's foreign trade. The Iraqi government was even able to maintain a cordial, albeit cool, relationship with the Shah. Domestically, the Baath increased efforts between 1975 and the start of the Iran-Iraq war to extend the party's political legitimacy. Economic development programs continued with renewed vigor.

The three years following the Algiers Treaty proved to be the quietest period in modern Iraqi history, but it was not destined to last long. In 1978, a crackdown on Communist party activities began, followed in mid-1979 by the revelation of an alleged plot to overthrow the government by a group of Baathists. The established Baath leaders, who had always believed that the party could only be threatened from within, executed the plotters. They were led by Saddam Husayn, Bakr's successor as president.

Causes of the Iran-Iraq War

The animosity displayed between the governing régimes in Iraq and Iran after the success of the Islamic revolution went one step further than the rivalry during the shah's time. Although hostility was not inevitable, the underlying differences between the two countries would have been difficult to reconcile because of a fundamental incompatibility between Arab nationalism and Islamic conservatism—the political ideologies propounded by the respective governing elites of Iraq and Iran. The definition of political legitimacy advanced by Ayatollah Khomeini was so exclusive that it posed a direct threat not only to the credentials of Arab nationalists but to the very unity of the Iraqi nation-state. This conflict was further complicated by the centuries-old Sunni-Shi'i and Arab-Persian differences.

When anti-shah demonstrations erupted in Iran in early 1978, Iraqi officials were apprehensive. The period shortly before the shah left in mid-January 1978 until Khomeini appointed Mehdi Bazargan in February 1979 to head a provisional government is revealing about official attitudes in Iraq. Iraqi media generally adopted a pragmatic wait-and-see stance, neither condemning the shah nor praising the Iranian revolution. Interviews with high-ranking Iraqi officials at the time, however, indicated more serious concerns about the nature of the new government. In late January 1979, Tariq Aziz, one of the five key members of Iraq's Revolutionary Command Council, gave an interview in which he recognized Shahpour Bakhtiar, who had been appointed prime minister by the shah, as the legitimate representative of the Iranian government. In the first week of February another interview was published in which an unidentified high-ranking Iraqi official was quoted as saying that "the entire situation [in Iran] awaits the emergence of another General Zahedi [who led the countercoup in 1953 against Musaddiq] who can quickly solve the issue." Besides actually listing many of the reasons for the shah's alienation from his people, this official surprisingly went on to ask, "Does this mean that the only way to punish the Shah is by dethroning him, that the régime can only be improved by a coup d'état ... ? Why don't they amend the Iranian Constitution ... ? Why doesn't the Shah turn into a mere sovereign who reigns but does not rule and thus returns to the country?"[2]

Both interviews stressed the positive aspects of the Algiers Treaty—the fact that outstanding problems between the two countries had been resolved and, even more important, that the treaty provided a legal foundation for the principle of noninterference by each signatory in the other's internal affairs. A statement issued by Iraq on February 9, 1979, requested closer ties with Iran even though the Iraqi media notably avoided discussion of Iranian religious leaders.

No one disputes that the Iran-Iraq war began in earnest in September 1980 when Iraq's regular army crossed the international boundary. But the events that occurred in the year prior to its outbreak are only dimly perceived in the West. Once the war began and received international attention, official Iraqi statements substantively changed, blaming the war on the inequality of the Algiers Treaty. This approach proved to be a short-lived pretext. Real Iraqi concerns, intimated earlier by interviews in Baghdad during January and February 1979, eventually surfaced: The specter of the installation of an Islamic government dominated by Khomeini and extreme Shi'i conservative leaders held serious implications for political stability in Iraq. So sensitive were sectarian topics to the Baath government that in interviews it denied that such divisions existed. In retrospect it is easy to understand why Iraqi officials had earlier acknowledged Bakhtiar's right to lead a constitutional government, asked for secular military intervention, and repeatedly emphasized one aspect of the Algiers Treaty—that of non-interference in the domestic affairs of neighboring states.[3]

At least one year prior to the war Iraq sustained a number of terrorist attacks by pro-Iranian Shi'i groups, including assassination attempts against members of the government. One attempt was directed at Tariq Aziz, the only Christian among the five key members of the government. Khomeini openly called for Iraqis to overthrow the Baath régime and establish an Islamic government. The pluralistic nature of Iraqi society, the physical concentration of its Shi'i population, and the presence within Iraq of the most holy Shi'i shrines in the Islamic world made religion a potentially divisive political factor. It has been utilized in the past by domestic opposition groups and by foreign countries for their own purposes. Official Iranian broadcasts during the war continued to exhort both Iraqis and Iranians to greater efforts to liberate the Shi'i areas in Iraq such as Karbala, al-Najaf, al-Kazimain, and Samarra. During 1983 and 1984 Iranian authorities promised not to bomb civilian areas that contained Shi'i shrines. No mention was made about Sunni mosques. Iranian tanks in the war bore the words "to al-Najaf." Iranian highway signs in Khuzistan indicated the number of miles before Karbala would be reached. Iran's ambassador to Italy, Nasir Sadat Salimi, stated in an interview: "There are millions of persons of Iranian origin in that country [Iraq]. Our Shi'ite saints are buried precisely in Iraq and that country is sacred to us, its territories are sacred."

As Arab nationalists, the Baath leaders rejected the notion that political unity in the Middle East should be achieved through the common denominator of Islam irrespective of one's origins. Rather, they believed that Arabism should be the shared ideal whether one was Muslim, Christian, or a member of any of Iraq's other religions or movements based on ethnic nationalisms. Among Arab nationalists, Baathists generally had advocated an extreme stance, that of Pan-Arabism or the elimination of all boundaries between Arab states, and unity under a single leadership. The exigencies of the Iraqi nation-state, however, forced Iraqi Baathists to modify this formulation. They went one cautious step further by trying to rationalize the inclusion of Kurds in an Arab state and by propounding Iraqi nationalism. This approach meant that a person should first identify himself or herself as an Iraqi citizen and only second as an Arab, a Kurd, a Shia, a Sunni, or a Christian. Therefore, when Iranian statements as early as March 1979 asked that both ethnic and state nationalisms be subsumed or eliminated for the greater unity of the Islamic revolution, serious concern began to arise in Iraq about the possibility of sectarian strife.[4]

As early as October 1979, Saddam Husayn emphasized at some length his fear of this fundamental disagreement between the two ideologies of Arab nationalism and Islamic conservatism. He first praised the "Arab revolution" as a "qualitative transformation" that derived its values from history and religion but then said that "in order for the Islamic revolution and any revolution to be Islamic, it must be a friend of the Arab revolution. . . . As an Arab revolutionary, I understand the matter as such . . . because a true Islamic revolution should absorb the Arab ideology . . . and remove any contradiction between it and this ideology."[5]

On February 8, 1980, Husayn made a significant declaration of Pan-Arabism that became known as the Eight-Point Pan-Arab National Charter.[6] In one sense, the charter itself produced no surprises and can be summarized as a call for all Arab states to reject the presence of any foreign army and the use of armed force against countries bordering the Arab homeland except in self-defense, to join as one Arab bloc in the defense of any Arab state that is invaded, to affirm international laws relating to the use of waters and air space and land unless a state of war exists, to commit themselves to nonalignment in international conflicts, and to establish constructive economic relations between themselves. In another sense, President Husayn's emphasis on Arab unity, protection of Arab rights to land, and Arab values was particularly noteworthy at a time when an extremely conservative Islamic government had just been installed in Persian Iran.

The introduction to the charter perhaps reveals even more about Iraqi concerns. It is one of the most succinct expositions against the Iraqi Communist party, relating in some detail Communist activities under the leadership of Abd al-Karim Qasim during the late 1950s and early 1960s in which the Communists exploited sectarian strife in Iraq. Husayn tells young Iraqis that they are not old enough to remember these horrors, which included torture and burying people alive, and that only the Baath party has been able to suppress these evils and overcome differences in the country. He then scoffs at people who say there is a difference between a Sunni and a Shia, an Arab and a Kurd, because "we in Iraq are one united people." Husayn warns them that there might be another attempt to divide the Arab homeland.

President Husayn was not the only Arab concerned about the Islamic revolution in Iran. Arab leaders, particularly those perceived as moderates by the West, anticipated significant political repercussions from the extremist interpretation of Islamic revolutionary ideology in their own countries. They included the leaders of Egypt, Jordan, Saudi Arabia, the Sudan, the Gulf states, and Morocco. Khomeini, in fact, labeled them as corrupt and as future targets in the export of the Islamic revolution whose religious-political ideology did not recognize state boundaries. It is not surprising, therefore, that a number of these Arab leaders offered verbal and monetary support to Iraq in the war and frequently consulted each other. In early February 1982, the Gulf Cooperation Council—including the countries of Bahrain, Qatar, Saudi Arabia, Kuwait, the United Arab Emirates, and Oman—publicly denounced inflammatory statements and acts of sabotage by Iran aimed at destabilizing the status quo of the Gulf region. Algeria professed neutrality. The only two Arab countries offering strategic support for Iran were Syria and Libya, which, in strong opposition to American intrusions in the Middle East had foreign policy goals similar to those of Khomeini.

One of the most succinct comments that explains the underlying reasons for the Iran-Iraq war, Iraq's role in that war, and the support for Iraq by moderate Arab states was made by King Husayn of Jordan:

> I am worried of what I believe is a very sinister, almost criminal attempt to create a rift between Muslims, between Shi'ites and Sunnis. This we saw very obviously at the very beginnings [of the Islamic revolution] and then obviously Iraq was a target. Fortunately Iraq and the area have withstood this attempt and I hope that it will not result in any success because it would be devastating. It would cause disintegration and far greater tragedy than this area has seen than any other. . . . Fortunately Iraq held as one nation and to my way of thinking—and that is an idea and opinion shared by many in the area—Iraq is a front line, not only for us in Jordan but for the entire area, for the Gulf, Saudi Arabia, and Oman as well.[7]

By spring 1987 there appeared to be little prospect for a settlement to the Iran-Iraq war. The Iraqi government and the Baath party remained fully occupied by the military conduct of the war and by its possible domestic implications. Iraq's failure to counter Iran's repeated advances in what became as early as 1981 a war of attrition clearly has serious implications for the Iraqi nation-state, the present Baathist leadership, and the other Arab states of the region.

Apart from the obvious dramatic consequences if Iran wins, Islamic conservatism would be given an immediate stimulus elsewhere in the region. Nevertheless, several predictions can be made about the course of Iraq's future policies regardless of whether the present leadership remains in power or is replaced by other political groups.

Determinants of Iraq's Domestic and Foreign Policies

A number of fundamental and interrelated considerations will shape the internal and external strategic concerns of future Iraqi governments regardless of their ideological inclinations or the foundations of their support. These considerations have serious implications for all foreign states that have or hope to have relations with Iraq. Domestically, there are at least five significant factors. First, the primary objective of any Iraqi government will be the internal consolidation of the nation-state and the establishment of a stable central governing authority that ultimately will achieve legitimacy

in the perceptions of Iraq's numerous particularistic groups. Second, over-
lapping and at times conflicting symbols of personal identity—such as those
of religion, ethnicity, and language—will remain strong vibrant factors in
Iraq's domestic political environment. Third, the availability of renewable
water resources in Iraq and the fact that some 30 to 40 per cent of the
Iraqi people remain employed in agriculture in contrast to less than 3 per
cent in the oil sector mean that the government must continue to focus
attention on both agriculture and irrigation. Fourth, there will be a continued
emphasis on the coordination and integration of the economic, political,
and social interests of the three dominant Iraqi cities—Mosul, Baghdad and
Basra—and on greater links between rural and urban areas. Finally, and
most important, Iraqis will continue to find their domestic affairs susceptible
to external interference, a condition inherent in Iraq's geographical position
as a frontier. Indeed, this frontier position has contributed to the pluralistic
characteristics of Iraqi society and continues to heighten and to multiply
Iraqi concerns.

At least three major foreign policy considerations will dominate the plans
of the Iraqi government. First, the nation's frontier position and the fact
that it is virtually landlocked, with a frontage of no more than 15 kilometers
on the Gulf, ensures that Iraqis will continue to have an acute sense of
their vulnerabilities. This sense has often impelled both offensive and
defensive solutions, although the leadership realizes that good relations
between Iraq and its neighbors are valuable, if not imperative. As one
Middle Eastener reflecting on relations between Iran and Iraq has said:
"You can divorce your wife, you can disown your son, but you can never
change your neighbor."[8] Not accidentally, Iraq was therefore one of the first
Arab countries to bring Turkey into the spheres of Arab commerce and
politics; Ayatollah Khomeini's talk of the export of the Islamic revolution
and the dangers of Arab nationalism was of direct and immediate concern
to Iraq even prior to the start of the war.

Second, as long as oil remains the major contributor to the Iraqi economy,
Gulf security and Iraq's access to the Gulf will be a constant source of
concern. Iraq will continue to diversify routes to ship oil, whether through
Saudi Arabia, Jordan, Syria, Turkey, or the Gulf. No future treaty or
agreement, whether with neighbors or superpowers, that does not effectively
quell Iraqi concerns can ever be expected to contribute to lasting peaceful
relations. Third, these strategic concerns will continue to make Iraq susceptible to superpower pressures, complicating the foreign relations of the
country.

Two solutions have been tried in Iraq's history, and both will probably
be tried again, as long as Iraq remains territorially integral after the conclusion
of the Iran-Iraq war. One is a policy of nonalignment and the diversification
of Iraq's economic and political ties. This solution has been pursued by
the present civilian wing of the Baath party and is reflected in almost every
sphere, such as the oil industry, in which the government bureaucracy has
control. The alternative is a situation where nonalignment is seen as a

weakness rather than a strength. The country's geopolitical vulnerabilities could then cause an Iraqi government to ally itself once again with a single strong partner as it did with the West prior to the revolution of 1958 or as successor governments did with the Soviet Union in the 1960s until the Baath took control in 1968 and actively began to pursue nonalignment in the mid-1970s.

Notes

1. For further information see John Rossant, *Iraqi Oil in the 1980s* (Petroleum Information International, 1983).

2. *Monday Morning*, January 22–28, 1979, pp. 18–22; and *al-Mustaqbal*, February 2, 1979, pp. 8–9.

3. For an analysis of Iraq's assumptions regarding domestic affairs in Iran prior to the war and Iraqi objectives once the war began, see Christine Moss Helms, "The Iraqi Dilemma: Political Objectives Versus Military Strategy," *American-Arab Affairs* (summer 1983), pp. 76–85, reprinted in the Brookings Institution Reprint Series, no. 398 (1983).

4. After the war started, Iraq went even further to state that Pan-Arabism was a moot concept. States should remain as they were presently constituted, and Arab governments should work together as neighboring states. Islamic conservatism in Iran, however, still recognized no territorial boundaries between states.

5. *Foreign Broadcast Information Service (FBIS)*, Middle East, October 17, 1979, p. E4.

6. FBIS, Middle East, February 11, 1980, pp. E1–E4.

7. FBIS, Middle East, March 2, 1982, p. F1.

8. Interview by Christine Helms with Shahpour Bakhtiar on May 5, 1983.

7

Iran

Robert S. Litwak

The rapidity and magnitude of change in Iran's domestic and foreign policy orientation have few historical parallels. In the wake of the 1973–1974 OPEC revolution, Iran appeared poised to supplant Britain as the paramount power in the Gulf region. The conception of Iran as a stabilizing, pro-Western pillar in the region was consciously fostered by the United States within the terms of the Nixon Doctrine. The centerpiece of the Shah's regional security policy was the containment of Iraq and the creation of a working relationship with Saudi Arabia. Half a decade later, the Iranian Revolution brought the collapse of the ancien régime and the advent of a successor government whose legitimacy rested upon an ideology that demanded a radical departure from previous policies. Within 18 months, the Islamic Republic was at war with its principal regional adversary and locked in crisis with its former superpower patron. The ability of the Western powers to assess and respond adequately to developments since 1979 has been hampered by the lack of a clear understanding of the dynamics of change within Iran. The prior set of assumptions guiding Western policy was overturned with the revolution—thus creating an intellectual vacuum that still exists.

Although revolutions are by their nature sui generis, they pass through broadly similar phases. Beginning more as a cause than a concrete program of action, successful revolutions are soon subject to the practical requirements of government. Although revolutions radically alter perspectives within the polity, they cannot change the objective realities of the state.[1] These realities—geographic position, demography, natural resources, and the regional environment—define the possibilities of state action. Given these inherent constraints, the inability of a revolutionary régime to implement doctrinally its broad vision of the new order invariably leads to schisms within the leadership. These splits between so-called pragmatists and radicals center on the degree of tactical accommodation (over issues such as the use of terror) that the régime must prudently make in order to further its long-term revolutionary objectives. The ongoing power struggle among the Tehran régime's multiple centers of power closely corresponds to this model. As

116

with previous revolutionary governments, however, the dilemma is obvious: At what point do cumulative tactical shifts in the name of pragmatism (e.g., Khomeini's support of Assad's campaign against the Ikhwani in Syria) begin to erode the legitimacy of the revolutionary vision? In the case of Iran, the requirements of legitimacy have led to a unique fusion of the clerical régime's domestic and foreign policies.

The purpose of this chapter is to survey briefly developments in Iran since the advent of the Islamic Republic. Attention will first focus on the internal dimension—specifically, the nature and structure of the theocratic régime, its social and economic program, civil-military relations, and the political strength of opposition forces (including leftist and national minority groups). The next section will examine the role played by Iran within its regional political environment. The central issue in this context is the devastating war of attrition with Iraq and its pervasive influence on Gulf stability. It will be shown that the factors at the heart of the Iran-Iraq war are precisely those that have complicated Iran's state-to-state relations with the other Arab states of the Gulf, as well as with Turkey and Pakistan. The final section of this chapter will assess the Islamic Republic's relations with the principal extraregional powers—the United States, the Soviet bloc, Western Europe, and Japan. The assessment of the postrevolutionary developments in Iran across these three levels of analysis will center on the interaction between trends that are presently manifest and those that could plausibly develop.

Domestic Politics and Security

Specialists on Iran commonly divide the period since the February 1979 revolution into four phases.[2] The first phase was the period of dual government beginning with Mehdi Bazargan's inauguration as prime minister in February 1979 and ending with his resignation in the wake of the seizure of the U.S. embassy in November 1979. The second postrevolutionary phase spanned the fall of the Bazargan government and Bani-Sadr's dismissal from the presidency in June 1981. Following the demise of the secular elements within the régime (as symbolized by the fall of Abolhasan Bani-Sadr), the clerical leadership initiated a third postrevolutionary phase with the explicit aim of consolidating and institutionalizing its control mechanisms. Public discontent with the arbitrary excesses of this period, however, prompted Khomeini to issue a decree in December 1982 ordering a reform of the nation's law enforcement procedures. Although arbitrary executions and arrests have continued during this fourth phase, some observers have pointed to signs of the régime's decreasing radicalization. The question remains as to whether such shifts are purely tactical or constitute a trend toward "Thermidor" (in Crane Brinton's terminology) and gradual normalization. Moreover, what would be the consequences of such a prospective deradicalization vis-à-vis the revolutionary régime's elusive quest for legitimacy and long-term stability? An exploration of these questions necessitates a more detailed analysis of the postrevolutionary phases through which Iran has passed. Such an exercise will permit the identification of the major determinants of social change and at least suggest a framework for assessing future developments.

The February 1979 revolution represented the culmination of a mass political movement cutting across ideological, national, and religious lines. Despite the plurality of the revolution, the ensuing periods witnessed an increasing centralization of political power in clerical hands at the expense of the movement's secular (so-called modernist) forces. The formation of the Provisional Government in early February, under Prime Minister Mehdi Bazargan, was viewed as a reassuring sign by the secular opposition.[3] The prevailing view in the immediate postrevolutionary period was that Khomeini would reside in Qum as the nation's spiritual leader but would not become involved in day-to-day politics. This belief was quickly dispelled, however, with the growing assertion of the Revolutionary Council as a rival power center to the Provisional Government. The Revolutionary Council was appointed by Khomeini upon his return to Iran from Paris and included a number of his former students (most notably Ayatollah Beheshti), as well as such radical secularists as Abolhasan Bani-Sadr and Sadiq Ghotbzadeh.

Within weeks of assuming office, Bazargan complained that the Revolutionary Council was usurping the powers and prerogatives of the Provisional Government. The problem of centralized control was further compounded by the operation of various autonomous organizations (such as the Islamic revolutionary courts under the control of Ayatollah Sadiq Khalkhali, the Pasdaran or Revolutionary Guards, and the revolutionary *komitehs*). On May 23, the prime minister baldly asserted that Iran had become a nation of "hundreds of chiefs." Several months later, in an interview with Italian journalist Oriana Fallaci, Bazargan expressed the fear that Iran was drifting toward a "dictatorship of the clergy" and aptly characterized the relationship between the Provisional Government and the Revolutionary Council: "They've put a knife in my hand, but it's a knife with only a handle; others are holding the blade."[4]

Dissension between the Bazargan government and the Revolutionary Council intensified during summer 1979. Khomeini, crediting the victory of the revolution to the fundamentalist clergy and the dispossessed classes, began to attack Bazargan's power base—the middle class—and to oppose secular candidates to the Constituent Council of Experts (Majlis-e-Khobregan). The council was the 73-member body empowered by Khomeini to draft the Islamic Republic's constitution. The sketchy electoral results announced on August 11 indicated that members of the clergy and other Islamic fundamentalists had gained 60 seats to the council. The election was followed by increasingly sharp attacks against the Bazargan government by Ayatollah Beheshti, then vice chairman of the Constituent Council of Experts and founder of the fundamentalist Islamic Republican party (IRP). Beheshti subsequently claimed that Khomeini had approached him and the IRP several times during 1979 to form a government, but they had responded that they were not sufficiently institutionalized to do so.[5]

Beheshti's admission is striking and sheds considerable light on the political strategy pursued by Khomeini upon his return to Iran from Paris. Far from auguring the withdrawal of the clergy from politics, the Bazargan appointment was a tactical decision based upon the balance of political forces within Iran in February 1979. With the IRP not yet fully organized and the imperial army still intact, Khomeini needed the support, or at least the quiescence, of the various secular groups (most notably, the Left, the "bazaar," and the middle class) who favored Bazargan. In so doing, the clerical leadership gained valuable time to establish independent lines of political control within the country. The major steps furthering this objective were the establishment of the IRP under Beheshti's direction, the strengthening of the Pasdaran, and the passage of the Islamic Republic's constitution. With the implementation of these measures, Bazargan became politically expendable. The hostage crisis, precipitated by the prime minister's meeting with Zbigniew Brzezinski in Algiers in late October 1979, should thus be seen as the occasion, not the cause, of Bazargan's resignation.

The election of Bani-Sadr to the presidency in January 1980 brought to political prominence a group of Islamic modernists more radical in their socioeconomic orientation than those associated with Bazargan. Having supported the attacks on the Provisional Government as a member of the Revolutionary Council, Bani-Sadr evidently believed that he would be more successful than Bazargan in politically outmaneuvering the fundamentalist clergy. The extent of Bani-Sadr's overconfidence was reflected in his claim on the morrow of the presidential elections that Ayatollah Beheshti was "politically dead."[6] The Bani-Sadr government, however, soon encountered the same limitations on secular authority that had plagued its predecessor. Lacking the clear-cut support of the Imam, Bani-Sadr was unable to weaken the principal instruments of clerical power, such as the revolutionary *komitehs* and the Pasdaran. Indeed, at every critical juncture in the first half of 1980, the newly incumbent president was rebuffed in his efforts to curtail the growing ascendancy of the IRP and its leader—Ayatollah Beheshti. The May 1980 parliamentary elections gave the IRP a sweeping majority of seats in the Majlis. Although Bani-Sadr and the leaders of Iran's remaining secular political parties levied charges of widespread voter fraud, Khomeini deemed the elections "fair."

Having contributed to the political demise of Bazargan for the sin of insufficient revolutionary fervor, Bani-Sadr was soon himself charged with excessive moderation. In mid-1980 Ayatollah Khomeini launched a cultural revolution and criticized Bani-Sadr, among others, for failing to establish a "truly Islamic country." Bani-Sadr's role in the hostage crisis was a symptom of his broader political predicament.

The identification of Bani-Sadr and Ghotbzadeh as moderates by Carter administration officials only served to undermine further their position with Imam Khomeini and the fundamentalist clergy. An indicator of things to come was the incarceration of Foreign Minister Ghotbzadeh for four days in early November 1980 on the charge of criticizing the nation's broadcasting service. As the schism between Bani-Sadr and Beheshti's IRP deepened throughout 1980, the president attracted support from a spectrum of national, liberal, leftist, and other secular groups. Most prominent of these was the Mujahedin-e-Khalq (People's Crusaders), a movement under the leadership of Massoud Rajavi, which had emerged as a party capable of mass mobilization in the wake of the February 1979 revolution. Although virtually none of these groups had previously been close to Bani-Sadr politically, they all viewed him as the best vehicle for channeling their opposition to the increasingly totalitarian control of the clerical leadership. Clashes between supporters of Bani-Sadr and Islamic fundamentalists in early March 1981 prompted Ayatollah Beheshti (in his role as chief justice of the Supreme Court) to urge that the president be brought to trial for inciting violence. In mid-March, Imam Khomeini summoned senior officials to Qum to order an end to infighting until the conclusion of the war with Iraq.

A constitutional crisis, however, developed in May 1981 when Bani-Sadr refused to sign legislation passed by the Majlis that would have further weakened the powers of the presidency. This act of defiance prompted Khomeini to issue a public warning that anyone who flouted the decisions of the Majlis would be "pursued" as a "corrupt person on earth" (such a crime normally punishable by death).[7] After his dismissal as commander-in-chief of the armed forces by Khomeini on June 8, Bani-Sadr was forced to go underground. Khomeini's political lead was quicky followed by the Majlis, which impeached the president on grounds of incompetence. The ouster of Bani-Sadr was accompanied by a governmental campaign to eradicate all opposition groups politically associated with the former president (the Mujahedin, the Marxist-Leninist Peykar movement, the Fedayeen-e-Khalq (People's Strugglers), Maoists, and national and religious minorities). The dominant opposition party, the Mujahedin, demonstrated the power of its own reach in a number of devastating bomb attacks against the IRP in summer 1981. The most serious of these was an explosion at the IRP's Tehran headquarters on June 28 in which some seventy party members, including Ayatollah Beheshti, were killed. The government's response to the Mujahedin bombing campaign was swift and massive: Pasdaran swept through entire neighborhoods arbitrarily arresting any persons whose age group and appearance suggested a Mujahedin affiliation. Former Prime Minister Bazargan, whose continued presence in the Majlis was intended to demonstrate the clerical régime's toleration of a secular opposition, was one of the few to speak out publicly against the summary executions and atmosphere of violence in Iran.

The fall of Bani-Sadr, followed by his flight with Mujahedin leader Massoud Rajavi to Paris in July 1982, marked the end of the second phase of the revolution. Over a two-year period, the fundamentalist clergy had divided and successively eliminated the secularist political forces. Khomeini had demonstrated his consummate skills as a politician, and the opposition had exposed its naiveté and romanticism. A common failing of the secularists was the reluctance to take Khomeini at his word. Khomeini was remarkably consistent in his pronouncements on the proper role of religion in Islamic society, while remaining ambiguous as to the timetable for the programmatic applications of these precepts. The romantic characteristic of the secular politicians lay in their tendency to read their own ideological preferences vis-à-vis questions of social justice and order into Khomeini's views. They were, as one observer phrased it, betrayed by their own illusions and in turn accused Khomeini of betrayals.[8] Throughout this period, the secularist forces were weakened by their own factionalism and their consequent failure to mount a credible institutional challenge to the IRP. Both Bazargan and Bani-Sadr had originally hoped to capitalize upon Khomeini's charismatic authority (as constitutionally vested in his title of *velayat-e faqih*) to out-maneuver their opponents and further their respective socioeconomic programs. Their failures were an inevitable consequence of Khomeini's utilization of the dictatorial potential implicit in the concept of *velayat-e faqih* for his own undisguised ends.

The preceding discussion has focused on the postrevolutionary power struggle between the contending clerical and secular factions. Within the clergy itself, however, some divisions have major policy consequences. Indeed, with the purging of the secularist elements from the régime, the significance of clerical factionalism has assumed heightened importance. Within the clergy, there is a broad dichotomy between the radical Khat-e Imam group and the moderate Hojjati faction. As its name suggests, the Khat-e Imam (followers of the Imam's line) favors the institutionalization of the *velayat-e faqih* and the continued centralization of clerical power. It further supports the nationalization of key industries and the tight regulation of foreign trade. The leading political figures associated with the Khat-e Imam group include Ayatollahs Ali Meshkini and Hussein Ali Montazeri, as well as Hojjat al-Islam Ali Khamenei (president of the Islamic Republic).

The Hojjati faction, in contrast, though acknowledging the necessity of a cultural revolution has been less doctrinal over policy matters. This attitude has been translated, for example, into the adoption of a more conservative stance on such issues as land reform, the nationalization of industries and trade, and labor law. Members of this faction are reported to have contacts with former Prime Minister Bazargan. Political figures identified with this line include Hojjat al-Islam Mohammed Reza Mahdavi-Kani, a member of the six-person Council of Guardians, and Ali Hashimi-Rafsanjani, the speaker of the Majlis. The dichotomy between the Khat-e Imam and the Hojjati offers a useful analytical framework to assess policy differences within the clergy. The realm of practical politics is, of course, less clear cut. Individuals may move from one faction to the other depending on the issue. Within this context, it would perhaps be more appropriate to view these factions as attitudes of mind rather than two distinct groups with conflicting political ideologies.[9]

The most important issue that divides the clerical leadership is the question of Khomeini's succession. On December 10, 1982, elections were held for the Council of Experts, an 83-member body that would preside over the selection of a successor to Khomeini. On July 7, 1983, Khomeini issued a statement that he had deposited with the Assembly of Experts a 30-page will to be read to the public upon his death. One month later, a clandestine radio broadcast announced that Khomeini had appointed a five-person provisional council (reportedly including Montazeri, Meshkini, and Mahdavi-Kani) to rule in the event of a deadlock within the Assembly of Experts.[10] Whereas the Khat-e Imam evidently favored the declaration of Montazeri as heir-apparent, the Hojjati and other social conservatives wanted a committee of clerical leaders to replace Khomeini as the *faqih*. The issue will probably become a theological dispute with one side asserting that Shi'i Islam favors the concept of a single spiritual leader and the other side opposing the institutionalization of *velayat-e faqih*. The resistance of the Hojjati to Khomeini's appropriation of the title imam during the immediate postrevolutionary period suggests the lines that will be drawn in the succession debate.[11]

The struggle for political power at the center since February 1979 has created new opportunities on the periphery for the assertion of autonomy by Iran's ethnic minority communities. The most serious challenge to central authority has been in Kurdistan where there are continuing clashes between local resistance groups (spearheaded by the Kurdish Democratic party) and government forces. The postrevolutionary period similarly witnessed the revival of autonomy movements in Baluchistan and Azerbaijan. In the latter, the opposition centered on political support for Ayatollah Karim Shariat-madari and the Muslim People's Republican party (MPRP). During the 1979 constitutional debate, Shariatmadari's opposition to the concept of *velayat-e faqih* precipitated a raid by Pasdaran on his residence and counterdemonstrations against the government. Under house arrest since 1981, Shariatmadari was implicated in Ghotbzadeh's alleged plot against Khomeini in April 1982. As one observer has noted, it is a testimony to Shariatmadari's influential position within the clergy that he was not formally charged and executed.

As with its secular opposition, the clerical régime has been loathe to accommodate the political interests of the ethnic minorities. Although the Islamic Republic's constitution contains provisions ostensibly protecting national minority rights (e.g., the preservation of ethnic languages and customs), official policy holds ethnic nationalism as a threat to the unity of Islam and a vehicle for external intervention.[12] Although regional opposition to the theocratic régime will certainly persist, the success or failure of these autonomy movements will rest on the long-term outcome of the Tehran power struggle. A weak central government will be less able to resist pressures on the periphery.

The resilience of the clerical régime has delighted its supporters and confounded its opponents. Its strongest political asset remains the charismatic appeal of Ayatollah Khomeini. The consolidation of clerical authority has been achieved through the implementation of tactically staged moves against the régime's secularist opponents. This process began with the political elimination of the moderates during the Bazargan period, continued with the purging of social radicals associated with Bani-Sadr and the non-Communist Left, and culminated most recently in attacks on the Tudeh (Communist) party. The neutralization of the political opposition has left no currently viable alternative to the Khomeini régime within Iran. The armed forces—the only interest group with the means to challenge clerical authoritarianism—has suffered multiple purges and remains preoccupied with the war with Iraq. The externally based opposition, ranging from monarchists to the Mujahedin, lacks broad popular support and the legitimacy of action that comes with it. In establishing the present structure of clerical rule in Iran, the Khomeini régime has proved singularly adept at overcoming the contradictions of revolution and statecraft. The ability of the fundamentalist clergy to maintain this political condition through a perpetual tour de force will be assessed in the concluding section of this chapter.

Regional Politics

Carl von Clausewitz observed that war has its own language but not its own logic. The Iran-Iraq conflict has been the most devastating and prolonged in the modern history of the Gulf region. The political dynamics governing Iran's continued participation in the war with Iraq reflect the broader patterns of the Islamic Republic's foreign policy in the region. These themes, in turn, provide some insight into the underlying logic of the clerical régime's actions.

Following the fall of the shah, a debate within the ruling circle centered on whether Iran should export its revolutionary experience to adjacent states in the region. In form, these discussions closely paralleled those that took place within the Soviet Central Committee in the 1920s over permanent revolution and socialism in one country. As opposed to the relative pragmatists who argued that Islamic republicanism should be consolidated within Iran, Khomeini asserted that the country's mission was to aid and foster revolutions of the oppressed Moslem masses elsewhere. This position was wholly consonant with the Ayatollah's Manichean worldview. At the same time, Khomeini's promotion of Iran's revolutionary self-image underscored the unique fusion of the Islamic Republic's domestic and foreign policies.

The example of a successful revolution in Iran, when coupled with the régime's inflammatory rhetoric, had a pervasive political effect within the Gulf region. Not surprisingly, Baathist Iraq and the Arab monarchies viewed the Islamic Republic as posing an ipso facto threat to the legitimacy of their régimes. Iranian efforts to destabilize the Gulf states centered on provocative radio broadcasts, as well as on the encouragement and financing of political agitation in areas with large Shi'i communities (such as Bahrain, Kuwait, and Saudi Arabia's eastern province).

Iran's postrevolutionary relationship with Bahrain offers a striking example of the manner in which a radical shift in the domestic structure of one state may lead to a transformation of the regional security environment.[13]

During the Shah's period, Iran's intermittently expressed irredentist claim to the Bahrainian archipelago was couched in the language of Persian nationalism. Reference was made to Persia's historical (albeit convoluted) connections to Bahrain. A 1970 UN-supervised plebiscite, conducted one year prior to the final British withdrawal from the region, confirmed the nation's independent status. At that point, this longstanding issue of contention was considered resolved. Yet, as the history of the Middle East demonstrates, interstate disputes are rarely settled per se; rather, owing to the perceived interests of the involved parties, they remain dormant or deferred—always bearing the potential to reemerge as a catalyst of conflict under the appropriate conditions. As suggested, these circumstances are largely determined by shifts on the domestic level. In the case of the Iran-Bahrain dispute, the overthrow of the shah created such a novel set of political conditions.

The postrevolutionary period witnessed the reassertion of Iran's claim to Bahrain, although now based on a wholly different set of criteria. Although the Shah's claim was premised on the traditional Persian connections to the islands, the clerical régime spoke of the special affinity between the states' Shi'i populations. The most influential and inflammatory advocate of this position was Ayatollah Sadiq Rouhani, who baldly warned the ruler of Bahrain to govern in conformance with Islamic principles or face popular overthrow. In an attempt to distance the Bazargan government from the Rouhani statement, the foreign minister, Ibrahim Yazdi, declared that the Ayatollah's declaration represented a personal view and not official policy. He further stated that Iran would not consciously export its revolution to adjacent states but could not prevent their "oppressed" populations from acting upon the inspiration of its example. This step in the direction of pragmatic accommodation was not sustained by Khomeini, who continued to stress the need to export revolution. As previously discussed, the relative moderation of the Bazargan government on this issue and the hostage crisis weakened its standing in the perspective of the imam. That development, in turn, allowed it to be outmaneuvered politically by the more radical secularist and clerical factions within the ruling circle.

The Islamic Republic's continued interest in the exportation of revolution was strongly suggested in the abortive coup in Bahrain in December 1981. The incident led to the arrest of over seventy conspirators and the expulsion of the Iranian chargé in Manama. Bahrain's prime minister charged that Iran had directly fomented the coup attempt via its political and materiel support for the Islamic Front for the Liberation of Bahrain. The Saudi interior minister alleged that the plot was part of a broader strategy to assassinate leaders in Saudi Arabia, Bahrain, and other regional states. The episode prompted Saudi Arabia in late December 1981 to conclude cooperative agreements with Bahrain and two other Gulf states on internal security matters.[14]

The dramatic revival of Iran's dispute with Bahrain by the theocratic régime carried two related sets of implications: one shaping the nature of regional relations, another specifically affecting the Islamic Republic's foreign policy behavior. On the regional level, it underscored that the activation of disputes and the perception of threat remain functions largely of the character of the régimes in question. A radical change in the domestic structure of a state results not only in a new régime but indeed in a wholly new set of circumstances. This political dynamic permits previously settled issues to be revived within a new context with reference to completely different criteria (e.g., the shift from historical to sectarian in the case of Iran and Bahrain). The degree of compatibility between the domestic structures of disputants is thus a major determinant of conflict.[15] In the lower Gulf region, the similarity between the domestic structures of the monarchical states limits the scope of territorial and resource disputes. This situation stands in sharp contrast to that of the Iran-Iraq war in which the conflict revolved around the question of legitimacy and the stakes were régime survival.

The Khomeini régime's contradictory handling of the Bahrain issue is a reflection of its broader dilemma: reconciling the competing demands of revolution and statecraft. The revolutionary component of its foreign policy is inextricably linked to the clerical régime's elusive pursuit of domestic legitimacy. The pragmatic nature of the Islamic Republic's current relationships with Turkey and Pakistan suggests some tactical accommodation;[16] yet the record of postrevolutionary politics within Iran indicates that the advocacy of such moderation has proved detrimental in the central power struggle. In view of this close linkage between domestic and foreign policies, the political prognosis is a continuing precedence of ideological over pragmatic considerations in the development of the Islamic Republic's regional relations. Iran's continued prosecution of the war with Iraq provides the most graphic and tragic illustration of this conclusion.

Prior to the revolution, the Shah had established a modus vivendi with the Baathist régime. The centerpiece of this relationship was the March 1975 Algiers agreement. In concrete terms, the understanding resulted in the equitable demarcation of the Iran-Iraq land frontier and the Shatt al-Arab waterway. Both sides also pledged to end "all infiltrations of a subversive character from either side"; this provision led to the cessation of Iranian support for the Kurdish nationalist movement within Iraq. The Baathist régime's limited rapprochement with Iran was one component of a broader Iraqi strategy of diplomatic activism. Baghdad's attempts during 1977–1978 to distance itself politically from Moscow (as manifested in criticism of Soviet policy in the Horn of Africa and Afghanistan, as well as in the suppression of the Iraqi Communist party) were coupled with the inauguration of bilateral security consultations between the Baathist leadership and Iran, Kuwait, and Saudi Arabia. Whether purely tactical in nature or not, the fragile bases of the post-1975 relationship between Tehran and Baghdad collapsed with the political upheaval in Iran.

Régime changes may precipitate radical shifts in security perspectives. The deterioration in relations between Iran and Iraq following the February

1979 revolution may be traced to a number of causes. In reaction to the ostensibly cordial relations between Tehran and Baghdad prior to February 1979, the attitude of the Khomeini régime toward the Baathist government was one of undisguised hostility. From the Iraqi perspective, there was the overriding fear that the clerical régime, as part of its drive to export revolution in the region, would seek to foment unrest among its large Kurdish and Shi'i communities. The Baathist régime, under the strong leadership of President Saddam Husayn, responded to Iranian provocations with a number of moves to preserve the regional balance of power while enhancing Iraq's Pan-Arabist credentials. For example, the revival of Iran's long dormant irredentist claim to Bahrain by Ayatollah Rouhani prompted an Iraqi counterpledge to repulse any such military threat.

The ideological nature of the struggle between the theocratic and Baathist régimes resulted in an expansion in the scope of conflict. This characteristic was manifested in late October 1979 when an Iraqi official first stated Baghdad's terms for an improvement in relations with Iran. This maximalist formulation included the following conditions: a revision of the 1975 Algiers agreement regarding navigation rights on the Shatt al-Arab; the return to Arab sovereignty of Abu Musa and the Tumb Islands (seized by Iranian forces in 1971); and the provision of self-rule to Iran's national minorities, such as the Arabs of Khuzestan. As reflected in this Iraqi statement, the ideological character of the Iran-Iraq dispute had the net effect of allowing differences in one area (the Shatt al-Arab dispute) to spill over and destabilize the entire range of their relations. From the time of the enunciation of Baghdad's maximalist demands—a clear exercise in domestic and inter-Arab politics—the frequency and intensity of skirmishes along the frontier increased. A major rhetorical escalation occurred in April 1980 when Khomeini branded Saddam Husayn "an enemy of Islam and the Moslems" and called upon the Iraqi people to "cut off the hand of America which has emerged from Saddam's sleeve."[17]

The timing of the Baathist régime's initiation of war against Iran was influenced by three conditions: (1) the Khomeini régime's self-generated diplomatic isolation as a consequence of the hostage crisis and its inflammatory rhetoric of revolution; (2) other events within the international system that diverted the attention of the superpowers (e.g., the U.S. presidential election campaign, the Polish and Afghanistan crises); and (3) the Husayn régime's perception of a decisive military tilt in its favor due to the degeneration of Iran's armed forces (through successive purges and the neglect of equipment). Against this background, Saddam Husayn evidently believed (perhaps on the basis of reports from Iranian exile groups receiving Iraqi assistance) that an Iraqi attack would likely trigger a domestic uprising against the Khomeini régime. Husayn's political miscalculation confirmed the traditional maxim—never invade a revolution.

The onset of open hostilities between Iran and Iraq came in mid-September 1980 following weeks of escalating border incidents. On September 17, Iraq took the formal step of abrogating the 1975 Algiers agreement.

Within four days, fighting spread to the Iranian port of Khorramshahr and to the area adjacent to Abadan airport. A major escalation in the conflict occurred on September 22 when Iraqi MIGs struck at air bases across Iran. This move was accompanied by the invasion of Baathist forces into Iran at four strategic points along the frontier. The important border town of Qasr-e-Shirin was quickly captured, and the refinery city of Abadan was besieged. Despite its prior pattern of provocations against the Baathist régime, the Iranian leadership depicted the conflict as an "imposed war"— the product of Iraqi-U.S. collusion against the Islamic Republic. Khomeini publicly embraced the war as "a blessing" that would breathe new life into the revolution.[18] The horrific human and economic costs of the conflict notwithstanding, the war with Iraq has had a positive political utility for the Khomeini régime: It has lent credence to the régime's claim that foreign enemies are seeking to strangle the revolution; it has provided a pretext for draconian domestic security measures, as well as a ready excuse for the country's poor economic performance; and it has kept the armed forces away from Tehran while occupied at the front.

The Iraqi assault on Iran in autumn 1980 was a strategic failure.[19] It neither neutralized the Iranian air and ground forces nor triggered the type of popular insurrection against the Khomeini régime that Saddam Husayn had reportedly anticipated. In January 1981, the shift in military initiative from Iraq to Iran was marked by an Iranian counteroffensive south of Susangerd. In September 1981, a combined operation involving the regular army and the Pasdaran successfully "lifted the siege of Abadan" (as Iranian propaganda described it). Two additional offenses in March and May 1982 resulted in the capture or expulsion of Iraqi forces from the majority of Iranian territory occupied since the early months of the war. In July 1982, Iran launched Operation Ramadan as its forces crossed the prewar frontier for the first time since the onset of hostilities and attempted to drive on Abadan. Iranian tactics have centered on mass attacks employing lightly armed Pasdar and Bassij volunteers. These "human wave" assaults, lacking any air or armored support, have failed to break through Iraq's Soviet-style fixed positions. A major factor adversely affecting the ability of the Iranian military to conduct the war has been the American arms embargo. With Iran unable to mount a war-winning offensive, the conflict has entered an attritional phase.

The paucity of available information makes impossible any precise assessment of Iran's human and materiel losses in the war. Estimates of dead and wounded have been placed anywhere from 150,000 to 500,000. Damage to Iran's economic infrastructure has been confined to the western section of the country and is estimated to be in the $100–150 billion range.[20] As described by Shaul Bakhash, the clerical régime's capital requirements— both to meet its economic needs and to prosecute the war with Iraq— have led to a pragmatic shift in its dealings with OPEC. By early 1982, the Khomeini régime's radical oil policies had led to the near exhaustion of Iran's foreign exchange reserves and the disruption of its prerevolution marketing networks. At that time, the precariousness of its financial position compelled the theocratic leadership to pursue a more assertive strategy to recapture markets (e.g., barter arrangements, discounted prices) and coordinate oil production levels within OPEC.[21]

Successive efforts since September 1980 by the United Nations, Islamic Conference, and other would-be mediators to negotiate a cessation to the Iran-Iraq War have led nowhere. The profound ideological hostility at the heart of the conflict continues to militate against the possibility of a mediated settlement. The predominance of this characteristic of the dispute ensures that questions of territorial disposition—the ostensible focus of any prospective negotiations—remain distinct from the underlying political objectives of the combatants. Because it is an ideological war (to use French philosopher Raymond Aron's phrase), the warring parties find it impossible to agree upon the political criteria of a settlement. In March 1975, the Shah and Saddam Husayn achieved a modus vivendi on the basis of non-interference in one another's domestic affairs. The structural nature of the dispute between Iran and Iraq—the conflict stemming from their contending notions of domestic legitimacy and national order—rules out the possibility of any such political accommodation in the current crisis.

In early 1984, an escalation in the conflict reflected the increasing frustration and desperation of both sides. In mid-March, Iraqi air strikes against Kharg Island prompted Iranian counterstrikes against commercial shipping in the Gulf. This expansion in the geographical scope of the conflict led Saudi Arabia, with American political and materiel backing, to provide some air cover for the major shipping lanes. On June 5, Saudi Arabian F-15s downed at least one Iranian F-4 fighter-bomber. The most serious military development during this period, however, was the confirmation by a UN team in mid-March of Iraq's battlefield use of chemical weapons.[22] As one observer noted, it was a testimony to Iran's political pariah status that this gross violation of international norms generated scant public outcry. Although the danger of further escalation remains, the possibility of a negotiated settlement will hinge on internal political developments in Iran and Iraq. The likely prognosis is a continuing war of attrition until a decisive shift takes place in the domestic power structure of either (or both) state(s).[23]

Relations with Outside Powers

The unique fusion of the Islamic Republic's domestic and foreign policies has been a leitmotif of this chapter. Domestic factors are the primary determinants of foreign policy choices; conversely, external policies are politically used by the régime to reinforce its precarious domestic legitimacy. In eschewing the shah's security perspective and policies, the clerical régime has defined threats in terms of dependence and cultural penetration. This analysis has led to the promulgation of a foreign policy whose basic tenets include genuine nonalignment and hostility toward the superpowers (as embodied in the slogan "neither East nor West"); increased cooperation with third world states; Islamic internationalism (e.g., the drive to export revolution and assist the world's dispossessed); and anti-Zionism. In the realm of foreign policy, two trends are evident: (1) the circumscribed ability of outside powers to influence the Islamic Republic's external policies and (2) the régime's propensity to display greater pragmatism on foreign as compared to domestic issues.

Soviet Union

Assessments of Iran's relations with the superpowers have tended to divide along the familiar lines of East-West controversies. A central issue of contention has been the extent to which the clerical régime's slogan of "neither East nor West" translates into true equidistance. Although one school emphasizes Soviet gains in Iran since the revolution, the other highlights the inability of Moscow to capitalize on political opportunities. A brief consideration of the evolution of Soviet policy toward the Islamic Republic would help to place this debate into perspective.

By all available evidence, the Soviet Union did not anticipate the accelerated collapse of the imperial régime any better than the United States did. When confronted with new objective circumstances, however, Moscow quickly adjusted both its rhetoric and policies. Soviet statements in the wake of Khomeini's triumphant return from exile emphasized a number of interrelated themes. The United States was depicted as the principal enemy of Iran that had callously exploited the country's mineral wealth and perpetuated the Shah's unpopular rule. The clerical régime's renunciation of Iran's membership in the Central Treaty Organization (CENTO) and the severing of its multifaceted security relationship with the United States were hailed in the Soviet press as a reassertion of Iranian sovereignty. Feeding upon the régime's campaign against the Great Satan, Soviet propaganda charged the United States with a host of anti-Iranian actions, most notably the abetting of a terrorist campaign against the clerical leadership.

Closely linked to the theme of anti-Americanism was Moscow's repeated emphasis upon the pluralistic character of the revolution that overthrew the Shah and, in particular, the contribution of leftist forces to that victory. The Soviet Union encouraged the revolutionary régime to forge closer ties with the Tudeh party and other progressive (pro-Soviet) elements. As for the Soviet role in the events of 1978–1979, Moscow subsequently portrayed itself as the protector of the revolution. Soviet commentaries asserted that President Leonid Brezhnev's warning of November 19, 1978, against foreign interference in Iran's domestic affairs had deterred an American intervention on behalf of the Shah. The contribution of the 1921 Soviet-Iranian treaty of friendship was depicted in similarly hyperbolic terms. The overall thrust of Soviet policy toward Iran since the revolution has been to ensure the irreversibility of Tehran's break with Washington.

The clerical régime's response to Soviet overtures has been mixed. Although the Soviet ambassador was the first foreign envoy to meet with

Khomeini in Qum in February 1979, the Ayatollah has denounced the Soviet system as an atheist form of government that does not respect the rights of its Muslim population. Iranian officials claimed that the advent of the Islamic Republic posed a direct ideological challenge to the Soviet Union as it represented an alternative model of revolutionary change. The activities of the Tudeh were tolerated by the régime, but its leaders were subject to arbitrary arrest and its publications were periodically suspended. An Islamic newspaper, presaging the régime's subsequent crackdown against the party after 1981, teased that the Communists "threw a mouse in the soup of the revolution and without shame shouted, 'Oh hajji, we are also a partner.' "[24] In the economic sphere, Soviet-Iranian relations suffered a setback in July 1979 when Tehran abruptly canceled the IGAT-II natural gas pipeline agreement. Moscow had sought a minimal, submarket increase in the price of natural gas exported to the Soviet Union on the theory that Iran would accept this low bid rather than flare the gas. Much to Moscow's evident surprise, the clerical régime suspended all natural gas shipments to the Soviet Union and broke off negotiations for the construction of a complement to the existing IGAT-I system.[25]

Soviet relations with Iraq and the Afghanistan crisis have further complicated relations between Tehran and Moscow. The Iranian response to the December 1979 Soviet invasion of Afghanistan has gone little beyond ritualistic denunciations of the Soviet Union. In comparing the fight of the Afghan resistance movement to their own struggle against the shah, the clerical régime has demanded the immediate and unconditional withdrawal of Soviet forces. The Afghanistan crisis further resulted in the Iranian boycott of the 1980 Olympic games in Moscow and has been a focal point of Iranian criticism within such international fora as the Islamic Conference. The régime has similarly refused to participate in the UN-sponsored negotiations on Afghanistan in Geneva on the grounds that participation would imply tacit recognition of the Karmal régime in Kabul. Despite its condemnation of Soviet actions in Afghanistan, the régime has provided only limited assistance to the Afghan resistance movement.

Apart from the Afghanistan crisis, the other major regional determinant of relations between Tehran and Moscow has been the Iran-Iraq war. The initial Soviet position upon the outbreak of hostilities in September 1980 was official neutrality. In view of the prior record of Soviet-Iraqi military cooperation, this ostensibly neutral stance translated into an implicit tilt toward Tehran. As with other third-world interstate conflicts (e.g., India-Pakistan, Ethiopia-Somalia), the problem for the Soviet leadership has been the dilemma of choice that it imposes. In this instance, Soviet policy was evidently driven by the desire not to alienate Iran at a time when its foreign policy orientation had just undergone a fundamental shift. Two developments in mid-1982, however, precipitated a reconsideration of this policy in Moscow: Iran's decision in July to cross the frontier into Iraqi territory and the régime's sharp crackdown against the Tudeh as part of its broader strategy to eradicate political opposition to clerical rule. This evolution of events led to a resumption of large-scale Soviet arms transfers to Iraq and a Soviet propaganda drive against the régime. In mid-1983, for example, Soviet commentaries spoke of the rise of "Islamic despotism" in Iran.[26]

Despite periodic setbacks, the Soviet Union retains a formidable comparative advantage vis-à-vis the United States in its relations with Iran. Most obvious is the continued presence of a Soviet diplomatic mission in Tehran, whereas Iranian-American relations remain at a nadir. The Khomeini régime's reluctance to sever diplomatic relations with Moscow, in light of Soviet arms shipments to Iraq and attempted internal subversion via the Tudeh, is a clear reflection of the pragmatic limits of Iranian criticism of the Soviet Union.[27]

United States

Since the advent of the Islamic Republic, the major determinant of U.S.-Iranian relations has been the political power struggle within the Tehran régime. American efforts to establish a working relationship with the Bazargan government were manifested in the provision of some military spare parts and specialized fuels. This policy of acceptance and nonprovocation was motivated by the desire not to appear threatening to the régime and thereby push it into a closer relationship with the Soviet Union. These tentative moves collapsed in the wake of the hostage crisis and the elevation of radical anti-Americanism to the status of official policy. As the "Great Satan," the United States is blamed by Khomeini for a multitude of sins, including the instigation of the war with Iraq and the Mujahedin's counterterror campaign against the régime. Direct governmental contacts between the United States and Iran have been limited to the negotiations to secure the release of the hostages and the Claims Tribunal in the Hague that is determining the disposition of Iranian assets frozen by the U.S. government.

In view of the link between Iran's foreign and domestic policies—and the continuing domestic utility of anti-Americanism to the Khomeini régime—any prospective improvement in relations between Tehran and Washington will rest upon the evolution of political events within Iran. Although the United States pledged noninterference in Iranian internal affairs, American policy during the Carter and Reagan administrations has centered on the containment of Iran. This policy has entailed the active political and materiel support of regional allies, such as Saudi Arabia and Oman. It has not, however, included the provision of arms to Iraq in the Gulf war despite the recommendation from many quarters for a U.S. tilt toward Baghdad. The resumption of low-level bilateral trade following the resolution of the hostage crisis (e.g., the Iranian purchase of American foodstuffs, the sale of Iranian oil to the United States) suggested a mutual desire to maintain some minimal contact.[28]

In November 1986, the Reagan administration made the startling revelation that it had initiated a series of arms transfers to Iran during the previous year using Israel as the conduit. The stated purpose of this "strategic diplomatic initiative" was to revive relations with the Islamic Republic by cultivating "moderates" in the régime. Former National Security Adviser Robert McFarlane subsequently likened the Reagan administration's actions to Nixon's secret diplomacy toward China in 1971—i.e., the courting of a strategically important country on the Soviet periphery. Critics of administration policy argued that this strategic rationale was a smokescreen for U.S. efforts to gain the release of American hostages held by pro-Iranian groups in Lebanon through the transfer of arms to the Islamic Republic. The consensus amongst Western specialists on Iran was that although the avowed U.S. goal of reviving relations with Iran was a sensible long-term objective, the Reagan administration's initiative was both ill timed (because domestic political conditions within Iran were not conducive to it) and ill conceived (because of its unwise reliance on arms transfers as an instrument of influence). The move greatly undercut the administration's anti-terrorist policy and complicated its relations with the Arab states in the region. For their part, Iranian officials have offered to assist the United States in securing the freedom of American hostages in Lebanon if the Reagan administration releases Iranian financial assets frozen in 1979. In addition, the Tehran leadership has called for the shipment of U.S. arms which were paid for by the Shah but never transfered following the collapse of his régime. The events of 1986 served to underscore the conclusion that the favorable evolution of U.S.-Iranian relations will remain largely contingent upon domestic developments within the Islamic Republic.

Western Europe and Japan

The clerical régime's desire to distance itself politically from both super-powers has prompted it to develop economic ties with Western and Eastern Europe, as well as with Japan. In 1983, for example, British exports to Iran rose by 90 per cent to $880 million, whereas West German exports more than doubled to $3 billion.[29] An Italian consortium is supervising the construction of new port facilities at Bandar Abbas at a cost of $1.5 billion; Japanese firms are reported to have some 16 major projects under way or pending, including the $4 billion petrochemical complex at Bandar Khomeini. Eastern European states have similarly increased their trade relations with Iran during the postrevolutionary period; Iranian imports from the Council of Mutual Economic Assistance (COMECON) countries, most notably Rumania, have tripled and now total approximately 15 per cent of Iran's purchases from abroad. Iran has consciously sought to increase trade with smaller states such as Spain, Austria, Finland, Denmark, and Sweden in order to increase its relative bargaining power in negotiations. This overall pattern of Iran's trade relations is consistent with the clerical régime's drive to reduce (or at least diversify) economic dependence and prevent cultural penetration.

Conclusion

Since the advent of the Islamic Republc in 1979, its politics have been dominated by the clerical régime's struggle to reconcile the competing demands of revolution and statecraft. The linkage between Iran's domestic and foreign policies is reflected in the workings of a subtle and complex feedback process. Although domestic politics determine the limits of diplomacy, foreign policy issues in turn are internally utilized by the régime as a legitimizing instrument. The early demise of the Bazargan government vividly demonstrates the manner in which foreign policy issues (e.g., the nature of Iran's postrevolutionary relationship with the United States) can affect the internal power struggle.

The relative stability and durability of the clerical régime remains a major point of contention. On the one hand, it is widely asserted that theocratic rule has been institutionalized within Iran. On the other hand, it is acknowledged that the death of Khomeini (whose own authority stems from his charismatic leadership) will precipitate a succession crisis. Max Weber's discourse on the difficulties of institutionalizing charismatic leadership highlights the contradiction between these positions. As in the case of leadership changes within the Soviet Union, the paucity of available information about the clerical régime and its institutional underpinnings makes any precise assessment of post-Khomeini succession politics problematic. In the continued absence of a credible internal or external opposition to theocratic rule, politics within Iran are likely to remain Islamic in substance and repressive in form.

Although the West can do little to affect the pace and nature of internal change in Iran, that is not a justification for benign neglect. Iran's intrinsic importance—its geographical position, the skills of its people, its natural resources—is not linked to régime changes. A continued Western interest in Iran will perhaps generate a better understanding of that country's internal political processes. Although such an understanding will not provide any ready answers, it will at least provide a basis for choice when inevitable political changes within Iran create new opportunities.

Acknowledgment

The author gratefully acknowledges the invaluable research assistance supplied by Kathryn Babayan in the preparation of this chapter. He is further indebted for the stimulation and ideas provided by the participants in the Iran Working Group—a series of three meetings on postrevolutionary Iran held on November 21–22, 1983, February 27–28, 1984, and May 14–15, 1984, at the Woodrow Wilson International Center for Scholars.

Notes

1. This theme is explored by Shahram Chubin in *The Foreign Policy of the Islamic Republic of Iran* (Geneva: Graduate Institute of International Studies, 1984), pp. 2–5ff.

2. See Shahrough Akhavi, "Clerical Politics in Iran since 1979," in Nikki R. Keddie and Eric Hooglund, eds., *The Iranian Revolution and the Islamic Republic:*

Proceedings of a Conference (Washington, D.C.: Middle East Institute/Woodrow Wilson International Center for Scholars, 1982), pp. 17–20ff.

3. For a discussion of political developments during this period, see Cheryl Benard and Zalmay Khalilzad, *"The Government of God": Iran's Islamic Republic* (New York: Columbia University Press, 1984), pp. 103–113.

4. Oriana Fallaci, "Everybody Wants to Be Boss," *New York Times*, October 28, 1979.

5. Cited in Benard and Khalilzad, *"The Government of God,"* p. 109.

6. For a sympathetic assessment of Bani-Sadr's political predicament, see Eric Rouleau, "Khomeini's Iran," *Foreign Affairs* 59, no. 1 (fall 1980), pp. 11–19.

7. *Keesing's Contemporary Archives* (1982), p. 31503.

8. This argument is developed by Azar Tabari in Keddie and Hooglund, *The Iranian Revolution and the Islamic Republic*, pp. 106–107.

9. Khomeini has spoken out against the rise of factionalism within the clerical régime. The Hojjati faction has reportedly been forced underground since July 1983.

10. Free Voice of Iran (in Persian) on August 7, 1983, in *Foreign Broadcast Information Service*, South Asia, August 9, 1983, p. I8.

11. Ervand Abrahamian in Keddie and Hooglund, *The Iranian Revolution and the Islamic Republic*, p. 39.

12. Cited in Benard and Khalilzad, *"The Government of God,"* p. 133.

13. For a discussion of the Iran-Bahrain dispute see Robert S. Litwak, *Security in the Persian Gulf, Vol. II: Sources of Inter-State Conflict* (London: Gower for the International Institute for Strategic Studies), pp. 41–48.

14. Cited in Shaul Bakhash, *The Politics of Oil and Revolution in Iran* (Washington, D.C.: Brookings Institution, 1982), p. 27.

15. Litwak, *Security in the Persian Gulf*, pp. 95–99.

16. For example, Iran has agreed to meetings with Pakistan and Turkey to reestablish the defunct regional cooperation for development organization; reported in *Middle East Economics Digest*, June 1, 1984, p. 11.

17. Cited in Bakhash, *The Politics of Oil*, p. 22.

18. Chubin, *The Foreign Policy of the Islamic Republic*, pp. 20–21.

19. For a discussion of military developments during the Iran-Iraq war, see Mark A. Heller, *The Iran-Iraq War: Implications for Third Parties* (Tel Aviv: Jaffee Center for Strategic Studies of Tel Aviv Unversity, 1984), pp. 7–11ff.

20. See *Strategic Survey 1983–1984* (London: International Institute for Strategic Studies, 1984), pp. 76–78.

21. Bakhash, *The Politics of Oil*, pp. 34–35.

22. See Eliot Marshall, "Iraq's Chemical Warfare: Case Proved," *Science* 224 (April 13, 1984), pp. 130–132.

23. Reports in late June 1981 suggested that Iranian hesitation to launch its long-awaited offensive (again code-named Ramadan) stemmed from divisions within the leadership over the continuation of the war. See Richard Halloran, *New York Times*, June 13, 1984. This dispute, however, appeared to revolve around the question of tactics, not the fundamental objectives of the war. For his part, Khomeini ruled out any possibility of peace with Iraq when he publicly asserted: "To compromise with the oppressor is, in fact, to assist in his oppression" (quoted in Paul Lewis, "Iraqis Say Jets Sank Five Ships, Downed a Plane," *New York Times*, July 2, 1984).

24. Quoted in *Strategic Survey 1982–1983* (London: International Institute for Strategic Studies, 1983), p. 84.

25. The IGAT-II project was revived in September 1982 when it was announced that it would be rerouted through Turkey. In November 1984, Iran and the Soviet Union resumed negotiations over economic ties, including the IGAT system.

26. See, for example, *Literaturnaya Gazeta*, 22 June 1983; quoted in *FBIS*, Soviet Union, June 30, 1983, p. H1.

27. Much of the information about the relationship between Moscow and the Tudeh party came to light in late 1982 following the defection of the Soviet vice-consul in Tehran to Britain.

28. The possibility of an eventual resumption in relations with the United States was suggested in a statement by Majlis speaker Hashemi Rafsanjani: "The policy of neither East nor West does not mean that we have to cut off all relations with the East and the West. Islam wants no such thing. . . . We could have relations with all these countries except Israel, whose existence is illegal, and South Africa which is racist." For the full text see *FBIS*, South Asia, July 1, 1983, p. I1.

29. *Middle East Economic Digest*, April 1984, p. 36.

PART TWO

The Palestinian Quagmire: Searching for a Way Out

8

Creating the Conditions for Israeli-Palestinian Negotiations

Herbert C. Kelman

The Egyptian-Israeli peace process that began with President Sadat's trip to Jerusalem in November 1977 has radically altered the context of the Arab-Israeli conflict. With Sadat's recognition of Israel, the signing of the peace treaty between the two nations, and the establishment of diplomatic relations, an important psychological frontier was crossed. Both the conflict and efforts to settle it must now be pursued in this new environment, in which firmly entrenched assumptions about what is possible and what is impossible are no longer valid. For the first time, the integration of Israel into the Middle East and the establishment of a stable peace and normal relations between Israel and its neighbors are realistic possibilities. Even if subsequent events were to lead eventually to a reversal in Egyptian policy, they could not entirely undo the restructuring of realities and perceptions that has taken place in the Middle East.

At the same time, the Egyptian-Israeli peace has been fragile from the beginning and has become more so as a result of the assassination of Sadat, the Lebanon War, and the failure of all peace initiatives during the first half of the 1980s. Although Egypt and Israel have strong interests in and commitments to maintaining the peace process, they have major differences in goals and expectations that have impeded the movement toward normalization and reconciliation and have created a state of "cold peace" between the two parties. A total breakdown of the peace process would provide evidence to each side that, even under the best of circumstances, the other cannot be trusted. Old stereotypes and attitudes may then reemerge with even greater intensity. In short, the Egyptian-Israeli peace has created enormous opportunities, but failure to grasp these opportunities may lead to a dangerous setback in the efforts to resolve the conflict.

This chapter is a shortened updated version of an article by Kelman that appeared in the *Journal of Conflict Resolution* 26, no. 1 (March 1982).

The principal difference between Egypt and Israel, of course, does not center on bilateral issues but on the steps required for an overall settlement of the Arab-Israeli conflict, particularly of the Palestinian problem. The Israeli government has tended to view the peace agreement as a bilateral process, whereas the Egyptian government has insisted throughout—starting with Sadat's Knesset speech in November 1977—that an Egyptian-Israeli agreement represents only the first step toward a comprehensive settlement, which must include a solution to the Palestinian problem. Increasingly, Israeli analysts of the conflict and strategic thinkers have come to accept these Egyptian pronouncements at face value and have concluded that the Egyptian-Israeli peace process cannot fulfill itself without a satisfactory solution to the Palestinian problem.

Resolution of the Palestinian issue is not only an essential condition for the fulfillment of the Egyptian-Israeli peace process but also a sine qua non for a genuine peace between Israel and its neighbors—a peace based on mutual acceptance and reconciliation and characterized by normal, cooperative relations between the various societies in the region. Since the competing territorial claims of Israelis and Palestinians represent the origin and the core issue of the larger Arab-Israeli conflict, there can be no peace without a resolution of the Palestinian issue that addresses the basic needs and concerns of both sides.

This chapter explores possible first steps toward such a resolution by focusing on ways to create the political and psychological conditions that might allow Israelis and Palestinians to begin the process of negotiating a mutually advantageous settlement. It examines, first, the assumptions on which such negotiations must—in my view—proceed. Second, it discusses the prospects for initiating negotiations based on these assumptions. Third, it analyzes the barriers to their initiation. Finally, it proposes a possible approach—both substantive and procedural—for overcoming these barriers.[1]

Assumptions for Israeli-Palestinian Negotiations

If negotiations are to produce not merely a tenuous nonbelligerency agreement but a stable, genuine peace, conducive to reconciliation between Israelis and Palestinians, they must meet certain special requirements. The negotiations must aim for a resolution of the conflict—an outcome that, though of necessity involving compromise, leaves both parties better off, is responsive to their basic needs and concerns, and is at least minimally consistent with their sense of justice. They must entail a process that helps to build mutual trust. And they must produce agreements to which the parties are and feel committed. To meet these requirements, negotiations must proceed on the basis of three central assumptions.

1. The negotiations must involve direct communication between Israelis and Palestinians. Clearly, the Israeli-Palestinian conflict is embedded in a larger conflict between Israel and the various Arab states which have a role to play in negotiating a settlement of the Palestinian issue. Third parties,

including the U.S. government, may facilitate and contribute to the negotiations process by using their power to compensate for power differentials between the parties, to provide incentives for negotiation and concession, and to offer necessary guarantees. A final agreement will almost certainly have to be ratified in a multiparty framework, but there is no substitute for direct negotiations between Israelis and Palestinians at some point in the process.

Only through direct interaction can the parties discover ways of redefining the conflict so that it becomes amenable to resolution and develop and test agreements that are maximally responsive to their mutual concerns. Even if it were possible for third parties (such as one or both of the superpowers) to impose an agreement on the Israelis and the Palestinians, or for Israel to work out a solution to the Palestinian issue with King Husayn, such agreements would not benefit from the mutual confidence and the sense of commitment that characterize those produced by the parties themselves. Many Palestinians would rather negotiate with the United States than with the Israelis, and many Israelis would rather negotiate with Jordan than with the Palestinians, precisely because an imposed or proxy agreement would allow them to sidestep the need for mutual acceptance and to postpone the painful process of coming to grips with the reality of each other's existence. But it is in the interest of the two parties that will have to live with each other to work jointly on an agreement that meets the needs of both and to which both are structurally and psychologically committed.

2. The negotiations must focus on development of a formula for sharing the land between the two peoples. Reconciliation requires solutions that allow each party at least a minimal satisfaction of its basic needs and national aspirations, rather than solutions experienced as defeat and subjugation by one of the parties. There may be exceptional cases (such as World War II) in which a humiliating military defeat forms the basis for reconciliation. In the Israeli-Palestinian case, however, the nature of the conflict, of the power relations between the parties, and of the international environment preclude building a stable peace and reconciliation on a settlement that spells total defeat for either party. Since the conflict centers on the competing claims of two peoples for the same land, the defeat of either would be equivalent to its national destruction—to a total loss on which nothing can be built. Since neither party has overwhelming power, each being marked by certain strengths and weaknesses relative to the other (e.g., Israel has a military advantage but the Palestinians benefit from the Arab world's advantage in population, resources, and strategic location), it is not possible for either to impose a stable settlement based on the other's defeat. And, finally, there is an international consensus that reflects a strong interest in avoiding such an outcome. If neither party is to be totally defeated, then some formula must be found that allows the two peoples—as peoples—to share the land they both claim.

The precise terms for sharing the land cannot be determined by absolute principles of justice or by recourse to historical rights. They require what

Walid Khalidi has called "pragmatic justice," which "takes cognizance of the imperative of both equity and reality" and "embraces both the changes brought about by the evolution of time and the historical context in which the changes took place."[2] The terms to be negotiated must, on the one hand, address the basic concerns of the parties—particularly their sense of injustice and their quest for security and national identity—and, on the other hand, take account of the current political realities, as defined by the resources that each party is able to bring to the negotiating table.

Whatever formula is negotiated for sharing the land must ensure the continued existence of Israel as an independent Jewish state. As a corollary to that requirement, it needs to provide special security arrangements that are responsive to Israel's real and understandable security concerns and cognizant of the military advantages that Israel currently enjoys and would have to renounce as part of a negotiated settlement.[3] By the same token, whatever formula is negotiated must ensure that the Palestinian people (not just the Palestinians as individuals) have a share of the land, a sense of ownership over part of it, and an opportunity to give political expression to their national identity within it. Anything less would fail to meet the minimal needs and aspirations of the Palestinians and would constitute a total defeat for them. It would also fail to take full account of one of their major resources: the support for Palestinian self-determination in the Arab world and in the larger international community.

Sharing land between the two peoples under present historical circumstances almost certainly means political partition. The precise borders along which the land is to be divided will have to be defined in the course of negotiations in which the parties' desire for borders that conform to their security and identity concerns are balanced against political realities. The strong international consensus in favor of Israel's return to its pre-1967 borders, with only some minor adjustments, is likely to be an important factor in the negotiation of this issue. The pre-1967 borders, though they may be arbitrary and flawed, have the great advantage of corresponding to international norms.

3. The negotiations must be designed to enable each party to benefit from the national and international legitimacy it has achieved. For both Israeli and Palestinian negotiators, two interrelated elements of legitimacy are of great importance: legitimacy in the eyes of their own populations and legitimacy within the international system. Both communities have large, attentive, and active political constituencies; negotiators' legitimacy in the eyes of these constituencies is an important potential resource—and lack of clear legitimacy an important constraint—in the negotiation process. Also, for both communities, international recognition of their legitimacy is a continuing central concern. These two elements of legitimacy mutually reinforce each other. International recognition enhances the legitimacy of national leaders in the eyes of their own people, and popular support in turn enhances their international legitimacy.

The Israeli rejection of the Palestine Liberation Organization (PLO) and search for alternative Palestinian interlocutors, as well as the Palestinian rejection of the Egyptian-Israeli peace process and search for an alternative negotiating framework, are problematic from this point of view. Both can be seen as attempts to deal with diminished partners, relegated to a past inferior status that they have long since overcome. Palestinians will not readily enter into negotiations that deny the widespread recognition their national cause has attained with the advent and growing influence of the PLO, nor will Israelis readily enter into negotiations that deny the new legitimacy in the region that the peace treaty and Egyptian diplomatic recognition have accorded them.

My analysis suggests that it would be neither possible nor helpful to find a substitute for the PLO as the Palestinian representatives in negotiations with Israel. For Palestinians (in the West Bank and Gaza, as well as in the diaspora) the PLO is not merely an organization but the symbol and embodiment of Palestinian nationhood. It is the only representative agency that speaks for Palestinians as a people and that is widely recognized in this capacity, not only in the Arab world, but in the general world community. As the internationally acknowledged repository for Palestinian legitimacy, the PLO at this time has a monopoly on legitimacy in Palestinian eyes.

In time and under changing circumstances, an alternative within the PLO may develop, for example, a leadership in which West Bank/Gaza figures are more heavily represented. It is highly unlikely, however, that any group of Palestinians (or King Husayn, for that matter) would be prepared to enter negotiations as an alternative to the PLO (that is, in lieu of or in opposition to the PLO). Palestinians entering negotiations on these terms would be relinquishing the important advantages in national and international legitimacy that the Palestinian cause has already attained but that only the PLO has at its disposal. Even if an alternative group of Palestinian negotiators could be found, their lack of legitimacy would reduce the value of any agreement they would reach since they would lack the capacity to obtain the commitment of the Palestinian community.

On the Israeli side, the assumption that each party must be able to benefit from the legitimacy that it has achieved implies that Israeli-Palestinian negotiations must be linked in some fashion to the Egyptian-Israeli peace process. This process, beginning with the Sadat visit to Jerusalem and including the establishment of diplomatic relations, has given Israel the kind of recognition and legitimacy that it had always hoped for but never expected from any of its Arab neighbors. This achievement and the desire to maintain and broaden it have created new opportunities and incentives for Israel to enter into serious negotiations with its Palestinian neighbors. It also gives Israeli decisionmakers greater flexibility in making concessions and compromises that might not have received sufficient popular support in the past. Thus, it would not be useful to design a negotiating framework that rejects or repudiates the Egyptian-Israeli peace process; nor are the Israelis likely to enter into negotiations that do not permit them to capitalize on the domestic and international advantages that Egyptian recognition and the peace process have provided.

Prospects for Negotiations

What is the likelihood that the Israeli government and representatives of the Palestinian people would be prepared, within the foreseeable future, to enter into negotiations on the basis of the kinds of assumptions that I have discussed? The official positions of the parties, the situation on the ground, and the international atmosphere make it difficult to assess the prospects optimistically.

Even if a Labor government were to replace the National Unity government established in Israel in 1984, it would not find it easy to meet the necessary conditions for negotiation. The Labor party's approach to the West Bank and Gaza is based on the principle of territorial compromise, and many of the party's leaders, including Shimon Peres, have at various times acknowledged the Palestinian people's right to decide their own identity. However, the party's specific proposals for realizing these principles fall far short of the Palestinians' minimal expectations. They call for retention of parts of the West Bank and Gaza under Israeli sovereignty (while offering to restore Arab sovereignty over the heavily populated areas); they envisage no compromise on Jerusalem; they reject an independent Palestinian state, offering instead to return the territories to a Jordanian-Palestinian state; and they rule out the PLO as a negotiating partner. There are various indications that Labor, freed from the constraints of the National Unity government, might pursue a more flexible policy, but the new facts on the West Bank and the increased strength of the annexationist elements in the Israeli political spectrum would severely constrain the party in any negotiations that contemplate withdrawal from the territories and dismantlement of the settlements. Since such policies would generate profound internal divisions and possibly violent resistance, any Israeli government would be inclined to postpone their implementation as long as possible, even if it were convinced of their ultimate inevitability.

The Palestinians, in turn, have vehemently rejected the Camp David agreements and boycotted the autonomy talks on the grounds that the structure and agenda of these talks preclude achievement of even their minimal goals. Whatever potential the autonomy talks may initially have had for moving toward a solution of the Palestinian problem, it became increasingly clear that the Begin government was not prepared to offer a meaningful degree of autonomy during the transition period or any hope for Arab sovereignty at the end of that period—a message visibly reinforced by the settlement policy. Efforts to broaden the concept of autonomy have failed and there is virtually no chance that autonomy talks as originally conceived can be resumed. More generally, the trends toward de facto annexation of the West Bank and Gaza, the failure of the Husayn-Arafat initiative of February 1985, and the Reagan administration's entire approach to the Middle East have deepened the Palestinians' pessimism about the chances for movement on the Palestinian issue. These attitudes tend to discredit the search for a negotiated settlement and to place further constraints on the Palestinian leadership in its pursuit of such a settlement.

The PLO, for its part, has not clearly indicated a readiness to enter into negotiations with Israel on the kinds of assumptions I have discussed. The official PLO position supports establishment of a Palestinian state on the West Bank and Gaza, but does not preclude the option of future efforts to take over the rest of Palestine. Thus, it falls short of a commitment to sharing the land between the two peoples. The many hints that the PLO is in fact prepared to end the military struggle with the establishment of a West Bank/Gaza state and that Arafat is much more flexible on the negotiating issues than the public PLO pronouncements would suggest have been discounted in Israel. Moreover, the Palestinians' total rejection of the Egyptian-Israeli peace process—just like the Israelis' total rejection of the PLO—precludes negotiations in which both parties start at the highest level of legitimacy that they have achieved in the international system.

Despite these dim prospects for Israeli-Palestinian negotiations, any attempt to arrive at an overall optimistic or pessimistic assessment on the basis of the current constellation of forces is likely to be misleading because of the dynamic character of the conflict at the present historical juncture. This character of the conflict can be attributed to a number of significant events that are changing the political, socioeconomic, and psychological environment and to the presence of sharp political and ideological divisions both within Israel and within the Arab world. Three sets of events, in particular, have altered the stakes in the Israeli-Palestinian conflict and continue to shape the perception of issues on both sides: (1) the evolution of an international consensus on a fair solution to the conflict—a consensus shared, incidentally, by the Soviet Union and, with some qualifications, by the United States; (2) the Sadat initiative (which was partly stimulated by this consensus) and the ensuing Egyptian-Israeli peace process; and (3) the Begin policies toward the West Bank and Gaza, including the increasing pace of settlement in populated areas, which changed the character of these territories and which continue under the Labor-Likud government set up in 1984.

The impact of these events on Israelis and Palestinians must be understood in the context of an ongoing struggle in both communities between two opposing tendencies: a pronegotiation tendency, which accepts however reluctantly the need for a negotiated settlement of the conflict based on a historic compromise, and an antinegotiation tendency, which rejects a political solution and remains instead committed to winning the conflict and achieving sovereignty over the whole of the land.[4] The three sets of events have evoked very different responses among the pronegotiation and the antinegotiation forces and have intensified the struggle between them, making the present situation particularly fluid. For pronegotiation elements on both sides, these events have created a sense of urgency and opportunity; among both, therefore, there is a strong feeling that now is the time to try to reach an agreement. At the same time, both are inhibited by powerful resistances to any moves toward political compromise on the part of the antinegotiation elements in their communities.

Reactions to the Sadat initiative and the Egyptian-Israeli peace process best illustrate the impact of events on the internal struggle within each community. The Sadat initiative transformed the idea of a settlement of the Arab-Israeli conflict into a more palpable reality, setting into motion a process that all the parties perceived as moving toward some definitive conclusion. The very fact that a concrete agreement could now be visualized intensified both the hopes and the fears engendered by such an agreement. It enhanced awareness of the new opportunities that had been created and provided a vision of a more desirable future; at the same time, it brought the dangers and threats entailed by an agreement into clearer focus. Reactions depended on the precise endpoint of the process visualized by people (and this perception itself has fluctuated over time) and on their attitudes toward that endpoint. For any given group, certain scenarios are exciting and others are threatening; perception of the endpoint, therefore, determines whether the predominant reaction is one of hope or of fear. Thus, for example, Palestinians have tended to be negative about the process because of the fear that they would be left out of it; some Israelis have tended to be negative because of the opposite fear that the Palestinians would be brought in.

One consequence of this interplay of forces is a tendency within each community to draw a sharp line between actions considered permissible and those considered treasonous. Cognizant of this line, even those committed to the search for a negotiated settlement refuse to engage in certain aspects of this process that are defined as beyond the pale. For Israelis, the dividing line has been discussions with the PLO; for Palestinians, it has been participation in the autonomy talks or any activity that might appear to be linked to such talks. It is no coincidence that these lines exclude precisely those activities that would tend to confirm the adversary's legitimacy. In short, the very movement toward peace initiated by the Sadat policies and the Egyptian-Israeli treaty has contributed to a political and psychological atmosphere in which certain steps toward Israeli-Palestinian negotiations seem to be categorically ruled out. Nevertheless, it is my contention that significant Israeli and Palestinian elements have a strong interest in a negotiated settlement—an interest accentuated by the Egyptian-Israeli peace process— and that this interest can potentially be mobilized in creating the conditions for negotiations.

In Israel, one of the major consequences of the new relationship with Egypt is that the Palestinian issue has moved to the center of political attention. From the very beginning, the Sadat initiative produced a dramatic shift in public awareness of the need to find a solution to the Palestinian problem, based on recognition that the future of the Egyptian-Israeli relationship itself and the possibility of a comprehensive settlement of the Arab-Israeli conflict depended on satisfactory movement toward such a solution. This linkage has aroused serious concern among proponents of an annexationist policy, some of whom opposed the peace treaty precisely because they were afraid that it would create the momentum and the precedents for withdrawing from the West Bank and Gaza.

The desire to counteract such precedents and to create new facts that would prevent extension of the peace process to the territories probably contributed to the stepped-up activities of ultranationalist settlers and their increasingly hostile posture toward the West Bank population. The Begin government supported these activities both out of its own policy and ideological preferences and out of its desire to reassure its nationalist constituencies. Some Israelis have taken comfort in the Reagan administration's rhetorical emphasis on the Soviet threat at the expense of local and regional issues. They have argued that the Palestinian issue is not a significant source of instability in the Middle East and that there is therefore no urgency to deal with it. Many Israeli analysts, however, reject this view as shortsighted. They continue to see the Palestinian issue as central to the Israeli-Egyptian relationship, and they feel a sense of urgency about its resolution.

The incentives that these Israeli elements have for seeking a peaceful, negotiated settlement of the Palestinian problem at this time can be linked to the three sets of events described—the evolving international consensus on a fair solution of the Palestinian problem, the Egyptian-Israeli peace process, and the changing character of the West Bank and Gaza.

1. Pronegotiation tendencies reflect a deep concern about Israel's increasing isolation from the rest of the world. Many Israelis see current Israeli policies toward the West Bank and Gaza as deviating from international norms and alienating even Israel's Western European friends. They also do not anticipate unqualified support from the United States to continue forever. They have understood from the beginning that, insofar as the Reagan administration bases its relationship with Israel on Israel's strategic value, it will not necessarily support Israeli policies (such as the West Bank/Gaza policy) that complicate U.S. relations with Saudi Arabia and other strategically important Arab states.

2. Pronegotiation tendencies reflect a view of the Egyptian-Israeli peace process as a historically unique opportunity for Israel to become integrated into the Middle East and to establish normal, peaceful relations with its neighbors. Many Israelis are afraid that this opportunity will be lost if there is no satisfactory resolution to the Palestinian problem. They accept Egypt's commitment to the Palestinian cause at face value, and they are afraid that Mubarak will be even less willing and able than his predecessor to maintain a separate peace with Israel without movement on the Palestinian issue. They do not necessarily expect a return to military confrontation between the two states, but they see their vision of normalization in Egyptian-Israeli relations (and Arab-Israeli relations more generally) to be seriously threatened by current Israeli policies.

3. Pronegotiation tendencies reflect a sense of dismay about the current situation in the West Bank and Gaza. Many Israelis see the continuing occupation as threatening the Zionist and democratic values of their own society. They are afraid that Israel may be approaching a point of no return in its West Bank/Gaza policy, which may culminate in an annexation that— apart from its international consequences—would undermine the Jewish and democratic character of the state.

In some Palestinian quarters, it seems, the Sadat initiative at first created a sense of opportunity and optimism, a feeling that the precedents it established and the process it started might open the way for settlement of the Palestinian problem. For other Palestinians, of course, these precedents and this process constituted a threat precisely because they raised the possibility of a settlement based on compromise. These elements, jointly with several Arab states, succeeded in defining involvement in the process as an act of treason, breaking Arab unity. The external pressures against involvement were reinforced by suspicions and fears throughout the Palestinian community that the Palestinians were being sold out, that Egypt was opting for a bilateral agreement, that at best the Sadat initiative represented an attempt to impose Egyptian hegemony on the Arab world. The Camp David agreements were taken as further evidence of betrayal of the Palestinian cause, and a strong taboo became attached to participation in the autonomy talks or in any other discussions that might appear to be related to these talks. The self-fulfilling effects of boycotting the autonomy talks together with the actions of the Israeli government helped to reduce Palestinians' sense of opportunity and to raise their sense of danger associated with the peace process. There remains, however, a strong interest among many Palestinians in finding an honorable way out that would allow them to end the conflict without accepting total defeat.

The incentives that these Palestinian elements have for seeking a peaceful, negotiated settlement now can be linked to the three sets of events described.

1. Prenegotiation tendencies reflect a concern that the advantage the Palestinians now have in terms of international support for their claims may dissipate if they are unable to capitalize on it and move toward a settlement. The proponents of a negotiated settlement, who have tried to tailor their position to the international consensus, have been unable to point to any visible successes of their policy. They have not elicited any concessions from Israel or any responsiveness from the United States. They have been eager, therefore, to promote any initiatives (such as the European proposals or the Fez plan) that point to a political settlement on terms acceptable to them. Support for such initiatives is a matter of special urgency to them, both to reassure the international community of their continuing commitment to a negotiated settlement and to demonstrate to their internal critics that the political route is capable of producing results.

2. Prenegotiation tendencies reflect a concern that the Palestinians will be left out as Egypt and Israel arrive at an accommodation and that they may be missing an opportunity to advance their own cause. Many Palestinians experience a sense of despair when they see the Egyptian-Israeli peace process moving forward despite Palestinian and other Arab opposition and, at the very least, reducing the military pressure on Israel. At the same time, they have probably experienced a new sense of opportunity with Mubarak's accession to the Egyptian presidency. There is an expectation that Mubarak will continue to be more responsive to Palestinian needs and Arab interests than Sadat was. Thus, many Palestinians may now be more

open to an Egyptian role in promoting an Israeli-Palestinian settlement, if a suitable vehicle other than the autonomy talks could be found.

3. Prenegotiation tendencies reflect a deep concern about developments in the West Bank. Many Palestinians are afraid that the expansion of Israeli settlements and other policies of the Israeli government may make it increasingly difficult to end the military occupation and avoid annexation. They are anxious, therefore, not to miss any opportunity for negotiations that offer the prospects of an eventual end to the occupation. They feel an added sense of urgency about negotiating a settlement because of the fear that new events (such as the outbreak of a war) may lead to even harsher measures in the territories, including large-scale expulsion of the population.

Barriers to Negotiations

A fundamental dilemma fuels the impasse between Israelis and Palestinians. To feel adequately reassured, each side wants from the other acceptance of its national identity and explicit recognition of its legitimate rights. But neither side is prepared to offer such acceptance to the other under the present circumstances because of the special type of zero-sum conflict in which they are caught up: a conflict in which acknowledging the other's legitimacy is perceived as compromising one's own legitimacy and in which granting rights to the other is perceived as abdicating one's own rights.

Not surprisingly, each party suggests that the other must take the first step. Palestinians argue that, since the Israelis are in a position of advantage vis-à-vis the Palestinians, they must take the initiative in recognizing the Palestinians. They regard it as self-evident that one cannot expect the occupied to recognize the occupier. Israelis, starting with the same premise, draw precisely the opposite conclusion: Since the Israelis are in a position of advantage vis-à-vis the Palestinians, the Palestinians must make the first move in recognizing Israel. They take it as equally self-evident that one cannot expect such a difficult initiative to come from those who are relatively comfortable with the status quo. Both sides are aware of the enormous obstacles within their own communities that impede recognition of the other, but they tend to underestimate the equally great obstacles faced by the other.

To understand why Palestinians and Israelis perceive acceptance of the other and acknowledgment of the other's rights as such threats to their own national existence, we must examine the psychological essence of the conflict. The Israeli-Palestinian conflict represents a clash between two nationalist movements, each struggling for its right to national identity and national existence and centering its claims on the same territory. Each sees the national identity and existence of the other as problematic because they cast doubts on its own claims. As a result, each refuses, as a matter of principle, to accept the other's national identity and right to exist as a nation. Despite the clear evidence that Israelis and Palestinians have the various characteristics that are usually associated with nationhood, there are persistent tendencies to deny each other's status as a bona fide nation. Though Palestinians and Arabs now generally acknowledge the reality of Israel as a Jewish state, many continue to argue that Jews represent a religion rather than a nation. Though Israelis now widely acknowledge the existence of a Palestinian people, many continue to deny the Palestinians' claim to distinctiveness and to define them instead as an ethnic Arab minority or as part of a Jordanian/Palestinian nation.

The perception of the two national identities as inherently incompatible is a direct consequence of the fact that the two national movements focus on the same land. But the issue of territorial claims touches directly on the more fundamental question of national survival. Israelis and Palestinians both see their nations as highly vulnerable; at stake for them in the conflict is the continued existence of the group. The themes of destruction, physical annihilation, and nonexistence play a central role in their self-images. Among Israelis, the destruction of European Jewry in the Nazi Holocaust is never far from the national consciousness. Among Palestinians, one hears recurrent references to their treatment as nonbeings (ranging from the description of Palestine by some early Zionists as a land without a people to the current status of Palestinians as people without passports). The members of each group are convinced that the ultimate intention of the other group is to destroy them. In fact, they believe that destruction of their group is inherent in the other's ideology. Thus, to Israelis, the PLO's project of liberating Palestine is synonymous with liquidating Israel. They do not believe that the PLO would stop with a West Bank/Gaza state but expect it to persist until it has liberated all of Palestine. They find evidence for the open-ended nature of the PLO's goals in the Palestinian National Council's reaffirmations of the Palestinian National Covenant and in the periodic appearance of statements that reassert the movement's commitment to liberating the whole of Palestine. To Palestinians, Zionist ideology is inherently expansionist, and Israel is prepared to eliminate Palestinian communities that impede the achievement of its goals. They find confirmation for the open-ended nature of Zionist goals in Israel's settlement, land, and water policies in the occupied territories. They see these policies as designed, in a repetition of the 1948 experience, to create new facts in the territories, to encircle the local people gradually, and to wait for an excuse to push them out. They see Israel's actions in southern Lebanon and in the Golan as further evidence of Zionist expansionism.

These existential concerns on both sides provide the context for their profound reluctance to accept the other and acknowledge the other's national rights, particularly to make the first move in that direction without any assurance of reciprocation. Thus, for reasons inherent in the conflict itself, it is extremely difficult to induce the parties to take the kinds of initiatives that might radically change the atmosphere and open the way to negotiations. There is indeed a procedural problem, caused by each side's refusal to make the first move. The refusal to go first, however, is not merely a delaying tactic or a bargaining ploy; it reflects the profound existential concerns aroused by the nature of the initiatives required.

This brings me back to the dilemma with which I began this section: To feel sufficiently reassured to enter into the negotiation process, each side wants from the other acceptance of its national identity and acknowledgment of its national rights. But neither side is prepared to offer such acceptance to the other under the present circumstances precisely because it sees such moves as threatening to its own rights. How, then, can negotiations begin? Is it perhaps possible, through a process of successive approximations, to create enough mutual reassurance even without formal mutual recognition so that the parties can enter into the process? The final section of this chapter addresses this question and offers some proposals for overcoming the barriers to negotiations.

Overcoming the Barriers

One can think of the road to negotiations as a process of successive approximations, in which the parties initiate communication at a level and in a context that represent a relatively low degree of commitment (in terms of official status, implied recognition, and expected outcome) and gradually move toward official negotiations, culminating in a binding agreement. The relatively lower degree of initial commitment should enable parties to accept a correspondingly lower degree of reassurance as the condition for talking with one another. This formula would make it possible, then, for each party to offer a degree of reassurance sufficient to draw the other into communication without endangering its own position. If the communication is carried out in a problem-solving mode, it should gradually facilitate both the emergence of new ideas and the development of mutual trust, allowing the parties to offer each other increasingly greater degrees of reassurance and encouragement. At some point, these should be sufficient to enable the parties to enter into official negotiations designed to produce formal mutual recognition as the final outcome.

Specifically, I want to propose a procedure designed to generate an understanding that could serve as a basis for the parties to begin the process of official negotiations. The understanding might take the form of a joint declaration or, more likely, of coordinated parallel initiatives. Whatever form it takes, the understanding that this prenegotiation procedure is designed to produce should meet the following criteria.

1. The procedure should make a clear distinction between the start of negotiations and the conclusion of negotiations. One of the barriers to negotiations has been the insistence of the parties on obtaining certain guarantees at the outset of negotiations that one can usually expect only at the end of the process. Clearly, mutual recognition is essential to a satisfactory settlement of the Israeli-Palestinian conflict. However, by demanding recognition from each other before even sitting down to negotiate, the parties have contributed to the present impasse. These demands cannot

be dismissed as mere bargaining tactics; they reflect genuine fears on each side that entering negotiations would create irreversible consequences not only in accentuating divisions within their own community but also in jeopardizing their vital interests. A clear distinction between the beginning and ending of negotiations may help to reduce these fears and enable the parties to accept terms for entering the process that they would regard as inadequate for a final settlement. It would be clear that, in agreeing to enter negotiations without full explicit recognition by the other, they were not agreeing that these terms would constitute a sufficient basis for a final settlement. Similarly, it would be clear that, in entering negotiations, they were not necessarily committing themselves to eventual recognition of the other beyond the level to which they have already agreed. Thus, the parties would not be relinquishing any of their own claims or acknowledging any of the claims of the other except those specified in the undertakings that form the framework for beginning negotiations.

2. The procedure should be announced simultaneously by both sides. Whether the outcome is a joint declaration or coordinated, parallel statements, simultaneous announcement helps to overcome the problem of who goes first. Making the first move is threatening to both sides since they have no assurance that the other will reciprocate. Simultaneous announcement presupposes prior communication between the parties (indeed, in my view, the understanding should ideally emerge out of a process of direct interaction between them) but in a context quite distinct from formal negotiations.

3. The procedure should avoid the language of rights and focus instead on concrete undertakings. I have argued that acknowledgment of the other's rights is highly threatening to both parties in this conflict because they see such a move as negation of their own rights. To overcome the barriers to negotiation, therefore, it is best not to invoke the language of rights at all but to find other ways in which each party can provide sufficient reassurance and encouragement to the other to begin negotiations without feeling that it is compromising its own interests. I propose that the reassurance take the form of operational commitments by each side, that is, specific undertakings to refrain from certain steps and to carry out certain other steps. Essentially, each party would reassure the other by agreeing to rule out certain options (not to take certain actions) that correspond to the other's central fears; each would encourage the other by agreeing not to rule out certain options that correspond to the other's central hopes and expectations. The operational commitments I have in mind are substantial and difficult to make, but they at least have the advantage of not going beyond what they say. They are commitments to specific acts rather than to general principles with unknown implications.

The specific undertakings can best emerge out of interaction between the parties themselves. But to concretize what I have in mind, let me suggest merely for illustrative purposes what the substance of such under-takings might be. To allay each other's fears, both sides could make it clear that they have no intention to appropriate the whole of the land: The

Israelis might indicate that they do not intend to annex the West Bank and Gaza or to occupy it in perpetuity; the Palestinians might indicate that they do not intend to use a possible West Bank/Gaza state as a base for continuing efforts to encroach on Israel. To enhance the other's sense of opportunity, both sides could agree that the negotiations would not preclude consideration of the outcomes that the other side considers vital to its national existence: The Israelis might indicate that they are willing to discuss the possibility of Palestinian self-determination, including an independent state, provided it does not unduly compromise Israeli security; the Palestinans might indicate that they are willing to discuss special security arrangements for Israel (e.g., Palestinian neutrality, arms limitations, observation posts, surveillance mechanisms), provided they do not unduly compromise Palestinian sovereignty. None of this implies that the two sides have agreed or will necessarily agree to any of these arrangements. Nor is there any implication that either side has acknowledged any of the adversary's rights or renounced any of its own rights. The illustrative undertakings that I have described merely state that each party is ready to enter negotiations with the understanding that the other's territorial aims are not open ended and that their own essential requirements are not closed out from the discussion.

To make it entirely clear that everything but these specific undertakings remains open to negotiation, it might be useful to list explicitly the various items that have yet to be resolved in the course of the negotiations. A list specifying what has yet to be agreed upon would reassure the parties that they have not made any implicit concessions on issues important to them by virtue of their agreement to enter into negotiations. Items that might be included in the list of negotiables are the precise borders of Israel; the timing of Israeli withdrawal from the occupied territories; political and military arrangements during any transition period before withdrawal is completed; the status of Israeli citizens currently living in the territories; the precise political form by which Palestinian national identity is to be expressed; the political status of the West Bank and Gaza and their relationship to Jordan, Egypt, and Israel; military and security arrangements for the territories; timing and phasing of a new political status for the territories; the status and governance of Jerusalem; the status of diaspora Palestinians and their relationship to the new political structure evolving in the territories; conditions for repatriation or compensation of Palestinian refugees; reciprocal arrangements for the settlement of Jews in Arab territories and compensation for Jewish refugees from Arab countries; and possible arrangements for demilitarization, early warning systems, security forces, international guarantees, or other security measures.

4. In deriving the authority for the negotiations, the procedure should utilize and transform the symbols of legitimacy crucial to each party. The understanding should spell out the structural framework for the negotiations—the precise definition of the parties, the choice of representatives, and the auspices under which negotiations are conducted—in a way that

accords the parties the benefit of the highest degree of legitimacy they have achieved internationally. Negotiations in which the Palestinian party is explicitly defined as an alternative to the PLO or the negotiating framework as an alternative to the Egyptian-Israeli peace process would be seen by the respective parties as placing them at a disadvantage and indeed representing a step backward in their struggle for legitimacy. Unfortunately, the symbols of one side's legitimacy are rejected by the other precisely because it sees them as a threat to its own legitimacy. There may be an advantage, therefore, to establishing a new channel for the negotiations, which draws on these important symbols of each side's legitimacy but transforms them in a way that reduces their threatening impact on the other. For example, though the structural framework for the negotiations might be new and independent, its task could be defined as extending the peace process to negotiation of the Palestinian issue as originally mandated by the Egyptian-Israeli agreement. The Palestinian representatives to the negotiations might be an independent task force, specifically created for this purpose, or part of a Jordanian-Palestinain delegation, but its members could be designated by the PLO and remain in close consultation with the PLO. Through some such arrangement, these crucial but controversial symbols of legitimacy for the two sides might be both acknowledged and transformed.

5. The procedure should contribute to an atmosphere of mutual trust in the seriousness of the other's intentions. The very fact that an understanding has been reached through a prenegotiation process would provide at least the minimal degree of working trust necessary for the negotiations to proceed. The atmosphere for negotiations would be further enhanced by certain gestures of good will included in or accompanying the understanding. For example, it may be useful to include a positive reference to the principle of sharing the land between the two peoples. It may also be possible for the parties to find language in which they express their human acceptance of one another, while staying away at this point from acceptance at the national political level. Most important, the process of negotiation would be greatly advanced if, as a gesture of good faith, the Palestinians undertook to suspend guerrilla actions against Israel and Israelis undertook to suspend settlement activities in the West Bank during the course of the negotiations.

An understanding consistent with these criteria, which could then serve as the framework for beginning official negotiations, would have to emerge from a prenegotiation process. In keeping with the view that there is no substitute for direct negotiations between Israelis and Palestinians, I also believe that this prenegotiation process should engage representatives of the two parties in face-to-face interaction with one another. To reduce the level of commitment at this early stage of the overall process, it would be best if the participants were not officials but politically significant and influential members of their own communities. Ideally, they should be designated, at least informally, by the responsible political policymakers, so that each party knows that its counterparts are speaking with some authority and so that the conclusions of their discussions can be readily fed into the policy process.

Such quasi-official designation may not be politically feasible at this time, since an effective prenegotiation process requires participants who, at some level, have come to terms with the idea that the land must be shared by the two peoples (even if they are not ready to make public pronouncements to that effect). For the initial steps, therefore, it probably be best if participants come in their private capacities. Representatives on the Palestinian side should be respected, politically active individuals who are close to the PLO but do not necessarily hold official positions within it. On the Israeli side, the participants might be political actors (including parliamentarians) affiliated with the ruling coalition or the opposition, as well as individuals who are not particularly identified with any political line but have a high level of credibility within the society as a whole.

Once the participants have reassured themselves that their counterparts are indeed relevant political actors who represent significant political tendencies within their respective communities, the two parties would begin substantive discussions designed to explore a framework for beginning negotiations. If these explorations prove promising, the conclusion that a mutually satisfactory understanding is within the realm of possibility can then be inserted into the political process. Once a favorable political climate has been created, decisionmakers can designate quasi-official representatives to complete the prenegotiation process.

These various steps in the prenegotiation sequences can best be arranged with the help of an unofficial third party, whose primary task is to create the context for and facilitate the process of constructive communication. A useful format for such communication can be provided by problem-solving workshops in conflict resolution, an approach that utilizes social scientists in a special third-party role.[5] The norms and procedures of problem-solving workshops, the context in which they are conducted, and the third-party interventions are conducive to new learning, to an analytical approach to the conflict, and to a cooperative problem-solving orientation. They can provide an opportunity for the parties to listen to each other, to share their perspectives, to learn about the other side's concerns, to explore the range within which mutually satisfactory solutions can be sought, to give and receive signals, and to identify necessary and possible steps for breaking the present impasse. Interaction in this kind of setting would allow the parties to probe the feasibility of creating the conditions for an understanding that might serve as the framework for beginning official negotiations.

I do not anticipate that it would be easy to produce the kind of understanding proposed here. Even if the parties can be brought together for prenegotiation talks, they may not succeed in arriving at a mutually agreeable formula. One or both parties may decide that the kind of commitment they would have to make in order to invite the other's reciprocation is more than they are prepared to offer. Alternately, one or both may decide that the kind of commitment the other is willing to make is less than they are prepared to accept. However, despite its difficulties, an understanding along the lines proposed here is less difficult to bring about because it consists of concrete, descriptive undertakings rather than statements about rights and principles. Moreover, by starting at a relatively low level of commitment, by clearly distinguishing between the beginning and the conclusion of the negotiation process, by providing for simultaneous announcement of the agreement by both parties, and by seeking to transform the controversial symbols of each party's legitimacy, the procedure proposed further helps to overcome the barriers to negotiations. All of these steps are designed to allow each party to give the other sufficient reassurance and encouragement to enter into the process without thereby threatening its own vital interests. I believe that large and important segments of both communities have strong incentives to achieve a peaceful settlement of their conflict and that there is, therefore, a reasonable chance that a systematic effort to open a process of communication may yet succeed.

Notes

1. For a more detailed description of the social-psychological methodology used in this chapter, see Herbert Kelman, "Creating the Conditions for Israeli-Palestinian Negotiations," *Journal of Conflict Resolution* 26, no. 1 (March 1982), pp. 41–43.

2. Walid Khalidi, *Conflict and Violence in Lebanon: Confrontation in the Middle East* (Cambridge, Mass.: Harvard Center for International Affairs, 1979).

3. It is sometimes argued that Israel does not require special security arrangements because of the military superiority it enjoys. As Davis Bobrow has pointed out, however, the issue for Israel is not simply whether it can provide for its security, but whether it can do so at a tolerable cost. Military superiority that requires a constant state of mobilization may entail an intolerable cost in economic well-being and quality of life and thus may not be sustainable over a long period of time. Thus, current capacity for military response does not necessarily obviate the need for longer term security arrangements. See Davis Bobrow, "The Autonomy Talks and the Camp David Framework," presented at the Fourteenth Annual Meeting of the Middle East Studies Association of North America, Washington, D.C., November 7, 1980.

4. These two tendencies, of course, correspond to different groupings within each society, which are typically referred to as moderates and extremists. I prefer to speak of pronegotiation and antinegotiation tendencies in order to underline the following assumptions: (1) Moderates and extremists are not fixed categories into which individuals or groups can be wholly and permanently placed; (2) the opposing tendencies exist not only within the society, where they are expressed in conflict between different political groupings, but also within each grouping and within each individual; and (3) moderates may turn into extremists under certain circumstances, since they are subject to external and internal pressures in that direction, and, similarly (though less commonly) extremists may turn into moderates under appropriate circumstances. The term *tendencies* implies that the conflict occurs within individuals and subgroups, as well as within the society, and that the definition of the opposing sides in that conflict must remain fluid.

5. Problem-solving workshops are part of a broader interactional approach to conflict resolution, pioneered by John Burton and his associates. See J. W. Burton, *Deviance, Terrorism, and War: The Process of Solving Unsolved Social and Political Problems* (New York: St. Martin's, 1979), and *Conflict and Communication: The Use of Controlled Communication in International Relations* (London: Macmillan, 1969). My colleagues and I have further developed this approach and applied it to the Arab-Israeli conflict. See H. C. Kelman, "The Problem-solving Workshop in Conflict Resolution," in R. L. Merritt, ed., *Communication in International Politics* (Urbana: University of Illinois, 1972); H. C. Kelman, "An International Approach to Conflict Resolution and Its Application to Israeli-Palestinian Relations" *International Interactions* 6 (1979), pp. 99–122; H. C. Kelman and S. P. Cohen, "The Problem-solving Workshop: A Social-psychological Contribution to the Resolution of International Conflicts," *Journal of Peace Research* 13 (1976), pp. 79–90; S. P. Cohen and E. E. Azar, "From War to Peace: The Transition Between Egypt and Israel," *Journal of Conflict Resolution* 25 (1981), pp. 87–114. This approach does not exhaust the role that third parties can play in resolution of the Israeli-Palestinian conflict. Some of the contributions of third parties, such as the U.S. government, are based on the deliberate use of their own positions of power. Without minimizing the potential value of such other approaches, I would argue that the problem-solving approach— with its emphasis on the facilitative, technical role of an unofficial third party—is uniquely suited to the prenegotiation process.

9

The Long Search for Peace:
A Progressive Israeli View

Simha Flapan

The Past

Unlike the conflict between Israel and the Arab states, the Israeli-Palestinian problem has not yet found a conceptual framework and machinery for even a partial and gradual settlement. When former Prime Minister Golda Meir issued her widely publicized pronouncement dismissing the existence of the Palestinian people, it escaped her critics that the view she expressed had been the cornerstone of Zionist policy from the very first. It was initiated in 1918 by Chaim Weizmann, the architect of the Balfour Declaration and the father and first president of the Jewish state.[1] David Ben-Gurion and his successors were orthodox followers.[2] It is ruthlessly applied today, despite abundant evidence that the Palestinians cling tenaciously to their national identity in the face of extreme adversity and even though their struggle for self-determination has become the crucial issue inhibiting a true peace process between Israel and the Arab world. Nonrecognition of the Palestinians' right to national self-determination and statehood was and remains a basic tenet of Israeli policymaking. It has been the essence of the Zionist-Palestinian confrontation that spawned the serial wars between Israel and the Arab states.

Shortly after the appearance at the beginning of this century of Theodore Herzl's manifesto on a Jewish state, which he predicted would become a reality within fifty years, a Palestinian, Naguib Azuri, authored the first manifesto of Arab nationalism, mainly addressed to the Palestinian question. As far back as 1905, he foresaw that within several decades, the Middle East would be the setting for a clash between the two nationalist movements and that this conflict would determine the fate of the region and perhaps of world peace.

Both prophecies proved true. A Jewish state has become a dynamic reality, a dominant factor for the Jewish Diaspora and a major power in the Middle East. At the same time, the conflict between Israel and the

Palestinian people has become the central and decisive issue for the prospects of peace and the future of the entire region.

A fundamental asymmetry in the objective situations of both peoples places the onus of the quest for a solution on Israel. The Jewish people have consummated their right to self-determination. They built a powerful state with an impressive track record of economic, technological, scientific, cultural, and military development. The Palestinians are a people of refugees, dispersed over the map, without a national home and self-government. They are mistreated, discriminated against, and oppressed by both Israel and the Arab régimes. Yet by no means does this exempt the Palestinians from the task and responsibility of formulating policies conducive to a solution.

A curious dynamic has characterized the pursuit of Arab-Israeli conflict resolution. Accompanying this eighty-year-old conflict has been a reversal of roles played by Israel and the Palestinians. Both sides have undergone fundamental metamorphoses in their attitudes but, unfortunately, in opposite directions. The 1948 war erupted because the Palestinians attempted to forcibly prevent Israeli self-determination in accordance with the UN resolution of 1947 that endorsed Jewish statehood in the framework of partition. Thirty-five years later, in 1982, the war in Lebanon broke out because of the Israeli resolve to block the self-determination of the Palestinians in the West Bank and Gaza envisioned by multiple UN resolutions and world consensus.

In an article entitled, "The Moment of Truth," an Arab thinker, Cecil Hourani,[3] claimed that the Arab debacle of the 1967 Six Day War was caused by emotional prejudice, misjudgment of capabilities, illusions of power, and the refusal to come to terms with reality as well as to accept a compromise, since this would indicate weakness. In rereading this article today, it is striking how these same maladies have taken root and now influence Israeli policy.

Although numerous factors have played a role and exacerbated and escalated the disagreement, no doubt the main point of conflict is the simultaneous claim of both peoples to the same territory, Palestine, as an exclusive base for their national development and sovereignty. Both peoples exhibit an astounding similarity in attitudes and policies in spite of the enormous differences in their cultures, social and economic structures, and problems of national revival.

Both officially deny the right of the other to have a state in Palestine or even in part of it. The PLO Covenant's aim to dismantle the Zionist state and Israel's violent opposition to the establishment of a Palestinian state are flip sides of the same coin. Likewise, both sides justify the use of force and violence for the achievement of their goals—indiscriminate acts of terror on one side, massive retaliation by armed forces on the other—with innocent civilians as the victims of both. Both sides have tried to reduce and weaken the demographic strength of the adversary. The Palestinians sought to arrest Jewish immigration and demanded the departure of Jews arriving in Palestine after a certain date; the Israelis encouraged the 1948 Arab exodus from the country and now encourage Arab emigration from the territories occupied in the war of 1967. Each side has been prepared to offer the other side personal and cultural, but not national, autonomy. However, the Palestinians in 1947 were ready to grant the Jewish minority proportional representation in the legislative and executive apparatuses of a Palestinian state, whereas the Likud governments (1977-1984) offered the Palestinians neither citizenship nor representation in the Knesset even after the incorporation of the West Bank and Gaza into the state of Israel. The party's program of autonomy and self-administration proposed for the five-year transition period deprived the Palestinians of the powers of legislation and of their right to self-determination.

Both the Palestinians and the Zionist leaders were Pan-Arab in orientation but for contrary reasons. The Zionist orientation toward Pan-Arabism was expedient; it was hoped that a miniscule portion of the greater Arab unity would be allocated for the Jewish homeland in exchange for Zionist support; and it provided moral justification for the idea of a transfer of Palestinian Arabs from Israel to the neighboring countries. Though never an official position, this idea had far greater repercussions on Zionist thinking than was usually admitted.

When Weizmann stated that the conflict between the Israelis and the Arabs is not one of right against wrong, but a conflict between two rights, he did not have in mind the rights of the Palestinians but those of Arab nationalism in general. Consequently, when he said that Jewish right has precedence over Arab right because a Jewish homeland in Palestine is a question of life and death for the Jewish people, while the loss of less than 1 per cent of their territory is not decisive for the future of the Arabs, he slighted the fact that for those who lived in Palestine, it was decisive.

The Palestinians were concerned lest they become the victims of a compromise between Arab nationalism and Zionism. Their Pan-Arabism originated in their sense of powerlessness, as a people numbering less than one million, to oppose the thrust of Jewish immigration and colonization initiated by a people ten million strong, without the backing of the whole Arab world. They were also intimidated by the adversary's connections at the apex of international finance and politics.

Zionist Policy, 1917–1947

During the period of the Palestinian mandate, the Zionist leadership followed a policy characterized by pragmatism, flexibility, and willingness to compromise. The emphasis was not on statehood and power but on immigration, settlement, and the building of a new society imbued with Jewish and universal moral values. The Revisionist party of Jabotinsky,[4] which preached conquest by "blood and fire," constituted the opposition and was excluded from the decisionmaking bodies of the Zionist movement, which was largely dominated by liberals, humanists, binationalists, and socialists. Thus, in spite of the escalation of the conflict from riots to civil war, the policy was one of restraint, political prudence, and moderation.

Although the Zionist leadership did not view the Palestinians as a national entity entitled to self-determination and hoped for an eventual transfer of the Palestinians to Jordan, it refrained from using violence as a means of forging its will. The principle of nondomination was repeated at nearly every Zionist congress; proposals for a legislative council were seriously considered on occasion, although never adopted as a program of action.

What rendered this realistic and practical approach futile and ineffective was the Zionist policy of economic and social separation that opened a chasm between Jews and Arabs, regardless of class. This approach contributed to the intransigence of the Arab leadership, which demanded an end to Jewish immigration and colonization as a precondition for any settlement. Important leaders and groups in the Yishuv and the Zionist movement labored to conceive a political program that would allow both Jewish immigration and settlement, as well as self-government and development of the Palestinians in the framework of a binational or federation state in which Arabs and Jews would enjoy equal power. Proponents of this parity formula never had the opportunity to influence Zionist policies. The moderate and realistic leaders in the Palestinian community were at the mercy of the intransigent leadership that rejected the idea of negotiations and settlement.

Partition Plans

Nonrecognition of Palestinian aspirations was the major reason for the collapse of compromise solutions that now and again enlisted the support of influential segments of the Palestinian movement as well as of Arab states. Various partition schemes, which emerged as the only realistic solution when the Zionist and Palestinian national movements advanced far along separate political trajectories, are a case in point. The British plan of partition floated in 1937 mainly foundered on two objections: (1) It proposed the unification of the projected Arab state of Palestine with Transjordan under the crown of Emir Abdallah, who was mistrusted by the majority of the Palestinians and the Arab states as the creature of the British Colonial Office, and (2) the Partition Plan was premised on the idea of a transfer of the Arab population from the projected Jewish state to Transjordan, either by consent or by a compulsory exchange of populations. The implications of this course for the Palestinians included the abandonment of their rich lands, citrus groves, wells, houses, workshops, and other assets and their relocation to an arid desert in a poor country.

For Ben-Gurion, then chairman of the Jewish Agency, the transfer of population became a condition sine qua non for acceptance of the partition scheme (which envisaged a small Jewish state containing 294,000 Jews and nearly 296,000 Arabs, the latter owning 75 per cent of the land). The transfer proposal prevented Nashashibi's Defense party from throwing its weight behind the plan, even though it was predisposed to accept partition in order to set up a self-governing Palestinian state in unification with Transjordan.[5]

Despite the ill-fated Partition Plan of 1937, the concept of partition became the main axis around which future attempts to solve the Zionist-Palestinian conflict revolved until it was adopted as the basis for the UN resolution of November 1947. This revised plan did not propose to cede part of Palestine to Transjordan but provided for the establishment of a self-governing Palestinian state alongside Israel and connected with it through an economic union. The Palestinian leadership, the Arab Higher Committee, and the Arab League shunned the plan and called upon the Palestinian people and the Arab states to frustrate its implementation by force.

The ensuing Jewish-Palestinian civil war culminated in full-scale war after May 15, 1948, between the newly proclaimed State of Israel and Arab states which, until then, had supported the Palestinians with money, arms, and volunteers. The struggle of the Palestinians against partition and the war initiated by the Arab states ended in a total collapse of the Palestinian political leadership and its military forces, as well as in a humiliating defeat of the invading Arab armies. The Palestinians became a people of refugees and the areas designated by the United Nations for the creation of a Palestinian state were either occupied or annexed by Israel, Jordan, and Egypt.

It would be wrong, however, to attribute the responsibility for this national calamity to the Palestinians and the Arab League alone. The Palestinians' struggle against the UN Partition Resolution had a very different character from their uprising against the British and the Zionist enterprise in 1937. The struggle reflected a new political mood in the people as a result of economic and social changes and the crisis of leadership, which condemned itself to exile because of its attempt to align the destiny of Palestine with the Axis war effort. Despite the appeal of the leadership to resist partition to the end, the masses demurred. Considerably fewer volunteers joined the fighting groups than in 1938.[6] Many villages signed agreements with neighboring Jewish settlements not to attack each other. In stark contrast to 1938, when the whole country was engulfed by the flames of the rebellion, in 1947 many areas remained quiet and untouched by the fighting.[7]

The opposition parties officially came out against partition but prepared themselves for this eventuality.[8] Scores of Palestinian merchants, landowners, community leaders, and their families left the country as self-displaced persons even before the massacre of Dir Yassin that unleashed panic and mass flight of unparalleled scale. The rebuff by the political forces to the call of the Arab Higher Committee to wage a war against the Jews was an unprecedented event in the history of the Jewish-Arab conflict.

Conspicuously absent against this backdrop were initiatives by the Israeli authorities to encourage these forces to improvise an alternative leadership which, contrary to the Arab Higher Committee, would work for the creation of a Palestinian state in accordance with the UN resolution. Instead, all contacts with the Palestinians and the Arab countries (and these were both numerous and influential) were exploited to promote an agreement with

Emir Abdallah based on annexation of Arab Palestine to Transjordan. Though there were several thorny and controversial problems in the negotiations with Emir Abdallah (such as his Greater Syria scheme, his double game in the Arab League, participation of his Arab Legion in the war, conflict over Israeli boundaries in the Triangle, Jerusalem, and the Negev, as well as the future of Gaza), there was a basic consensus that Abdallah's Arab Legion and the Iraqi forces dispatched to Palestine would remain within the borders of Arab Palestine and would not attack Jewish areas in return for Israeli acquiescence to his annexation of the West Bank. This agreement was mutually respected and implemented.

The nonrecognition of the Palestinians as a people entitled to a national entity was epitomized by the absence of Israeli attempts to capitalize on the economic unity plan provided for in the UN resolution (which the Jewish Agency endorsed) as a means of attracting Palestinian acceptance of partition. Instead, the Israeli authorities looked to the potential benefits to be extracted from the chaotic disintegration of the Palestinian community— its curtailed military potential and the projected demographic edge for the Jewish state. Weizmann hardly concealed his relief when he described the flight of the Palestinians as a "miraculous simplification" of the problem. Although some Israeli leaders, like Moshe Sharett, left open the prospects of return under certain political conditions, the Israeli authorities took pains to minimize this possibility by razing entire villages deserted by the Palestinians.

The special "refugee committee" set up by Ben-Gurion to handle the flight and refugee problem was called the "transfer committee" even though there was no connection between this flight and the mass immigration of Jews from the Arab countries in terms of timing, country of origin, and motivation. Jewish immigration from Arab countries came in the main after the war, from Morocco, Iraq, and Yemen. Neither Morocco nor Yemen was involved in the fighting, and the Palestinians, fleeing from the war, were concentrated in refugee camps in the West Bank, Gaza Strip, and the adjoining Arab states. Very few Zionist leaders appreciated the extent to which the refugee question would radicalize the conflict. (Ironically, Ben-Gurion intimated his apprehension by suggesting that the Palestinian refugees should be confined to one Arab state, Iraq, rather than dispersed throughout Israel's neighboring countries.) The concept of transfer was used to explain and rationalize a posteriori an event of an entirely different nature.

Israeli policy was intended to undermine the Palestinian national movement and its claim to independent statehood through a settlement with the Hashemite kingdom. At the Jericho Conference of December 1948, which was attended by delegations from towns and villages in the Jordanian controlled part of Palestine, a resolution was passed calling for the unification of Jordan and Palestine under the Hashemite crown. Although this was rejected by King Faruk and by Azzam Pasha, the secretary-general of the Arab League, as well as by Syria, Lebanon, Saudi Arabia, and the All-Palestine government in Gaza, Israel, represented by Eliahu Sasson, prevailed upon the emir to implement the resolution as soon as possible in order to present his rivals with a fait accompli.[9]

The idea of a Palestinian state did not evaporate, however, with the annexation of the West Bank by Abdallah. It was raised again and again by Egypt, Syria, Saudi Arabia, and the Arab League, all of whom were violently opposed to Abdallah's annexation of the West Bank and insisted on the Palestinians' right to determine their future status. Israel's refusal to consider even partial repatriation of the refugees contributed to the failure of the UN Palestine Conciliation Commission (PCC), which attempted between the years 1948 and 1951 (in the Conferences of Lausanne, April 27–September 15, 1949; Geneva, January 16–June 21, 1950; and Paris, September 10–November 19, 1951) to bring about a peaceful settlement of the Israeli-Arab conflict.

Examination of these protracted conciliation efforts proves beyond doubt that the decisive reason for their doom was not the extremist and inflexible refusal of the Arab states to accept the reality of partition and the existence of the Jewish state. The Arab states voted against UN Resolution 194 of December 1948, which called for the repatriation of the refugees, "wishing to return to their houses and to live in peace with their neighbors . . . at the earliest practicable date." The Arabs rejected the resolution for the same reasons that the Israeli representative present at the UN debate did not oppose it, though he qualified the terms of its implementation. It was viewed as an acceptance of the 1947 UN Resolution of Partition and a legitimization of Israel's right to exist. However, following the hapless Arab military intervention in Palestine, the conclusion of armistice treaties, and domestic social unrest in Arab countries, the Arab governments soon displayed a fundamental reversal in their policies. They agreed to cooperate with the Conciliation Commission, even though its task was to work for the implementation of the UN resolutions that they had previously rejected.

The Refugee Problem

The change in Arab policies was expressed as a willingness to accept, under certain conditions, the new realities created by the UN resolution of 1947, the war of 1948, and the emergence of the well-structured and dynamic Jewish state. The main condition was Israel's acceptance of the 1947 borders and the implementation of the UN resolution on the refugee problem. On this basis, a transition from armistice treaties to peace treaties seemed within reach.

The Arab demand for the repatriation of the refugees was not a maneuver to create an impasse in the negotiations and to paralyze the work of the PCC or to destroy the Jewish state from within through a mass return of refugees who would engage in terror and guerrilla warfare. This was evident from the limitation of the Arab demand for repatriation to refugees who left the areas earmarked by the United Nations for the Palestinian state and from the readiness of the Arab governments to discuss the problem of resettlement in their countries of refugees who did not wish to return to Palestine, the problems of territorial adjustments and demilitarized zones, and the problems of transition from armistice to peace treaties.[10]

The pressure for a settlement was also exerted by the refugees themselves, who made up the majority of the Palestinian people. They demanded that the Arab governments "make peace if they can't make war," and they also offered Israel their support for a peace settlement based on the recognition of their rights. Unfortunately, Israel's objective at this stage was not the achievement of peace treaties but the legitimization of its territorial war gains, the organization and absorption of a mass immigration, and the building up of an economically and militarily powerful state able to withstand and survive a confrontation even with a united Arab world.

Israel was facing a fateful decision in its long-range political orientation. A struggle for hegemony raged in the Arab world between the Hashemite Dynasty, supported by Great Britain, and the more radical elements of the Arab Nationalist movement, led by Egypt, which was in the throes of a political struggle to remove the British military presence. In an attempt to counter Emir Abdallah's plans for the annexation of the West Bank and hegemony over Syria, Cairo supported the Palestinian Arab Higher Committee, helped it to set up an All-Palestine government in Gaza, but at the same time tacitly explored through secret contact with Israel the possibility of a Palestinian state in part of Palestine.

The choice was made by Ben-Gurion who, in conformity with Weizmann's strategy, excluded the option of an anti-British alliance with the Arabs. He had little sympathy for their struggle against foreign domination. Ben-Gurion was well aware of Egypt's central role in the Middle East, but he was influenced—apart from his despairing of Arab anticolonialism and beneficent view of the West as the embodiment of morality, democracy, and social justice—by the fact that an agreement with Abdallah offered to Israel the legitimization of its territorial gains in the 1948 war and the removal of the Palestinian problem from the agenda.

The Jordanian option proved to be an illusion. Israel's refusal to accept the principle of refugee repatriation and to deal with the Palestinians led to the termination of the Palestine Conciliation Commission. But peace with the Hashemite Kingdom of Jordan was not signed, not only because of the assassination of Abdallah in 1951. It is doubtful whether he would have been able to sign a peace with Israel, as he was unable to persuade his own government to approve the far-reaching concessions he was forced to make.[11] The unsolved refugee problem concerning the majority of the Palestinians remained on the agenda.

To most Israelis the war of 1948 seemed to vindicate the policy of nonrecognition of the Palestinian people. Jordanian annexation of the West Bank and Palestinian dispersion within the region nurtured the illusion that the Palestinian national problem had disappeared, leaving only the residual humanitarian question of the refugees to be solved. Nearly twenty years had to pass before it became clear that the refugee problem had not liquidated but had aggravated the Israeli-Palestinian conflict.

Israel's policy was to place the entire responsibility for the refugee problem on the Arabs and to link the problem of compensation with that of the loss of Jewish property in Arab countries for which the Palestinians were not responsible and were unable to solve. This policy played into the hands of those who, motivated by the powerful urge to vindicate the humiliating defeat of 1948, wanted to use the refugee problem as a weapon against Israel. The refugee problem became an excellent instrument for anti-Israeli propaganda, boycott, and ostracism. Meanwhile, the Palestinian refugee camps became hotbeds of a militant nationalist movement of fedayeen aiming to restore the status quo ante through infiltration, terrorism, and sabotage, though not always with the blessing and often against the wishes of their host countries. The refugee problem became, between 1948 and 1967, the major source of conflict and escalation of tension between Israel and the Arab states. The absence of a solution generated a revolt among the younger generation of refugees against the perpetuation of their homelessness and misery.

Palestinian Involvement in Arab Politics

With the rise of the movement for Arab unity in Syria and Egypt in 1954, many young Palestinians urged a policy of belligerence and confrontation with Israel. They became the militant wing of the Baath and of Nasserism and spearheaded the efforts for unification, in the hope of achieving the liberation of Palestine.

Israeli Prime Minister Golda Meir opposed the return of Arab refugees to Israel on the grounds that they would become a "time bomb." She failed to see that the bomb, if not dismantled, would explode on Israel's doorstep. It was again Meir who used a variation of the Israeli security argument to justify the 1967 occupation and rule over the 1.2 million Palestinians of the West Bank and Gaza, including half a million refugees.

Although the aim of the massive Israeli retaliations was to compel the Arab governments to constrain the fedayeen, the result was a vicious cycle of escalating violence. The consequences of this policy were ruinous. The Arab countries that had been a factor of moderation in the Zionist-Palestinian conflict (as evidenced in the diaries of Prime Minister Moshe Sharett among others) became Israel's main enemy and security problem. But, in spite of the hostility of the Arab leaders and their thirst for revenge, the ongoing convolutions following the 1948 war (as expressed in coups d'état, upheavals, revolutions, and inter-Arab conflict) rendered inoperative all plans for renewed Arab aggression.

The policy that Israel pursued, however, confirmed Arab fears of Israeli expansionism and conspiracy with the historical enemies of Arab nationalism. Israeli collusion with Great Britain and France in the war of 1956 and the support for French colonialism and war against the Front de Libération Nationale (FLN) in Algeria left bruises darker than those from Israel's military actions themselves. Concomitant with these ever-spiraling military clashes, Israel's foreign policy and socioeconomic development were subordinated to the building up of a military deterrent and of preemptive actions to control the military balance in the region. A corollary of this was Israel's belief in its role as a "regional power" able to match the combined strength of all Arab states and to prevent any substantial uncongenial change in the political and military structure of the Middle East.

In spite of the fedayeen activities, the Palestinian problem was obliterated from Israeli political thinking. The Arab states, and particularly Egypt since the coup d'état in 1952, were seen as arch enemies and as a major threat to Israel's existence. Little can be found in the Israeli literature between 1948–1967 that predicts the reemergence of Palestinian nationalism in the refugee camps. The fedayeen were seen as agents of the Arab military rulers preparing for a war of revenge. Israel accused the Arab governments of a deliberate policy to prevent rehabilitation and absorption of refugees in order to maintain hotbeds of hostility and tension and to use the refugees for guerrilla warfare, harassment, and violations of the fragile armistice-treaties.

The 1967 Watershed

The war of 1967 put an end to the effacement of the problems. The future of the West Bank and Gaza, with more than one million Palestinians, representing the largest sector of the Palestinian people, became the chief problem of Israel's policy. The encounter with the people in the West Bank and Gaza was a shock for Israeli people and resulted in a change in public opinion, destroying the myths of nonexistence of the Palestinian people and the artificiality of the refugee problem. For the Palestinians, the new direct exposure served to counterpoise the old demonic propaganda with the human face of the enemy, whereas the oppressive military occupation bred resistance and hostility.

The intoxication with the blitz victory in the Six Day War of 1967 produced a spontaneous reaction expressed in the sudden emergence of a mass movement for undivided Israel. This time it was made up not only of those who opposed partition in 1947 (the right-wing parties of Herut and the Liberals and the left-wing party of Ahdut-Avoda) but also of some of the most prominent intellectuals, writers, leaders, and generals of the Labor movement, including Nathan Alterman, Moshe Shamir, Chaim Guri, Eliezel Livne, and Avraham Yaffe. The movement called for abolition of partition and new "strategic frontiers" and a "new historical era" marked by a massive concentration of the Jewish people in Eretz Israel and a leading role for Israel in the Middle East. Undivided Israel was not a political opposition but a massive pressure group for unilateral settlement in the West Bank, Jerusalem, and the Gaza strip. The so-called Allon Plan initiated by Deputy Prime Minister Yigal Allon tried to synthesize territorial expansion with the Jewish character of the state through a network of rural and urban Jewish settlements around Jerusalem, in the Gushe-Etzion, the Jordan Valley, and Golan Heights, and in half of the Sinai peninsula, while giving back to Jordan or to local leadership the densely populated areas in the West

Bank. This approach meant the annexation of 30 to 35 per cent of the area of the West Bank, including nearly 50 per cent of its cultivatable land.

At the time (1968–1969), a number of important Palestinian and Israeli politicians proposed the establishment of a Palestinian entity in the West Bank that would be the first to negotiate a peace treaty with Israel. On the Palestinian side, Shaikh Ali al-Ja'abari, Ayoub Musallem, Aziz Shehada, Taji al-Faruqi, Hamdi Kana'an, Hikmat al-Masri, Anwar Nusseiba, and others expressed their readiness to set up a self-governing authority in the West Bank, although they differed among themselves on the future status of this entity. Some hoped to develop it into a Palestinian state, whereas others aspired to reunite with Jordan. Their conditions for negotiations included an Israeli renunciation of annexation and rule over the West Bank.

Among the Israelis who suggested the creation of a Palestinian entity were ministers, intellectuals, and exgenerals, including Abba Eban, Shlomo Hillel, Yehoshafat Harkabi, Elad Peled, Mati Peled, Shlomo Avineri, Chaim Herzog, and Mordechai Gazit. They conceived of the state, however, as remaining under Israeli military occupation and under conditions set down by Israel concerning the delineation of frontiers, foreign policy, and defense so as to prevent it from becoming a new base for aggression for the Arab armies. Because this proposal emerged alongside a policy aimed at annexing at least part of the Sinai and the Golan Heights, many of the Israeli peace forces regarded it as a proposal for a colonial protectorate, a Bantustan completely dependent on Israel's good will for its economic and social needs. Deprived of any contacts with the Arab world, it would have been stigmatized as a puppet state run by quislings, and would have produced nationalist and revolutionary opposition from the Palestinians living outside its borders and from the Arab states that suffered a loss of territories in the 1967 war.

The idea of a Palestinian state was rejected, however, by the Israeli cabinet, which represented at that time a national coalition with Begin. The initiative was killed not only by Begin's pressure for the annexation of the West Bank but also by the intoxication of many Labor leaders with the military victory and their belief that Israel, with its overpowering military capacity, could acquire new territorial dimensions and new strategic frontiers. The Allon Plan, by unilaterally creating faits accomplis, obfuscated the ideological differences between Labor and Begin and paved the way for Begin's advent to power. Endorsing a policy of "peace from strength," the Labor leaders sacrificed their historical vision and far-sighted statesmanship for short-term and dubious war gains.

Although the Allon Plan was not formally adopted by the government, which included Likud party members (Begin considered it too minimalist), it was not rejected; it became the guideline for setting up Jewish settlements in the occupied territories, amounting de facto to a policy of unilateral annexation. The Likud backed the implementation of the Allon Plan as a starting point for the realization of its Great Israel vision.

The rationalization for the unilateral action was that it would prompt the Arabs to negotiate sooner out of fear that loss of time would mean loss of territories. However, the insistence on new strategic frontiers and direct negotiations made talks impossible. Thus the settlement policy of Allon, who was regarded as a leading dove, served to unite rather than divide the doves and the hawks. Because of the blurred distinction between Labor and Likud on the vital issue of war and peace, crossovers (Moshe Dayan, Ahron Uzan) and new alliances became possible. Begin could claim at crucial junctures in Israeli-Arab relations that he was only following—more consistently and literally—the policies advocated by Allon. This explains the tragic paradox that the Labor party, heading the coalitions between 1967–1977, presided over the disintegration and dismantling of the values of pioneering Zionism and socialism and over the collapse of its own hegemony and the ascendancy of its historical rival, Begin.

The Ramadan–Yom Kippur War, 1973

The war of 1973 did not produce an atmosphere conducive to a comprehensive peace settlement and a new approach toward the Palestinian problem, despite the Geneva Peace Conference and the military disengagement agreements with Syria and Egypt in 1975–1976 initiated by U.S. Secretary of State Henry Kissinger. Kissinger's step-by-step strategy produced an impasse: The U.S. government, anxious to avoid antagonizing the American Jewish community in an election year, refrained from taking any active steps to promote a final peace settlement or to stop Israel's faits accomplis in the West Bank and Jerusalem despite reservations of some prominent men from the foreign policy establishment like George Ball and William Scranton who demanded a more even-handed policy in the Middle East.

The main result of the 1973 war was a new emphasis on Israeli military preparedness. An enormous effort has been made to reorganize, reequip, and strengthen the Israeli Defense Forces for any future emergency. The new cabinet headed by Rabin and Peres refused to consider any move, even tactical, to break the impasse over the Palestinian problem, though its centrality became obvious after the 1973 war in which the Palestinians played no role. One year after the war the PLO received international recognition when the United Nations voted 105 to 4 to invite Yasir Arafat to address the General Assembly.

In the same month the Arab League meeting in Rabat unanimously affirmed the PLO as the sole legitimate representative of the Palestinian people on any liberated Palestinian territory. Israel reacted by boycotting the session of the UN Security Council attended by PLO representatives and by blocking attempts to resume the Geneva peace talks with the participation of the PLO. The majority of the Israeli public and decisionmakers did not understand that the shift of the Palestinian issue to the forefront of the peace process originated in the inner logic of the military disengagement process. The more the Arab states disengage themselves from the military confrontation with Israel, the more concerned they must become about finding a solution to the Palestinian problem. The Palestinians act as a catalyst for explosive social and political conflicts within the Arab world, and the only way to stop their involvement in these conflicts is to engage them in building a nation of their own.

The decision of the Rabat summit was not meant to block the way to a second Geneva Conference but to ensure that the Palestinian problem was dealt with there. After the affirmation of the PLO as the sole representative of the Palestinian people, the Rabat summit called upon Egypt, Syria, Jordan and the PLO to work out a formula governing their relations in the peace negotiations. Despite a last minute agreement by Moshe Dayan (the foreign minister in Begin's new cabinet) to PLO participation as members of a united Arab delegation, the Geneva Conference was not resumed. This failure was the result of the fierce opposition of Israel and its supporters in the United States to the Cyrus Vance–Andrei Gromyko agreement (on October 1, 1977) and to the sudden visit of Anwar al-Sadat (November 1977) to Jerusalem, which initiated the Camp David peace process.

The years 1975–1976 mark the beginning of a dialogue between the Israelis and the PLO on mutual recognition and a two-state solution to the conflict. PLO representatives Said Hammani, Sabri Jiryis, Issam Sartawi, Abdallah Hurani, and others issued statements on a new peace strategy and on the possibility of a Palestinian state alongside Israel and entered into contacts with Israeli Zionists Lova Eliav, Mati Peled, Uri Avneri, Yaakov Arnon, and Simha Flapan. In Israel the Yariv-Shemtov formula, proclaiming readiness for negotiations with any group of Palestinians, including the PLO, that will recognize Israel's right to exist and renounce terrorism, received support from a wide range of political forces: Abba Eban, Itzhak Navon, and many others in the Labor party and the academic and business community. The Mapam (United Workers party) adopted the formula as its official policy, and, though it gave preference to a Jordanian-Palestine state as a solution, it declared its recognition of the Palestinian self-determination in a separate state in the West Bank. The newly formed Israeli Council for Israeli-Palestinian Peace (ICIPP) headed by the venerable Elie Eliashar and directed by General Mati Peled, Member of Knesset Lova Eliav (former secretary general of the Labor party), Yaakov Arnon, and Uri Avneri called for direct negotiation with the PLO and established close contacts with its special representative, Issam Sartawi, and later with its chairman, Yasir Arafat. All this, however, came too late to prevent the advent to power of the right-wing Likud in the 1977 elections.

The Present

Between 1967 and 1977, Israeli society underwent a dramatic transformation. The rule over 1.25 million Arabs engendered the influx of cheap laborers from the occupied territories, to which Israel had to provide sources of employment in place of the previous labor markets in Jordan and other Arab countries. This stimulated the movement of Jewish workers away from production. The continued belligerence and clashes with Arab states stimulated the growth of a war economy exempt from public control and economic competition and the import of enormous quantities of capital for arms production. Nearly $15 billion were invested in the Sinai peninsula, money that proved to be wasted when the land was restored to Egyptian sovereignty. All these complications induced a fundamental change into the Israeli economy, a change from a well-planned, productive economy and a labor-based society imbued with ideas of democracy and social justice to an unbridled capitalist economy and a consumer mentality ready to capitalize on quick profits, tax evasion, and speculation.

The unconditional support of Diaspora Jewry, which basked in Israel's prowess, and American nurturing of Israeli policy with massive economic and military aid fueled the militarization of Israel's political thinking and bolstered a view of Israel as a dominant regional power and an indispensable ally for U.S. regional and global strategy. Many sections of the Labor elite were lured by military careerism, easy profit making, and the sweets of power. Corruption, which crept into the highest echelons of the Labor party, contributed to its downfall in 1977. Much to their chagrin, some of the leaders of Labor witnessed this process but tried to arrest it by exalting the old-fashioned values of Labor Zionism. They failed to understand that the disintegration of these values resulted from socioeconomic changes caused by the ongoing war, the escalation of the arms race, exploitation of cheap Arab labor, and the military rule over the Palestinians. They failed to see that only by ending the occupation of Arab territories and by attaining a peace settlement could this process have been controlled.

But the peace settlement was precluded by the Israeli policy of "no return to 1967 borders," as well as by its insistence on direct negotiations and on the Jordan Option and the Allon Plan as the only political and territorial compromise. Denial of the Palestinian right to self-determination, nonrecognition of the PLO as a representative of the Palestinian people, and the harsh repression of PLO sympathizers in the occupied territories led to an erosion of the moral, ethical, and humanistic values in Israeli society and to a collapse of its image as a liberal democratic and peace-aspiring nation. The practices of the military administration in the West Bank voided the Zionist declarations on peace, justice, and nondomination. This policy benefited Begin's revisionist ideology and the movement for the Greater Israel that pressed for acceleration of Jewish settlements in the occupied territories. The ground was thus fertile for Begin to come to power with his policy of massive Jewish colonization in the West Bank.

The Likud Policy

The change in policy, however, could only be implemented by brutal force and oppression: dismissal of democratically elected mayors, expulsion of scholars and teachers, closure of journals and universities, enforcement of collective punishments, demolition of houses, imposition of curfews on entire villages, dispersion of student demonstrations by gunfire, and prohibition of cultural and political activities expressing Palestinian national aspirations. These measures were employed with an eye toward proposing a collaborationist leadership that would accept the autonomy plan of Begin, which deprived the Palestinians of control over land and water as well as of legislative powers and the right to self-determination. The aim of Begin's peace treaty with Egypt was to eliminate the military potential of the largest and strongest Arab country from Israel's confrontation with Syria, Jordan, and the Palestinians who opposed Israeli annexation of the West Bank and Gaza and insisted on the restitution of these territories and of the Golan Heights to Arab and Palestinian sovereignty. This approach could only lead to the war in Lebanon, which (to use the Clausewitz definition) was the continuation of politics in the West Bank. Its main objective was the liquidation of the PLO, viewed by the overwhelming majority of the Palestinians in the occupied territories as their only legitimate representative.

Begin declared the war in Lebanon to be a political choice that would end the trauma of the Yom Kippur War of 1973, liquidate once and for all the PLO and its terrorist action, lead to a peace treaty with liberal, pro-Western Phalangist-dominated Lebanon, deliver a crushing and humiliating blow to Syria and to Soviet positions in the Middle East, and open the way in the West Bank and Gaza to a new, realistic leadership that would acquiesce to Israeli rule and annexation. Jabotinsky's political philosophy that the Great Israel vision could be realized by military power and conquest was tested under the most optimal conditions: overwhelming military superiority, tacit but full support of the United States, nonintervention of the USSR, and tragic isolation of the PLO in an impotent, conflict-ridden Arab world. However, none of these objectives was achieved, and the war became a turning point in Israel.

The war generated a national crisis of unprecedented depth and revealed the erosion of Israeli moral and social values; it exposed the centrality of the Palestine problem and the impossibility of eradicating by military means the aspirations for independence among the Palestinian people. It increased the prestige and influence of the PLO for a time, even though by the mid-1980s the future of the PLO was in doubt. The objectives and the nature of the war, which led to the massacre at Sabra and Shatila, as well as its political ramifications and consequences—in particular, the increased prestige of Syria, the abrogation of the Lebanese-Israel peace agreement, and the growing popular resistance in southern Lebanon—dealt a blow to Likud's political concepts and generated a nationwide movement of protest and criticism that strengthened the demand for a change of government and policy.

The moral and political setbacks experienced by Israelis in the Lebanon War undermined two of Begin's major arguments against the PLO. Before the war, most Israelis believed that a Palestinian state in the West Bank, bent on irredentist guerrilla action and serving as a forward base for hostile Arab states and the USSR, would pose the greatest threat and danger to Israel's security. Such a state existed in southern Lebanon, and it was liquidated in two days at the price of 26 dead and 75 wounded Israeli soldiers. The enormous military superiority of the Israeli army, equipped with the most sophisticated artillery, tanks, warships, and air force, demonstrated the absurdity of the propaganda-incited fear of a small Palestinian state that lacked the industrial technology needed for modern warfare. After the war, larger segments of the public began to question the danger of a small Palestinian state established in the framework of a peace settlement. Also, the image of the PLO as a band of gangsters who took control of the refugee camps by acts of terror and intimidation withered, giving way to confusion and a moral dilemma when the Israeli soldiers discovered that the PLO members were in fact the leading cadres, firmly rooted and running the schools, hospitals, workshops, and social services in the refugee camps, and that they fought courageously against a powerful army.

The opposition—even when it came to power under Shimon Peres and a National Unity government that included the Likud—has not yet formed a clear-cut alternative to Begin's policies and still hesitates or refuses to recognize the PLO and accept its demand for independent statehood. It still clings to the Labor party's Jordan Option and the idea of a territorial compromise, a policy that brought Begin to power. But it is becoming increasingly clear—partly because of the many failed attempts to lure King Husayn into talks during 1984, 1985, and 1986—that Husayn can enter the play only in cooperation with either the PLO or other Palestinians designated by the Palestinians themselves and only on the basis of a commitment to respect in due course the Palestinians' right to self-determination. There is also a widespread awareness in Israel that the present policy toward the Palestinians can be continued only through brutal oppression of elementary human rights and that Jewish terrorism and reaction as well as the destruction of Israel's democratic-liberal values would be the liabilities of this policy. Attendant upon this scenario would be a new cycle of violence, an undermining of the peace process with Egypt, growing isolation in the world, a potential crisis of relations with Diaspora Jewry, and a new round of turbulence in the region, which might threaten, sooner or later, the special relationship with the United States.

National Crisis in Israel

The national crisis in Israel is only beginning. The opposition is not only a movement of protest against the war; it revives the historical struggle in Zionism and in Israeli society between the liberal-humanistic-socialist trend aspiring for peace and coexistence and the ethnocentric, militaristic, expansionist, and chauvinistic Zionism for which power and territory are the primary objectives. The outcome of this struggle depends also on the position of Diaspora Jewry, on U.S. policy in the Middle East, and on the line the PLO will take regarding a political solution.

The consensus in the Israeli peace camp is that the occupation and rule over the Palestinian people have a corrosive effect on the human and moral values that succor Israeli society and therefore must end. There is also agreement that no peace is possible without a solution to the Israeli-Palestinian conflict. Linked to these beliefs is the growing realization that the only way to a real peace is to negotiate with the PLO in one form or another. But the precondition here is that the PLO must adopt a clear-cut, unambiguous policy in favor of a full peace settlement. This approach would require from the Palestinians a radical revision from nonrecognition, or at best equivocal and ambiguous quasi recognition, to recognition of the Jewish people's right to self-determination and statehood in Palestine. The PLO Covenant that denied this right embraced an ideological credo that also became a program for action when al-Fatah took over the leadership of the PLO. Significantly, modifications in PLO positions have corresponded to failures and setbacks in the attempt to implement the covenant.

Al-Fatah's strategic and political thinking was heavily influenced by the Algerian struggle for independence, the war in Vietnam, and the theory of the popular war of liberation propagated by the Syrian Baath. The strategy of a guerrilla war and the policy to mobilize the Arab world for a confrontation with Israel have taught the PLO the infeasibility of implementing the covenant. A few examples of the PLO tactics that came to naught were the abortive guerrilla tactics in the West Bank and Gaza; the attempt to take over power in Jordan; the creation of an independent semistate in south Lebanon and cooperation with the Lebanese Moslem and left-wing opposition; the defunct diplomatic campaign for Israel's expulsion from the United Nations; a united front with oriental Jewish communities against the Zionist state. The PLO's financial dependence on Saudi Arabia and Kuwait and the limitations on policymaking imposed by Syria and other host countries also contributed to the failure of these tactics.

Nevertheless, the PLO scored a stunning success in corralling world support for its role as sole legitimate representative of the Palestinians in their struggle for self-determination and statehood and as an active participant in negotiations. The PLO's signals of readiness to negotiate a political solution to the conflict must be perceived against this background. The passivity of the Arab régimes during the war in Lebanon, their submission to U.S. pressure, their consent to the dismantlement and evacuation of the PLO bases in Lebanon, the inability of the USSR to stop the war and prevent this outcome, and the sensational demonstrations in Israel against the war, and the Sabra and Shatila massacres have all had a dramatic impact on the Palestinians.

The PLO is now compelled to evolve a new strategy in view of its dispersion among all Arab states and the absence of a territorial base and sanctuary. In the past, the Palestinians were unable to perceive the internal struggle in Zionism as relevant to their destiny. They viewed it as a Jekyll and Hyde phenomenon of the same movement; Jabotinsky was seen as the true spokesperson of Zionism, and Weizmann, as a hypocritical mask of its real expansionist aims. This distinction can be understood in view of the fact that the liberal, humanistic, and socialist ideas had little practical application in Zionist policies. Today, however, the PLO cannot afford to disregard this internal struggle since its outcome will be fateful for its own as well as Israel's future.

The present dilemma for the PLO, following the expulsion of Yasir Arafat from Damascus, the on and off relations with Jordan, the Syrian sponsored mutiny of Abu-Mussa and Abu-Nidal and the continuing challenge within the PLO to Arafat's leadership by George Habash and Naif Hauwatmeh arises from the PLO's crucial choice between a moderate-realistic policy and a continuation of the futile struggle for a secular-democratic state and the remobilization of the Arab world for a new confrontation with Israel.

Israeli responses to various PLO signals that it desires to negotiate a settlement based on mutual recognition, Israeli security, and Palestinian self-determination continue to be diverse in the extreme. At present, the support for the different attitudes in Israel can be summarized as follows:

1. Annexation of the West Bank and Gaza as number one priority, by all available means and regardless of the price to be paid in relation with the United States, with the Jewish Diaspora, with international public opinion, and with the Arab world, and regardless of its consequences for the future of the Israeli state and society. This view is put forth by Ariel Sharon and his supporters in Herut, the Tehiya party of Yuval Neeman, the Kach party of Rabbi Meir Kahane, the Morasha party of Rabbi Druckman, and about 30 per cent of Gush Emmunim (Block of the Faithful) and its settlers in the occupied territories—altogether about 15 to 20 per cent of the Israeli vote.

2. Annexation of the West Bank and Gaza, but in a more expedient and gradual manner to avoid a crisis with the United States, loss of economic and military aid, too sharp a strain with Diaspora Jews, and a collapse of the peace agreement with Egypt. This position is supported by the Herut section led by the more moderate wing of David Levy and Cohen Orgad, by most of the Liberals in Likud, and by the National Religious party led by Yusef Burg. Altogether, this group makes up about 20 per cent of the Israeli vote.

3. Restitution of densely populated Arab areas of the occupied territories to Arab sovereignty, that is, to Jordan or to a local leadership, in return for a peace settlement, rectification of frontiers, security guarantees, and no enforced dismantlement of Jewish settlements, but opposition to an independent Palestinian state run by the PLO. About 45 per cent of the Israeli society support this line, which is officially adopted by the Labor party.

4. Restitution of the West Bank and Gaza, with minor rectification of frontiers, to Jordan in return for a peace treaty and security guarantees, but no opposition to a subsequent self-determination of the Palestinians in a separate state, which would adopt the obligations of the peace treaty. This is the official position of the Mapam, which represented about 15 per cent of the Labor Alignment before Mapam broke from Labor when the National Unity government was formed in 1984. As an independent party, Mapam may represent 6 to 7 per cent of the Israeli voters.

5. Recognition of Palestinian right to self-determination and to an independent state in the West Bank and Gaza, in the framework of mutual

recognition and coexistence with Israel. Rakah, the Communist party that usually receives about 50 per cent of the Israeli-Arab vote (but only 3 to 4 percent of the general vote) is the major party supporting this solution. Some Jewish factions hold this position including General Mati Peled, journalist Uri Avneri, Yaakov Arnon, who together with Mohamed Meari established the "Progressive List for Peace" and achieved two seats in the Knesset, the remainder of the Sheli party and of "Peace Now," who joined the "Citizens' Rights" party headed by Member of Knesset Shulamit Aloni. Also a number of Jewish and Arab committees support the two-states solution and call for direct negotiations with the PLO. About 7 to 10 per cent of the Israeli people favor this solution. About twenty-two Israelis from these groups went in November 1986 to Romania to meet an official delegation of the PLO, in spite of the law prohibiting contacts with this organization.

The constellation of forces within Israeli politics is neither stable nor fixed. International circumstances, U.S. policy, regional development, Diaspora Jewry's attitudes, and Palestinian strategy may cause considerable fluctuations and changes. The costs of occupation and the benefits from a settlement with Palestinians may play an important role. The Labor party itself is not immune to criticism and pressure from within and without. Though it is officially committed to a line resembling the Allon Plan, the consequences of its past mistakes have created more flexibility and open-mindedness. The door to contact with the PLO—if the PLO succeeds in formulating a policy paving the way for its integration into the peace process—will not remain closed especially if Labor is able to form a government without the Likud in the future. Many Labor members of parliament already support new peace initiatives based on the principle of self-determination of the Palestinians and mutual recognition. A new Labor-dominated coalition will not block, with the help of the U.S. Jewish community, a revival of the Reagan peace plan, which, with some corrections, could be synthesized with the Fez plan and thus open the way to negotiations on a comprehensive peace in the Middle East. A revival of the Reagan peace plan, however, may depend more on a change in U.S. global strategy than in Israeli policies.

The Future

The reluctance of the Labor party to accept the fact that peace is not obtainable without talks and negotiations with the PLO is based on the conviction that the PLO would suffer a permanent decline and lose its influence both in Arab politics and over the Palestinians under Israeli rule. This idea has been renewed in recent years particularly after the PLO's loss of sanctuary, territorial base, and infrastructure in Lebanon, the rebellion against Arafat's leadership, and most recently the break between King Husayn and the PLO. The idea is that the Palestinians in the West Bank and Gaza, constituting one-third of the Palestinian people, and facing accelerated Jewish colonization that threatens to impose irreversible demographic and economic changes, will sooner or later opt for what they have hitherto rejected. This course would involve serving as an alternative to the PLO, abolishing the covenant and the idea of "a secular democratic Palestine," recognizing Israel, and negotiating with it concerning the creation of a ministate committed to respect Israeli conditions of security and peace.

A wide range of U.S. political analysts share this view of the inevitability of the PLO's decline, the irreversibility of the Israelization of the West Bank, and the emergence of a new, more realistic and collaborationist leadership in the West Bank. They claim that this view is based on an analysis of the different segments and interests of the Palestinian people from a socioeconomic perspective. According to this view, the two million Palestinians dispersed in the Arab world pursued the unrealistic vision of a secular democratic state in the whole of Palestine because they hail from areas that form the pre-1967 State of Israel. Their policies were motivated by the desire to regain their lost homes and assets. The PLO leadership reflected in the main the unrealizable interests of the refugees, according to these analysts.

By contrast, the 1.25 million Palestinians currently under Israeli control in the West Bank and Gaza represent an indigenous population with a national-economic infrastructure. Their land and property are in jeopardy unless a political accommodation is soon secured with Israel. After the evacuation of the PLO from Beirut, loss of the military base, dispersal of their cadres, the center of gravity moved to the West Bank, which has become the focal constituency and the last territorial base for a Palestinian national entity. Present conditions are ripe for the Palestinians in the West Bank to initiate a policy of self-salvation, which in turn could create an opportunity for the Palestinians in the Diaspora to achieve partial repatriation and compensation.

Although this analysis sounds very persuasive, it has many weaknesses. The differentiation between the "haves" and the "have-nots" does not correspond to the categories of the West Bank–Gaza population and the Palestinians abroad. Refugees who lost their property in present-day Israel form the majority of the people in Gaza and a considerable portion of the population in the West Bank. Also, in Jordan, refugees from Israel as well as from the West Bank still live in the camps. On the other hand quite a number of refugees from abroad, especially large property owners, tried to come to terms with the state of Israel. Although economic interests influence political aspirations, programs, and strategies, these are not the most crucial factors.

West Bank Palestinians have played an important role in PLO policies for some time. They did not accept the idea either of a Vietnam-style resistance and of a secular-democratic state in the whole of Palestine. They have proposed a Palestinian state alongside Israel, usually in coordination with Arafat's PLO, not because of their own particular economic interests but because in the 16 years of day-to-day interaction with the Jewish state they have learned the futility of armed struggle and the likelihood that in a common state with the Jews they would be the woodcutters and water-drawers, suffering from economic exploitation and political oppression. But at the same time they have always refrained from establishing an alternative leadership to the PLO and initiating separate negotiations on the grounds that severance from the rest of the Palestinian people would condemn them to surrender and submission to the most discriminating and humiliating conditions set down by Israel.

It is no accident that the West Bank Palestinians reacted even more sharply to the autonomy plan envisaged by Camp David than did Arafat, who was ready to discuss an autonomy idea under certain conditions. The West Bank Palestinians fought not for local self-government but for an overall solution of the national problems—homelessness, refugee camps, dispersion, and lack of a national economy and sovereignty—from which they suffer no less than other sections of the Palestinian people. The Jewish community in Palestine before 1948 refused to renounce its Zionist aspirations in order to settle down with the Arab majority. Likewise there is little chance that West Bank Palestinians will give up a common struggle with the rest of their people in order to save what is left of their assets. Indeed, when King Husayn broke off relations with Arafat in February 1986 and called on the West Bankers to join him in talks with Israel, they instead rallied around Arafat.

The argument that the Palestinians might otherwise lose the last chance for national sovereignty because the West Bank would become irreversibly incorporated into Israel is factually wrong. The Likud government launched feverish efforts to change the demographic, economic, and political structure of the West Bank in a way that would make its incorporation into Israel irreversible. But after seven years of efforts to redesign the ethnic map of the West Bank and 19 years of occupation, no more than 50,000 Jews (representing less than 4 per cent of the population) reside in the occupied territories. Even the most ambitious plans for rural and urban settlements will hardly increase the percentage, whereas the implementation of these plans encounters more and more obstacles and a rising wave of doubts and opposition. And under the new National Unity government and Prime Minister Peres, the idea of further settlement has greatly receded.

The galloping inflation and the economic crisis in Israel necessitated limiting the budget for new settlement, whereas many of the established settlements—troubled by economic and social malaise—register waning memberships. Bankruptcy menaces government-sponsored construction firms engaged in housing schemes, and opposition to the settlement plans in the West Bank from underdeveloped townships and poverty areas in Israel is mounting. Among the moral and political repercussions have been the criticism from international and Jewish public opinion and the security problems raised by the arrogant behavior of fanatic settlers. A terrorist Jewish underground has come into its own, provoking stout protest among the Israeli public and leaving government circles embarrassed. On the other hand, the Palestinians in the West Bank, solicitous of the looming annexation, have mounted a strenuous campaign of reconstruction of their villages and towns—building schools, universities, and cultural clubs to inculcate the spirit of Palestinian nationalism into the younger generation.

No amount of intimidation and oppression by the military administration or of fanatic settler vigilantism is likely to defeat this spirit. The determination of the Palestinians in the West Bank to remain on their land and to cultivate their national consciousness and aspirations seems even more resolute today than before. On the Jewish side, the discovery of underground terrorism, which until now was conducted with impunity, has produced consternation and hampered the momentum of the settler movement. The war in Lebanon has proved that it is not the military balance of forces but the social and political dynamics that arbitrate the outcome of the battle. The Shia—the poorest, least organized and militarily weakest community—emerged as one of the most politically decisive factors in Lebanon; indeed it forced an Israeli withdrawal. Likewise, the future of the West Bank and Gaza will be determined not in the field of economic and military warfare but by psychological, political, and social dynamics.

Israel has the physical military power to dismantle and destroy an organized national structure in the West Bank, as it did in Lebanon. However, deprived of political freedom and a national, cultural, and economic infrastructure, proponents of Palestinian national aspirations would be likely to express themselves through unorganized and uncontrollable groups of suicide fighters engaged in blind desperate acts of vengeance and terror against those responsible for the Palestinian tragedy, including the United States. It is a historical fact that this kind of terror can not be prevented even by highly organized and powerful states: A state cannot prevent acts of terror perpetrated by small groups of fanatics—that indeed was the basic lesson of southern Lebanon. The continuation of oppression in the West Bank would spoil the last chance for a peaceful resolution to the Israeli-Palestinian conflict.

The Jews of the Arab World

The most spectacular and sophisticated acts of Palestinian terror took place in the early years when the PLO did not have an infrastructure and was not generally recognized as an authority in control by most of the Palestinians. Another wave of terror on an international scale arose after the destruction of the PLO headquarters and infrastructure and was followed by the expulsion of all PLO political and military cadres from Jordan by King Husayn in 1971. Although the Palestinian movement is now undergoing a very difficult internal crisis, it is far from disintegrating or losing its impact in the Arab world. The Zionist movement also underwent periods of crisis and division before 1948, but the objective situation of the Jewish people revived and revitalized it time and again.

The Palestinians are now the Jews of the Arab world. They have no choice but to struggle against their homelessness, dispersion, and lack of sovereignty; the Arab world has no choice but to support their struggle. The Arab world is today more divided and conflict ridden than ever. The Palestinian problem reflects all the internal contradictions and struggles, which increase the fermentation among the masses and endanger the stability of the régimes.

Glaring gaps divide the conservative states that fear the spread of communism and the Soviet Union and the so-called radical states that profess to follow socialist programs; this division has arisen even though neither group wants to become a tool in the superpowers' rivalry or a battlefield for their wars. A social gap in every state creates a wedge between the masses of workers and peasants living in traditional patterns of Arab-Islamic culture and the class of merchants, businesspeople, and landlords profiting from oil trade, government contracts, capital influx, and real estate and leading a cosmopolitan, mercantile lifestyle. Between military oppressive bureaucratic régimes and intellectuals, professionals, and trade unionists striving for popular participation in government, a serious struggle rages. In all of these fields, the Palestinian cause has become a symbol and a battle cry. For the Socialists and Communists, the Palestinians have symbolized the cause of the have-nots and the oppressed who aim at radical changes in Arab society and structure; for the radical nationalists, they have represented the vision of Arab unity; for the conservatives, the Palestinian cause is seen as a channel to divert the revolutionary mood of the refugees from social struggles in their countries toward the construction of their own national state.

In his dramatic initiative Anwar al-Sadat sought an answer to all these tensions and contradictions through a solution of the Palestinian problem and acceptance of Israel as a Middle Eastern state. The Israeli-Egyptian peace was to serve as a model for a peace settlement with all other Arab states which, it was hoped, would lead to a restoration of Arab sovereignty over the territories lost in 1967, to the actualization of Palestinian national rights, and to the integration of Israel into the Middle East. This settlement would have "lifted the nightmare of renewed military confrontation from the suffering anguish of our peoples,"[12] and allowed them to find ways "towards building peace together and beating their swords into ploughshares."

However, the Camp David meetings yielded something entirely different: a separate peace between Egypt and Israel shaped in the spirit of cold war strategy and a realignment of forces in the context of the U.S.-Soviet confrontation. The Palestinian problem was not resolved, the conflict between Israel and its adversaries in the East remained in full force, and the arms race escalated—sabotaging potential solutions to urgent social and economic problems. Begin's unilateral annexations of the Golan Heights and East Jerusalem, advances on the West Bank, suppression of Palestinian rights, invasion of Lebanon, and maintenance of military superiority over the whole Arab world could not but create a deadlock in the Camp David peace process—which, if perpetuated, will ultimately abort it. The Egyptian people and the intellectual political elite have paid the steep price of isolation and ostracism for their signature of separate peace. Though they regained all the territories they lost in 1967, they feel extremely frustrated and angry at Israel's exploitation of the peace treaty, for the invasion of Lebanon, for the unilateral annexations, and for the oppression of the Palestinians. Although Egypt gave up the military option for the solution of its own and the Palestine problem, it did not give up its commitment to Palestinian rights and to the principle of Egyptian centrality in the Arab world.

The United States' perceived complicity in Israeli policies has nurtured anti-American sentiment in Egypt and elsewhere in the Arab world. It has called into question U.S. credibility as a disinterested peace broker and the viability of the Camp David agreement. This complicity—taken together with Washington's failure to curb Begin's passion for building settlements, the lame pursuance of the September 1982 Reagan plan, the continuation of massive American aid to Israel in spite of the settlements in the West Bank, which the United States itself defines as an obstacle to peace, the strategic understanding that the Israeli Defense Forces should be superior to the combined Arab force, the U.S. refusal to initiate formal talks with the PLO—accounts for the growing disillusionment in the Arab world with the United States and its peace initiatives. The U.S. role in Lebanon, the interception of the Egyptian aircraft carrying Abul Abbas, and the April 1986 bombing of Libya have further inflamed Arab public opinion. Even the most pro-Western and pro–United States Arab countries are now despairing of America's willingness to conduct an even-handed policy leading to peace. The influence that the United States could potentially exercise over Israel's recognition or nonrecognition of the Palestinians is deemed considerable, and hence its non-use is all the more frustrating in Arab eyes.[13]

Events in mid-1987 reflected growing support for an international conference to deal with the Arab-Israeli conflict. Reports of an unofficial London meeting in April 1987 between Shimon Peres and King Husayn suggest that an acceptable formula may have been developed on the framework for such a conference that would allow participation of Palestinian representatives who are not members of the PLO in the Jordanian delegation.

While such reports are initially encouraging, optimism fades as one considers some of the other dynamics at work. Peres's discussions with foreign leaders about an international peace conference are strongly opposed by Prime Minister Shamir's Likud bloc. More serious is the fact that in May 1987 Peres brought the issue of an international conference before the Cabinet in an attempt to break up the National Unity government, but he failed to win sufficient support for his proposal to dissolve the coalition. Even if elections should somehow be held with an international conference as the major issue, there is no guarantee that Peres would succeed in winning majority support for his position. Implementation of the reported Peres-Husayn formula is further complicated by disputes between the various factions of the PLO. During the first meeting in three years of the Palestine National Council in Algiers April 20, 1987, Arafat was able to reunify the

PLO and win an endorsement, for the moment, of his leadership of the movement, but at a price. Arafat was obliged to abandon the 1985 agreement he had made with King Husayn (previously renounced by the king) under which the two leaders would seek a joint approach to negotiations with Israel.

The Palestinians and Arafat in particular are potentially key to the solution of the Arab-Israeli conflict, to the restarting of a real peace process, and to stability in the Middle East. But they are also a time bomb which, whenever it explodes, may ignite a new period of turbulence. The solution of this problem will also greatly affect the prospects of democracy, economic development, and social progress in all the countries concerned. In short, Israel today faces the basic choice of following the moral, ethical, and social values from which it drew its strength or of giving credibility to the charge that Zionism equals racism, apartheid, and militarism.

Notes

1. Chaim Weizmann thought that the focus of Arab interest is the Hedjar and the "triangle formed by Damascus, Mecca and Baghdad" and that the Palestinians presented not a political problem but an economic one, which in due time would be solved. Details are presented in S. Flapan, *Zionism and the Palestinians* (London: Croom Helm, 1979), pp. 56–57.

2. "There is no conflict between Jewish and Palestinian nationalism because the Jewish Nation is not in Palestine and the Palestinians are not a nation." Ben-Gurion's speech to the Inner Action Committee, Jerusalem, October 12, 1936, *ibid.*, p. 131.

3. See *Encounter*, November 1967.

4. Zeev Jabotinsky (1880–1940) was the founder of the Revisionist movement in Zionism, who appointed Menahem Begin as the leader of the dissident underground organization Irgun Zvai Leunir, which engaged in acts of terror against the British and the Arabs in Palestine and later established the Herut party in Israel. The party demanded and struggled for a Jewish state on both sides of the Jordan river and opposed the partition of Palestine.

5. For details on the debates on transfer in the Zionist movement, in the Jewish Agency Executive, and in the Histadruth, see Flapan, *Zionism and the Palestinians*, pp. 59, 259–265.

6. See *Political and Diplomatic Documents*, published by Israel State Archives and Central Zionist Archives, Jerusalem 1979; E. Janin to E. Sasson, January 4, 1948, Document 90, pp. 126–129.

7. See Ben-Gurion's diary, "The War of Independence," published by the Ministry of Defense 1982, January 4, 1948, pp. 112–114, and March 7, 1948, pp. 283–284.

8. Ben-Gurion's diary, p. 97; also report of A. Eban, December 16, 1947, in *Zionist Archives*, 525/5353.

9. *State Archives*, document 181, p. 331.

10. See *UN Palestine Conciliation Commission: Third Progress Report*, A/927, p. 8; Rony E. Gabbay, *A Political Study of the Arab-Jewish Conflict* (Geneva: Librairie E. Droz, 1949), p. 246.

11. See *Foreign Relations of the United States*, 1951, pp. 735–737. On June 28, 1951, King Abdallah said to Fisher, an officer of the PCC, in a personal and confidential talk, "I know that my time is limited . . . and that my own people

distrust me . . . because they suspect [me] of wanting to make peace without any concessions from Israel. . . . Without any concessions from them I am defeated before I can start." The king declared that he and his government were prepared to defy the Arab League, but "we cannot defy our own people." Among the concessions he regarded necessary were territorial adjustments in the triangle or elsewhere, a corridor to the Gaza Strip, and permission to propertied refugees to go to Israel to settle their affairs "to ensure at least income from their property if not the property itself."

12. See his message to the 20th Anniversary Symposium of New Outlook in November 1977, Tel Aviv, conveyed through Mark Bruzonsky. Before his departure from Jerusalem, Anwar al-Sadat also emphasized the centrality of the Palestinian problem in his meeting with a delegation from the symposium composed of Nahum Goldmann, Pierre Mendès-France, Inge Gebel, Shimon Shamir, Saul Friedlander, Sam Rubin, Dan Gillon, David Shaham, David Susskind, and the Editor of *New Outlook*, Simha Flapan.

13. These views have been well discussed and documented in Mark Bruzonsky, "The Second Defeat of Palestine," *Journal of Palestine Studies* 59, no. 1 (spring 1986), pp. 30–52.

10

The Palestinian Problem
and U.S. Policy

Bruce R. Kuniholm

The Palestinian problem derives from conflicting Palestinian and Israeli claims to Palestine. In its present form, the problem is essentially a clash between Israel's search for security and the Palestinian quest for self-determination. Meron Benvenisti, the former deputy mayor of Jerusalem, has emphasized the zero-sum nature of the conflict—"the perception, equally shared by both Israelis and Arabs, that what one side can win equals what the other side must lose"—and has argued that third parties have under-estimated difficulties associated with its resolution. Nevertheless, several U.S. administrations have asserted that the conflict is not a zero-sum game, that a mutually beneficial compromise is possible, and that the establishment of a Palestinian entity in the territories now occupied by Israel could be in the interests not only of the Palestinians but also of both Israel and the United States. Clearly, much would depend on the structure of the process to evolve such an entity, the guarantees that Israel would receive, and the overall context within which these developments would take place. History may offer scant hope for amelioration of the problem, but the imperatives that drive U.S. foreign policy demand that means be found to mediate and, if possible, reconcile the conflict between Arab and Jew. Even if reconciliation seems impossible, these imperatives suggest that an effort must nevertheless be made.[1]

The Question of Palestinian Self-Determination

This chapter examines the Palestinian problem and discusses its impli-cations for U.S. policy. As a means to this end, arguments for and then against Palestinian self-determination are considered in some detail. Since self-determination, unqualified by anything other than normal constraints, would lead to the establishment of a state for the Palestinians, the question of a Palestinian state will also be examined.

Establishment of a Palestinian state is not a solution that the U.S. government supports. Although Palestinians insist on it, the plan proposed by the Reagan administration in September 1982 opposes it, and the Israelis totally reject the notion. Instead the Reagan plan (in an approach similar to that favored by President Carter) proposes a compromise between Palestinian and Israeli desires—Palestinian self-government in association with Jordan.[2]

The extent to which the Palestinians should have self-government on the West Bank and Gaza—whether or not in association with Jordan—is the subject of serious controversy in all deliberations over the requirements for a comprehensive settlement of the Arab-Israeli conflict. Disagreements arise in debates within the Palestine National Council, the de facto Palestinian parliament, and within the World Zionist Congress and Israel. More than for any issue, the discussion of Palestinian self-government raises the question of entitlement to the West Bank and Gaza, which in turn lays bare the psychological and emotional factors at the root of the conflict. These factors explain why both the Palestinian leadership and the Israeli government until recently have rejected the Reagan administration's attempt to address their concerns, and to some extent they corroborate the judgment of those who see the Arab-Israeli conflict as a zero-sum game.

In view of these profound differences, the question of whether or not the Palestinians can or should determine their own future in the West Bank and Gaza Strip serves as a convenient framework for discussing the Palestinian problem. Presented in stark terms, the question may be somewhat artificial because whatever the outcome, the result will have to be a compromise; neither self-determination for the Palestinians nor its denial by Israel will be without qualification. Arguments for and against self-determination are not necessarily mutually exclusive and are subject to qualification and compromise. Nevertheless, approaching the question from two general points of view helps to focus the debate between the Israelis and Palestinians and allows for a relatively clear exposition of their primary concerns.

Our focus will remain on the Palestinian problem. We want in particular to avoid being distracted by the complications stemming from the war in Lebanon. The Israeli invasion of Lebanon was precipitated by the Palestinian problem, and Lebanon's future will depend as much on satisfactory resolution of that problem as it will on reform of the Lebanese political system. Our intention here is to provide those concerned about the broader questions of U.S. policy with some insight into the Palestinian context of the Arab-Israeli question; to illuminate the fundamental problems that continue to separate so many Palestinians and Israelis; to illustrate why certain concerns affect their differing perceptions of President Reagan's peace initiative of September 1, 1982; to provide a better sense of the gaps that will have to be bridged if a settlement is ever to be achieved; and to explore how the United States might encourage the process.

Arguments in Favor of Palestinian Self-Determination

The line of reasoning leading to the conclusion that the Palestinians need a state of their own begins with the premise that the creation of a Palestinian state (which the Palestinians want, and which would be consistent with their legitimate right to self-determination) would rectify previous injustices and restore Palestinian dignity. The Egyptians understand the importance of this psychological process. President Sadat's visit to Jerusalem in 1977 was made possible by the erasure in 1973 of Egypt's humiliating defeat of 1967.

The Israelis, too, should understand the importance of this process. The trial of Adolf Eichmann served as a first opportunity for many Israelis to face their past squarely. According to Amos Elon, the Eichmann verdict played a role in preparing the emotional ground for the resumption of normal relations with all things German. If Israel, with the help of the United States, addresses legitimate grievances and develops a fair solution to Palestinian problems, the Palestinians may finally come to terms with the Israelis.[3]

The 1982 war in Lebanon, which included the massacre of hundreds of Palestinians by Christian Phalangist militiamen, and for which the Israelis bear indirect responsibility, has underscored the Palestinians' need for a home of their own. Like the Jews before them, the Palestinians in their diaspora have been forced to conclude (with the help of the Jordanians in 1970–1971, the Syrians in 1975–1976, Lebanon's Christian Maronites in 1982, the Syrians again in 1983, and Lebanon's Muslim Shia in 1985) that only self-rule in a state of their own can ensure them control over their lives.

Like Israelis and Jews all over the world, Palestinians identify with the land of Palestine. Palestinians lived on the land for centuries. Before being ousted from a part of Palestine in 1948, Palestinians owned most of the land and constituted two-thirds of the population. Since then, Palestinians have lived under Jordanian, Egyptian, and Israeli rule and in exile. Israel has granted citizenship to Palestinians in Israel but has given them unequal treatment. Arab countries, except for Jordan, have not offered the Palestinian refugees citizenship, nor have the Palestinians desired assimilation. They prefer to maintain a separate identity, based on ties to the land from which they came and maintained by a developing sense of themselves as a nation in exile. A Palestinian state, which is consistent (as Israeli sovereignty over the occupied territories is not) with UN Security Council Resolution 242 and which is consonant with the ideal of self-determination embodied in the UN Charter, would meet their needs and fulfill their dreams.[4]

Most Palestinians—particularly those who live in the occupied territories— recognize that they cannot recover all of Palestine. They seek that part in which many still live: the West Bank (including East Jerusalem) and Gaza. A state formed from these territories, many believe, would not need to be a place of residence for all Palestinians. Some, under UN General Assembly Resolution 194 III of 1948, would seek compensation for their property rather than return. For others, the main issue is attainment of a political identity. But a Palestinian's right to return, most argue, must be no less than that accorded Jews under Israel's law of return, which provides every Jew a right to immigrate to Israel. Absorption, if it is a problem, should be one for the Palestinians to solve.[5]

Walid Khalidi, a prominent Palestinian scholar and member of the Palestine National Council, declared that only a Palestinian state is likely to effect a psychological breakthrough for the Palestinians under occupation and in the diaspora.[6] This approach explains the Palestine Liberation Organization's (PLO) condemnation of the September 1982 Reagan initiative. President Reagan's opposition to an independent Palestinian state meant that he rejected what the Palestinians regard as their inalienable right to self-determination. Instead, the United States continued to ask the Palestinians to recognize Israel without a quid pro quo (that is, without Israeli recognition of Palestinian national rights). Sabri Jiryis, an Israeli-Arab lawyer who subsequently became director of the PLO Research Center in Beirut, has observed that "recognition, like marriage, must be mutual." It should be the task of the United States to facilitate mutual recognition of national rights, the Palestinians would argue, because peace is possible only on the basis of mutual respect and dignity.[7]

If mutual recognition leads to the establishment of a Palestinian state, many of the factors that now fuel Arab hostility and Palestinian irredentism could be diminished. As the Fez Summit in September 1982 indicated, the Arab countries (with very few exceptions such as Libya or the People's Democratic Republic of Yemen) would endorse a solution acceptable to a majority of Palestinians. A Palestinian government, under the control of nationalists—who predominate in both the Palestine National Council and (even after the rebellion within its ranks) in the Fatah wing of the PLO— would probably be anxious to respect Israeli sovereignty and prevent terrorist attacks by ideologues and extremist groups. Why? To avoid the consequences of Israeli retaliation. Palestinians would now have something to lose, some-thing for which they themselves would be responsible. A port on the Mediterranean would serve the same function (that is, a hostage to fortune) that the city of Suez served on the Gulf of Suez in the rapprochement between Israel and Egypt.

Daily interaction between Israelis and Palestinians (approximately half of the West Bank's labor force now works in Israel) provides a reason to believe that, if the Palestinians are given the opportunity to be responsible for their own fate, mutually beneficial economic interaction would continue and even improve.[8] Brian Van Arkadie, who undertook a study of the West Bank and Gaza economies for the Carnegie Endowment, argued that the territories could benefit from wider leeway to define and pursue their own economic self-interest.[9] Whatever the case, the issue of economic viability may be irrelevant. Israel would not be economically viable without U.S. aid, whereas the moderates in the Arab world, led by Saudi Arabia, could provide financial support sufficient to ensure the viability of a Palestinian state and thereby limit Soviet influence over it. Furthermore, the inter-dependence between the economies of Israel, Jordan, and a Palestinian state could serve as a foundation for a common market economy. With over 50,000 university graduates and thousands of civil servants employed through-out the Arab world, the Palestinian human resources pool is better educated and more capable than that of most countries of the third world. In addition, the West Bank already has an indigenous political system with viable social, administrative, political, and institutional infrastructures that could serve as a nucleus for a national entity.[10]

Some prospect for resolution of the problem of Jerusalem is essential for progress on a political settlement. Palestinians regard access to the city as crucial because of its symbolic, emotional, political, and economic significance. Walid Khalidi has asserted that "without East Jerusalem, there would be no Palestinian state."[11] A number of analysts have examined imaginative alternatives for resolution of conflicting Palestinian and Israeli positions on Jerusalem. No one denies the difficulty of this issue, and most agree that it should not be dealt with at the outset of discussions; many believe that a solution is workable in the context of a comprehensive agreement on other issues. Their judgments are based on the feasibility of inventive formulae that establish a borough system or create two municipalities that circumvent thorny debates over territorial rights. Although not without problems, such proposals suggest that the positions of Israelis and Palestinians are not irreconcilable and that this most difficult problem need not preclude the establishment of a Palestinian state nor prevent an overall settlement of the Arab-Israeli conflict.[12]

On the important issue of security, Israel will always have a crucial deterrent: the power to crush the Palestinians should punitive action be required. If a Palestinian state were to be established, Israel obviously would have a difficult time deciding which hostile actions warranted various levels of punitive responses. It would have to develop a sophisticated concept of deterrence. Such a problem, however, is not insurmountable. The legitimacy and recognition accorded the Palestinian state, meanwhile, could foster the goodwill and predictable behavior necessary for peace. According to Major General Mattityahu Peled, former member of the Israeli General Staff in 1967, any knowledgeable Israeli who argues for keeping the occupied territories on security grounds is consciously lying. A Palestinian state, he has asserted, would provide Israel with far greater security than possession of that same territory ever could. Peled's opinion, however, is not repre-sentative of Israeli judgments.[13]

Another means of approaching the security question is through American guarantees, which could compensate for the loss of strategic depth and reinforce Israel's deterrent posture. Those guarantees could be made more credible by an Israeli stake in the NATO alliance (air bases, prepositioned project stocks, land-based air, and a role in defending strategic maritime areas in the eastern Mediterranean), which could establish the principle of interdependence between the United States and Israel.[14] In addition, security threats to Israel could be diminished by the broader context of a comprehensive Palestinian settlement. The Japanese and Austrian peace treaties after World War II contain useful precedents in that those countries chose to accept constitutional restraints on their military capabilities and their conduct of foreign policy, respectively. The Palestinians could do the same.

Many of the arguments that say that a Palestinian state would be in Israel's best interests are based on the limited nature of Israel's resources. Israel's enormous defense expenditures, which account for nearly 30 per cent of its national income (GDP), have contributed to triple-digit inflation since 1979 (117 per cent for 1981, 131.5 per cent for 1982, 190.7 per cent for 1983, and 444.7 per cent for 1984). Such rates cannot be sustained indefinitely.[15] Israeli trade deficits ($5.1 billion in 1983 and $5.2 billion in 1984) have also been problematic, and Israel's foreign debt of $24.4 billion is, in per capita terms, the largest in the world. According to one estimate, approximately 35 per cent of the budget is required to service the national debt.[16] Clearly, though peace would be expensive, continued hostility between Arab and Jew will cause an even greater long-term drain on Israel's resources, affecting not only the economy but, because of the trials of being an occupying force, the very psyche and identity of the nation. A Palestinian state, on the other hand, offers the possibility of true peace, a decreasing defense budget, a viable economy, and ultimately prosperity for both Arab and Jew.

Current demographic trends do not bode well for Israel's long-run viability as a Jewish state if it continues to hold on to the occupied territories. These trends include declining Jewish immigration (less than 11,000 in 1981), increasing emigration (20,000 in 1981), and the wide disparity between Arab and Jewish birthrates in Israel (the Israeli Arab population has a growth rate of 3.5 per cent, double the 1.8 per cent growth rate for Israeli Jews). Together these trends suggest that the 700,000 or so Arabs living in Israel (a figure that does not include those living in the occupied territories) will continue to increase relative to the approximately three million Jews who live there (an additional 500,000 Israeli Jews live outside Israel). If Israel retains control of the West Bank and Gaza (with a combined population of 1,240,000 Palestinians) over the next two or three decades, and demographic trends of the last decade continue, Jews could constitute a minority in Israel and the occupied territories[17] unless Israel chooses to step up repressive policies to drive the Palestinians out.[18]

If Israel persists in rejecting Palestinian self-determination, whether by repression or eviction, the foundations of Israeli society can only be eroded by the resulting hostility. According to a comprehensive study, Israel's methods of control over its minority Arab population will have to become more repressive if control is to be maintained. Repression is certainly characteristic of Israel's policies toward the Arabs in the occupied territories. Confiscation of land for the establishment of new Israel settlements, control of West Bank water resources, closure of Palestinian universities, censorship of library materials, dismissal and deportation of freely elected officials, prohibition of political assembly, detention without trial or explanation, curtailment of financial support for municipal services and development, and promotion of the so-called village leagues (armed and financed by the Israelis in spite of rejection by every well-known West Bank figure)—all are part of a policy that increasingly alienates the Palestinian Arabs, the vast majority of whom continue to support the moderate factions of the PLO.[19]

Israeli policies toward the Palestinians will also create difficulties for Israel's Jewish citizens who value the humanistic traditions of Judaism. Avraham Ahituv, who formerly headed Shin Bet (the Israeli equivalent of the FBI), in August 1983 publicly charged that Israel's settlements encouraged lawlessness and served as a psychological hothouse for the growth of Jewish terrorism. Settlers, he argued, have learned that illegal activities are sanctioned because the Likud government is politically sympathetic to their aims. Less extremist Israelis, according to Jonathan Kuttab, a Palestinian lawyer who is the director of a human rights office in the West Bank, are being inured to violence by a dehumanization of Palestinians (e.g., references by public officials to "two-legged animals" and "drugged cockroaches in a bottle"). In an essay styled as a eulogy for the humanistic tradition in Israel and a plea for a new beginning, Meron Benvenisti observed that the prospect of ruling over more than a million Arabs without full democratic rights raises serious concerns about Israel being either Jewish or democratic. It also raises the profound question of whether the entire Zionist conception can be made to fit the situation developing in Israel and the occupied territories.[20]

Israel, it can be argued, is progressively losing control over its own fate, and not just because of the erosion of its humanistic traditions. As a result of its limited financial resources and vast defense expenditures, Israel's gross foreign debt was $24.4 billion at the end of 1984 and rising steadily. In 1985 it cost Israel $4.265 billion to service its foreign debt (with over $1 billion in interest going to the United States, to which Israel owes $10.235 billion). Foreign aid generates approximately half of Israel's GNP, and 75 to 80 per cent of that aid, if one counts all means of support, comes from the United States. Economic and military assistance from Washington (not including private transfers, economic infrastructural support, contingency economic support, or consequential aid) has fluctuated since the Camp David accords between a high of $4.9 and a low of $1.8 billion a year. This amount, former Undersecretary of State George Ball has pointed out, equals roughly $3,500 to $4,000 per year for every family of five in Israel.[21] Recent trends, moreover, suggest that this dependency will increase. The amount of U.S. aid to Israel in FY 1985 was $2.6 billion—all in outright grants. In April 1985 a supplemental economic grant of $1.5 billion (to be split between FY 1985 and FY 1986) was approved by the U.S. Congress, and Israel was scheduled to receive an additional $3 billion in outright grants in FY 1986.

Financial dependency on the United States has unsettling implications for Israel. In recent years, an international consensus has emerged that one prerequisite for international security is an even-handed settlement of the Arab-Israeli problem (one that includes self-determination for the Palestinians). A reflection of this consensus was the August 1982 UN General Assembly resolution that called for the right of Palestinian self-determination and national independence "in Palestine." The vote in favor of a Palestinian state was 120 to 2 (only the United States and Israel dissenting) with 20 abstentions. If events should cause the U.S. Congress to reorder its current pro-Israeli priorities, there is an increased likelihood that the American government—until now steadfast in its support of Israel—could begin to reflect this international consensus. A logical consequence of this shift in attitude would not mean an abandonment of Israel but a gradual increase in acceptability of the concept that withholding military and financial aid to Israel is an appropriate means of encouraging cooperation. To the extent that Israel wants greater control over its own fate, it should take major initiatives on issues such as the Palestinian problem now rather than be subject to external pressures later.[22]

Arguments for Palestinian self-determination demonstrate that time is not on Israel's side. The risks of bold and meaningful initiatives for peace are dwarfed by those that could arise from a continuation of the status quo. The October War of 1973 made clear that maintenance of the status quo—which best describes the strategy followed in the aftermath of the 1967 war—was a prescription for continual unrest. On a symbolic level, the death of Anwar Sadat made the same point about the stalled autonomy talks. Neglect of the Palestinian question is not a viable policy. That problem has contributed to every major Arab-Israeli conflict, and in spite of periodic attempts to downplay its salience—a trend evidenced after the Israeli destruction of the PLO military infrastructure in Beirut in 1982, again after the Syrian ouster of the PLO from Tripoli in 1983, and most recently after the Palestinian-Shi'i conflict in southern Lebanon in 1985—the Palestinian problem has consistently reasserted itself as an issue whose resolution is central to any long-term peace. Sizable Palestinian populations remain in Lebanon, Jordan, Syria, and the West Bank, and the Palestinian problem will not go away.

Although Israel's defenses are more than adequate for the near future, projections of the Arab world's population (currently over 100 million), petroleum resources (well over 350 billion barrels of proven reserves), and military capabilities suggest that in the long run Israel (with its limited resources) can only lose by failing to tackle the Palestinian question in all its aspects. The ultimate well-being of Israel necessitates risks that can only grow with time, particularly if an unbending attitude toward the question of Palestinian self-determination, encouraged by the United States, lulls successive hardline Israeli governments into complacency and causes them to lose the opportunity for peace.

Deliberations in the twelfth Palestine National Council (PNC) in Algiers in February 1983 evidenced a profound concern that time, in the short run, was not on the Palestinians' side either. Gradual Israeli annexation of the occupied territories, some felt, could be prevented only if the PLO responded to the Reagan initiative and sought a "state" in confederation with Jordan. Arguing for a green light for King Husayn to participate in American-sponsored peace talks were moderates who hoped that, if Husayn joined the peace negotiations, the Reagan administration would give him strong support and work to obtain a full freeze on Jewish settlements in the occupied territories. Arguing against it were those who believed that painful concessions would lead nowhere in the face of Israeli intransigence and domestic American politics, leaving the PLO worse off than before. In the end, the Palestine National Council refused to accept the Reagan plan because it denied the Palestinians self-determination. The most that President Reagan has offered the Palestinians is "something in the nature of a homeland." The PNC did not, however, reject the plan outright—a conscious act designed to leave the door open for negotiations. The position of the PNC constituted at best a yellow light for King Husayn: The PLO did not approve of his negotiating on its behalf, but it did not intend to attack him if he did so.[23]

Ultimately, pressures within the Palestinian movement forced Yasir Arafat to opt for the cohesion of the PLO over the promise of limited self-government. Even then, his long deliberation over the choice led to destruction of the cohesion he sought to protect. Radicals supported by Syria—which has no stake in the Reagan plan and primarily seeks to ensure that its interests are not overlooked—objected to his leadership as well as to his conservatism. Fearing a sellout of what they regarded as their birthright, the radicals under Colonel Said Musa started a rebellion that for a time turned into a virtual civil war within the PLO. The dissidents' ties with Syria and Arafat's expulsion from Damascus in June 1983 appeared to discredit the rebels among the PLO's 20,000 fedayeen and led to enhanced support for Arafat among the Palestinians in Lebanon, Jordan, and especially the West Bank. But massive Syrian assistance to the rebel forces in northern Lebanon forced the expulsion of the PLO chairman from Tripoli in December 1983. As a result, Arafat's authority eroded, and though the Palestinian problem remained as important as ever, the direction of the Palestinian nationalist movement, subject to extended debate at the meeting of the thirteenth PNC in Amman in November 1984 and in key Palestinian councils after Arafat's February 1985 agreement with King Husayn on a "framework for common action," was in question.[24] At the PNC in Algiers in April 1987 Arafat was able to reunify the PLO and once again assert control over the nationalist movement. The price of cohesion, however, was isolation from Syria *and* Egypt and cancellation of the Amman Agreement of 1985.

A number of Israeli leaders have indicated a sensitivity to Palestinian needs. Former Foreign Minister Abba Eban has expressed his belief that an Arab destiny on the West Bank is inevitable and that Israel should consider how best to rescue its basic interests through steps such as modest but crucial territorial change, demilitarization, military balance, and mutual accessibility. Defense Minister Yitzhak Rabin has noted that the PLO cannot be eliminated by force and that the only solution to the problem of Palestinian attacks must be political. Shimon Peres, before he was elected prime minister, said that if his party came to power he would seek to open talks with Jordanians and Palestinians over the future of the West Bank and would limit the construction of Israeli settlements. As prime minister and then as foreign minister in Israel's National Unity government, he has sought to achieve these goals. The sentiments of these officials are not isolated. One 1982 poll in Israel found that over half of the population favored a return of territories in exchange for peace,[25] and a poll released by *Haaretz* in February 1985 indicated that 51.7 per cent of Israelis questioned opposed building more West Bank settlements (a sizable shift from October 1981, when only 29.2 per cent opposed more settlements).

On the other hand, Menachem Begin, while prime minister, expressed an intention to assert sovereignty over the occupied territories. During Begin's tenure in office, Israel asserted sovereignty over Syria's Golan Heights and unilaterally annexed East Jerusalem, where some 70,000 to 80,000 Jews now live within the expanded Jerusalem limits. During Begin's tenure, the West Bank's Jewish settlement population also increased sevenfold from 3,500 to at least 25,000, and the number of settlements more than tripled from 32 to 110.[26]

Meron Benvenisti has asserted that the effective annexation of the West Bank has very nearly been completed. Though a consensus concerning what to do about the West Bank has yet to emerge, de facto annexation clearly continues. Ze'ev Ben Yosef, spokesperson for the settlement office of the World Zionist Organization, said in August 1983 that the Jewish population of the West Bank would reach 70,000 by October, when 7,000 new family apartments were taken over by their owners. The Jewish Agency's projection of 100,000 settlers on the West Bank by 1985, though overstated (in March 1985 Benvenisti's best estimate was 42,600), is within reach by 1990 if Israel's housing industry maximizes its capabilities (3,000 cheap, subsidized flats a year, housing 12,000 to 15,000 people). If realized, such developments will make it increasingly difficult for any Israeli government to return occupied territory to Arab control and virtually impossible to effect a political solution to the intractable Palestinian problem. As a consequence, many believe that those who desire a peaceful resolution of these issues should press Israel to terminate any new settlement activities and support creation of a Palestinian state—or, at the very least, some viable form of Palestinian self-government—in the West Bank and Gaza before it is too late.[27]

Arguments Against Palestinian Self-Determination

Creation of a Palestinian state in the West Bank and Gaza poses serious ideological and security problems for Israel. Israelis are divided over alternative solutions to the Palestinian question, but they are with few exceptions united in opposing an independent, fully sovereign Palestinian state. As a result, many Israelis assert that American espousal of such a policy would eliminate the credibility of the United States in Israel, undermine U.S. influence with Israel in the peace process, and thereby jeopardize its interests in the region as a whole. Their reasoning illuminates the Reagan administration's advocacy of a Palestinian entity in association with Jordan. Officials in Washington did not in principle oppose the concept of self-determination; for them it was a question of what was acceptable within the context of U.S.-Israeli relations.

The Begin government, which saw such a Palestinian entity as a potential state and therefore rejected the Reagan plan, believed that the conflict between Israel's search for security and the Palestinian quest for self-determination was a zero-sum game. For Begin and his followers, Palestinian self-determination (which has become a codeword for an independent Palestinian state) directly challenged the government's claim to sovereignty over Eretz Israel (the biblical land of Israel) and threatened its very existence.[28]

Israel's rejection of a Palestinian state and insistence on sovereignty over the occupied territories derive in part from an understandable concern for security of the Jewish state. Two thousand years of persecution and the unspeakable trauma of the Holocaust together have instilled in the survivors what Amos Elon has called an existential sense of self-assertion in adversity. Zionist settlers who established Israel, Elon observed, were imbued

> with the relentless drive of drowning men who force their way on to a life raft large enough to hold both them and those who are already on it. If they were deaf to the legal protestations of the latter, it was not only because they considered the raft a birthright. . . . but because they were swept away in a storm so ferocious that conventional legality inevitably appeared in their eyes as a tragedy and mockery of higher justice.[29]

Former Prime Minister Begin, his successors in the government of Yitzhak Shamir, and the Likud faction in the unity government now headed by Shamir all share the beliefs and determination of those settlers described by Elon. Begin believed that Eretz Israel, including Judea and Samaria (the Biblical names he uses to refer to the West Bank), is a birthright promised in the Bible, and he refused to characterize as "occupied" what he insisted is "liberated" territory: "You cannot annex your own land. This is the land of our forefathers. You annex foreign land." Begin vowed never to divide again or hand over any part of Judea, Samaria, and East Jerusalem to foreign rule or sovereignty. Former Defense Minister Moshe Arens has declared that Israel will eventually annex the West Bank; and Yitzhak Shamir, when he was sworn in on October 10, 1983, as Israel's seventh prime minister, pledged to follow Begin's policies although he said he has no intention of annexing the West Bank. Shamir, referring to Israeli settlements on the West Bank and Gaza, told the Knesset that "this sacred work must not stop. It is the heart of our existence and life."[30]

The dedication, conviction, and sense of righteousness of Begin, Shamir, and their supporters in the Herut party and the Likud coalition, together with Israel's de facto control over the territories in question, appear to preclude any compromise on the issue of sovereignty and particularly any compromise on the question of a Palestinian state. This interpretation was corroborated, in the wake of Begin's August 1983 decision to resign, by failed negotiations over a government of national unity and was underscored by irreconcilable differences over settlements in September 1984 when a national unity government was formed. The denial of Palestinian self-determination, implicit in the Likud coalition's refusal to accept the position of the Labor party on the occupied territories, follows logically from the premise of Israel's claim to Eretz Israel and is rooted in a fundamental concern: Recognition of Palestinian rights would constitute acknowledgment that Jewish claims to the land of Israel were questionable. For Likud supporters, to divide the raft described in Elon's metaphor even now would be to sink it.[31]

Numerous supporters of Israel have attempted to rationalize this existential concern through a kind of moral calculus. Barbara Tuchman has argued that Palestinian refugees should be the responsibility of the 21 Arab states whose population is 40 times that of Israel and whose territory is 600 times the size of Israel. She and others also suggest that Arab states should be responsible for accommodating the 725,000 refugees (a UN estimate) from the 1948 war, their progeny, and the refugees from the 1967 war. They see this solution to the problem of Palestinian refugees as fair because Israel has had to accommodate approximately 500,000 Jews displaced by Arab states in the years following the creation of Israel. More recently, some have argued that, with the return of the Sinai to Egypt, Israel gave up 92 per cent of the territory it captured in 1967; the West Bank is an insignificant part of the whole and need not be given up. These and other arguments generally proceed from the assumption that Palestinians have no distinct national identity (i.e., they are Arabs), that distinctly Palestinian claims to the land are not legitimate, or that Palestinian claims are less legitimate than those of Israel.[32]

The implications of recognizing Palestinian claims have created problems for Israeli governments. If certain beliefs are crucial to national ideology and that ideology is regarded as central to national survival, challenges to the legitimacy of such fundamental beliefs directly threaten the nation's capacity to sustain itself. This line of reasoning helps explain why Israeli governments—led by both Labor and Likud—have consistently denied the legitimacy of Palestinian rights and a distinctly Palestinian national identity. It explains why Prime Minister Golda Meir in 1972 prevented the inhabitants of two Arab villages in Israel from returning to their land. The issue concerned pro-Israeli Christians from Bir'im and Iqrit who had been uprooted by the Israelis, whose homes had been destroyed, and whose land had been handed over to Jewish immigrants from Iran. Their plight became a *cause célèbre* among Israeli liberals. Among the reasons the prime minister gave for preventing their return was concern that it might intensify doubts about the righteousness of the Zionist cause. She feared that these doubts might

contribute to an erosion of Zionist ideology and prove to be a danger—
perhaps Israel's greatest—against which "not even Phantom fighter planes
can help."[33]

The threat posed by any compromise on the issue of historical rights
and sovereignty is central to the concerns of the Likud coalition, and it
helps explain the assertions of Yitzhak Shamir, Moshe Arens, and former
Defense Minister Ariel Sharon that "Jordan is Palestine."[34] Following World
War I, what is now Jordan was part of the land designated as Palestine
and mandated to the British by the League of Nations. It was later separated
from the Palestine mandate by the British, who restricted application of
the Balfour Declaration to the region west of the Jordan River. Although
the British had no intention then of creating a predominantly Jewish state
in all of this smaller area, many Israelis now apparently do. Because of the
influx of Palestinian refugees from various Arab-Israeli wars, a majority of
Jordan's population (approximately 65 per cent) is now Palestinian. Relating
this demographic development to the tenuous designation of Jordan as
Palestine, some Israelis, including Sharon, welcome a Palestinian takeover
of Amman. The resulting partition of "Palestine," for this group, would
absolve Israel of the obligation of making further territorial concessions
and would be consistent with Israeli claims to sovereignty over the West
Bank and Gaza.[35]

Many Israelis, particularly supporters of the Labor party who do not
necessarily reject a Palestinian state on ideological grounds, still reject this
course for reasons of security. The worst Israeli fear is that a radical
Palestinian state, with Soviet and Arab support, would attempt to realize
the goals articulated in the 1968 Palestine National Covenant and adopted
by the Palestine National Council. Palestinian endorsement of armed struggle
to liberate and exercise sovereignty over "Palestine" (i.e., Israel and the
occupied territories) heightens Israeli anxieties and reinforces the Israeli
belief that no compromise is possible.[36]

Israeli apprehensions about military security are well founded. Since
World War II, over 10,000 Israelis have been killed in battle against Arab
foes. Terrorism has also taken its toll. According to statistics compiled by
the Israeli Defense Forces, in the years from 1967 to 1980 a total of 3,174
terrorist attacks took place in the occupied territories and 1,306 in Israel.
In the course of these attacks, 230 Israelis were killed and 3,303 injured.
For many Israelis, the lesson of these statistics is clear: Israel cannot afford
the luxury of trusting a sovereign Palestinian state. Creation of such a state
would leave Israel with a narrow strip of land connecting its northern and
southern territories; it would expose 80 per cent of Israel's people to long-
range guns and rockets in the West Bank.[37]

From an Israeli perspective, territory and security are closely related.
The West Bank is essential as a buffer; control over it provides reasonable
assurance that it will not serve as a springboard for a large-scale attack on
Israel; access to it allows Israel to place early warning and control systems
and to deploy military forces along the Jordan Valley and in the central

mountain range. Palestinian sovereignty over the West Bank would decrease Israel's capacity to safeguard its security through these mechanisms of control. Road networks, constructed with Israel's defense in mind, and groundwater acquifers, whose mismanagement would cause irreversible salination of the acquifers in Israel's plains, would be subject to Palestinian control. Palestinian jurisdiction over Israeli actions on the West Bank, moreover, would cause hopeless complications, making an effective Israeli defense extremely difficult. As a result, if Palestinian sovereignty were not strictly qualified to the point where it became almost meaningless, Israel would be forced to return to a pre-1967 strategy of preemptive attacks when it felt sufficiently threatened.[38]

The difficulties associated with a strategy of preemption are suggested by the fact that Israel, though it possessed the plan for Operation Badr, was subject to strategic surprise during the 1973 war. Richard Betts attributed Israel's surprise to several factors: excessive reliance on the military balance of forces, an underestimation of ideological and psychological factors, the consequences of alert fatigue, and a reliance on stategic preconceptions that degraded the perception of tactical indicators. Clearly, without a territorial buffer (let alone a canal) to protect its eastern flank, Israel would constantly face the difficult task of interpreting risks. As the October War illustrated, this is no easy matter. Israel would also constantly have to assess the question of how much evidence warranted the costs involved in preemptive military action. These costs would be enormous, both for Israel and for regional stability.[39]

Terrorism presents Israel with an additional problem. Major General Raphael Vardi, a former head of the military government in the occupied territories and later comptroller of the Defense Establishment (Israel), believes that an effective strategy against terrorism necessitates freedom of action on the West Bank. Bitter experiences with terrorists have taught Israel that orderly life requires internal security. Internal security, in turn, requires a strategy of reprisals that places responsibility for terror on the states from which it originates. If one accepts Vardi's analysis, Israeli security requirements are incompatible with the concept of Palestinian sovereignty.[40]

For some Israelis, the problems associated with implementing an agreement on a Palestinian state, even if the sovereignty issue were capable of being resolved, are virtually insurmountable. What guarantees would Israel have? Who would ensure those guarantees? UN actions in recent years have failed to give Israel any confidence in that body. U.S. guarantees are also suspect. Israelis were not impressed by previous American commitments concerning the Straits of Tiran, nor were they pleased with the U.S. failure to monitor and then address Egyptian violations of the cease-fire between Israel and Egypt in 1970. As American Marines participated in the Lebanon peace-keeping force in the first months of 1983, Israeli officials complained that American troops were acting as a buffer behind which PLO terrorists were withdrawing after ambushing Israeli troops. The withdrawal of American troops from Lebanon in early 1984 further undermined confidence in the will of the United States to sustain a commitment in the Middle East. If Europeans occasionally doubt U.S. commitments to NATO, how could Israel doubt American commitments any less?

The refugee problem also poses practical difficulties for many Israelis. Israel, they believe, should exercise at least some control over Palestinian immigration. If a Palestinian state were established, who could return? How many? Who would monitor the process? If all Palestinians chose to come back to a new state, its absorptive capacity would be overtaxed and the immigrants could stimulate irredentism either toward Israel or toward Jordan (over half of whose population is Palestinian). The latter course could result in a radical Palestinian-Jordanian state. In any case, instability would be chronic. Arabs in Israel would demand incorporation in a Palestinian state, and the status of Israeli settlers on the West Bank would present constant problems. The trauma of removing 2,000 settlers from Yamit in the Sinai in April 1982 and the costs, both emotional and monetary, that were involved suggest the kinds of problems that would be posed by this issue which, like most issues in Israel, has security implications. As Attorney General Aharon Barak told President Carter at Camp David, settlers can serve as justification for the movement of Israeli forces into a region. This is one reason why Israel does not intend to remove its settlers from the West Bank. Yamit, former Defense Minister Ariel Sharon has stated, is the "Red Line" of Israeli concessions.[41]

If all these issues could be resolved, a Palestinian state would still face serious problems. What would ensure its moderation? Which countries would monitor the process and with what success? The experience of the Arab Deterrent Force and UN International Force in Lebanon is not promising. Many Israelis fear that the political and social gaps inherent in Palestinian society would quickly become manifest and serve as a source of instability. Would such an entity be economically viable? A small, poor state would be vulnerable to external manipulation by a host of countries, such as Syria, that have supported dissident factions within the PLO and that bear Israel ill will. How could one control external aid? Feuds between rivals such as Syria and Iraq and struggles between moderate and radical power alignments would play themselves out in a Palestinian state. Restrictions on military forces and weapons have never worked and would be resented. Verification would be a constant problem and would only stimulate nationalist fervor.

Israelis also worry that rejectionist groups such as the National Palestinian Salvation front, or subsets of this coalition of guerrilla factions such as George Habash's PFLP, would see a small state as only the first step in realizing long-term Palestinian goals and play on unfulfilled nationalist yearnings for a democratic, secular state in all of Palestine. They doubt that the state could prevent their attacks on Israel from bases in the state. Yasir Arafat was unable to curb the PLO, and King Husayn could not control the Palestinians in Jordan in 1970–1971.[42] Arafat's recent difficulties in Lebanon with the Abu Musa-led rebellion within the ranks of the PLO are hardly reassuring, particularly since Syria's President Hafiz al-Asad has made it clear that there can be no solution to the Palestinian problem without addressing Syrian interests. Syrian support for dissident activities within a Palestinian state and promotion of attacks against Israel from that state would force the Israelis to retaliate. The consequences of Israeli retaliatory policies would only add fuel to the fire. Eventually, many Israelis believe, whatever Palestinian government there was would fall or be overthrown and renege on its agreements. Chaos would reign.

The issue of sovereignty, for many different reasons, is at the heart of Israeli objections to a Palestinian state. As a brief review of recent attempts to mediate the problem will show, matters relating to the issue of sovereignty remain a major constraint on U.S. attempts to devise a constructive solution to the Palestinian question.

The United States as Mediator

At Camp David, the Carter administration sought to define a process that would temporarily circumvent the issue of sovereignty over the occupied territories. This approach would have permitted the Palestinian Arabs political self-expression while the Israelis maintained a presence that safeguarded their security and fulfilled what they regarded as their right to be there. Under the Camp David accords, Israel and Egypt agreed to provide full autonomy to the inhabitants of the West Bank and Gaza. Full autonomy was to be exercised through a freely elected self-governing authority during a five-year transitional period, with the status of the West Bank and Gaza and its relationship with its neighbors to be decided at the end of the period.[43]

President Carter apparently believed that the ambiguous formulation of autonomy for the Palestinians—a concept which, he noted in his memoirs, was debated for hours and never successfully defined—would allow for eventual agreement. In time, he hoped, agreement on autonomy would make it possible for Israelis and Palestinians to demonstrate their ability to live in peace and would lead to a solution that fulfilled the legitimate objectives of both.[44]

Prime Minister Begin's goals appear to have been both different and more limited: a separate peace with Egypt and, along with rejection of the concept of a Palestinian state, as free a hand as possible for Israel in the occupied territories. From a Palestinian perspective, full autonomy was a euphemism for Israeli control, which was never acceptable. From the Israeli government's perspective, full autonomy clearly meant something less than sovereignty, and it was to be exercised by the inhabitants of that land over themselves, not over the land itself. Begin subsequently reserved the right to assert Israel's claim of sovereignty to all the West Bank in negotiations on its final status and asserted that he would do so. His settlement policies, which his Likud successors support, suggest that at least his party intends to keep his pledge.[45]

Israel's early rejection of the Reagan plan of September 1, 1982, appears to corroborate this assessment of the Likud's intentions. The Reagan Plan asserts that peace cannot be achieved on the basis of Israeli sovereignty over the West Bank and Gaza but must be based on UN Resolution 242's formula of territory for peace. The plan opposes the creation of a Palestinian state on the West Bank and Gaza and instead states its preference for self-government by the Palestinians in association with Jordan, with the extent of Israeli withdrawal determined by the quality of peace offered in return.[46]

Prime Minister Begin's reaction was predictable. Rabbi Arthur Hertzberg, former president of the American Jewish Congress, put it succinctly: "The new American initiative has now made it clear, even to those who have preferred not to see, that if the forces of heavenly angels themselves were deployed to protect an Israel that had lost sovereignty over the West Bank, Menachem Begin would nonetheless stand before God and demand that He keep His promise to return the whole of their homeland to the Jews." Yitzhak Shamir, who was foreign minister at the time and who is now prime minister in the National Unity government, has insisted that Israel would never part with Judea and Samaria and that if the Reagan plan had been put forward as the American position at the time of Camp David, Israel would not have signed the accords.

This assertion, though undoubtedly correct, is misleading. As President Carter noted in his memoirs, Prime Minister Begin at Camp David rejected UN Security Council Resolution 242's stipulation that the acquisition of territory by war was inadmissible; instead, Begin argued that the 1967 war was a defensive act that gave Israel the right to keep and occupy lands taken in its own defense. Neither the United States nor Egypt accepted Israel's position or interpretation. If the ambiguous formulation on autonomy had been defined according to Israeli desires, neither Sadat nor Carter would have signed the accords. What they did sign, and what Begin signed, was a document sufficiently flexible to allow for compromise should good faith prevail. President Carter, meanwhile, reserved the right to put forward compromise proposals. Over two years after the date set as a goal for establishment of a self-governing authority for the West Bank and Gaza, no agreement had been reached in the autonomy talks; good faith had not prevailed.

The Reagan plan, drawn up in response to these developments, is consistent with the guidelines followed by Carter in the course of the negotiations at Camp David.[47] Differences of interpretation raise the question of whether it is in Israel's best interests to accept the Reagan plan as a basis for negotiations. Many Israelis, particularly those who support the Labor party, oppose the Likud's determination to retain sovereignty over all the occupied territories. They also share a number of the concerns voiced by proponents of a Palestinian state. They have serious problems, however, with the idea of sovereignty for the Palestinians—unless the concept is markedly qualified by safeguards essential to Israel's security. These safeguards, they reason, would be a fair exchange for the risks Israel would have to take were it to support full autonomy for the Palestinians. For this reason, they look to proposals that modify sovereignty and that include some combination of self- and shared-rule between a Palestinian entity, Jordan, and Israel.[48]

Meanwhile, the vociferous reactions of Begin, Shamir, and the Likud coalition to the Reagan plan—which calls for Palestinian autonomy in association with Jordan—make it obvious that espousal of a Palestinian state by the United States, however desirable in terms of some abstract principle of justice, and however consistent with the principles of self-determination of peoples codified in the UN Charter, is not likely to lead to it. None of the main political parties in Israel would support creation of a Palestinian state. The concept does not have any substantial support in the United States, and no serious presidential candidate was prepared to endorse it during an election year. Such a proposal would cause grave anxieties among Israelis, damage any possibility of a constructive alternative to the Israeli government's current policies on the Palestinian question, and undermine the American role as mediator and treaty guarantor.

Clearly, a modus vivendi is required. A number of Israelis who oppose a Palestinian state, and many Arabs who might prefer one, regard the Reagan plan as a constructive response to this situation. They see such an approach as a pragmatic alternative that deserves careful attention. The problem they have had with the Reagan plan is not so much with its proposals as with the administration's lack of political will in attempting to implement them.[49]

Despite events since the Reagan plan was announced, peace is not unattainable. Rather, the fundamental problem is a lack of political will on the part of the Israelis to compromise on the question of territory and Palestinian rights, on the part of the Palestinians to recognize and negotiate with Israel, and on the part of the United States to use its influence to facilitate a process of mutual accommodation that must take place if there is to be a peaceful settlement. Concerned institutions and individuals, such as those who collaborated on the Brookings Report in 1975, have isolated problems that need to be addressed. They have attempted to define principles that would govern a settlement and to explore the contents of a possible agreement. In the course of their endeavors they have examined the importance of safeguards, demilitarized zones, great-power guarantees, and various forms of assistance in reinforcing commitments. In an effort to avoid pressures for one-sided implementation of any agreement, they have considered carefully the role of stages in the process of implementation and reflected on the linkages between stages of withdrawal from occupied territory and manifestations of peaceful intent. To preclude military actions, they have looked hard at the interposition of force, limitations on military equipment, the creation of physical barriers, and zones of separation and denial. Their writings lead one to believe that practical implementation of a solution is not impossible and that it is not even the main problem. The most difficult problem, recent history suggests, is mustering the political will necessary to set the peace process in motion and encourage its realization.[50]

The key to thinking about a constructive solution to the Palestinian question is to avoid becoming immobilized by categorical positions and semantics and to support mechanisms that will permit the Palestinians to have as much real authority as possible over themselves, the West Bank and Gaza, and their resources, while simultaneously making it possible for the Israelis to avoid the security risks that they believe would be inherent in an independent, sovereign Palestinian state.

What Is to Be Done?

If one can accept the logic of these arguments, it follows that the American government, following the collapse in February 1986 of King Husayn's year-long peace initiative, has basically three options: letting things drift, trying again to revitalize the peace process, or pursuing an alternative strategy for addressing the Palestinian question in all its aspects. If the United States chooses to let things drift, it will leave the initiative to others; in such circumstances, it will have little option but to respond to events precipitated by Palestinian terrorism or resulting from Israeli policies such as the invasion of Lebanon and de facto annexation of the West Bank.

If the United States chooses to confront the Arab-Israeli conflict, on the other hand, and to address the Palestinian question whether through pursuit of the Camp David framework and the Reagan plan or some alternative, it must to some extent be able to count on Arab acceptance of the idea. Such receptivity was evidenced by President Anwar al-Sadat's willingness to go to Jerusalem in November 1977. Whether the opportunity will present itself again under King Husayn depends in part on the ability of the United States to draw Syria into the peace process (and undoubtedly relates to the prospects of the Golan being returned to Syria). It also depends on Arafat's courage in making some difficult choices and on the Reagan administration's willingness not only to come to terms with the Palestinian movement but to mediate the problem of mutual recognition of national rights. Finally, it depends on Israeli policies toward the West Bank.[51]

Israel's annexationist policies toward the occupied territories, more than any other problem, Carter administration officials believed, kept the United States from facilitating a process of mutual accommodation between the Israelis and Palestinians.[52] If this is still so and one accepts the argument that the practical problems of peace are not insurmountable, the crucial question concerns the extent to which the United States can exercise the political will necessary to set the peace process in motion. Because massive U.S. assistance to Israel to a great extent determines the constraints on Israeli policies and because Israeli policies have the potential not only to work against U.S. interests in the Middle East but to draw the United States into a global confrontation with the Soviet Union as well, it is only reasonable for the American government to consider carefully how and to what degree it can constructively influence Israel to cooperate in the peace process. The problem was not examined seriously during the 1984 election year, and has so far failed to be addressed by the second Reagan administration, whose opportunity to do so relatively free from domestic political pressures is quickly slipping away.

Carrots or Sticks?
The Question of U.S. Influence over Israel

A former member of the National Security Council staff, William Quandt, observed that during their terms in the White House, Presidents Nixon and Ford each subscribed to both of the following views at different times:

> If Israel is to feel sufficiently secure to make the territorial concessions necessary to gain Arab acceptance of the terms of a peace agreement, she must continue to receive large quantities of American military and economic aid.
>
> If Israel feels too strong and self-confident, she will not see the need for any change in the status quo. United States aid must therefore be withheld as a form of pressure.[53]

Though recognizing the complexities and importance of other factors, both presidents clearly sought some combination of carrot and stick that would cause Israel to take the steps necessary for peace. Since the period of the Nixon and Ford administrations, the search for an appropriate combination of inducements and pressures to influence Israeli policies has been central to the concerns of the Carter and Reagan administrations as well.

All recent American presidents and their closest foreign policy advisers, though conscious of the political liabilities involved, have sought repeatedly to exercise whatever influence they can muster in order to induce and prod Israel to be more responsive to American interests.[54] President Reagan and Secretary Shultz, in spite of their strong support for Israel, have not been exceptions. According to one well-informed correspondent, President Reagan promised King Husayn in December 1982 that the United States would try to halt the construction of Israeli settlements in the West Bank and Gaza. The president also reportedly told the king that he intended to press the peace plan outlined in his September 1, 1982, initiative, even though he knew that as a consequence he could lose the Jewish vote in 1984. Subsequent developments, however, proved the president's resolution to be limited. In March 1984 King Husayn announced that he was not prepared to enter into U.S.-sponsored negotiations with Israel on the problem of the West Bank. His decision was precipitated by the administration's refusal to support a draft resolution in the United Nations calling Israeli West Bank settlements illegal and by the president's rejection of the king's request to use his influence with Israel to facilitate the attendance of moderate West Bank leaders at the November 1984 meeting of the Palestinian National

Council.[55] Following the February 1985 agreement between Husayn and Arafat, equally problematic complications attended the acceptability of Palestinians to the joint delegation of Jordanians and Palestinians who might meet with U.S. representatives and possibly participate in negotiations over the future of the occupied territories. In February 1986 King Husayn terminated his efforts to coordinate plans with the PLO, and in April 1987 the PNC in Algiers formally cancelled the agreement with Husayn. While the United States strongly endorsed the idea of an international peace conference, the question of who should represent the Palestinians remained one of several major impediments to its realization.

It is doubtful that a second Reagan administration will be any more successful than its predecessors in influencing Israel to take the steps necessary for peace. Israel's massive settlement activity on the West Bank (not to mention the determination of the Likud coalition to annex the West Bank and Gaza) will pose serious obstacles to progress. The American presidential campaign in 1984 showed both major candidates pledging complete support for Israel and avoiding any specific discussions of the requirements for peace in the region. The National Unity government installed in Israel in September 1984 is seriously divided and promises little more than *l'immobilisme* of the Fourth French Republic, especially since Yitzhak Shamir is now prime minister.

In the meantime, speculation over presidential strategy continues, particularly by some who view the Reagan Plan as having had a hidden agenda which is still valid. The United States would have been naive, they assert, to believe that Begin's mind could ever have been changed. As a consequence, they conceive of the plan as intended not to influence Begin or his successors but rather to draw King Husayn into the peace process (in a manner that exhibits greater commitment than his initiatives to date). The importance of Husayn's involvement, they believe, would be to precipitate within Israel a movement responsive to his initiative and opposed to the policies pursued by the Likud coalition. If a movement were to develop, it would be significant because it could precipitate a coalition crisis, a new election, and a clear Labor majority in the Knesset. Foreign Minister Peres's inability to obtain government support for an international conference, however, and his inability to force new elections in Israel in May 1987 (they are not required until October 1988), suggest that hope for the development of such a movement is at best premature. In its absence, the United States is forced to focus on procedure over substance since it is difficult to legitimize opposition within the United States to the policies of the Likud. U.S. pressure on Israel would be much more effective if it were correctly characterized as anti-Likud rather than anti-Israeli. Common ground between the U.S. government and the Labor party within Israel would also help destroy the credibility of polemicists in this country who could confuse the ensuing debate by accusing anyone who criticizes policies espoused by the Likud of being anti-Semitic.[56]

In a thoughtful analysis, political scientist Ian Lustick has argued that American initiatives should be designed to affect Israeli politics rather than

Israeli policies and suggested a possible course by which to create conditions supportive of substantial shifts in Israeli politics. Because his proposals could affect the mindsets of the negotiating parties, Lustick has offered a constructive contribution to a resolution of the Arab-Israeli conflict.[57]

The United States, Lustick asserts, must stop characterizing the present as a not-to-be-missed opportunity; instead, it should prepare for years of patient diplomacy, backed by concrete measures that shape the context of Israeli policies. He opposes direct use of Israel's military and economic dependence on the United States to manipulate Israeli policies or politics. Such a course, he argues, would generate a severe backlash in Israel, raise a storm of protest in the United States, and send a dangerous signal to the Arabs that concessions from them are unnecessary. Lustick would prefer to use leverage in a less confrontational, more indirect manner. One of the measures he suggests is voicing opinion about the legal status of the settlements. According to the 1907 Hague Convention and a unanimous declaration by Israel's High Court of Justice, he points out, any "permanent" settlement is ipso facto illegal.[58]

According to former Secretary of State Cyrus Vance, the long-standing U.S. position on settlements is that they are contrary to international law and an obstacle to peace. President Reagan's position, however, has been more difficult to define. It includes a statement in February 1981 that the settlements might have been ill advised and unnecessarily provocative, but not illegal; a statement in May 1983 that Israeli settlements did not pose an obstacle to peace; and a veto in August 1983 of a UN Security Council resolution that said Israeli settlements in the West Bank had no legal validity and were a major and serious obstruction to peace. The administration's objection to the resolution rested in part on the view that characterization of Israeli settlement policy as having no legal standing is inconsistent with the views of the United States. A State Department spokesperson also asserted that the resolution's call for dismantlement of existing settlements was impractical and that the implication that Israel was expelling the Arab population from the occupied territories was unfounded. King Husayn has refused to accept the U.S. explanation of its veto, which he regards as "totally unacceptable, inadequate and unsatisfactory." Unless the United States can clarify its position and speak with one voice about the settlements, voicing opinion about their legality (or illegality) will have little effect on Israel. Israeli settlement activity, according to American and Egyptian officials, more than anything else undermined the credibility of the Camp David process. Until such activity ceases, it is hard to see how the United States can have any credibility as a mediator in the Arab world.[59]

Lustick also advocates giving concrete effect to U.S. opposition to Israeli settlements. He supports deducting from aid to Israel amounts estimated to have been spent in the previous year on settlements in the occupied territories. "The key to success," Lustick observes, "lies in the convincing promotion of U.S. ideas that affect the rhetorical and political resources available to competing Israeli groups." Although former Defense Minister

Moshe Arens has said that Israeli expenditures on the West Bank "are the last investments we would give up under the most stringent conditions because we feel that our very physical security depends on what we do in Judea and Samaria," Lustick's suggestion, particularly if it were carried out on a progressive basis, could have considerably more influence than Arens is willing to acknowledge. Israel is not spending millions of dollars on West Bank settlements; it is spending billions.[60]

Ultimately, finding the right combination of carrot and stick that would cause Israel to take the steps necessary for peace requires more imagination and will than recent administrations have devoted to the task. Clearly, the United States can provide a considerable number of incentives—beyond massive economic aid—for Israel to cooperate with well-conceived initiatives. Security arrangements and U.S. guarantees, for example, could help to compensate for the loss of strategic depth on the West Bank; such guarantees could be made more credible by an Israeli stake in the Western alliance and could establish the important principle of interdependence between the United States and Israel.[61]

But providing Israel with guarantees, aid, and support, without a constructive Israeli response to American interests in general and to White House peace initiatives in particular is counterproductive because it deprives the United States of important leverage in the negotiations that must take place.[62] Such a course of action reduces one of Israel's primary incentives to freeze its settlement activities; it also eliminates one of the factors most likely to bring home to the Israelis the enormous cost of continuing their unenlightened policies toward the West Bank and Gaza.

The United States can wield a stick, force the Israelis to respond to U.S. interests, and coerce them into supporting U.S. peace initiatives only at the risk of feeding their worst fears and causing them to become absolutely intransigent. Clearly, the impetus toward autonomy for the Palestinians, and hence toward a settlement of the Palestinian problem, must come from the Israelis themselves; it must come from internal debates and careful assessments of their current policies. This development is possible, however, only if the United States allows it to evolve naturally and does not impede it by making it possible for the Israelis to avoid the economic, political, and moral consequences of the policies they choose to pursue. The argument here is that the United States should provide the carrot, but in such a way that it allows the Israeli government to confront the fact that it wields its own stick.

Notes

1. Meron Benvenisti, *Jerusalem: Study of a Polarized Community* (Jerusalem: West Bank Data Base Project, 1983), p. 121.

2. For Carter's preference that the Palestinians have a homeland tied to Jordan or a larger confederation, see Cyrus Vance, *Hard Choices: Critical Years in America's Foreign Policy* (New York: Simon and Schuster, 1983), p. 177.

3. Amos Elon, *The Israelis: Founders and Sons* (New York: Bantam Books, 1971, 1972), p. 280.

4. Those who seek to legitimate the Palestinian cause argue that the Palestinians deserved the right to independence after World War I. Among the factors contributing to this judgment are President Woodrow Wilson's espousal of autonomous development for nationalities under Ottoman rule in his Fourteen Points; the agreement in 1915 between the Emir Husayn, sherif of Mecca, and Sir Henry McMahon, the British high commissioner in Egypt, which under one reasonable interpretation promised independence to the Arabs in Palestine; and the Arab revolt against the Turks in 1916, which fulfilled the terms of the agreement. Instead, against the wishes of the people (as evidenced by the findings of the King-Crane Commission), the British mandate ignored the right of the Arabs in Palestine to self-determination and imposed upon them a pro-Zionist solution that could only be carried out by force of arms. See George Antonius, *The Arab Awakening: The Story of the Arab National Movement* (New York: Capricorn Books, 1946, 1965), pp. 164–183, 413–427, 443–458. During the course of the mandate, others argue, an important part of the Balfour Declaration was disregarded (the clause noting the clear understanding "that nothing shall be done which may prejudice the civil and religious rights of existing non-Jewish communities in Palestine"). The 1947 UN decision to partition Palestine continued the history of bias against the Palestinians; it was reflected not only in how the boundary lines were drawn (56 per cent of the land went to one-third of the population, which only owned 6 per cent of it) but in who voted for and against partition (i.e., former colonial powers and their friends against emerging third world countries). See Fawzi Asadi, "Some Geographic Elements in the Arab-Israeli Conflict," *Journal of Palestine Studies* 6 (autumn 1976), pp. 79–91.

5. As Palestinian author Fawaz Turki has written, "Palestine is no longer a mere geographical entity, but a state of mind. The reason, however, that Palestinians are obsessed with the notion of Return, though indeed there is no Palestine to return to as it was a quarter of a century before, is because the Return means the reconstitution of a Palestinian's integrity and the regaining of his place in history. It is not merely for a physical return to Palestine that a lot of men and women have given or dedicated their lives, but for the right to return of which they have been robbed." (*The Disinherited: Journal of a Palestinian Exile*, second edition [New York: Monthly Review Press, 1972, 1974], pp. 175–176.) International acceptance of a Palestinian identity is relatively recent. The Balfour Declaration (1917) referred to Palestinians (then 90 per cent of the population) as one of the "existing non-Jewish communities," whereas UN Security Council Resolution 242 (1967) referred to Palestinians as "the refugee problem." For elaboration of the argument that the Palestinians have a legal right to self-determination under international law, see W. Thomas Mallison and Sally V. Mallison, "The National Rights of the People of Palestine," *Journal of Palestine Studies* 9 (summer 1980), pp. 119–130.

6. Walid Khalidi, "Thinking the Unthinkable: A Sovereign Palestinian State," *Foreign Affairs* 56 (July 1978), pp. 695–713.

7. Sabri Jiryis, "On Political Settlement in the Middle East: The Palestinian Dimension," *Journal of Palestine Studies* 7 (autumn 1977), pp. 3–25. For a reiteration of this formula in November 1982 by Khalid Hassan, chairman of the foreign relations committee of the Palestine National Council, see the *Christian Science Monitor*, November 4, 1982. Hassan believed that Israel would not recognize the PLO even if the PLO recognized Israel's right to exist and that this is why the United States wanted Jordan to negotiate for the Palestinians. At present, the United States will not talk with the PLO unless it accepts UN Resolutions 242 and 338

and recognizes Israel's right to exist (conditions stipulated in 1975 in an agreement between Israel and the United States). See Philip Geyelin, *Washington Post*, May 8, 1985, and the letter by Mel Levine, May 25, 1985. The problems this policy poses for moderate Palestinians continue to be stumbling blocks.

8. Meron Benvenisti pointed out that officially 39,000 (29 per cent) out of 131,000 are employed in Israel but that 20,000 are unofficially employed and 15,000 are employed in local West Bank enterprises that serve as Israeli subcontractors (Meron Benvenisti, *The West Bank and Gaza Data Base Project*, Interim Report no. 1 [Jerusalem: The West Bank Data Base Project, 1982], p. 5). According to Trudy Rubin, *Christian Science Monitor*, August 16, 1983, 38,000 Palestinian laborers commute daily to fields, factories, and construction sites in Israel.

9. Brian Van Arkadie, *Benefits and Burdens: Report on the West Bank and Gaza Strip Economies Since 1967* (New York: Carnegie Endowment for International Peace, 1977), p. 154; Vivian Bull, *The West Bank—Is It Viable?* (Lexington, Mass.: Heath and Company, 1975); and Elias Tuma, "The Economic Viability of a Palestinian State," *Journal of Palestine Studies* 7 (spring 1978), pp. 102–124.

10. Emile Nakhleh, *The West Bank and Gaza: Towards the Making of a Palestinian State* (Washington, D.C.: American Enterprise Institute, 1974), p. 65. John Cooley, *Green March, Black September: The Story of the Palestinian Arabs* (London: Frank Cass, 1973), p. 69, put the number of university graduates at 50,000.

11. Khalidi, "Thinking the Unthinkable," p. 705.

12. Evan Wilson, *Jerusalem: Key to Peace* (Washington, D.C.: Middle East Institute, 1970); Eugene Bovis, *The Jerusalem Question* (Stanford, Calif.: Hoover Institution Press, 1971); Meron Benvenisti, *Jerusalem, the Torn City* (Minneapolis: University of Minnesota Press, 1976); and Benvenisti, *Jerusalem: Study of a Polarized Community.*

13. "Israel on the Edge of Elections: An Israeli General and Two Palestinian Mayors Talk About the Future," *Village Voice*, May 27–June 2, 1981; a variation of this idea was expressed by King Husayn to Secretary Vance: "Security is less a matter of geography and borders than a state of mind and a feeling of wanting to live in peace" (Vance, *Hard Choices*, p. 176).

14. For discussion of this issue, see Shai Feldman, "Peacemaking in the Middle East: The Next Step," *Foreign Affairs* 60 (spring 1981), pp. 756–780.

15. See Samih Farsoun, "Begin's Distractionism," *New York Times*, August 2, 1982; *International Herald Tribune*, August 11, 1983; *Jerusalem Post* (International Edition), November 17, 1984; and CRS Issue Brief IB85066 (updated April 30, 1985).

16. See Bernard Avishai, "The Victory of the New Israel," *New York Review of Books*, August 13, 1981; Trudy Rubin, *Christian Science Monitor*, August 26, 1983; and CRS Issue Brief IB84138 (updated April 30, 1985), Table 4.

17. Samih Farsoun, *New York Times*, August 2, 1982; see Dwight Simpson, "Israel After Thirty Years," *Current History* 76 (January 1979). Arthur Hertzberg more recently has argued that this demographic argument is probably not true. The high rate of emigration from the West Bank, according to Hertzberg, means that the high birthrate in the region does not dictate a growth in the Arab population. Hertzberg, "Israel and the West Bank: The Implications of Permanent Control," *Foreign Affairs* 61 (summer 1983), pp. 1064–1077. Uziel Schmelz of the Israeli Bureau of Statistics, however, has observed that in 1982 net emigration from the West Bank dropped by half in comparison with that in recent years because of the slide in the oil economy of the Gulf and the greater political problems for the Palestinians in their diaspora (Trudy Rubin, *Christian Science Monitor*, August 16, 1983).

18. According to sources cited by Arthur Hertzberg, former Defense Minister Ariel Sharon hoped the Lebanese War would start a flight of Palestinians to the

eastern borders and, eventually, to Jordan. Hertzberg, "The Tragedy and the Hope," *New York Review of Books*, October 21, 1982. Joseph Harsch in the *Christian Science Monitor*, November 9, 1982, also noted that the Israelis "are frank about their intention to push most of the Arabs out of the West Bank and Gaza into Jordan." Palestinians, needless to say, are not assured by off-hand remarks such as deputy Knesset speaker Meir Cohen's comment that present troubles could have been avoided if 200,000 to 300,000 Palestinians had been driven from the West Bank in 1967 as they had been expelled in 1948. Fears of being forced to leave were heightened by violence in Hebron in summer 1983 (Meir Cohen, *Christian Science Monitor*, August 11, 1983). See also Jonathan Kuttab, "Palestinians See Expulsion Coming," *International Herald Tribune*, August 4, 1983. For similar concerns in Lebanon, where the Lebanese government desired to evict as many as 300,000 Palestinians, see Bernard Gwertzman, *International Herald Tribune*, August 18, 1983. In light of events, it seems clear that Fouad Ajami's assessment is correct: "The war in Lebanon was a war for the West Bank" (Ajami, "The Shadows of Hell," *Foreign Policy* 48 [fall 1982], pp. 94–110). This opinion is echoed by former Assistant Secretary of State Harold Saunders, who argued that the Israeli invasion "was designed to destroy once and for all any hope among the people of the West Bank and Gaza that the process of shaping the Palestinian people into a nation could succeed. It was designed to break any final resistance to total Israeli control" (Harold Saunders, "An Israeli-Palestinian Peace," *Foreign Affairs* 61 [fall 1982], pp. 100–121). Ironically, the Israeli ambassador to London Shlomo Argov, whose shooting was used as a pretext for the invasion, has charged that the "senseless" adventure has weakened Israel (*Christian Science Monitor*, July 11, 1983).

19. Ian Lustick, *Arabs in a Jewish State: Israel's Control over a National Minority* (Austin: University of Texas Press, 1980), pp. 266–271; see also Bernard Avishai, "Do Israel's Arabs Have a Future?" *New York Review of Books*, February 19, 1981.

20. Ann Mosely Lesch, *Political Perceptions of the Palestinians on the West Bank and Gaza Strip* (Washington, D.C.: Middle East Institute, 1980); for more recent evidence of West Bank support for Arafat, see Trudy Rubin, *Christian Science Monitor*, July 1, 1983; David Ottaway, *International Herald Tribune*, July 13, 1983; Edward Walsh, *Washington Post*, August 24, 1983; Trudy Rubin, *Christian Science Monitor*, August 25, 1983; and Meron Benvenisti, "The Turning Point," *New York Review of Books* 30, October 13, 1983, pp. 11–16.

21. Trudy Rubin, *Christian Science Monitor*, December 8, 1981; Thomas Stauffer, *U.S. Aid to Israel: The Vital Link* (Washington, D.C.: Middle East Institute, 1983); "Washington's Commitment," *New York Times*, August 8, 1982; George Ball, "Recast Ties to Israel," *New York Times*, July 28, 1982; David Francis, "Total U.S. Aid to Israel—Its Dimensions, Implications," *Christian Science Monitor*, August 9, 1982; the *Jerusalem Post* (International Edition), November 17, 1984; *Christian Science Monitor*, May 1 and 3, 1985; and CRS Issue Brief IB84138 (updated April 30, 1985).

22. "Demand for a Palestine State is Renewed in a Vote at U.N.," *New York Times*, August 20, 1982.

23. Robin Wright, *Christian Science Monitor*, February 15 and 16, 1983; Trudy Rubin, *Christian Science Monitor*, February 15, 18, 23, and 24, 1983; Harry Ellis, *Christian Science Monitor*, February 23, 1983; and Hedrick Smith, *New York Times*, February 24, 1983.

24. For assessments of Arafat's position, see Thomas Friedman, *International Herald Tribune*, June 4 and 5, 1983; Trudy Rubin, *Christian Science Monitor*, July 6, 1983; Eric Rouleau, "The Future of the PLO," *Foreign Affairs* 62 (fall 1983), pp. 138–156; and more recently, Herbert Denton, *Washington Post*, March 26, 1985, and Mary Curtius, *Christian Science Monitor*, June 5, 1985.

25. See the editorial in the *New York Times*, June 10, 1979; David Shipler, *New York Times*, June 13, 1980; Benvenisti, *The West Bank and Gaza Data Base Project*, pp. 62–63, noted that the Labor party supports annexation of 40 per cent of the West Bank; Hertzberg, "Israel and the West Bank," pp. 1069–1070; *Jerusalem Post*, September 3, 1982; *New York Times*, September 4, 1982, and August 6, 1985. Of 1,937 adults interviewed, 51.2 per cent were willing to give up parts of occupied territory in return for peace; 53 per cent opposed annexation and favored compromise; 46.8 per cent, on the other hand, were opposed to giving up even one inch of territory. See also Mary Curtius, *Christian Science Monitor*, February 5, 1985.

26. Trudy Rubin, *Christian Science Monitor*, September 2 and 3, 1982, and August 15, 1983; Ned Temko, "The Struggle for the West Bank," *Christian Science Monitor*, January 4, 1982. The third Drobles Plan calls for the establishment by 1987 of 57 new settlements, 20 of which have already been approved (*Christian Science Monitor*, August 17, 1983).

27. "First Step to a Solution," *New Outlook*, May 1981; David Shipler, *New York Times*, September 12, 1982; Trudy Rubin, *Christian Science Monitor*, November 5, and 10, 1982, and August 17, 1983; Benvenisti, *The West Bank and Gaza Data Base Project*, p. 55; Hertzberg, "Israel and the West Bank," p. 1070; *Christian Science Monitor*, March 29, 1985. For an articulate examination of a Palestinian state as being Israel's best strategic choice among relatively less appealing alternatives, see Mark Heller, *A Palestinian State: The Implications for Israel* (Cambridge, Mass.: Harvard University Press, 1983).

28. Vance, *Hard Choices*, pp. 183–184.

29. Elon, *The Israelis*, pp. 240, 259. Arthur Hertzberg, in explaining the popularity of Begin's West Bank policy among those who do not share his ideological motivations, noted that it speaks for one of the deepest emotions of world Jewry: "anger at the results of Jewish powerlessness in the age of Hitler" (Hertzberg, "Israel and the West Bank," p. 1066). See also Christopher Sykes, *Crossroads to Israel, 1917–1948* (Bloomington, Ind.: Indiana University Press, 1965), pp. 269, 277.

30. U.S. Congress, House, *Perspectives on the Middle East Peace Process*, December 1981, Hearings, Subcommittee on Europe and the Middle East, Committee on Foreign Affairs (Washington, D.C.: Government Printing Office (GPO), 1981) pp. 50–51, 113. *International Herald Tribune*, September 9, 10, and 11, 1983; Trudy Rubin, *Christian Science Monitor*, October 7, 1983. Irreconcilable issues that surfaced during negotiations between Labor and the Likud following Begin's resignation included Labor's desire for the principle of territorial compromise and for limitation of new settlements to areas that Israel considered essential to its security. The Likud, of course, rejected Labor's desires.

31. Edward Walsh, *International Herald Tribune*, October 1–2, 1983; Trudy Rubin, *Christian Science Monitor*, October 7, 1983; and the *Jerusalem Post* (International Edition), September 2–8, September 9–15, October 6, 1984.

32. Barbara Tuchman, "A Task for the Arabs," *New York Times*, July 25, 1982; U.S. Congress, House, *Perspectives on the Middle East Peace Process*, pp. 113–114.

33. Joseph Ryan, "Refugees Within Israel: The Case of the Villagers of Kafr Bir'im and Iqrit," *Journal of Palestine Studies* 2 (summer 1973), pp. 55–81.

34. Trudy Rubin and Daniel Southerland, *Christian Science Monitor*, September 2, 1982; George Will's columns in the *Washington Post*, September 2, 5, and 9, 1982; U.S. Congress, House, *Perspectives on the Middle East Peace Process*, p. 51; Yitzhak Shamir, "Israel's Role in a Changing World," *Foreign Affairs* 60 (spring 1982), pp. 789–801. Some of these matters are clarified by Bernard Lewis, "The Palestinians and the PLO: A Historical Approach," *Commentary* 59 (January 1975),

pp. 32–46, and by L. Dean Brown, The Land of Palestine: West Bank Not East Bank (Washington, D.C.: Middle East Institute, 1982), which underscores the speciousness of the "Jordan is Palestine" campaign.

35. Arthur Hertzberg, New York Review of Books, October 21, 1982. For discussion of the Balfour Declaration, see Leonard Stein, The Balfour Declaration (New York: Simon and Schuster, 1961). The Balfour Declaration, an important source of legitimacy for Israel, was quoted in full in the British mandate for Palestine, which was sanctioned by the League of Nations.

36. Excerpts from the covenant along with the Palestine National Council's Ten Point Program are reprinted in Wolf Blitzer, ed., Myths and Facts, 1976 (Washington, D.C.: Near East Report, 1976), pp. 72–79.

37. According to Trevor Dupuy, the number of Arabs and Israelis killed in action in the various Arab-Israeli Wars is

	Israelis	Arabs
1948	6,000	15,000
1956	189	1,650
1967	983	4,296
1967–1970	627	5,000
1973	2,838	8,528
Total	10,637	34,474

(Elusive Victory: The Arab-Israeli Wars, 1947–74 [New York: Harper and Row, 1978], pp. 124, 212, 333, 369, 609). One reasonably reliable estimate of the lives lost during the 1982 Palestinian-Israeli war in Lebanon puts the Arab number at 17,825 (New York Times, September 2, 1982). The Israelis in early September 1982 reported 340 Israelis killed and 2,200 wounded in action (Ed Walsh, Washington Post, September 6, 1982). On the eve of Israeli withdrawal in June 1985, Israeli losses were reported as 654 dead and 3,195 wounded (Mary Curtius, Christian Science Monitor, June 4, 1985). For the impact of terrorism, see Daniel Elazar, ed., Judea, Samaria, and Gaza: Views on the Present and the Future (Washington, D.C.: American Enterprise Institute, 1982), p. 188. For another estimate see Michael Jansen, The Battle of Beirut: Why Israel Invaded Lebanon (Boston: South End Press, 1982), p. 130.

38. For discussion of Israeli concern for water resources, see J. Schwarz, "Water Resources in Judea, Samaria, and the Gaza Strip," in Elazar, Judea, Samaria, and Gaza, pp. 81–100; Benvenisti, The West Bank and Gaza, pp. 19–23; and John Cooley, "The War Over Water," Foreign Policy 54 (spring 1984), pp. 3–26.

39. Richard Betts, Strategic Surprise (Washington, D.C.: Brookings Institution, 1982), pp. 68–80, 104.

40. Raphael Vardi, "The Administered Territories and the Internal Security of Israel," in Elazar, Judea, Samaria, and Gaza, pp. 171–190. The relative severity of Israeli reprisals is indicated by one estimate that between the October 1973 war and the 1978 invasion of Lebanon, the number of Israelis killed by Palestinians was 143, whereas the number of Palestinians and Lebanese killed by Israeli reprisals was 2,000 (Time, March 27, 1978).

41. Jimmy Carter, Keeping Faith: Memoirs of a President (New York: Bantam Books, 1982), p. 382; John Yemma, Christian Science Monitor, April 26, 1982.

42. Cooley, Green March, Black September, pp. 108ff.

43. Harold Saunders, The Middle East Problem in the 1980s (Washington, D.C.: American Enterprise Institute, 1981), pp. 40–41; the Camp David Accords can be

found in *The Middle East: US Policy, Israel, Oil and the Arabs*, fourth edition (Washington, D.C.: Congressional Quarterly, 1979).

44. Carter, *Keeping Faith*, pp. 335, 428.

45. From remarks made at Duke University by Yochanan Ramati, chairman of the foreign policy committee of the Leam wing of the Likud Party, on a visit to Durham, N.C., November 1982; "Text of Israel's Communique on the Reagan Plan," *New York Times*, September 3, 1982; Trudy Rubin, *Christian Science Monitor*, September 2–3, 1982; Carter, *Keeping Faith*, p. 397; and Vance, *Hard Choices*, pp. 225–228.

46. The text is in the *New York Times*, September 2, 1982; see also "Text of 'Talking Points' Sent to Begin by President," *New York Times*, September 9, 1982, for clarification of the plan; and two public addresses by George Shultz: "President Reagan's Middle East Peace Initiative," September 10, 1982, U.S. Department of State, Bureau of Public Affairs, *Current Policy* no. 418, and "The Quest for Peace," September 12, 1982, *Current Policy* no. 419.

47. Hertzberg, *New York Review of Books*, October 21, 1982; David Shipler, *New York Times*, September 9, 1982; "Israeli Authorities in Sharp Opposition to Reagan Proposals," *Washington Post*, September 2, 1982; Carter, *Keeping Faith*, pp. 333, 354, 367, and 386.

48. For the Labor party's response to the Reagan plan and Shimon Peres's characterization of it as a basis for dialogue, see *New York Times*, September 3, 1982. For the tentatively favorable responses of the American-Israel Public Affairs Committee (AIPAC) and B'nai B'rith, see the articles by Bernard Gwertzman, *New York Times*, September 7, 9, 1982; see also "Dissent & Israel: An Exchange," *New York Review of Books*, November 18, 1983, pp. 73–77.

49. For discussion of Labor party attitudes see Yigal Allon, "Israel: The Case for Defensible Borders," *Foreign Affairs* 55 (October 1976), pp. 38–53; Abba Eban, "Camp David: The Unfinished Business," *Foreign Affairs* 57 (winter 1978/79), pp. 343–354; Shimon Peres, "A Strategy for Peace in the Middle East," *Foreign Affairs* 58 (spring 1980), pp. 887–901. In a thoughtful article, "America's Palestinian Predicament: Fallacies and Possibilities," *International Security* 7 (summer 1982), pp. 93–110, Mark Bruzonsky analyzes the semantic confusion surrounding solutions to the Palestinian question.

50. For the Brookings report, see "Toward Peace in the Middle East," *Report of a Study Group* (Washington, D.C.: Brookings Institution, 1975). Its members included Zbigniew Brzezinski, Nadav Safran, and William Quandt, whose book, *Decade of Decisions: American Policy Toward the Arab-Israeli Conflict, 1967–1976* (Berkeley: University of California Press, 1977), is particularly thoughtful.

51. Husayn's role is central. For a recent U.S. assertion that the territories-for-peace assumption of the Reagan plan applies to all Israeli fronts including the Golan Heights, see Don Oberdorfer, *Washington Post*, February 17, 1985.

52. For Egyptian and American officials' assessments of Israel's annexation policies, see Vance, *Hard Choices*, pp. 237, 254. Henry Kissinger and Harold Saunders have both said that the United States cannot accept annexation of the West Bank. See Daniel Southerland, *Christian Science Monitor*, September 1, 1983.

53. William Quandt, *Decade of Decisions: American Policy Toward the Arab-Israeli Conflict, 1967–1976* (Berkeley: University of California Press 1977).

54. For discussion of this issue see Bruce Kuniholm, "Carrots or Sticks? The Question of U.S. Influence over Israel," *International Journal* 38 (autumn 1983), pp. 700–712.

55. Karen Elliot House, *Wall Street Journal*, April 14, 1983; and the interview with King Husayn, *New York Times*, March 15, 1984.

56. See, for example, Norman Podhoretz, "J'Accuse," *Commentary* 74 (September 1982), pp. 21-31, and the discussion in the December 1982 issue.

57. Ian S. Lustick, "Israeli Politics and American Foreign Policy," *Foreign Affairs* 61 (winter 1982/83), pp. 379-399.

58. Lustick, "Israeli Politics and American Foreign Policy," pp. 392-398.

59. Vance, *Hard Choices*, pp. 185, 231, 237, 254; Evans and Novak, *Washington Post*, June 20, 1983; Ian Black, *Washington Post*, August 4, 1982; *Washington Post*, August 21, 1983; *International Herald Tribune*, August 4, 1983; *New York Times*, March 15, 1984.

60. Lustick, "Israeli Politics and American Foreign Policy," pp. 390, 393-394; for Arens' statement, see Lally Weymouth, *Washington Post*, July 24, 1983. On November 29, 1982, the Israeli press carried estimates by Michael Dekel, deputy minister of agriculture, that the cost of every Jewish family settled in the West Bank ran from 4 to 5 million shekels. Current exchange rates would have made that $90,000 per family, or $630 million for 7,000 families; housing was to be available before October 1983. Required government financing for the third Drobles Plan, named after the head of the settlement department of the World Zionist Organization and tacitly if not formally approved by the Israeli government, which calls for the establishment of 57 more settlements by 1987, runs to 12 billion Israeli shekels, or $240 million annually. Another report suggests that costs may be as high as $1.5 billion over the next three years (Trudy Rubin, *Christian Science Monitor*, August 17, 26, 1983). Harry J. Shaw, senior associate of the Carnegie Endowment for International Peace, estimates the annual cost of Israel's West Bank settlements at $400 million (*Christian Science Monitor*, December 19, 1984). The majority of settlers, particularly in the urban settlements that serve as dormitory suburbs for Jerusalem and Tel Aviv, are not motivated by ideology. They are mostly young, middle-class Ashkenazim, responding to the fact that the cost of subsidized housing on the West Bank is 50 to 60 per cent of that in Israel. These observations are based on the author's conversations with Palestinians and Israelis and travel in the West Bank and Israel in April 1983.

61. Israeli leaders have repeatedly rejected as meaningless U.S. guarantees of a comprehensive settlement. In March 1977, Prime Minister Yitzhak Rabin told President Carter that the only commitment Israel wanted from the United States was to supply arms (Vance, *Hard Choices*, p. 173). Such a commitment, of course, would give the Israelis license to do what they wanted without consideration for U.S. interests. As President Nixon told leaders of the American Jewish community in June 1974, hardware alone was a policy that no longer made sense. Each new war would be more costly, there were more Arabs than Israelis, and whether Israel could survive over a long period of time against these odds was questionable. In addition, the United States would inevitably be drawn in as it was in 1973. Nixon's recommendation was that Israel seek a settlement now, while it was in a position of strength. His message was clear: Israel could not have a blank check when it came to American arms. See Richard Nixon, *The Memoirs of Richard Nixon* (New York: Grosset and Dunlap, 1978), p. 1007.

62. In June 1983, Secretary of Defense Weinberger noted that the military cooperation agreement, signed on November 30, 1981, and suspended on December 18, 1981, over the extension of Israeli civil law to the Golan, might soon be revived (Hedrick Smith, *International Herald Tribune*, June 16, 1983). The quid pro quo presumably had to do not with settlements but with Israeli willingness to withdraw from Lebanon. This interpretation was borne out in November when, according to Prime Minister Shamir, the United States and Israel established a joint military-

political committee to coordinate enhanced cooperation. The United States also agreed to increase military grant aid to Israel and to negotiate a free-trade agreement with Israel (*Washington Post*, November 30, 1983). The question that should be posed is whether or not the United States should back away from greater military cooperation with Israel and avoid further relief of Israel's financial burdens until there is a quid pro quo on the problem of settlement activity.

PART THREE

The Great Powers, Oil, and the Middle East

11

Middle East Oil
and the Industrial Democracies:
Conflict and Cooperation
in the Aftermath of the Oil Shocks

Robert J. Lieber

Acrimonious differences between the United States and its European allies over Middle East issues have waxed and waned since at least the time of the Suez crisis of 1956. The flare-up of tension in response to a series of terrorist attacks in late 1985 and early 1986 (the *Achille Lauro*, Rome and Vienna airports, the Berlin discotheque), followed by American reprisals against Libya, was thus part of a long pattern of disagreements among the industrial democracies in response to regional crises. Although the subject can be approached from a variety of vantage points, the purpose of this chapter is to examine U.S.-European differences in light of the two major oil shocks (1973–1974 and 1979–1980) of the past decade. Although other factors have influenced alliance disagreements, the experiences of the twin oil crises have left a deep imprint. These events have significantly shaped the divergent ways in which Europe and the United States have reacted to subsequent Middle East-related crises. A detailed examination of allied conflict and cooperation in the immediate aftermath of the two oil shocks may therefore contribute to better understanding of European-American friction over subsequent events.

Allied Conflict and Cooperation over Middle East Oil

Since the onset of the first energy shock in October 1973, Middle East oil has posed a particular problem for the industrial democracies. Moreover, it has done so in ways that are less apparent and more complex than they initially appeared. In essence, the problem has encompassed relations among the Western countries and Japan as much as it has the security or price of Middle East oil.

It is not surprising that the responses of the Western countries and Japan have varied over time and in response to dramatic oscillations in the urgency of the oil problem. The diversity of these allied responses has sometimes caused great strains in mutual relationships; yet ultimately it has not had the acutely divisive consequences that initially seemed possible. The cumulative experience of two oil shocks (1973–1974 and 1979–1980), two gluts (1976–1978 and 1982–1986), and other perils (for example, the Iran-Iraq war and threats to the Gulf) suggests that though policy differences over oil and other Middle East issues can occur repeatedly and sometimes intensely, there are limits to the extent of allied disagreement. More important, in a complex international environment, in which the United States is the most important single player economically, politically, and militarily, the record of the 1970s indicates that European and Japanese room for maneuver is significantly constrained. By themselves, these countries are unable to cope effectively with the consequences of the Middle East oil situation or with wider problems of regional instability. They thus find themselves inextricably linked to the United States, even when other national priorities may pull them in different directions.

The importance of oil to the United States and its allies caused both the Carter and Reagan administrations to treat Gulf security as a vital interest. In the words of Jimmy Carter's January 1980 State of the Union Address: "Let our position be absolutely clear: An attempt by any outside force to gain control of the Persian Gulf region will be regarded as an assault on the vital interests of the United States of America, and such an assault will be repelled by any means necessary, including military force."[1] Just over a year later, the importance of this region was reiterated by a leading figure in the Reagan administration: "The umbilical cord of the industrialized free world runs through the Strait of Hormuz into the Arabian [Persian] Gulf and the nations which surround it. . . . We cannot deter [the Soviet long range objective of denying access to oil by the West] from seven thousand miles away. . . . We have to be there in a credible way."[2]

Cooperation in dealing with this area appeared to be important; yet from the American perspective the Europeans and Japanese failed to maintain a unified response. This was exemplified by the scramble for oil contracts after the October 1973 war, and later when Japanese and European governments tried to strike deals with oil producers and engaged in competitive bidding for oil supplies. There did exist important achievements in constructing the International Energy Agency (IEA) and its emergency oil-sharing program. Yet during the 1979–1980 oil crisis touched off by the Iranian revolution, the industrial democracies achieved only minor improvements in cooperation, despite extensive consultation and other efforts.

Not only did the Carter doctrine not elicit active allied cooperation where oil supply was concerned, the United States did not always find the allies' response adequate in the face of related developments during this period. These included the Iranian hostage crisis and the Soviet invasion of Afghanistan (both beginning in late 1979), and American efforts to

Table 11.1
OFFICIAL SELLING PRICE OF SAUDI ARABIAN LIGHT MARKER CRUDE OIL

Date	Dollars per Barrel
January 1, 1970	$ 1.39
October 4, 1973	2.70
January 1, 1974	8.32
March 1, 1974	10.46
January 1, 1977	12.09
January 1, 1979	13.34
June 1, 1979	18.00
November 1, 1979	24.00
January 1, 1980	26.00
April 1, 1980	28.00
July 1, 1980	30.00
November 1, 1980	32.00
October 1, 1981	34.00
March 14, 1983	29.00
February 1, 1985	28.00
March 1986	(approximately) 15.00[a]

[a]Saudi Arabia had discontinued a fixed official selling price. Extensive Saudi use of "net-back" deals, beginning in late 1985, resulted in fluctuating per barrel prices based on the value of refined products produced from a barrel of crude oil.

Sources: Exxon Corporation, *Middle East Oil*, second edition (September 1980), p. 26; U.S. Department of Energy, Energy Information Administration, *Weekly Petroleum Status Report*, June 5, 1981, p. 20; U.S. Central Intelligence Agency, *International Energy Statistical Review*, December 22, 1981, p. 21; *New York Times*, March 15, 1983 and January 31, 1985.

promote peace between Israel and Egypt. In the early stages of the Iran-Iraq war, however, allied collaboration did succeed in preventing competitive bidding for oil on the spot market, limiting oil market disruptions, and deploying British, French, and American naval forces in the Indian Ocean.

The obstacles to cooperation go far beyond allied unwillingness to follow a U.S. lead. For one thing, oscillation between oil crisis and glut, as well as sharply fluctuating oil prices, has caused concern over energy security to develop unevenly (see Table 11.1). Even now confusion persists in interpreting cause and effect. The vulnerability that results from dependence on Middle East oil does not stem uniquely from possible forcible interruptions of oil supply routes by the Soviet Union. Nor, despite a widely held European view, is the solution of the Israeli-Palestinian conflict the key to Middle East energy security.

In fact, neither the Arab-Israeli nor East-West conflict fully explains the energy security problem. Of equal or greater significance are other sources of regional conflict (a point more readily accepted after the September 1980 outbreak of the Iran-Iraq war than before it), as well as serious uncertainties about long-term domestic stability within the major oil exporting countries.

In analyzing the difficulties that the Middle East oil problem creates for the industrial democracies, this chapter briefly examines the context in which European policies are made. It then considers the significance of European policies toward the Iranian hostage crisis, the Euro-Arab dialogue, and the Arab-Israeli conflict. What emerges is a picture of remarkable constraint on Europe's role in the Middle East. An understanding of these constraints helps to explain the mixed pattern of conflict and cooperation in Western policies toward this region. The Arab-Israeli conflict, Middle East regional stability, and the energy crisis are sometimes treated as nearly identical, but each poses a much more distinct and independent set of problems than commonly assumed.

Europe and the Middle East

European policies toward the Middle East are partly shaped by a historical role that has left cultural, commercial, and other ties of long standing. In most cases, these are matters of individual national relationships (e.g., France with Lebanon, Britain with the Gulf), which originally involved competition among the former European powers (and sometimes with the United States) for political influence and access to oil. The 1956 Suez crisis illustrates how severe the divergences among the Western countries can become. Thus the notion that the countries of the Atlantic Alliance should and can develop common policies toward the Middle East, in light of the region's strategic oil significance, overlooks a history of periodic disagreements.

Interrelated concerns involving oil have been superimposed upon the early pattern of European interest in the Middle East. These have included not only access to supply but matters of price, export markets for Western and Japanese goods and services, and access to petrodollar recycling. At times, the relevance of oil has been depicted as secondary to historical, cultural, and geographic motivations. Thus former French President Giscard d'Estaing maintained that, "The allusions, here or there, to the fact that our policy is dictated by petroleum considerations are absurd."[3] Despite this disclaimer, however, petroleum considerations starkly shaped European and Japanese policies toward the Middle East in the oil decade.

During and after the two oil shocks, each of the major oil-consuming countries sought to maintain its political-economic equilibrium in the face of sharply increased oil costs. Throughout the postwar period, the governments of these countries had been held responsible for successful operation of their welfare states and managed economies; thus electoral concerns made individual governments particularly attentive. Given these domestic concerns for Britain, Germany, and France, the result has been a considerable degree of policy continuity in responding to the problem of Mideast oil.

Britain presents an important case in point. In January 1981, the UK achieved net self-sufficiency in oil. Its problem was not the need to obtain or pay for petroleum imports but the requirement of finding or maintaining sufficient export markets to aid its embattled industries and cope with the threat of massive unemployment. Both Conservative and Labor governments were sensitive to the commercial, financial, and strategic importance of the Middle East, and there were no profound divergences in their policies during the decade after 1973. (Perhaps the chief difference for a Labor government was its lesser readiness to dispatch naval forces to join those of the United States in the Gulf, as the Thatcher government did after the outbreak of the Iran-Iraq conflict and as it may be prepared to do in future allied efforts. In addition, it is doubtful that Labor would have provided the kind of support for the U.S. reprisal against Libya that Prime Minister Thatcher gave in April 1986.)

For Germany, it is difficult to envisage major changes in policy under alternative governments. The dependence on imported oil, the need for export markets, and concerns about international financial stability all created major constraints. The foreign policy of both Social Democratic and Christian Democratic governments reflected substantial inputs from their centrist Free Democratic party coalition partner, which controlled the Foreign Ministry. Chancellor Helmut Schmidt did not favor sending German forces into the Gulf, nor later into Lebanon when the peace-keeping force was constituted, but he explicitly offered cooperation in Europe to facilitate the dispatch of U.S. and other allied troops. His successor, Helmut Kohl, pursued similiar policies.

A succession of Gaullist and center-right governments in France followed consistent policies from 1967 to 1981. These originated in Charles de Gaulle's shift to a pro-Arab policy and in an effort to establish privileged relations between France and the oil-producing countries of the Middle East. Until the early 1960s, France's national interests led to cooperation with Israel. Both countries shared a common antipathy toward President Nasser of Egypt—who was a key source of arms aid to the Algerian nationalists. Once France liquidated its Algerian involvement, however, de Gaulle had political as well as economic reasons for his shift in Middle East policy. These reasons stemmed from Gaullist aspirations for greater foreign policy autonomy, as well as the fact of oil import dependence and a desire to cultivate improved links with the Arab World.

The government of François Mitterrand and the Parti Socialiste (PS), which came to power in 1981, was somewhat more sympathetic to Israel than its predecessors, but its policies continued to be shaped by the need to find outlets for exports of manufactured goods and armaments. Oil import dependence also caused continued pressure toward cooperation with other oil-consuming countries. In sum, in France as in Britain, Germany, and presumably Japan, there has been a great deal of policy continuity.

European Policy in the Iranian Hostage Crisis

The Europeans' actions during the hostage crisis reflected their internal differences as well as problems in relations with the United States.[4] In addition, their responses illustrated important aspects of the Middle East problem that have little to do with the Arab-Israeli conflict.

At the time of the November 4, 1979, seizure of the U.S. embassy and the taking of 53 American hostages, the individual European states offered verbal support for the United States, along with hopes for an early end to the problem. They also undertook individual diplomatic efforts in this direction. Subsequently, France and Britain voted for the January 13, 1980, UN Security Council resolution that would have blocked sales and deliveries of exports to Iran (except medicine and food), banned new contracts for services and new credits, and called for the reduction of Iran's diplomatic personnel stationed abroad. However, this resolution was vetoed by the Soviet Union. Finally, on April 2, the European Economic Community (EEC) heads of government approved a sanctions policy in principle. In doing so, they reaffirmed their solidarity with the United States and agreed upon a two-stage procedure for implementation. The first stage consisted of mostly symbolic actions: reduction of the number of European diplomatic personnel stationed in Iran and of Iranian diplomats in Europe, the reinstitution of visa requirements for Iranians wishing to travel to EEC countries and a halt to arms sales to Iran. They also agreed to impose trade sanctions by May 17 unless decisive progress toward securing the hostages' release had been made.

In the absence of further progress, the EEC foreign ministers proceeded with trade sanctions against Iran, but they limited these restrictions to contracts signed after the hostage seizure. This represented a step away from the original UN resolution, which had covered all trade with Iran apart from medicine and food. Even this agreement among the EEC nations, however, proved incomplete. Almost immediately, the British Parliament rejected the terms. Despite Prime Minister Thatcher's solid Conservative majority of more than 40 seats in the House of Commons and strong verbal support for sanctions, her government did not throw its full weight behind the measure by making it a matter of party loyalty in the House. As a result, the British position was revised so that it would not be retroactive to November 4 but would instead affect only contracts arranged after the sanctions policy had been decided upon.

Ultimately, these sanctions were diluted still further when the Department of Trade announced that new contracts would be forbidden after May 30, 1980, but that the limitation would apply only to new contracts by new traders; that is, firms already doing business with Iran would still be able to expand existing contracts or even agree on new ones, provided these continued "an established course of business." Thus, a major contract of the British Talbot (Chrysler) automobile firm was not jeopardized, and no more than 10 per cent of Britain's Iranian exports of $1.6 billion per year would be affected.

The other countries of the EEC, though critical of Britain's position, adopted regulations to put the trade restrictions into effect. By finally arriving at this position some seven months after the hostage incident had begun, the EEC gave tangible form to its position, while protecting most of its economic interests: Seven billion dollars in French capital projects, large German business deals, and $3 billion in Italian construction contracts (including a port and a steel mill) were involved. In 1979, EEC exports to Iran had represented no more than 1 per cent of its total exports, and oil imports from Iran had amounted to just 5 per cent of the community's 1979 total. Yet the vulnerable situation of the EEC's energy balance, its members' concerns to maintain the employment and industrial base supported by export markets, and a general skepticism that sanctions could produce the hostages' release all worked against tougher policies.

The European position exacerbated U.S.-European relations; the United States perceived European measures as foot dragging and half hearted with respect to Iran as well as to Afghanistan, whereas the Europeans expressed criticism of inconsistent U.S. leadership and then dismay at both the idea and the failure of the American hostage rescue mission.

Limits on Europe's Role in the Middle East: The Euro-Arab Dialogue and the Venice Declaration

As a result of French initiatives, the nine member countries of the European Economic Community began a dialogue in July, 1974, with the 21 states represented in the Arab League. It gradually became apparent, however, that tangible results from this dialogue would be slow in coming. The two sides spent the first year in disagreement over Palestinian representation. The working groups established in June 1975 were confined to technical topics such as agricultural development, infrastructure projects, and technical cooperation.[5]

The dialogue offered a vehicle for European involvement in an area that the United States and the USSR tended to dominate. But the impact of the dialogue itself remained meager. The crucial subjects of the Arab-Israeli dispute and of oil price and supply were explicitly absent from consideration. Divisions within both sides dictated the former omission,[6] whereas the fact that the Arab League included important nonproducers of oil and excluded non-Arab oil producers and that important oil consumers such as the United States and Japan were absent from the European side worked against the inclusion of energy issues. Nor were these the only limitations. European preferences for bilateral negotiations, the slowness of the EEC's political machinery, continued divisions among Arab participants, and periodic differences over the Palestinian issue ensured a restricted agenda.

With the Camp David agreement in early 1979, the already moribund Euro-Arab dialogue came to a halt. The isolation of Egypt from most of the other Arab states, its separation from the Arab League, the transfer of the league's headquarters from Cairo to Tunis, and general division among the Arab states caused temporary suspension of the dialogue.

The Europeans sought to reactivate the dialogue in early 1980. In this effort, they meant to avoid becoming the target for increased Arab demands, and they expressed a willingness to include political issues. Nevertheless, the dialogue itself remained limited. Arab states used it as a means of exerting pressure on the Europeans over Middle East issues, and at a November 1980 meeting in Luxembourg, they demanded European recognition of the Palestine Liberation Organization. The Europeans, meanwhile, reiterated their view of the need for Israel to withdraw from occupied territories, for the Arabs and Palestinians to recognize Israel's right to exist, and for the Palestinians to have the opportunity to express themselves on the issue of self-determination.[7] As usual, questions of oil and energy remained absent from these discussions, which continued a long-term pattern of delay and lack of tangible achievement. In any case, the outbreak of the Iran-Iraq war of September 1980 further exacerbated divisions within the Arab League and substantially diminished the immediate salience of the Palestinian issue.

Ultimately, the Euro-Arab dialogue had little relevance as a vehicle for EEC involvement in the Middle East, and the factors impinging upon it reflected the limited ability of the Europeans to shape major events in the region.

The European community countries also experienced limits on their margins of maneuver at the United Nations. There they sought a Security Council resolution to go beyond Resolution 242 to provide for Palestinian participation in a comprehensive Middle East settlement. This approach was strongly opposed by the United States on the grounds that it would interfere with the Camp David process. It also contradicted the American position that the PLO must first accept UN Resolution 242 and Israel's right to exist before it could be accorded any negotiating role. As a result, this effort came to a halt when President Carter pledged to veto any such European move within the Security Council.

Elsewhere, the Europeans extended their own efforts to reach understandings with the Arab countries. In late 1979, for example, the French government made high-level contact with Yasir Arafat to indicate that it would receive him on an official visit to Paris on the condition that he explicitly accept the existence of Israel. He was also asked to agree to an additional precondition regarding the role of the PLO in Lebanon. These French efforts failed, however. Subsequent European gestures included such symbolic steps as French President Giscard d'Estaing's March 1980 trip to the Gulf, in which he stressed the need for Palestinian self-determination, and British Foreign Secretary Lord Carrington's statement to the House of Lords on March 17, 1980, that he did not believe that the PLO is "a terrorist organization as such." There were also a number of major weapons export deals, including large French and Italian sales to Saudi Arabia and Iraq. In addition, there was a contract for the purchase by Jordan of highly advanced British Shir II tanks (an export version of the Chieftain formerly intended for the shah's army), equipped with chobham armor and advanced fire control systems not yet supplied to the British Army itself. And by early 1981, the Saudis embarked on additional major purchases of European arms. These included a $3.4 billion contract for French ships and requests to buy 200 Tornado Fighter bombers from Britain and 300 Leopard 2 tanks from West Germany.

Other European efforts to court Arab governments went well beyond any aspects of the Arab-Israeli conflict. Thus, for example, the West German government pressured the West Berlin city administration to release two Iraqi diplomats detained on charges of preparing a terrorist bomb attack against a group of Kurdish students.[8] In late May, Denmark signed a three-year oil contract with Saudi Arabia, in which it agreed to avoid behavior that could "discredit" the Saudi monarchy, government, or institutions.

The most ambitious European initiative, however, came with the meeting of the European Council (the EEC heads of state and government and the ministers of foreign affairs) in Venice on June 12–13, 1980. The Venice Declaration of the EEC reiterated a number of previous European positions.[9] It also restated the right of all states in the region, including Israel, to existence and to security. However, it broke new ground in several key respects, particularly in regard to Palestinian self-determination and the need to associate the PLO with negotiations. In addition, the nine countries declared that they were prepared to participate "within the framework of a comprehensive settlement, in a system of concrete and binding international guarantees." The Venice Declaration was noteworthy for two additional reasons: It constituted the most cohesive European proposal yet presented on the Middle East and it called for a specific follow-up. The president of the EEC Council of Ministers was thus directed to make contacts among all concerned parties and report back on what form the European initiative could take.

The fate of the Venice Declaration illustrates the limits of European room for maneuver in the Middle East. On June 15, the PLO criticized the statement for failing to recognize it as the sole legitimate representative of the Palestinian people and described it as a response to U.S. pressures and an effort to draw some Arab states into the Camp David process. Although the PLO also "welcomed" the Europeans' move, it called on them to "free themselves of the pressure and blackmail of U.S. policy." On the same day, the cabinet of Prime Minister Begin bitterly denounced the Venice Declaration for attempting "to bring into the peace process that Arab SS which calls itself 'the Palestine Liberation Organization.'" It also characterized the European document as "a spur to all those seeking to undermine the Camp David accords and derail the peace process in the Middle East."[10]

As an emissary of the European Economic Community, the Luxembourg foreign minister, Gaston Thorn, made a series of visits to Arab states and to Israel in August and September 1980. Given the response of the PLO and of Israel, it is not surprising that the effort produced little tangible result. The EEC countries themselves backed away from their own initiative, and the Thorn mission received no substantive discussion at a subsequent EEC foreign ministers' meeting. Thorn's mission was then virtually buried by two coinciding events: the abrupt end to his visit to Israel in late September over a disagreement with the Begin government on the circumstances for his travels to the West Bank, and the outbreak of the Iran-Iraq war. The latter event left the Arabs themselves bitterly divided and turned attention within the region at least temporarily away from the IsraeliPalestinian conflict; it also served as a reminder that other profound sources of instability existed in the Middle East.

An Assessment of Europe's Role

Some observers regard Europe's role in the Middle East as positive and constructive. In June 1980, for example, European policymakers claimed that Secretary Cyrus Vance and U.S. State Department members had privately expressed the view that it was useful for Europe to pressure both Israel (over its position on the West Bank and the role of the Palestinians) and moderate Palestinians (over recognition of Israel). From a related perspective, it was argued that European efforts to establish or expand special relationships in the region (for example, that of France with Iraq) helped to maintain a Western link to the region at a time when America's intimate relationship with Israel might otherwise force a dangerous choice between the United States and the Soviet Union.

Europeans also claimed that their efforts sought to move the peace process beyond Camp David to include the Palestinians, who would otherwise constitute a major destabilizing factor, and that their position had the virtue of insisting upon both the right of Israel to existence and security and recognition of the legitimate rights of the Palestinians.

Further, the EEC countries did appear to have moved toward a greater degree of mutual agreement and cooperation on Middle East issues than had previously characterized their foreign policies. The gap between the Dutch, the Danes, and to some extent the Germans, all of whom had previously been more sympathetic to Israel, and the French and Italians, more favorably disposed toward the Arab and Palestinian perspective, seemed to have narrowed, with the European consensus moving more in the direction of the French position. This was evident at the United Nations on the question of a Palestinian state: On a controversial General Assembly resolution, the abstention of the EEC countries in July 1980 represented a shift away from the pattern of previous years when the French had abstained while their partners voted against the resolution.[11] At the same time, the policies of the Begin government over West Bank autonomy, settlements, the annexation of Jerusalem, and the June 1982 Lebanon war may have affected the position of some European governments previously more favorable toward the Israeli position. The 1977 defeat of the Israeli Labor government had also weakened a source of support within the Socialist International, particularly among the West Germans. Moreover, the European dependence on Arab oil continued to shape the environment in which policies were made.

The implicit factors driving Europe's position on Middle Eastern issues were energy dependence and a desire for export markets at a time of petrodollar surpluses. Above all, European policies in the region were designed to establish a modus vivendi with Arab oil producers in order to buffer European countries against the consequences of the continued Arab-Israeli problem and of some future exacerbation of the conflict.

What, then, was the balance of these European efforts, not only in their own terms but also as they affected the Arab-Israeli conflict as well as Europe's energy security? In essence, these policies were not overwhelmingly successful. Former Israeli Foreign Minister Abba Eban criticized the European initiatives as undercutting the Camp David peace process and rewarding intransigence. In Eban's words, "If Europe grants recognition to the PLO before any Palestinian organization has accepted the axiom of Israel's statehood, it squanders one of the incentives which . . . might have induced moderate impulses in the Palestinian community."[12] Further, many Israelis who opposed the Begin government's policies were nevertheless quite critical of the European role. Israeli resentment at a European tilt toward the Arabs deprived the EEC of an effective role as an *interlocuteur valable*. Eban, for example, noted the absence of any constructive European contribution to the series of conciliation efforts between 1973 and 1979: "Having placed a parochial and mercantile approach above Israel's survival and Western solidarity, Europe could not expect to be taken seriously as a disinterested conciliator in later months."

Ironically, this distancing from Israel undercut not only Europe's role as an intermediary but even its stature with the Arab world because it lacked the influence with Israel that the United States, by contrast, possessed. In addition, the tangible achievements for the Europeans in energy security remained decidedly limited. From 1973 to 1979, the Europeans, including the French, received no substantial quantities of oil that would not otherwise have been available to them, and they enjoyed no price concessions. Although an increased number of state-to-state oil deals were negotiated (for instance, between France and Iraq), a major supply disruption, regardless of the cause, would trigger the emergency oil-sharing system of the International Energy Agency (IEA). Although France is not formally an IEA member, it is indirectly associated through participation in a more limited sharing arrangement of the European Economic Community, all of whose other members belong to the IEA.

In sum, the efficacy of the EEC's Middle Eastern policies remained limited. The Europeans had struck a pose that established their sympathy with Arab concerns. But Europe's oil import dependence, its lack of substantial military assets in the region, and its fundamental security dependence upon the United States all limited the Europeans' ability to shape events in the Middle East—whether in the Israeli-Palestinian conflict, the Iran-Iraq war, or elsewhere. Subsequent events, including the Lebanon war

and Libyan- and/or Syrian-inspired terrorist actions within Europe, simply
tended to reconfirm this pattern. Even apart from the EEC's own specific
attributes, including problems of agreement and lack of a political secretariat
to direct its cumbersome political cooperation machinery, the broader limits
on the room for maneuver by individual European states mean that these
constraints are likely to prove enduring.

Problems in Allied Relations

Divisiveness among the United States, Europe, and Japan has often
occurred over Middle East issues; at times it has been bitter. In reaction
to half-hearted allied measures following the Iran hostage crisis and the
Soviet invasion of Afghanistan, an American editorial writer lashed out at
"Europe's shopkeeper cupidity" and singled out France for special condemnation by observing: "To call France an ally today is to mistake nostalgia
for reality."[13] (Equally sharp words were later exchanged when Germany,
Italy, and France opted not to support the American airstrike against Libya
in April 1986.)

The October 1973 war gave rise to sharp differences between the United
States and its allies over Middle Eastern issues. During the conflict, the
Europeans refused landing rights for U.S. aircraft engaged in resupply of
Israel. This action was followed by a series of strategies that aimed (largely
unsuccessfully) at establishing privileged relationships with individual Middle
Eastern oil-producing countries. Later, European support for Camp David
was muted at best. The United States, Europe, and Japan also failed to
devise an effective strategy for coping with the Iranian oil curtailment
following the outbreak of the Iranian revolution, and, as we have already
noted, responses to the Iranian hostage incident were varied. Even the
Soviet invasion of Afghanistan did not produce a decisive and coordinated
Western response. Furthermore, throughout the decade of the 1970s, there
was not a sufficiently firm response to terrorist incidents when those involved
were in some way associated with the Middle East.

For most of these differences, Americans blamed the Europeans; from
the European perspective, however, the United States was also at fault.
First, insofar as oil was concerned, there was the problem of rising American
imports. From 1973 to 1978, U.S. oil consumption climbed by 11.8 per
cent and imports by a stunning 28.5 per cent. For the Europeans and
Japanese, whose consumption had declined by 2.3 per cent and imports by
2.2 per cent in the same period[14] and who observed the United States
using up to twice the amount of oil per capita as the French, these patterns
were harmful. Growing U.S. oil imports also ensured continued strong
demand for Middle Eastern oil and thus greater world vulnerability to price
increases and disruptions of supply. The sharp reduction in U.S. oil imports
during 1980, which declined to 6.4 mbd (million barrels/day) from 8.0 in
1979 (see Table 11.2) however, did help to lessen allied resentment over
this problem. The experiences of the Iranian revolution and the Iran-Iraq

| | | | | Share of U.S. Imports | | | |
| | Total Oil | | | OPEC | | OAPEC | |
Year	Consumption (mbd)	Net Imports (mbd)	%	(mbd)	%	(mbd)	%
1973	17.3	6.0	35	3.0	50	0.9	15
1974	16.7	5.9	35	3.3	56	0.8	14
1975	16.3	5.8	36	3.6	62	1.4	24
1976	17.5	7.1	41	5.1	72	2.4	34
1977	18.4	8.6	47	6.2	73	3.2	38
1978	18.8	8.0	43	5.8	73	3.0	38
1979	18.6	8.0	43	5.6	70	3.1	39
1980	17.0	6.4	38	4.3	67	2.6	41
1981	16.1	5.4	34	3.3	61	1.8	33
1982	15.3	4.3	28	2.1	49	0.9	21
1983	15.2	4.3	28	1.9	44	0.6	14
1984	15.7	4.7	30	2.0	43	0.8	17
1985	15.7	4.3	27	1.8	43	0.5	11
1986	16.1	5.3	33	2.8	53	1.1	21

Table 11.2
U.S. OIL IMPORT DEPENDENCE

Source: Calculations based on data from U.S. Department of Energy, Energy Information Administration, *Monthly Energy Review*, May 1985, pp. 37, 42, 109; March 1987, pp 43, 48, 119.

war also led to a climate in which the Europeans were somewhat more willing to cooperate than in the past.

Differences in U.S. and European policies toward the Arab-Israeli conflict resulted, in part, from divergent beliefs about the efficacy of the Camp David process versus a comprehensive approach. But the Americans and their European allies often cited other factors as influential in shaping each other's Middle East policies. The Europeans pointed to U.S. domestic politics, which some of them believe led the United States to identify closely with Israel. American observers noted that the European dependence on Middle Eastern oil led them to tilt in the Arab direction and to pay insufficient attention to Palestinian intransigence.[15]

West Europeans sometimes perceived a lack of correspondence between America's stated Gulf objectives and its capabilities. Although the January 1980 Carter doctrine labeled the protection of Gulf oil supplies as a vital U.S. interest, there remained a question as to whether the U.S. actually possessed the ability to guarantee oil supplies by military means. Meanwhile, Europeans and Japanese sometimes attempted to ensure the continuity of their oil supplies by measures that appeared pusillanimous to the United States.

Can effective cooperation between the United States and its partners be achieved where Middle East oil is concerned? The possibilities may be less bleak than sometimes assumed, though the risks are considerable. But cooperation is far more than a matter of rapid deployment forces: It concerns a combination of foreign policy choices, international and domestic energy strategies, military options, and an ability to achieve agreement on broad outlines of policy.

The period from the first oil shock in 1973 to the aftermath of the second shock in 1980 did see some improvement in U.S.-European-Japanese cooperation. Participants did, often grudgingly, seem to recognize that isolated policy responses were inadequate to ensure sufficient supplies of imported oil at stable prices. Coordination of policy through the IEA and summit mechanisms thus increased to some degree.

There were also signs of greater political and military coordination among the countries of the Atlantic Alliance and Japan, as well as action by individual nations that benefited other allied countries. Thus France provided discreet but helpful assistance to the Saudis in ending the takeover of the Grand Mosque in Mecca. In addition, French and British naval contingents were dispatched to join those of the United States in the Indian Ocean after the Iran-Iraq conflict erupted in September 1980. At the same time, the Federal Republic of Germany made clear its willingness to support a "division of labor." In the words of Chancellor Helmut Schmidt: "The truth is: Number one, we cannot send troops into the Persian Gulf. We have constitutional inhibitions. Number two, we have no inhibitions on seeing American troops being moved from Europe to the Persian Gulf. On the contrary . . . there should be a division of labor in the western defense alliance."[16] Schmidt added that Germany was "prepared to be helpful in taking up the slack" in Europe if American troops were sent to the Gulf. In effect, this reflected a German desire to facilitate the protection of Western oil supplies by complementing the U.S. direct military role.

Regional Problems and Energy Issues

Interrelations among the Arab-Israeli conflict, Middle Eastern regional stability, and Gulf oil supply are complex and indirect. These are by no means synonymous problems. Nevertheless, the view prevails in Europe that the linkage is quite direct. As expressed by a prominent European observer, "The settlement of the Palestinian conflict would do more to secure Western oil supplies than any other single development that could be devised."[17] Yet in all probability, such a settlement—however difficult or improbable—would only slightly lessen the risks to secure Middle East oil supplies.

Indeed, there might be no net gain in oil security at all. The removal of that element of common purpose provided to the Arab world by having Israel as a shared enemy could well unleash even greater divisive tendencies than already exist. In this regard, the observation of Fouad Ajami is worth quoting at length. He judges that a major Middle East peace initiative by the United States would greatly inflame the passions of the extremists, and he observes:

It is a false reading of a large civilization to say that the terror springs from the impasse between Israeli and Palestinian. It springs from that but only partly so. More broadly, it springs from deeper social, economic and political pressures within Middle Eastern society, from the traumas of dislocated, newly urbanized youth, from the sense of men and women caught in terrible times that their world is being torn asunder.[18]

In view of the actual or potential conflicts between Iraq and Syria, Libya and Tunisia, Morocco and Algeria, South Yemen and Saudi Arabia, and Jordan and Syria, to mention a few, there is little reason to expect regional stability would be enhanced if an Arab-Israeli settlement removed the most unifying of antipathies from the long list of regional disputes.

The lack of appreciation for the distinctions among the problems of oil, regional instability, and Arab-Israeli conflict helps to explain why European policies toward the Middle East have produced such meager results in energy security. Neither collectively nor individually have the Europeans or Japanese succeeded in obtaining guaranteed supplies and production levels or any insulation from OPEC price increases. The experience of France provides an important case in point.

From 1973 to 1981 the French governments of Pompidou and Giscard d'Estaing tilted consistently toward the Arab position yet reaped few tangible advantages in supply or price. In terms of oil cost, France remained a price taker rather than a price maker. Its special relationship with Iraq did not really alter France's overall situation of oil import dependence. Even in overall trade, the French did not benefit disproportionately. Thus, France's share of OECD exports to the OPEC countries, which stood at 10.7 per cent in 1972-1973, declined to 9.8 per cent in 1979. By contrast, the share held by the Netherlands, ostensibly more sympathetic to Israel, actually increased from 3.4 per cent to 3.8 per cent.[19] (Only in the area of arms sales, which increased at double the rate of industrial exports during the 1970s, did France achieve tangible gains.) Even French hospitality for Ayatollah Khomeini in the months prior to the shah's overthrow conveyed no real advantages, nor did it protect France from cancellation of industrial and nuclear contracts or insulate the country from the impact of steeply higher OPEC oil prices in the year following the Iranian revolution.

Perhaps in recognition of the limits of what the West Europeans could achieve on their own, much of their Middle Eastern policy was symbolic rather than substantive. Gestures of sympathy and support for the Arab and Palestinian position were offered at the United Nations and in diplomatic exchanges. These were conditioned by a desire to mollify opinion among the Arab oil producers. Yet, in essence, there developed a kind of cynical reciprocity: no tangible enhancement of oil security or price stability for Europe in exchange for largely ritualistic expressions of European understanding and sympathy for the Arab position.

Except in the event of another Arab-Israeli war, the Palestinian issue is not likely to be the chief threat to Middle East oil supplies. Such a war remains extremely unlikely as long as two conditions are satisfied: that Egypt remains apart from other potential Arab belligerents as a result of its peace treaty with Israel and that Israel maintains credible deterrence vis-à-vis its potential adversaries. On the other hand, movement to any broader Arab-Israeli peace agreement is not likely to take place without Syria; yet its inclusion could require major political change within that country.[20]

The peace agreement between Israel and Egypt significantly decreased the near-term risk of another major Arab-Israeli war and thus constituted the first major step in the direction of a mutually satisfactory and stable peace. From this perspective, European criticism of Camp David (as too limited in view of the need for a comprehensive settlement) missed the point. It also failed to take into account that, though a viable and comprehensive settlement remains highly desirable over the long run, it will be very difficult to reach. Thus, by failing to give sufficient support to the significant achievement that had been made and by adopting policies that had the effect of encouraging Palestinian intransigence, the European efforts were counterproductive.

Conclusion

The industrial democracies' failure to cooperate in the oil embargo of 1973–1974 produced damaging results. Five years later, in the aftermath of the Iranian revolution, the major oil-consuming nations remained wedded to national strategies that failed to prevent disruptions in oil supply patterns and a 170 per cent oil price increase.

Together, the two oil shocks cost the industrial democracies approximately $1.4 trillion in lost economic growth. These events also exposed them to threats of political blackmail and, in the case of the United States and the Netherlands, an attempted oil embargo. Moreover, the oil crises precipitated serious political acrimony between the United States and Europe. Were these unique occurrences? And under what circumstances might these experiences be relevant to future differences among the allies in confronting Middle East events? Although any conclusions are necessarily speculative, the following inferences seem warranted based on the experiences of the oil decade.

1. Europe's problem becomes most acute and the potential for disagreements among the allies most marked at times when world oil supplies are tight, that is, when even small increments in demand or reductions in supply are difficult to meet or can only be obtained from Middle East oil producers. These circumstances have occurred twice, in 1973–1974 and again in 1979–1980, but the oil glut of the mid-1980s has made it unlikely that they will recur in the near future. (For 1985, OPEC's production had fallen to 16 mbd from nearly 31 mbd in 1979. This drop implied a huge unused production capacity of 15 mbd, overhanging the market.) Although uncertainties abound, there is, however, a real risk of a tightening in world oil supplies at some point in the 1990s.

2. The effects of high oil prices intensified the economic problems of the industrial democracies in the decade after 1973. Inflation, unemployment,

lagging economic growth, and other economic pressures created conditions for intensified competition over export markets. They also enhanced the propensity to seek means of political leverage in order to gain market advantage. Factors such as these exacerbated differences among the industrial democracies.

3. Other things being equal, alliance tensions are likely to be less acute during periods of ample oil supply and stable or falling real oil prices. This may suggest why such events as the Iran-Iraq war and the Israeli invasion of Lebanon did not cause any worsening in intra-allied relations.

4. For better or worse, the United States is likely to take a global view of Middle East issues. This policy reflects its position as both an economic and military superpower and the fact that it possesses substantial (though not comprehensive) means for seeking to influence events. The countries of Western Europe, however, are more likely to proceed from a local or regional perspective on events in the Mediterranean and Middle East. These will often lead them to promote narrower national interests, even at the expense of broader allied concerns. In practical terms, countries have sought to profit from export markets for industrial products, high technology and weapons, no matter the identity of the customer nor the reasons why the market niche had suddenly become available. Not infrequently, individual European countries have also turned a blind eye to terrorism in the hope of being able to avoid its ravages on their own soil, regardless of what happens nearby. The judgment may seem harsh, but it reflects the record of the 1970s and early 1980s, as well as the limits on room for maneuver of middle-sized powers with generally limited means for influencing outcomes.

5. The lessons of the oil decade suggest that there remain basic limits to the degree of alliance acrimony, even under the most unfavorable circumstances. These limits result, first, from practical experience. Go-it-alone strategies do not in fact provide a realistic means for coping with either the price or supply consequences of actual oil shocks. The participation of the Europeans, Japanese, and Americans in the International Energy Agency reflects this lesson; it is also visible in the fact that a modest identifiable increase in allied cooperation did take place in the aftermath of the revolution in Iran and the Iran-Iraq war. A second, even more fundamental circumstance has little to do with the Middle East per se: Europe remains dependent upon the United States for effective deterrence of the Soviet Union. As long as this situation and the perception of it continue, there will be inherent limits to the division between Western Europe and the United States—notwithstanding the status of policies toward Qaddafi or the PLO.

Acknowledgment

In part this chapter is based on a paper (later extensively revised) presented in the Middle East Core Seminar of the Woodrow Wilson International Center for Scholars, March 24, 1981. For comments I wish to thank Samuel

Wells, Ronald Morse, Dominique Moisi, and Helga Haftendorn. For a more comprehensive treatment of the subject, see also Robert J. Lieber, *The Oil Decade: Conflict and Cooperation in the West* (New York: Praeger, 1983, and Lanham, Md.: University Press of America, 1986.)

Notes

1. U.S. Department of State, Bureau of Public Affairs, "President Carter: State of the Union Address," Washington, D.C., January 23, 1980 (*Current Policy* no. 132).

2. Statement before the Senate Armed Services Committee, March 4, 1981. Text in *New York Times*, March 5, 1981.

3. *Le Monde*, June 28, 1980.

4. This discussion of the European Economic Community and the Middle East draws substantially on Robert J. Lieber, "The European Community and the Middle East," in Colin Legum, ed., *Middle East Contemporary Survey*, vol. 4 (London: Holmes and Meier, 1981). For a broader discussion of the hostage crisis, see Gary Sick, *All Fall Down: America's Tragic Encounter with Iran* (New York: Random House, 1985), pp. 175–249.

5. For a discussion of the inception of the Euro-Arab dialogue, see Robert J. Lieber, *Oil and the Middle East War: Europe in the Energy Crisis* (Cambridge, Mass.: Harvard Center for International Affairs, 1976). The interim period is discussed in Udo Steinbach, "Western European and EEC Policies towards Mediterranean and Middle East Countries," in Colin Legum and Haim Shaked, eds., *Middle East Contemporary Survey*, vol. 2, 1977–1978 (New York and London: Holmes and Meier, 1979), especially pp. 42–45.

6. See Dominique Moisi, "Europe and the Middle East Conflict," in Steven Spiegel, ed., *The Middle East and the Western Alliance* (London: Allen and Unwin, 1981). For a comparison with Japan, see Ronald Morse, ed., *Japan and the Middle East in Alliance Politics* (Washington, D.C.: Wilson Center, and Lanham, Md.: University Press of America, 1986.)

7. See, for instance, *Le Monde*, November 14 and 15, 1980.

8. *New York Times*, August 21 and September 16, 1980.

9. These included support for UN Security Council Resolutions 242 and 338, as well as previous European Council declarations of June 19, 1977, September 19, 1978, and March 26 and June 18, 1979.

10. The texts of the EEC statement and of the official Israeli and PLO reactions are reprinted in *Survival* (London), September/October 1980, pp. 227–230. The circumstances for the peace initiative were hardly auspicious, even before Venice. Thus, in early June, a resolution of al-Fatah at its congress had included a commitment to the "liquidation of the the Zionist entity." After this threat was reported in Beirut newspapers and in the U.S. press, PLO representatives claimed the organization's position had been "misrepresented." See *New York Times* June 5 and 7, 1980.

11. The General Assembly vote of July 29, 1980, called for establishment of a Palestinian state in Israeli-occupied areas of the West Bank and Gaza and omitted any reference to Israel's right to exist. The resolution passed by a vote of 112 to 7, with 24 abstentions. Among those voting against the resolution were Norway, the United States, Australia, and Canada.

12. Abba Eban, "The West Bank: Why Have Europe's Diplomats Played Such an Unimpressive Role?" *The Times* (London), June 22, 1980.

13. *The New Republic*, June 14, 1980.

14. Figures for oil imports exclude the UK and Norway, Calculated from OECD *Economic Outlook* (Paris), no. 25 (July 1979), pp. 63 and 140.

15. The view of European policy as appeasement at the expense of Israel is expressed, for example, by Walter Laqueur in *The New Republic*, March 7, 1981.

16. Excerpts from an interview with the chancellor of the Federal Republic of Germany, Helmut Schmidt. Broadcast on the ABC television program "Issues and Answers" on November 16, 1980, *Relay from Bonn, Statements and Speeches* (New York: German Information Center, vol. 3, no. 15, November 17, 1980).

17. David Watt in *The Economist* (London), quoted in Walter Laqueur, *Commentary* 71, no. 2 (February 1981), p. 39.

18. Fouad Ajami, "How the U.S. Became a 'Demon,'" *New York Times*, 17 April 1986.

19. OECD, *Economic Outlook* (Paris), no. 28 (December 1980), Table 55, p. 124.

20. See especially Moshe Ma'oz and Avner Yaniv, eds., *Syria Under Assad: Domestic Constraints and Regional Crises* (New York: St. Martin's, 1986), pp. 157–178, 251–263.

12

Soviet Decisionmaking for the Middle East

Dennis Ross

Although the United States has been aware of its vital stakes in the oil-rich Gulf region for some time, American concern about the vulnerability of the U.S. position in that region is more recent. Historically, the internal stability of the region was of little concern because the area was controlled by conservative monarchies with small and relatively docile populations. Also, the general security of the region seemed ensured by the British, who acted as the arbiters of local disputes and the guardians against external threats. When the British withdrew from east of Suez in 1971, the United States sought a new formula for regional security and settled on a twin pillar approach, depending on the Iranians and to a lesser extent the Saudis to guarantee regional security. With the collapse of one pillar and the instability exhibited in the other (which was in any case never a military power), the United States became aware of the need to find a new basis for regional security.

Adding urgency to this search was the growing shadow that Soviet power cast over the area. Improved Soviet ability to project power, the erosion of northern tier barriers to Soviet access to the region, and the growing Soviet naval presence in the south—all fundamentally affected the security calculus of the local states and made Americans far more concerned about the Soviet threat in an already shaky, yet critical, region. Not surprisingly, the Soviet invasion of Afghanistan served to crystallize U.S. concerns about countering Soviet threats in the Gulf region.

Though some threats to U.S. interests in the region are internally generated and may be independent of the Soviets (the war between Iran and Iraq being a case in point), the purpose of this chapter is to discuss

This chapter originally appeared as "Considering Soviet Threats to the Persian Gulf" in *International Security*, vol. 6, no. 2, fall 1981, and is reprinted with permission of the MIT Press.

the somewhat more narrow theme of Soviet threats to the Gulf. Nevertheless, in the course of outlining Soviet options for furthering its goals in the area, I will at least indirectly note some of the sources of regional instability (for instance ethnic-sectarian fragmentation, conflicting claims and ambitions to regional dominance), since these various causes of local conflict and instability provide the Soviets with opportunities to establish greater local presence and to exercise increased local coercion.

Any discussion of Soviet political-military options and related threats to the Gulf would be of limited value if it only catalogued these in the abstract. Soviet options and threats must be placed in the more general context of global Soviet perspectives, goals, and risk-taking propensities. In this chapter, I will outline general Soviet attitudes and orientations, the Soviets' preferred operating style for pursuing their goals, the types of concerns that could trigger more extreme or militant Soviet options, and the character and shape these options could potentially take in the Gulf. The concluding section of this chapter will touch briefly on some of the options the United States may have to counter the Soviets in the area.

Risks and Opportunity: The Soviet Style of Operation

Some people see all Soviet moves around the globe as fitting neatly into a master plan for world domination calibrated according to time and place. The Soviet invasion of Afghanistan is seen as presaging a move into Pakistan, and the Soviet position in the People's Democratic Republic of Yemen (PDRY) is seen as portending direct threats against Saudi Arabia and Oman, all according to a conscious plan and a finely developed timetable.[1] Although the master plan argument has a superficial plausibility, it does not take into account the inherent Soviet belief in the need for flexibility in exploiting trends and developments in the world—not all of which are precisely predictable—and the socialization of Soviet leaders that leaves them with a strong sense that they should avoid unnecessary risks that could threaten the natural unfolding of the historical process.

Although the Soviets may not have a master plan, they do have a strategic vision of the world and of the direction in which they want it to go. The Kremlin's view is colored by the assumption that the Soviet Union is locked in a struggle with the forces of imperialism. Although this is an era of nuclear weapons, Soviet leaders see the need to avoid triggering a nuclear war and indeed to take steps that minimize the chances of war so that the world will remain safe for competition with the West.[2]

In essence, the Soviet perception of the struggle means that the Soviets must try to erode and undermine U.S. positions and influence around the globe and ultimately supplant them with their own. At the same time, because such supplanting can be risky if attempted too directly in areas of real importance to the United States, the Soviet strategy for eroding U.S. positions has tended to be indirect—exploiting available opportunities or creating opportunities but carefully avoiding overt challenges that might elicit unpredictable and dangerous Western responses.

The Soviet Union exploited two political opportunities to broaden its scope for diplomatic maneuver when it established diplomatic relations with Oman in September 1985 and with the United Arab Emirates (UAE) in November 1985. Western observers reacted with some surprise to these two moves, particularly the agreement with Oman—given the longstanding Soviet antipathy towards the Omani régime as a result of its close ties with the United States. But it is apparent that these moves responded to desires evident in these countries. Oman viewed the move as an opportunity to send a political signal to the United States that it should not take its security relationships in the Middle East for granted, and the UAE felt such a move was a useful way to distance itself from Saudi Arabia, and by extension, from the United States.

Though persistently pressing to improve their international position and global standing—as they feel they must—the Soviets have been guided by a basic cautiousness, and for the most part, a low propensity to take risks.[3] Several factors account for this approach. The Soviets take great pride in their achievements; moreover, they believe that history is on their side; thus they need not take great risks.[4] In addition, the Soviet decisionmaking process and the leadership's perception of the high cost of failure contribute to a cautious style and outlook among the current Soviet leadership.

Consensus and Risk Sharing in Soviet Decisionmaking

Decisionmaking in the highest councils of the Soviet system has increasingly become based on elite consensus. Following the turmoil and contention of the Khrushchev period (and Brezhnev's own perception of what got Khrushchev in trouble), Brezhnev and his Politburo colleagues forged a process in which all the leading interests or leadership elements essentially had to be minimally satisfied before major decisions were made. In this kind of coalition-maintenance, decisionmaking environment, lowest common denominator policies naturally emerged and in general militated against bold departures and high risk actions.

Although this process produced stability, it also produced a sense of stagnation that Andropov and his supporters seemed determined to overcome by infusing new energy and dynamism into the political process. Whether he and his bureaucratic allies could have succeeded is unclear, given the leaders with important vested interests who saw this effort as a threat to their positions and perquisites. In any event, his early incapacitation and long illness guaranteed that these plans would be forestalled. Chernenko's succession to Andropov saw a return to "Brezhnevism without Brezhnev." Chernenko's main appeal was his continuation of the Brezhnev style of rule, a style that tended to work against risk taking.

The impact of Mikhail Gorbachev on Soviet policy, foreign and domestic, remains a topic of intense interest and speculation. Two points seem firmly established. The new Soviet leader clearly intends to project a new image of openness and decisiveness, and he is quite determined in his effort to reform the Soviet economic system and open it to greater exchanges with countries beyond the Warsaw Pact. Yet it is far from certain whether his economic reforms can overcome the bureaucratic interests and rigidities of the present structure. With evidence incomplete and contradictory, opinions differ on the nature and extent of change in Soviet foreign policy under Gorbachev. One Soviet specialist has observed that Gorbachev's initial foreign policy appointments represented an interesting mixture of change and continuity that gave few clues to his own views or to the nature of the influences on him. He concluded that the long-term consequences of this foreign policy mix are currently unclear.[5]

At any time, but particularly during periods of succession, the perceived high cost of failure probably also reduces the willingness of Soviet leaders to run serious risks. The surest, safest, and most legitimate way to challenge a Soviet leader and oust him from his position—the thing Soviet leaders value more than anything else—is to pin a significant policy failure or humiliation on him. Since losing one's position means becoming a nonperson, the lesson for Soviet leaders since Khrushchev has been to seek cover in collective responsibility, to be content to muddle along, and to avoid bold and inherently risky and uncertain initiatives.

None of this discussion suggests that the Soviets cannot be decisive in the pursuit of opportunities or that they are not prepared to take risks. They can and they are, under some circumstances.

Defending Socialist Gains: The Cost of Failure

The Soviets are quick to exploit opportunities that appear to involve low risks or costs. They see themselves not as passive observers of the march of history but as part of a vanguard responsible for furthering its progress—something that requires them to exploit available opportunities.[6] In effect, failure to seize opportunities that involve low risk may constitute a kind of failure for which a Soviet leader could be held accountable.

Paradoxically, the need to avoid being charged with a failure may lead Soviet leaders to shed some of their basic cautiousness. To preempt a potential failure and its high costs, for instance, Soviet leaders may be prepared to run risks and act decisively. Indeed, it is in this light that one can best understand Soviet military interventions in Hungary, Czechoslovakia, and Afghanistan. In each case, the consequences or costs of not acting were perceived to be quite severe, in effect constituting a major failure that would have been difficult to accept and for which the presiding leadership would have been held responsible.

In Hungary and Czechoslovakia, the basic question of the Soviet hold over Eastern Europe was at issue. The Hungarian leadership, after fits and starts, had declared its intention to drop out of the Warsaw Pact, become neutral, and inaugurate a multiparty system. Aside from introducing a major gap in Soviet defenses along its western frontier, the Hungarian moves—especially in light of earlier intimations of a U.S. roll-back policy—promised to set a very dangerous precedent that the rest of Eastern Europe would follow unless decisively checked. Similarly, in 1968, the Prague Spring posed an unmistakable threat to party rule that could potentially spread and infect not only the rest of Eastern Europe but the Soviet Union as well.

In both cases a fundamental threat to a basic Soviet achievement that legitimizes further party rule—the creation and security of the socialist commonwealth—was involved. If unanswered, that threat to such a fundamental goal posed a major danger for the Soviet Union and its leadership. It should be noted that the Soviets will do whatever it takes and will be prepared to run very significant risks in responding to perceived threats to the Soviet Union or its principal achievements.

In cases where the stakes are lower, Soviets may still act decisively and run risks if the costs of inaction are deemed to be high. Afghanistan is a case in point. In Soviet eyes, if Moscow did not act, a pro-Soviet Marxist régime along the Soviet border would have been toppled and replaced not by neutralist elements but by Islamic fundamentalist forces hostile to the Soviet Union. A hostile presence along the Soviet border is threatening (partly because it could be used to contain Soviet movement and influence in peacetime and might be a launching point for attacks in wartime); this threat alone might have been sufficient justification for invasion. After the Iranian revolution, the Soviets were probably also concerned about the impact that another fundamentalist Islamic régime along its border might have—and about assessments by their own Muslims, more independently minded east Europeans, and clients and foes in the third world—of Soviet willingness to see this happen. Indeed, allowing a clear defeat and reversal of the revolutionary process to occur in their own backyard, at a time when the correlation of forces looked increasingly favorable, was something no Soviet leader could do without being charged with a serious lack of political will, as well as with responsibility for a significant failure.

In these cases, the Soviets have demonstrated an ability to act decisively, but in each case, they were impelled to act by the prospective costs of not acting, and not by the expected gains of their action.[7] One might conclude from these cases that the Soviets are far more prepared to run risks in defense of their gains—thereby preempting or averting potential failures—than they are over attempts to extend their gains.

Although this basic inclination—reflecting the systemic factors that produce caution in the Soviet leadership—is not likely to change, the Soviets in the future may feel compelled to defend gains in more distant, noncontiguous areas. The continuing Soviet need for external successes as signposts of progress, in conjunction with the deeply felt desire to have the full trappings of global power and status, has led them to broaden the scope of their interests and internationalist responsibilities.[8] Given their perception of the retrenchment of U.S. power, their own ability to project and support their forces in more distant areas, and international trends that are yielding a more favorable correlation of forces,[9] the Soviets seem increasingly determined to emphasize their global role and rights.

In this connection, Soviet officials and commentators appear to be going beyond their earlier declarations of Soviet status as an international arbiter, exemplified by Gromyko's assertion that "no [international] question of any significance . . . can be decided without the Soviet Union or in opposition to it."[10] They are suggesting that Soviet standing and power give them the same rights of global intervention as those enjoyed by the United States.[11] The significance of this is not that the Soviet inclination toward caution is likely to change soon; rather, it is that as the Soviets define their interests and global commitments more broadly, threats or losses to these more distant interests may be cast as failures and may therefore impel the Soviet leadership to act more decisively and run greater risks (or at least convince the West that they will) in areas farther from the Soviet Union.

In relating this particular trend to Soviet behavior in the Middle East/ Gulf region it seems likely that the Soviets will find it more difficult to accept reversals in this region, especially given its importance for Soviet access to the third world and its international standing. Specifically, this means the Soviets are probably prepared to run greater risks and go to greater lengths to support and stand by (or at least create the impression that they will stand by) their clients in the area (e.g., Syria, PDRY, Libya).[12] Similarly, it probably also means the Soviets are less willing to let the clock turn back in a strategic sense in the Gulf region; the Soviets may not simply acquiesce in U.S. attempts to recreate containment along their southern periphery or in the reestablishment of Iran as a strategic barrier to the projection of Soviet power and influence.[13]

Thus, because the Soviets may increasingly consider that the costs of acquiescing in such American efforts constitute an unacceptable setback— one whose cost exceeds the costs of countering U.S. moves—they may be willing to run somewhat higher risks in the Gulf. This is not to say that they will pursue reckless or adventuristic policies that invite confrontation; it does mean the Soviets will probably pursue more assertive policies designed to intimidate the United States and the West, to prevent local powers from cooperating with U.S. initiatives, and to secure Soviet objectives in the region. What are the specific objectives that the Soviets have in the Gulf region? What kinds of options do they have to achieve these objectives?

Why the Gulf Region?

In discussing Soviet objectives in the Gulf, it is useful to divide Soviet goals along defensive and offensive dimensions. On the defensive side, the Soviets see the Gulf area—like any on its periphery—as a potential launching point for intrigues and threats. Along all their borders or nearby regions, the Soviets favor weak states with régimes that are friendly and responsive to Soviet concerns and needs. In this way, the Soviets can minimize the threats they face and in real terms meet a fundamental Soviet objective: pushing threats farther and farther away from the Soviet homeland.

The Gulf as Staging Area

This strategy requires that the only foreign ties or presence permissible in nearby areas are those sanctioned by the Soviets, and it therefore necessitates ongoing efforts to undermine the ties and erode the presence of hostile powers (especially the United States) in contiguous areas such as the Gulf. This strategy fits naturally with the general Soviet policy to erode and then supplant U.S. influence and presence in any case. Largely for defensive reasons, the Soviets strive to impose some measure of limited sovereignty on the state along their periphery.

In the Gulf this impulse has certainly found historical expression in Soviet policies and attitudes toward Iran. In the late nineteenth and early twentieth centuries, the Russians protested against internal developments in Iran (e.g., building railroads) that might have military utility. Subsequently, Soviet concern about the use of Iranian territory for attacks on the USSR led to the conclusion in 1921 of a treaty that gave the Soviets the right to send troops into Iran if a third party intervened militarily there or used Iranian territory as a base for an attack on Soviet territory (Articles 5 and 6). Though subsequent Iranian governments have renounced the treaty as unfair,[14] the Soviets continue to insist on its validity,[15] and in fact used the treaty to warn the United States against intervention during Iran's upheaval in late 1978.[16] Even though the Soviets have not succeeded in imposing limited sovereignty on Iran or the other Gulf states over the last two decades, this goal is probably seen as achievable in degree or in stages. In any event, it is more achievable now with an Iran less politically and militarily able to resist Soviet pressure and therefore less capable of being a barrier to Soviet influence in the Gulf.[17]

The notion of removing potential barriers to the southern expansion of Soviet influence is important and probably reflects both defensive and offensive impulses. Though it goes beyond the main Soviet defensive concern about the Gulf, it responds to traditional Soviet fears of Western encirclement. To break Western-inspired containment is a goal the Soviets consider critical to their ability to compete with the United States and also critical to their achievement of a universally recognized superpower status.

The Gulf as Land Bridge

In this light the more offensive side of Soviet goals in the Gulf region comes into focus; breaking the northern tier barrier is important precisely because it will allow the Soviets to establish a presence in the Middle East/ Gulf area and from there to project their power internationally. Indeed, because the Gulf area is a land bridge to Africa and the Indian Ocean basin, the Soviets must establish a secure foothold there if they are to improve their strategic power and influence internationally. Hence, even without the oil resources of the area, the geopolitical centrality of the region was bound to foster great Soviet interest in establishing a meaningful presence and the kind of dominion or arbiter status that the British had once enjoyed in the area, both because of the impact this would have on the perception of Soviet international standing and because sitting astride this strategic passageway would facilitate Soviet power projection and impede or check that of Soviet adversaries.

From a geopolitical standpoint alone, the Kremlin's success in building its presence and leverage in the Middle East/Gulf would have great utility against not only the imperialists of the West but also the social imperialists of the East. In this latter sense, though the Soviets have persistently fought Western containment, they seem to believe that they must contain, encircle, and isolate the Chinese; to be able to do so, the Soviets need to have established their power and influence in the Gulf and adjacent areas.

The foregoing discussion explains the significant attraction of the Middle East/Gulf area to the Soviets, even if the Western world were not as dependent on the region's oil. The fact that it is, however, enhances the Soviets' interests in establishing their presence and leverage within and among the countries of the region. Establishing such leverage and appearing capable of disrupting the flow of oil from the area promise the Soviets big payoffs. At the very least, the Soviets could manipulate European and Japanese dependency to erode the cohesion of the Western Alliance and make America's allies more responsive to Soviet interests.[18] More overt Soviet control over Gulf oil would, no doubt, fundamentally alter the global balance of power in favor of the Soviets.

Soviet Oil Interests and Leverage

Soviet leaders are not blind to the strategic payoffs of gaining some leverage over or becoming an arbiter of oil flows. Although disclaiming any intent to interfere with the flow of oil, the Soviets have been positioning themselves in countries that sit astride the oil sea lines of communication (SLOCs)—PDRY, Ethiopia, Libya, and Afghanistan; though Soviet presence may create the image of being able to disrupt the oil flow to Western countries, the SLOCs are not the sole or probably even the major determinant of the Soviet presence in these countries. The Soviets have hinted that in the future they too may be a user of Gulf oil and have suggested that a conference of users, including themselves, should be convened to discuss how to guarantee access to and the flow of oil from the region.[19]

Here two points should be noted. First, any such conference would establish the precedent—to which the Soviets would demand adherence in the future—of Soviet involvement in the discussion and determination of Western oil supplies; this would represent a first step toward granting the Soviets one of their long-term goals—arbiter status with respect to the flow of oil to the West.

Second, the possibility that the Soviets may become a user of Gulf oil is indicative of a deeper problem—that of potential oil production difficulties in the Soviet Union. Even if the estimates of Soviet energy problems prove to be unfounded,[20] the Soviets are still likely to seek access to Gulf oil at concessionary rates, if not for themselves, then for their Eastern European clients. Here it seems likely that the Soviets will not be able to meet Eastern

European needs (they have already suggested that their clients look for alternate suppliers); yet if these countries have shortfalls in their energy supplies or simply cannot afford their oil bills, they are likely to suffer serious economic problems which, as the events in Poland indicate, are bound to have serious political repercussions. Hence to avoid potential political problems in Eastern Europe, with all that this situation threatens for the USSR, the Soviets are likely to have increasingly strong incentives to gain access to Gulf oil at favorable rates.

In short, Soviet interests in the Gulf may now be fueled not only by the proximity of the area, its geopolitical centrality, and Western dependency on the region's oil but also by the Soviets' own or their allies' increasing oil needs.

Soviet Leverage and a Diplomacy of Coercion

What instruments or political-military options do the Soviets have for gaining access to Gulf oil? Indeed, what instruments or options do the Soviets have for achieving any of their near and longer term goals in the Gulf: to reduce and eventually remove U.S. influence and presence in the area, to build and formalize their own presence, to create Soviet leverage within the area both to ensure local responsiveness to Soviet needs and interests and to achieve Soviet arbiter status over local decisions?

The Soviets have a wide range of options for realizing many of these goals at relatively low risk. The indirect nature of many of the Soviet options reduces the level of risk to the Soviets, especially because it tends to pose threats that are ambiguous or often difficult to respond to, while still promising achievement of Soviet goals. Some of the Soviet options by their very nature may seem benign, though still capable of yielding results.

Development Aid

One option the Soviets have for acquiring Gulf oil and gas is to engage in economic development or barter arrangements. The Soviets have taken this approach in the past in Iran and Iraq. For example, in Iran the Soviets constructed a steel mill in Isfahan and a heavy machinery plant in Arak. Payment was made to the Soviets in natural gas. Similarly, the Soviets developed the North Rumaila oil field in Iraq and were repaid in Iraqi oil. Following the visit of Iraq's Deputy Prime Minister Ramadan and Foreign Minister Aziz in May of 1984, a similar deal was struck.

The Soviets and Eastern Europeans can be expected increasingly to offer to construct heavy industrial facilities and to explore and develop oil fields in exchange for local oil or gas. Though the West certainly has a clear advantage in oil technology (with regard to exploration and extraction), political calculations may figure importantly, as in Iraq's case.[21] Such considerations may lead some of the local countries to turn to the Soviets for developmental assistance.

In the case of heavy industrial development, at least some of the locals (Iran or Iraq) may turn to the Soviets simply because they are more likely to come in and support industrial ventures that do not look economically sound but are of considerable symbolic value to the given country. Not only will the Soviets or bloc countries receive oil/gas and political payoffs in return; they will also have an opportunity (which they rarely pass up) to insert significant numbers of KGB or security people into the host country.[22]

Arms for Oil

Of course, a far less benign form of barter is also available for the Soviets—simply to swap arms for oil. The Soviets have tremendous stockpiles of advanced conventional arms and no shortage of production lines.[23] The countries of the Middle East have demonstrated a large appetite for advanced weaponry because of local rivalries, the desire to underpin claims to regional primacy, and the need to deter external threats, to respond to internal challenges, and to keep their own militaries happy. Although the Soviets have played on Middle Eastern arms appetites to establish a presence and some dependency in Iraq, PDRY, Syria, Libya, and Algeria (three of which are oil states), they can be expected to emphasize the hard currency, or more likely the oil returns, even more in the future. Hence, the Soviets are likely to see not only the political and military benefits of providing arms to the locals but also the economic logic of doing so; one should look for indications that the Soviets are pushing arms sales to oil-producing states and indeed even seeking to have oil producers pay (perhaps in oil) for the arms transferred to nonoil states in the region.[24]

While arms transfers have provided the Soviets with access to the area, allowed them to build a military presence in key places in the region, and may in the future offer them a relatively low-cost way to acquire local oil, it also enables them to manipulate local régimes with threats.[25] In this way, arms transfers are an integral part of a general Soviet strategy of coercion designed to increase Soviet leverage over regional states. The success of this strategy has increased, as evinced in the growing awareness of Soviet strength near the area,[26] the heightened visibility of Soviet forces within the region itself, and the demonstrated willingness of the Soviets to use their military forces directly in Afghanistan and indirectly to support their friends in Ethiopia and in the PDRY. In this strategy of coercion the Soviets have a variety of covert and overt means of applying pressure against (and perhaps even toppling) local régimes. In addition, the character of the region has ensured local instability and conflict, providing the Soviets with plenty of opportunities to use their various instruments of coercion in support of groups or régimes that seek to challenge the local or regional status quo.[27]

Those instruments include Soviet disinformation, clandestine activities, and military aid (including all manner of arms, logistic support and training, battlefield management and planning, and proxy forces), which can be used to support the following groups:

- Ethnic-separatist movements, for instance, Azerbaijanis, Turkomen, and Kurds in Iran, Kurds or Shia in Iraq, Baluchs in Pakistan.
- Internal-revolutionary insurgencies or guerrilla movements directly or indirectly through Soviet client states, such as a potential Palestinian uprising in Kuwait, PDRY renewal of the Dhofar rebellion in Oman, or the insurgency in North Yemen.
- Interstate threats or wars (PDRY vs. any of its neighbors—North Yemen, Oman or even Saudi Arabia;[28] Ethiopia vs. Somalia; Iran or Iraq against any of their neighbors, including each other, depending on Soviet stakes and its relationship with each régime).

Added to the Soviets' ability to manipulate threats against local régimes is their willingness to be quite cynical and expedient when it suits their larger purposes. Soviet treatment of local Communists (especially Iraqi Communists) and the Kurds is a case in point. Though they have supported both, the Soviets have largely acquiesced in the purges and executions of Iraqi Communists and in 1974–1975 actually provided the Iraqis the means to crush the Kurdish insurgency. Despite this, the Soviets have apparently maintained ties with both. Their thinking seems to be that continued ties with these groups remain a useful lever to employ against countries like Iraq to remind them of the potential costs of trying to draw away from Soviet influence, as well as to hedge their bets if that eventuality were to occur.[29]

The Soviets also have a variety of indirect means and options for exerting leverage against friendly and unfriendly régimes in the Gulf area. Because most of these régimes feel vulnerable to internal pressures that can be manipulated from the outside and to more overt military threats from hostile neighbors, they may be responsive to a Soviet Union that seems in a position to relieve them from internal and external threats. In effect, should the Soviet Union appear to be able to offer Mafia-style protection (assuring a régime, for instance, that it need not worry about an internal insurgency or a neighboring threat so long as it remains responsive to the Soviets' legitimate needs), Gulf régimes may be prepared to cut the appropriate deals with the Soviets.

From the Soviet standpoint, the pursuit of such a strategy, which requires modulating its instruments of coercion, carries low risks if for no other reason than the threat to the United States may appear (or can be made to look) opaque. Yet it promises the gradual achievement of many Soviet objectives in the area, and it is very much in keeping with the Soviet operational style. As such, the Soviets' use of indirect means to achieve their goals in the area is far more likely than any direct use of Soviet military force.

This does not mean that the Soviets will not use military forces to achieve their goals in the Gulf. Just as in past situations the Soviets (for reasons explained earlier) are most likely to intervene with their forces in situations in which they are defending their gains or their international prestige as a superpower and not in which they are exploiting an opportunity to achieve a major new success. Indeed, unless the Soviets feel there is a very low risk of a U.S. response, they are most likely to use their forces directly only in those circumstances that they consider to be defensive or extreme. Those might include defending a client such as the PDRY from an external threat; responding to instability and turmoil along their border triggered by a civil war in Iran; responding to or trying to preempt a U.S. military intervention and potential presence in Iran by seizing the northern part of the country; seizing Iran down to the Gulf and perhaps also Saudi oil fields either because the Soviet need for oil becomes very great in an extremely grim economic situation that threatens political stability and the security of the system or because a major, unprecedented crisis in Europe leaves the Soviets the option of going to war there; or striking a major blow against the Western Alliance by going after the marginally less risky targets in the Gulf. Although this list does not exhaust the circumstances under which the Soviets might militarily intervene in the Gulf, it indicates the types of situations that might lead them to do so.

Soviet Military Invasion: How Possible? How Likely?

In any circumstances under which the Soviets might conduct an invasion in the Gulf, they will emphasize achieving their military goals quickly and, if possible, confronting the United States with a fait accompli. This approach offers the greatest chance of preempting an American response and minimizing the risk of escalation.

As for the style or character of the operations, Soviet doctrine dictates the use of airborne and special operations forces to seize critical transportation and communication nodes (e.g., mountain passes, bridges, communication-relay and rail stations, air fields, and ports) and subsequent linkup with heavy ground forces.[30] The purpose of the airborne/special forces assault against this array of targets is to facilitate and secure the rapid movement of Soviet mechanized ground forces through potential choke points, to deny strategic positions to countering forces, to sow confusion and disrupt the enemy's ability to coordinate a defense, to make reinforcement or supply of enemy forces difficult, and to prevent forward enemy air bases from being used against Soviet forces while also making them potentially available to Soviet tactical aircraft. (More distant ports or airfields that may be difficult to seize but remain potential staging areas for local or external supporting forces are likely to be the targets of Soviet bomber forces.)

In relating this style of operation and these objectives to Soviet military moves into Iran or the Gulf, it seems clear that a limited land seizure in northwest Iran, down to perhaps Qazvin and including Azerbaijan and Kurdistan, poses the easiest challenge for the Soviets. Under current circumstances it is the only option the Soviets have in which they would be able to provide air cover for the insertion, resupply, and defense of their airborne forces. (Here it should be noted that the range of Soviet strike aircraft, in general, is limited; the distances to the northern Gulf, the Strait of Hormuz, and Saudi oil facilities and northern airfields greatly exceed these ranges.)[31]

Aside from the very major advantage of air cover, which is critical given the preferred Soviet style of operation, proximity creates other advantages as well. Additional forces deployed locally can play a leading role in the invasion without necessarily requiring major augmentation from other Soviet military districts (a fact that will cut down on American warning indicators). Airmobile (heliborne) forces are deployed in the area, and though having limited range, could be used to seize critical points or facilities, that otherwise would require airborne division elements. Similarly, forces with an amphibious capability and emphasis are deployed in the Caspian Sea area and could also be called upon to assume some of the missions that airborne units might otherwise have to carry out, including securing vulnerable points along the main roadway running down the Caspian coast to Rasht.[32]

In addition to advantages such as shorter supply lines, a limited northwest seizure boasts additional attractions to Soviet planners. First, the Soviets are familiar with the territory and actually have operational experience, having seized the area down to Qazvin in 1941. Second, once they achieve a military presence in the north, the Soviets would be in an excellent position to exert leverage against any central régime. Moreover, a subsequent move to the Gulf would be far easier to support logistically and with air cover once they establish and build up a presence in the north.[33]

Although a limited Soviet move to seize the northwestern area of Iran may seem suited to Soviet doctrine, more ambitious moves to the Gulf seem far less so. The distances involved mean that Soviet airborne divisions, which are very light on support and have only limited organic air defense, would be exceedingly vulnerable (assuming no tactical air cover). The resupply itself is likely to be vulnerable to air interdiction or ground fire since it will be conducted by slow-moving air transports, with the linkup on the ground not likely to occur for at least two weeks.[34]

Much evidence indicates that the Soviets might have a difficult time getting to and supporting airborne units deployed to the Gulf. Of course, they might deploy these forces to the Gulf anyway in the hopes that the shock value of seizing Abadan, Bandar Abbas, or critical oil facilities and airfields in Saudi Arabia would be great enough to disrupt local defenses and preempt any U.S. response. This approach would involve a major gamble, but if the situation and stakes were extreme enough and/or U.S. credibility and capability were perceived to be low enough, the Soviets might try it.

Two things would greatly facilitate the Soviets' ability to execute their preferred military strategy throughout the Gulf and into Saudi Arabia. The first—building and establishing a secure military presence in Afghanistan—is already under way. Should the Soviets secure their presence and lines of communication (LOCs) within the country and also construct bases in southwest Afghanistan, their ability to project power to the Strait of Hormuz and the entrance to the Gulf would be greatly enhanced. As a result, the Soviets could provide air cover for the insertion of airborne elements into Bandar Abbas or Chah Bahar. In addition to reducing the vulnerability of these forces and the ground forces and logistics units that might go overland along the Helmand River–Zahedan–Bandar Abbas or Zahedan–Chah Bahar axes to link up with them, a Soviet combat air and bomber presence in Afghanistan could keep U.S. carrier forces farther from the Gulf and threaten all shipping transiting the Strait of Hormuz.

Second, a Soviet presence in Iraq or the Soviet ability to use Iraqi bases would greatly enhance the Soviet threat to the northern Gulf area and Saudi Arabia. Iraqi bases would bring these targets within range of Soviet tactical aircraft.[35] They could be used to protect the forward deployed Soviet airborne divisions, cover the Soviet land routes through Iran and air and land routes to Saudi Arabia, and also bomb potential land and sea entry points for U.S. or other forces in the Gulf/Arabian peninsula.

Put simply, usable Soviet military presence in Afghanistan and Iraq could make more ambitious Soviet military moves to the Strait of Hormuz, on the one hand, or to the northern Gulf/Saudi Arabia, on the other, more feasible. Even so, the Soviets would face enormous operational difficulties in conducting such long distance airborne assaults, designed to achieve rapid successes and a fait accompli.

Conclusion

Although the purpose of this chapter has been to consider Soviet threats to the Gulf and not to describe measures to counter them, it is useful to offer a few thoughts on the types of steps the United States might take to respond to the range of Soviet political-military options that have been outlined.

If the United States is to counter and, more important, deter Soviet military options in the Gulf, it needs to be able to frustrate the major objectives of the Soviet strategy while playing upon its key vulnerabilities. For example, if the Soviet strategy emphasizes rapid successes and the achievement of faits accomplis to minimize the threats to Soviet forces and to limit the chances of escalation, the United States must convince the Soviets by American actions and capabilities that rapid successes are not achievable, that their losses will be high, that their forces are likely to get bogged down, and that the chances of escalation are great. Clearly the U.S. counterstrategy requires the capability to threaten vulnerable Soviet airborne forces (as they are deployed and once they are on the ground), interdict airlift aircraft to limit resupply, and interdict and disrupt Soviet air/ground LOCs so that Soviet ground movement (especially in the northern and central mountains) is slowed and made very difficult.

To employ this strategy, the United States will obviously need a significant air presence, with air-to-air and air-to-ground capabilities, available in the region before any Soviet move. It will need presence not only in the lower Gulf region but also in the northern reaches of the area; a presence in Turkey may be especially important to be able to threaten Soviet movement into northwest Iran.

At the same time, an American capability to defend critical points (e.g., oil facilities, air and sea staging areas) in the air and on the ground will also be essential to convince the Soviets that they cannot achieve a fait accompli or preempt American involvement. Such a strategy requires a buildup of local air defenses and the capability to insert limited ground elements rapidly to hold and defend these points of great strategic significance.

Although more needs to be done, this strategy clearly would represent a good basis on which to deter direct Soviet military threats. Perhaps the most important measure the United States must take to deal with less direct Soviet options in the area is to ensure local countries against external threats—from outside the region or from hostile neighboring states. Building an American presence in the region in ways that demonstrate U.S. willingness to take risks will be important in this regard. Indeed, if local countries are more susceptible to coercion because they do not feel they can rely on the United States in the crunch—an impression that gained added force from U.S. behavior in Lebanon—the United States needs to take military steps that not only upgrade its capabilities in the region but also indicate America's seriousness about protecting its interests, regardless of the reaction within and outside the region.

Coping with internal threats to friendly régimes that the Soviets may be able to manipulate is more difficult. If local régimes do not have the will to face internal insurgencies, the United States cannot provide it for them; if, however, they merely require the means and other forms of assistance, Americans, the British, the French, or local actors can provide those. Indeed, because U.S. presence in some instances may only exacerbate internal problems, the American role in many insurgencies may simply be to facilitate the help of others, for instance, providing the means and making it safe for Jordan or Egypt to support the Omanis or Saudis.

Besides helping others combat internal insurgencies (through material support and protection from external threats), American leaders may want to consider how the United States can put pressure on local Soviet clients that provide sanctuaries, training facilities, transit points for Soviet arms, and other forms of support for insurgents. Here the United States should remind the local régimes and the Soviets that internal vulnerabilities can be exploited from the outside by either side, involving friends of the Soviets as well as those of the United States. (Indeed, because of sharpening ethnic tensions and growing challenges to secular authority in the area, Soviet clients [PDRY, Syria, etc.] may be more susceptible to internal problems than are America's friends there.)

If the United States is to bolster its local friends and also give the Soviets incentives to exercise restraint, it needs a strategy that goes beyond merely reacting to threats; the United States needs a strategy designed to enable it to cope with threats and to take advantage of (and even create) opportunities; it also needs a strategy that drives up the costs of Soviet competition without so threatening defensive Soviet interests (the kinds most likely to trigger military intervention) that the Soviets respond militarily.

Achieving such a strategy is obviously no simple matter: It will require the use of the full array of U.S. political, economic, and military instruments to make it clear that it pays to be an American friend and it may cost to be an American foe. It will also require the establishment of a local military presence that, though taking account of local sensibilities, provides the United States enough local capability to make it clear to the Soviets that resisting an American force or exercising their military options will be very costly.

If the United States means to fashion a strategy that responds to the internal complexity of the area and the broad spectrum of Soviet threats, subtlety and a clear vision of what the United States wants to happen in the region will be required. Although the task is difficult, the continuing stakes and the challenges that the United States faces in the area seem to demand it.

Notes

1. For an example of this kind of thinking see Robert Moss, "Reaching for Oil: The Soviets' Bold Mideast Strategy," *Saturday Review*, April 12, 1980.

2. By definition, détente cannot rule out ideological competition with the United States; that would run counter to Marxist-Lenin creed. In this regard, Soviet commentators have said: "It is an objective fact that even in conditions of peaceful coexistence, which historically is one of the forms of class struggle, between two systems, friction and considerable difficulties are inevitable in the relations between capitalist and socialist states." V. Nikitin, "Peaceful Coexistence and Soviet-American Relations," *Mezhdunarodnaia zhizn'* (May 1974), pp. 9–10. Note also A. Aledimov's comment: "It is perfectly obvious . . . that, even given good interstate relations between the USSR and U.S., the principled ideological struggle and the historically inevitable competition between socialism and capitalism in various spheres, including, of course, the international sphere, will continue." "From Positions of Realism," *SShA*, October 1977, p. 91.

3. There are notable exceptions, of course, especially those in which Moscow did not realize how risky certain initiatives were (for example, the Cuban missile crisis).

4. Here it should be noted that although Soviet leaders are imbued with the belief that they must grease the historical wheels, as it were, they must also be careful not to take steps that could trigger a nuclear cataclysm that could destroy all their hard-won achievements and the historical process itself.

5. Thane Gustafson, "Will Soviet Foreign Policy Change Under Gorbachev?" *The Washington Quarterly*, fall 1986, p. 155.

6. The need to exploit opportunities also grows out of an internal legitimizing impulse. In this regard, Soviet leaders require signposts of success—growing international recognition and legal trappings of Soviet international standing (e.g., Strategic Arms Limitation Talks, treaties of friendship) and imperialist defeats (such as those

in Vietnam, Angola, Ethiopia, Iran)—not only to reassure themselves that things are happening as they should be but also to justify their right to rule.

7. This does not mean that the Soviets would ignore the potential gains to their strategic position of going into Afghanistan; it does mean that the fear of a loss and not the expectation of a gain drove them to act.

8. For an Afghan corollary to the Brezhnev doctrine see the editorial in *Novoe Vrema* that concludes by saying that "to refuse to use the possibilities at the disposal of the socialist countries would signify virtually eroding performance of *internationalist duty* and returning the world to the times when imperialism could throttle at will any revolutionary movement" (emphasis added).

9. For a good discussion on Soviet views of the correlation of forces, see Vernon Aspaturian, "Soviet Global Power and the Correlation of Forces," *Problems of Communism* 29, (May-June 1980), pp. 1-18.

10. From Gromyko's speech to the 24th Party Congress (*Pravda*, April 4, 1971).

11. For a particularly blunt Soviet view on this, see the interview with a high official in Thomas Kielinger, "A Soviet Diplomat: We Bridle Slowly But Do Some Fast Riding," *Die Welt*, January 14, 1980, translated *FBIS*, USSR, January 15, pp. A4–A6.

12. Soviet provision of SA-5s and other air defense weapons (along with a significant advisory presence) to Syria during an uncertain phase of the conflict in Lebanon suggests as much, particularly because the Soviets had to know they were running risks of getting embroiled in a conflict or escalatory cycle that might not easily be controlled if the Begin-Sharon government preempted against such systems.

13. Note Soviet statements that imply this; for example, B. Ouchinnikov, "What then is Interference?" *Pravda*, January 13, 1979.

14. They renounced it in 1959 and then again in October 1979. There was, however, a clause in the treaty that precluded unilateral abrogation.

15. See Shahram Chubin, "Soviet Policy Toward Iran and the Gulf," *Adelphi Papers 157*, spring 1980 (London: International Institute for Strategic Studies), p. 11.

16. *Ibid.*

17. A point to note here is that the shah's own military buildup was, in part, motivated by his desire to resist Soviet efforts to constrain Iranian sovereignty. Although his close association with the United States and the development of his military machine limited the extent and impact of Soviet pressure on Iran, it also heightened Soviet concerns about the role Iranian military infrastructure and equipment (American developed and produced) might play in any future regional or more expansive U.S.-Soviet wars. If nothing else, preventing Iran from ever again becoming a potential front must represent an important Soviet objective.

18. If there is any doubt about this, note how the Europeans have failed to support Washington's Middle East policy (including resupply for Israel during the 1973 war) out of fear of jeopardizing their oil supplies.

19. See Portugalov's statement in *Tass*, January 29, 1980.

20. Marshall I. Goldman, *The Enigma of Soviet Petroleum: Half Empty or Half Full?* (London: Allen and Unwin, 1980).

21. For a good discussion of these considerations, see Francis Fukuyama, "The Soviet Union and Iraq Since 1968," the Rand Corporation, N-1524-AE, pp. 36-40.

22. Vladimir Sakharov, *High Treason* (New York: Putnam's Sons, 1980).

23. The Soviets turn out several thousand tanks, APCs, and so on every year.

24. In early 1979, following the rapprochement that proved short lived between the Iraqis and Syrians, the Soviets sought to have the oil-rich Iraqis pay for Syria's

arms. Though this did not pan out, the Syria-Libyan merger promises to have oil-rich Libya paying the Soviets for Syrian arms. See Gur Ofer, "Soviet Military Aid to the Middle East," *Soviet Economy in a New Perspective*, Joint Economic Committee of the Congress of the United States (Washington, D.C.: Government Printing Office, 1976).

25. This can be used to threaten states that are pursuing policies unfriendly to the Soviets as well as states that might consider drawing away from the Soviets. In this regard, the Iraqis have limited the extent of their distancing from the Soviets and now have engaged in significant fence-mending with the Russians.

26. With Iran no longer a barrier to the Soviets, the relative Soviet proximity to the region and the military forces the Soviets have positioned in the Transcaucasus and Turkestan military districts (19 divisions, including two airborne, 180,000 men, 4,500 tanks, and 940 aircraft) are probably more apparent to the local countries. See Chubin, "Soviet Policy Toward Iran and the Gulf," p. 3; Chubin uses figures from the IISS (International Institute for Strategic Studies, London).

27. Here the ethnic-sectarian fragmentation, new-found wealth and widespread corruption, political and social upheavals associated with the impact of modernity on traditional structures of authority, radical socialist opposition to conservative-monarchical régimes, and local ambitions and rivalries over regional dominance provide fertile breeding grounds for local turmoil and conflict.

28. A PDRY military humiliation of Saudi Arabia—say, for example, the defeat of the Saudi garrison opposite the PDRY border—could cause severe domestic dislocations in Saudi Arabia. Given the small size and relatively low quality of the forces on both sides, Soviet support and Soviet proxy forces might well tip the scales in the PDRY's favor.

29. See Fukuyama, "The Soviet Union and Iraq," on the use of the Kurds, local communists, and so on.

30. The standard Soviet works cited in the West on Soviet doctrine by Siderenko and Savkhin should be noted here. For a spirited portrayal and description of the airborne role and mission, see the interview with Col. Gen. D. S. Sukhorukov, commander of airborne troops, in *Sovetskiy voin*, no. 14 (July 1980), especially p. 3.

31. See for these figures, Jane's *All World's Aircraft* and Charles Fairbanks, "On Possible Soviet Threats to the Persian Gulf," outline paper prepared for the European-American Workshop, Eletham Hall, Great Britain, June 27, 1980.

32. In this regard, note that coordination between airborne and amphibious forces is also a basic part of Soviet doctrine.

33. Given the disaffection of the Kurds, Azerbaijanis, and Turkomen, the Soviets might also calculate that they would not face a hostile population in the north whereas they would in any more extensive moves into Iran; the latter could give them pause after their experience in Afghanistan.

34. For a detailed discussion of the logistics of and obstacles to such a Soviet advance, see Joshua M. Epstein, "Soviet Vulnerabilities in Iran and the RDF Deterrent," in *International Security* 6, no. 2 (fall 1981).

35. Baghdad to Abadan is 530 km and to Dhahran is 960 km. Staging from more southern bases in Iraq would reduce these numbers.

13

Soviet Policy
in the Middle East

Shahram Chubin

Renewed and intensified superpower competition in the Middle East and Gulf region has come at a time when the region is undergoing historic transformation. On a profound level it is anachronistic to see two states contend for power and influence over a region neither understands, cares for, or is likely to be able to influence more than marginally. On another level the process and result of the competition could seriously affect the autonomy and prospects of the peoples of the region.

The sense of powerlessness, lack of control, and susceptibility to manipulation by outside forces have of course been increased by the jockeying for position, solicitation of diplomatic support, and request for base and access rights of the great powers. This intensified pressure for alignment, according to which local actions are interpreted in terms of the East-West competition, increases the sense of impotence of the local states, which watch the game being played out over their heads. The precise relevance of this game to their needs is as shrouded in mystery as the eventual outcome is a source of anxiety. The possibility of superpower arrangement made at the expense of these local states worries the regional powers almost as much as more pressing and immediate security threats. As small states, the regional powers' interests are local whereas those of their patrons are global; the possibility that their interests may be sacrificed in a wider arrangement is therefore ever present. A related concern is the possibility of conflict in the region unrelated to the region itself; if the invasion of Afghanistan was a Soviet breakout from potential encirclement, the Arabs and Iran, not China, paid the costs.[1] Even this regional theater thus can be an arena for, rather than a stake in, great power rivalry.

This chapter originally appeared as "Gains for Soviet Policy in the Middle East" in *International Security*, vol. 6, no. 4, spring 1982, and is reprinted by permission of the MIT Press.

The Competition of Superpower Intrusion

Undoubtedly the most disruptive force in the Middle East and especially in the Gulf region is modernization. Constituting a multiple challenge that requires often contradictory responses, it is intrinsically destabilizing and immune to fine-tuning. The simultaneity of its demands and the disorientation it wreaks politically, socially, economically, culturally, and psychologically are nowhere identical and never entirely predictable. Such forces cannot be controlled or influenced by outside powers with even the best intentions, although they may be exacerbated. Neither of the superpowers is therefore likely to touch the deeper forces within these societies, and neither is more than marginally relevant to the most profoundly destabilizing trend in the region. Each can, however, reduce these complexities by supporting moderate or progressive régimes and by interpreting the interplay of social forces tactically. On this level it may be argued that with so little knowledge of the area and with so little relevance to its variety of development needs, the most useful role for outside powers is to balance one another. The Soviet Union may be unattractive as an economic model, limited as a technological partner, unacceptable as an atheistic state, and undependable as a military ally. Faced with local nationalism and the complexities of modernization, the Soviets would, some argue, perhaps inevitably learn the limits of influence.

There are several problems with this proposition. First, the Soviet Union is not alone in its ignorance of the region. Indeed the West, and particularly the United States, has been the major disruptive (that is, culturally intrusive) force in these societies. The U.S. approach has generally been instrumental, often mindlessly reactive, and framed in terms of the Soviet threat[2] or of access to oil. Its specific policies have been less than reassuring even to European allies.[3] Second, though neither superpower is able to control events, each is able to aggravate developments and exploit them to the other's short-term disadvantage. Third, the ideal of a balance between the superpowers that allows the regional states to get on with the disruptive business of modernization, without messy alignments or involvement, has long been just that. Since the beginning of the cold war, commentators from Walter Lippmann to George Kennan have argued against a global crusade, that props up every dictator who professes to be anti-Communist, and in general makes common cause with states so culturally different. The difficulty has been how to establish a balance of power that deters outside intervention when the opportunities for it are plentiful and local and when the occasions for its occurrence are not easily identified or dealt with after the fact.

Soviet Power and Proximity

Undoubtedly a major factor conditioning the perceptions of local states is the growing military power of the Soviet Union. These regional states are impressed (perhaps overly impressed) by military power. They believe that a military balance can restrain the aggressor and that intentions are influenced by the prevailing balance. They have seen that the rise of Soviet military power has affected the West's propensity for intervention by raising both its risks and costs. They have also seen that it has enabled the Soviet Union to do things it was unable to do earlier—to project power and sustain and succor régimes some distance from its homeland. They have seen a modern Soviet navy plying the Gulf of Oman and heard mysterious reports about the upgrading of Soviet divisions in the Transcaucasus from Category III to Category II or I state of readiness.[4]

The Soviet Union is now closer to the region both politically and militarily. The crumbling of the northern tier and erosion of constraints on air access, together with an enhanced projection capability, have virtually brought the Soviet Union into the Arabian Peninsula. Proximity confers undoubted advantages in the shadowy world of influence. It virtually guarantees persistence by nullifying the prospect of retreat. It allows for a greater tolerance toward setbacks and reverses and affords the Soviets the advantage of measuring their progress there in terms of a longer time horizon. It enhances claims to a legitimate interest, be they Monroe Doctrines or formulas like "Defense of the Homeland" and "cannot remain indifferent to events in an area of close proximity to the borders of the Soviet Union." Such claims, remarkably, have been extended recently to the Gulf region from their traditional zone, Persia, with very little notice in the West. Finally, contiguity multiplies options. It takes little effort to impress at this distance. The shadow of power can inhibit, modify expectations, and encourage adaptation with little overt effort. It is a useful adjunct to an indirect strategy. It also makes the reversal of gains harder.

The growth of Soviet power and the shrinkage of distance have naturally been felt by neighboring states. The Saudis and Iranians noticed the Afghan coup of April 1978. The Iraqis' calculation of threats to their régime also seems to have undergone a change since that year. Arguments that the West's past global predominance was unnatural and bound to change do not alter the central fact that the shift has come with a lurch, requiring adjustment by regional states. Even less comforting for them is the argument that Soviet expansionism is not a general but a regional impulse largely dictated by "the traditional Russian tendency to border expansion."[5]

The Local Context and Regional Priorities

Modernization is the most serious disruptive force in the region; though resistant to influence, it can be exploited. But there are other issues of general consequence in the region. The shift in the military balance has been alluded to, and the Iranian revolution and the Arab-Israeli conflict will be considered in following sections. Besides these, there are issues of more local concern that preoccupy the states of the Middle East. Foremost among these are the issues of régime security and stability. A direct Soviet military invasion, though of concern, is given much less priority and assigned much less probability than indirect threats to state security. The threats may originate from internal dissidence, regional rivalries, and the assistance of outside powers, or from a combination of the three; but the Middle East provides fertile ground for all of these. Furthermore, these destabilizing factors provide opportunities for exploitation by outside powers in ways that cannot be clearly identified or met. And the United States has shown itself either unable or unwilling to deal with these murky threats or willing to do so only in ways that destabilize the state it seeks to protect.

The Middle East states' deep ambivalence regarding the West requires little elaboration. At one and the same time, the Western powers are credited with omnipotence and undependability. The American connection with Israel undermines the Arab leaders associated with Washington.[6] Western assistance is irresolute when required (in regional conflict or internal unrest) or dangerous in the way it is extended when it is forthcoming (by being public, conditional, and polarizing among states within the region). The intrusiveness of the Western embrace can be as dangerous as the West's neglect, calling forth images of imperialism, puppets, and the Baghdad Pact. Although ultimate dependence on the West may be inescapable, many Middle Eastern leaders are coming to believe that the search for options must be intensified.

The American weakness in meeting its allies' need for régime security arises not merely from priggishness about definition (internal vs. external threats) or to a quixotic quest for pure contingencies in which military power may be used clearly. It derives from the overall U.S. position in the region, notably the relationship with Israel. The Soviet Union is the beneficiary of position in that it may be said to have played a constructive role historically for the Arab world on the Palestine question. Without the Soviet Union as a countervailing power, the Arabs would have been forced to accede to Washington's dictates on Palestine. Such change as has been evidenced in the stance of the United States comes from Soviet power and the prospect of war and confrontation with the USSR. The Soviet Union has thus helped the Palestinians and the Arab cause, a fact that cannot be denied by even the most pro-Western Arab state. Furthermore this positive feature of Soviet policy makes it difficult for the Arab states concerned about the growth of Soviet power to condemn it (in the context of some strategic consensus, for instance) and to embrace that of the United States— such a recalcitrant ally on the issue of Palestine. As a result, Soviet influence in the region, which largely derives from the West's handling of the Arab-Israeli issue, is transmitted through the Arab consensus into the Gulf, where the Soviet Union's diplomatic base is otherwise poorly established.

The attractiveness of the Soviet Union as a potential partner could be argued either as a function of the West's unattractiveness or on its own terms—for the pressure it might alleviate and for the protection it might purchase. Above all, the factor that enhances Soviet influence in the region is the growth of its relevant power. Moscow is in a position to meet many of the security needs of the regional states: to airlift massive supplies of arms; to ensure state security through the provision of a praetorian guard (perhaps through East Germany); to assist in resisting another state's irredentism; and to quell internal secessionist movements.

The Soviets' ability to establish their influence in the Middle East is facilitated by the belief—most prevalent in Arab countries some distance from the Soviet Union—that domination of other states is not imperialism unless it is exercised across an ocean (the saltwater fallacy). Combined with this belief is the difficulty that many nonaligned states have in criticizing régimes with an explicitly progressive ideology. Furthermore, Marxism-Leninism provides rationale for dictatorship,[7] which is comforting to one-party states.

The Soviet Union furthermore is a revisionist state, a stance in tune with régimes that profess to be revolutionary—such as those of Iran, Libya, or Algeria. The turmoil in the Middle East is bound to attract Soviet interest and involvement to promote anti-West trends, block anti-Soviet trends, respond to revolutionary duty or historic opportunity, or inhibit enemies and encourage friends. The Soviet propensity for probing and for indirect action through proxies or Communist parties is likely to be far more directly relevant to the security problems of the Gulf states than any Western recipe. From the point of view of leaders in the Middle East, the reality of Soviet power should be accommodated for a variety of reasons:

- To reduce dependence on the West, establish a balanced superpower relationship, and increase options, including the preemption of a possible superpower "deal."
- To seek reduced Soviet support for dissidents, minorities, and autonomist movements.
- To reduce the prospect of Soviet support for a regional adversary (e.g., the People's Democratic Republic of Yemen for Saudi Arabia or Oman).
- To counter Soviet criticism, as well as propaganda communicated directly and through fronts and communist parties.
- To reduce uncertainty about Soviet mischief-making during the domestic upheavals associated with modernization that lies ahead.

Soviet power for mischief-making in the region may appear to some to be exaggerated—perhaps it is. What is incontrovertible is that in the region the perception of Soviet power has changed appreciably, a product partly of the relative decline of Western power and of the insecurity generated by the Iranian upheaval. But it is also the result of the Soviet Union's expansive definition of security and of an indirect and incremental Soviet strategy in the region that is difficult to counter. As Henry Rowen has noted in reference to the Soviets' piecemeal accretions of power: "What matters most is the vector of all the instruments used and the positions built."[8] This power is derived not because the Soviet Union is an attractive socioeconomic model, nor from pure military power, nor indeed from a large-scale presence or influence in the Gulf, nor even because the regional states are duped into believing that the Soviet Union is more altruistic than the West. It comes rather from the conjunction of three factors: growing Soviet military capability, an expanded interest or motivation in seeking influence in the region (whether offensive or defensive), and the prevalence of regional opportunities for achieving this.

Regional instabilities will provide ample opportunity for exploitation by the determined outside power. Whether the issue is interstate war (Iran-Iraq), or secession or autonomy for a particular group (as in Dhofar or Kurdistan), the Soviet position will be important. Domestic instability, ranging from coups to minority (perhaps sectarian) discontent and the possibility of outside support for opposition forces, also raises the question of the Soviet attitude in these circumstances.[9] Soviet training of and assistance to opposition groups that practice terror tactics, groups that are not subject to its strict or direct control (and which are hence, "deniable"), are also of considerable importance to regional states, which feel both vulnerable to such groups and easily inhibited by hints of retaliation for policies they might otherwise wish to pursue. In all these areas the combination of regional opportunity and the proximity of relevant Soviet power guarantees a preoccupation by the local states with Soviet policy in the region.

The compression of the multiple crises of national integration, state building (institutions), legitimacy, identity, and participation in a short period makes for an explosive brew.[10] The instability associated with modernization in the Middle East is likely to be prolonged and is unlikely to be neutral. The status quo in the Gulf region has generally been consistent with U.S. and Western interests. Change is unlikely to come peacefully, and as a result, much of a régime's legacy, including its foreign orientation, is likely to be rejected by its successor régime. In this respect the Soviet Union stands to benefit by emphasizing the West's responsibility for the disruption of these societies by its "technological neo-colonialism."[11] Soviet optimism about the impact of modernization on the global correlation of forces is certainly not disguised.[12] The struggle will be waged in this area, and the Western position is most vulnerable.[13] Related to this is the natural expectation that frustration on the stalemated issue of Palestine will provide the Soviet Union with a growing constituency of young and radicalized Arabs, disgusted with their own governments and with their Western patrons.

The Soviets' optimism regarding the opportunities afforded by Middle East modernization does not merely derive from their faith in its anti-Western tendencies, which will therefore favor the USSR. It is more assertive than that. Although revolutionary change is unstoppable and doomed to failure, counterrevolutionary change (that is, developments against Soviet interests) must and should be blocked.[14] The assertion of irreversibility of change that favors the Soviet Union contrasts starkly with the West's proclivity to adapt to and accommodate change, or so it must appear to the regional states. After all, whatever else Soviet policy in the region has entailed in recent years, it has shown the Soviets' willingness to defend allies. Support for a preferred faction in Kabul and willingness to involve itself formally with the beleaguered régime of Hafiz al-Asad contrast strongly with the United States' scramble to abandon allies.

Decisiveness does not mean that there are not problems of choice. Some Western commentators gleefully point out problems the Soviets face in supporting two antagonistic states (Iraq and Syria, or Iraq and Iran). But these problems derive from power, not weakness, and they can be useful: The recalcitrant or defecting state can be pressured by assistance to its adversary and the prospect of Soviet arbitration between the two is always present. Investment in several places acts as a hedge against a setback in any one place. The Soviet Union appears to have resigned itself to the complexities of the region's politics; as Alvin Rubenstein has noted: "Influence building in the Arab world is an untidy business."[15]

Nor is Western optimism about the Soviets' disadvantages related to their atheism well founded. Propaganda aside, most states are pragmatic in their foreign relations: The issue of Soviets butchering Afghan Muslims has not had the effect one might have expected, partly because of the West's identification with Israel and the latter's treatment of Arab Muslims, partly because the West is seen as the culturally disruptive power that has challenged or undermined Islam in these societies. Whether Islam and its purported revival is a potential vulnerability or an asset[16] for the Soviet Union remains to be seen. I am, however, impressed by the possibilities open to the Soviet Union to develop the fact of its large Muslim population into an entrée into the Islamic world,[17] to use its southern provinces as showcases for the reconciliation of Islam and development,[18] and to purposefully develop contacts with the clergy in the Muslim states.

Soviet Policies and Regional Responses

Soviet policy in the Gulf region has been to exploit opportunities to decrease Western influence and to undermine an order in which it has little stake. Even in areas where one might expect the Soviets to be interested in predictability and stability (for instance, on its frontier in Iran), their temptation to score off the West has overridden any innate conservatism about border security. To intensify anti-Western pressures, which it sees as a natural outgrowth of revolutionary change and the struggle for national liberation, the Soviet Union has been prepared to act as patron and ally, to supply arms, and to furnish diplomatic support to states with coinciding interests.

Soviet policy is thus two-sided—defensive and offensive—and though it is usually unproductive to attempt to dissect any particular act as to the precise mix of these components, it is helpful analytically to note them:

Defensive. Ensure security of the homeland. This policy includes securing borders, maintaining friendly régimes on borders, containing Islamic contagion, and preventing encirclement, as well as countering the U.S. Rapid

Deployment Force. It is a short step from this strategy to preclusive intervention, the nailing down of the area in a period of uncertainty, and the insistence on compliant régimes on its border.

Offensive. Establish military dominance to be in a position to threaten to deny Gulf oil to the West and thereby divide Europe and the United States; to pressure and inhibit the Gulf states and Pakistan; to reassure its regional allies and "protect" change.

*   *   *

To the Gulf states the Soviets argue that the major threat to the region comes from the United States, which seeks to seize the oil fields or to cow the producers into selling their oil at a price and quantity that suits Western capitalists. To the anti-Western states the Soviets observe that the United States is a continuing threat to Iran's revolution, to progressive régimes, and to struggles for national liberation. Although acknowledging the Europeans' vital interest in Gulf oil, it denies any such interest on the part of the United States.[19] Furthermore, the Soviets reject the view that any state may make special claims to specific regions (e.g., the Carter doctrine) as a cloak for intervention. A consistent message to regional and Western states alike is that no problem in the region can be settled without consultation with the Soviet Union. According to the April 1971 party congress formula: "There is no question of any significance which can be decided without the Soviet Union or in opposition to it."

In the Gulf region, however, this doctrine is linked with both the growth of Soviet military power and local preponderance and the prevalence of regional instability. Here it means something more than consultation: It means the recognition of the Soviet Union's legitimate interest in the region and its acknowledgment as an equal by the West. Without this, it is implied, there is simply no prospect of stability or restraint in the region. The implied offer of restraint is in exchange for the joint management of the region that is implicit in the various Soviet offers (Portugalov proposal of February 1980; Brezhnev's offer to link Afghanistan and the Gulf at the party congress in April 1981).[20] Any neutralization formula is unlikely to appeal to the states located adjacent to Soviet power. The idea, however, of the Soviet Union's permanent presence as comanager or security manager of the region is communicated skillfully. To the United States, the Soviet Union argues that it provides a basis for stabilizing a region in which both superpowers have interests; to the Europeans it is depicted as an alternative to costly arms races, uncertain bases, and dangerous confrontations. Exclusion, it is implied, guarantees a spoiler role for the Soviets.

With the regional states, the Soviets are much tougher. They resist anything likely to constrict Soviet choices. The Soviet Union supports Gulf regional cooperation but not in defense or security affairs. Such cooperation would necessarily be part of an American pact structure such as the Central Treaty Organization (CENTO). The only basis for cooperation in the Soviet view is solidarity with the Steadfastness and Confrontation front and opposition to U.S. bases in the region. Although seeking co-equality, the Soviet Union is adamant in refusing to accept any equation of the two superpowers, even when the formula "exclusion of superpowers" from the Gulf is a concession by pro-Western states in its favor.

In pursuit of recognition of its minimum right to be a comanager and possibly even a regional security manager, the Soviet Union has made considerable progress in the past two to three years. Regional instabilities, the risks of confrontation, and the costs of military equipment may encourage the West to seek a cheaper solution in the near future.

Regionally, the Soviet Union has sought to inhibit ties with the West, weaken existing links, and impede Western access. Although encouraging nonalignment, the Soviets have made it clear that only a nonalignment tilted anti-West is acceptable. The Soviet Union's overtures to the West for an overall regulation of the problems of the area—in the Middle East, in the Gulf, in Afghanistan, whether individually or together—are bound to encourage the regional states lacking ties with Moscow to reconsider their policies so as to have some influence with both superpowers when they negotiate the future disposition of the region. In some respects this has already occurred in the past several years, as evidenced by Saudi Arabia's loosening of its ties with the United States, Jordan, Kuwait, and the other Gulf states and its friendly noises in the direction of the Soviet Union. Note also the opening of diplomatic relations with Moscow by Oman and the United Arab Emirates. In any case, Soviet ability to hurt and cause trouble for these régimes in the future will encourage them to appease and accommodate Soviet power in an effort to deflect its wrath. Kuwait is the outstanding example of a state that has elevated the purchase of protection[21] into a diplomatic art, but the perception of pressure is a general one. In July 1980, the Iranian Foreign Minister Ghotbzadeh, referring to differences with the Soviet Union, observed: "As we have no intention of being either pro-West or pro-East we are not going to pay protection-money to anyone."[22] It is testimony at least to the rhetoric of nonalignment, if not to Soviet pressure, that none of the Gulf states (with the single exception of Oman) was prepared to admit that the Gulf Cooperation Council was conceived largely for security reasons. Similarly, although Saudi Arabia was frantically requesting AWACS in October 1980, it was also calling for the exclusion of the superpowers from the Gulf.

A Soviet presence in Afghanistan, uncertainty in Iran, and the hint of superpower discussions on the region's future may well encourage a policy of accelerated reinsurance with the Soviet Union by the Gulf states. If Soviet influence is likely to be a permanent feature in the Gulf, it may make sense to acknowledge it.

Saudi Arabia

Saudi Arabia is a prize for Soviet policy in the Middle East. Saudi activism in Arab politics makes it important in issues outside the Gulf, whereas its leadership on the peninsula virtually guarantees that the smaller shaikhdoms would follow suit if Riyadh established diplomatic relations. Soviet policy in recent years has been to demonstrate to the Saudis that the USSR is a reliable ally on Arab issues, to show that differences in social structure and ideology[23] are not an obstacle, and to hint that simple prudence would dictate that the kingdom take out insurance by establishing normal ties with the Soviet Union.

Some progress has been made on several fronts. Saudi unwillingness to offer the United States permanent access to its facilities has earned Soviet gratitude, whereas Riyadh's continued public emphasis on the primacy of the Israeli as opposed to the Soviet threat and the Saudis' refusal to support the Camp David accords have encouraged the Soviets to believe that relations are steadily improving.[24]

To be sure, the Soviet invasion of Afghanistan resulted in Saudi condemnation, boycott of the Olympics, criticism in the Islamabad and Taif summits, and derecognition of the Kamal government (on April 7, 1981). But it also underscored the reality of Soviet power that required recognition, a point hinted at by Prince Fahd.[25] Despite this, the Saudis have observed that the positive contribution the Soviet Union has made to the Arab cause does not give Moscow the right to "interfere in the internal affairs of other states."[26]

The Soviets for their part have sought to depict Saudi criticisms on Afghanistan as U.S.-inspired and as an attempt to weaken Saudi relations with the Soviet Union.[27] They have sought to encourage the split with the United States on Camp David[28] and to depict the United States as a threat to Saudi stability.[29] Aware of divisions within the Saudi royal family on foreign policy (and especially on the U.S.-oriented versus the Arab-oriented components of it), Moscow has sought to show its own support for the Saudis' rejection of U.S. bases and insistence on the primacy of the regional states in ensuring Gulf security.[30] It has depicted Saudi dependence on the United States for military supplies as being in conflict with Riyadh's support for a genuine settlement of the Middle East problem.[31]

Although the invasion of Afghanistan has temporarily halted any further progress toward the establishment of diplomatic relations, the trend in this direction will continue. In the view of a senior Saudi official, the Soviet Union seeks to establish a basis on which to ensure a guaranteed oil supply.[32] Its overtures to the Saudis do not consist exclusively of carrots. The Soviet position in South Yemen—and potentially through that country and through arms supplies to North Yemen—provides a pressure point on the Saudis that might be alleviated if the Saudis are more forthcoming. Soviet power, proximity, and ability to pose indirect threats to the Saudi régime will constitute a continuing incentive to the Saudis to avoid offending the Soviet Union and to acknowledge its interests. Saudi policy recognizes this. It sought Soviet support for the Fahd peace plan, while offering as inducement the possible resumption of diplomatic relations. Overtures to the Soviet Union are helpful to the Saudi image in balancing the country's clear dependence on the United States for security and in offsetting the image created by the clamor surrounding the sale of AWACS to Riyadh.

The Soviet Union and Iran

The future of Iran is an issue of pervasive concern to all the states of the Middle East. The Iranian revolution clearly dealt a severe blow to the United States, but its course has not converted it into an asset for the Soviet Union. How far Iran will be permitted to evolve in its own way and at its own pace will be an indicator of Soviet intentions. The Soviet distinction between contiguous states, which it views in narrow terms of the defense of the homeland, and others, in which it tolerates more uncertainty, will surely be tested in Iran. Left to itself, Iran is likely to be highly unstable, providing opportunities and pretexts for intervention. The emergence of an indigenous Communist Popular Front or a condition of unsettled violence that attracts Soviet intervention are seen by the regional states as two equally unattractive but by no means unlikely outcomes in Iran. An eventual Soviet domination of Iran would alter the entire context of politics in the Gulf, making an accommodation to Soviet power a necessity for any prudent state.

Soviet Policy Since the Revolution

Soviet policy has been characterized by a number of persistent themes that merit brief discussion before an assessment of future prospects is attempted. The dominant feature of Soviet behavior throughout and after the Iranian revolution has been opportunism and the attempt to use the revolution against the West. No matter how much it may have complicated Soviet calculations (by its unpredictability, its Islamic dimension, and the uncertain supplies of gas that it caused), the revolution in Iran has clearly hurt the West more, with a potential for even more damage in that respect. In this zero-sum approach, therefore, the revolution has "objectively" favored the Soviet Union and is welcomed in the Kremlin.[33] The Soviet aim has been to intensify Iran's anti-Western component, deepen its radicalization, and prevent any possibility of normalization. In so doing, the Soviets have stressed the continuing dangers to the revolution posed by the West (especially the United States) and encouraged the elimination of those groups within Iran that seek a balanced relationship between the superpowers. They have sought to equate criticism of the Soviet Union with counterrevolution, to portray themselves as the protectors of the revolution, and where possible to increase the régime's dependence on the USSR.

A few examples suffice. The continuing threat of the West—a theme essential for the revolutionary leadership in Iran—has been a constant in Soviet propaganda. It has enabled the Soviet Union to pose as the protector of the revolution (by constant reference to Brezhnev's declaration of November 1978 warning against outside power interference), to reject any equation of the two superpowers, and to argue that such spurious evenhandedness in practice masks support for the West.[34] Soviet protection in turn is used to justify the 1921 treaty, which the Soviets insist guarantees Iran's independence and made possible Iran's resistance to British imperialism.[35] Soviet support for Iran's independence also lends itself to another Soviet concern. Since the Soviet Union defends Iran's independence against threats, Iran ought to respect the independence of other states, including that of Afghanistan.[36]

The attempt to prevent any normalization of relations with the West is best illustrated by Soviet policy during the hostage crisis. The Iranian Communist party (Tudeh) was explicit in supporting the retention of U.S. hostages for this very reason.[37] The Soviets encouraged the Iranians, terming the action "understandable" and intimating that U.S. espionage indeed threatened the revolution. Throughout the crisis American comments about instability in Iran were depicted as a rehearsal for direct military interference as in Chile.[38] Soviet attempts to prevent the removal of this obstacle to any possible reconciliation continued until the very eve of the hostage release, with the threat of an imminent attack by the United States as its central component.[39]

Within Iran there were officials who maintained a vigilant eye on Soviet activities and sought to retain a semblance of balance in relations with the two superpowers. In February 1980, after reports of Soviet troop maneuvers on Iran's borders, Iranian officials were quoted to the effect that these were designed to inhibit criticisms of Soviet policy in Afghanistan.[40] Later in the year, Foreign Minister Ghotbzadeh sought to gain support for a policy of equidistance by directly criticizing the Soviet Union and sending a stiff note that called for a reduced Soviet diplomatic presence in Iran. Refusing to take the bait and be provoked into a reaction that could justify those arguing for hostility toward Moscow, the Soviet government nevertheless tirelessly criticized Ghotbzadeh. The Soviet Union depicted his criticisms as counterrevolutionary and proimperialist and his aim as "a course based on pro-Americanism; on the subordination of the country to imperialist *diktat*; and on anti-Sovietism. Such a course is against the interests of the Iranian people."[41] Ghotbzadeh was not without supporters on this issue. Tehran Radio delivered a scathing commentary on the "allegedly greater benevolence on the part of the Soviet Union," which it considered irrelevant in the light of its exercise of military pressure, its invasion of Afghanistan, and its treatment of its own Muslim peoples.[42] President Bani-Sadr also criticized the Soviet Union in March 1980, accusing it of wanting to seize parts of Iran. But he was upstaged by Ghotbzadeh's anti-Soviet comments. After the latter's removal, Soviet commentaries concentrated on Bani-Sadr, insisting that Iran's leaders must determine who their true friends were.[43]

Opinions vary as to the success of this Soviet policy to date. Any analyst who seeks to portray Soviet policy toward Iran as successful will encounter serious qualifications: Iran's criticisms of Soviet policy in Afghanistan, Khomeini's warnings,[44] divergences on fixing a gas price, the schisms in

Arab solidarity vis-à-vis Israel arising from the Iran-Iraq war, and the contribution Moscow's cynical policy on the hostage issue made to American public opinion's support for a larger defense budget (including that of the Rapid Deployment Force) and a harder line against the Soviet Union. Yet these too are subject to modification, particularly if Iran's actions rather than declarations are examined, and if American public opinion is unable to channel its militance into productive policies that stop subversion.

Soviet gains, some of them intangible, and Soviet opportunities, arising out of the unrest in Iran, are more impressive than Soviet losses. The turmoil in Iran, the elimination of any center, and the radicalization of a young and expectant people provide ample scope for Soviet power and influence; in this the clerics in Iran have helped the Communists.[45]

As the revolutionary consensus has evaporated in Iran with the resultant fragmentation among its supporters and a bloody power struggle in progress, a key consideration for the Soviet Union has been the prospect of maintaining the revolution's radicalism. Even a most cautious observer surveying the Iranian scene in June 1981 noted that though the clerics may have been unable to deal with Iran's problems, Bani-Sadr's support came from the "pro-Western bourgeoisie," including the bazaar, which had defected from Khomeini. The ambivalence was evident: an incompetent clerical régime versus a better (but presumably less desirable) moderate régime.[46]

The ensuing showdown between the Mujahedin-e-Khalq and the Islamic Republican party (IRP) posed a greater dilemma for the Soviet Union. True, the Tudeh party maintained its precarious freedom by continuing to support Khomeini. But there were some differences within the IRP on the question of whether this should be allowed to continue. Furthermore, the execution of a prominent Mujahedin supporter, Mohammad Reza Sa'adati, for alleged spying for the Soviet Union, threatened to link the threat of the Mujahedin to that of the Soviet Union and result in the repression of the Tudeh and greater hostility toward Moscow.[47] To counteract this the Soviet Union emphasized that the bombing of the Islamic party's headquarters was evidence of continuing U.S. hostility to the régime, requiring—by implication—a strong link to the Soviet Union for protection.

The Soviet Union's support for the radicalization of Iran is clearly intended to facilitate the extension of Soviet influence. The elimination of the liberal nationalists (who are pro-Western), the repression of competing ultraleftist groupings, and the inevitable discrediting of the clerics (which requires little Soviet assistance) will leave the Tudeh as the only secular grouping in the country. In the meantime, the virtual international isolation of the country will have ensured the growth of Soviet influence.

The Soviets' continuing reminders of the threats confronting the revolution—particularly from the West—are designed to increase Iran's sense of isolation and vulnerability and to accentuate the pressures for reliance on the Soviet Union. By increasing Iran's dependence on the Soviet Union and offering assistance and protection, the Soviet foothold in the country would be expanded legitimately. The Soviet Union has sought to restore and expand trade relations.[48] More significantly, it has offered Iran protection on a number of occasions in the past two years that merit brief mention. These are significantly different from the Soviet veto of a Security Council resolution on the hostage issue in January 1980 or the subsequent offer of spare parts for Iran's oil and gas industry in March 1980. They concern assistance in the military-security area and could be the basis for a significantly new and probably irreversible trend in the relationship.

- In January 1980 the Soviet chargé in Mexico City offered Soviet troops to defend Iran against a U.S. invasion.
- In mid-1980 the Tudeh party (presumably through Soviet intelligence) warned the Iranian régime of an impending military coup.[49]
- In autumn 1980 Soviet Ambassador Vinogradov offered to provide Iran with arms in its conflict with Iraq, after having warned Iran of Iraq's impending attack.
- Throughout winter 1980-1981 Soviet arms were supplied to Iran indirectly (but presumably with Soviet consent) from Poland, North Korea, Syria, and Libya.
- After the bombing of the IRP headquarters, the Soviet Union offered security assistance to the régime, presumably in the form of counter-intelligence expertise.[50]

It is known that Soviet diplomats in Tehran have consistently warned Iranian officials of the serious threats confronting the revolution and offered them any assistance they might require.[51] As the clerical régime finds itself beleaguered and under attack, the temptation to rely on Soviet expertise for physical security may increase. There is no reason to expect that this would conflict with ideological principles if it were done to protect the revolution. For the Soviet Union, an arrangement whereby it ensures the régime's security would constitute a major breakthrough, conferring upon the Soviets not only the power to identify threats to the authorities but also the prerogative to withhold such information.

A third theme in Soviet policy (besides encouraging the revolution's radicalization and offering it protection) is irreversibility. There is little to suggest that the Soviet Union has a clear conception of the outcome of the revolution or its eventual stopping point. But slowly and with some success, the Soviet Union has sought to narrow the range of possible outcomes and to be in a position at least to inhibit (and possibly to veto) what it considers unacceptable or intolerable. In this it has been considerably abetted by the Washington practice of leaking internal policy debates and memoranda. When newspapers report that the United States expects the Soviet Union to invade northern Iran if the United States attacks that country[52] and ignorant discussions of the 1921 treaty refer to a general Soviet right to intervene in Iran, then the Soviet Union may be excused for believing that Iran has been conceded as being in its sphere of influence.

What would the Soviet Union find unacceptable in Iran? Certainly a pro-Western and probably an independent leftist régime. It is most unlikely that a leftist régime in Iran will be entrenched without Soviet aid; it is equally unlikely that a pro-Soviet left-wing régime could be reversed. Despite considerable evidence in support of the proposition that the superpowers' competition—at least in the Middle East—is not zero sum, that both superpowers can, and indeed frequently do, suffer setbacks simultaneously, Soviet policy persisted from 1979 to 1983 in cultivating the volatile anti-Western régime in Iran. That revolutionary Iran contained many political currents that could not be judged as pro-Soviet did not have a perceptibly constraining effect on Soviet policy. Revolutionary optimism and opportunism took precedence over national conservatism concerning stable frontiers or predictable neighbors. The régime of clerics in Tehran, restrained in its criticisms of its atheistic superpower neighbor, having dispatched its other domestic enemies, turned attention at last to the Tudeh, which had enjoyed at least partial immunity from previous purges. The timing of the crackdown on the Tudeh in Iran was related less to the Tudeh itself than to Tehran's relationship with Moscow.

Soviet overtures to Iran from the outset of the Iraq-Iran war reflected two primary considerations: (1) Iran was the greatest strategic prize whose orientation was uncertain and whose potential as an ally was considerable, whereas Iraq, in any case less geopolitically important, had shown signs of drift since 1978; (2) the Iraqi attack on Iran, undertaken probably against Soviet advice and possibly also without its foreknowledge, encouraged Moscow to tilt toward the defending state. By late 1982, neither of these considerations remained; Iran had shown itself to be no less anti-Western than before, but it also was now clearly less of a "catch" for the revolutionary camp with its obscure medieval ravings and its potential for catalyzing a superpower confrontation. Furthermore, by mid-1982 Iran, no longer on the defensive, appeared intent on expanding the war into Iraq and the Gulf states, carving up southern Iraq, and establishing its political hegemony in the other Arab littoral states. On both counts Iran appeared to menace Soviet interests and especially to risk a direct American intervention on the side of the Arab states. Soviet policy from autumn 1983 was therefore a tilt back toward Baghdad and the resumption of arms supplies to seek to redress the balance of power in the Gulf. A further Soviet consideration was the wider Middle Eastern picture, which had seen a clear Israeli military dominance (in mid-1982) of Syria and had demonstrated yet again the divisions in the Arab world in supporting its Palestinian brethren. Both the failure of Soviet arms in Lebanon and the diminishing number of entry points for Soviet influence in the Middle East must have argued for an emphasis and commitment to the Iraqi connection.

Tehran's reaction to the resumption of Soviet arms supplies to Iraq—to the supplier of missiles that landed in Nezfal and other western Iranian towns—was also predictable. The Tudeh leadership was rounded up, paraded, and eventually tried. Some of its members, but not its leaders, were executed in mid-1983. Iranian criticisms of Soviet policy in Afghanistan were renewed, and Tehran's emphasis on "neither East nor West" was revived. Tehran was careful not to sever commercial or diplomatic relations because it remained dependent on the USSR for an important transit route. Nevertheless, by mid-1983 the relationship was neither correct nor cordial, and it was unlikely to be improved as long as the Gulf war continued to sputter on without a definite conclusion.

The schism between Tehran and Moscow and the tone of Soviet commentaries in 1983–1984 certainly suggested that both sides, and particularly the USSR, had lost no illusions about the potential for progress in relations between the two states. The gap between them was simply too wide. Nevertheless, the clerics in Tehran, having come very close to establishing a security relationship with Moscow, were now in danger of drifting to the farther shore and threatening Soviet interests by opposition. The perennial dangers for a government in Tehran of too much dependence on the USSR (which encourages appeasement and fraternal intervention) and excessive distance (which could be construed as unnatural and provocative) still persist. The clerics' drift away from Moscow must be moderate and well managed if it is to steer between the two extremes that seem to characterize Soviet security perspectives. This moderation will not emerge spontaneously from the revolutionary policies of Iran in the post-Khomeini era, and therefore the risks of Soviet displeasure—and more—will remain.

The Soviet Union and the Future of Iran

The prospects of political stability in Iran in the foreseeable future are dim and grow dimmer by the day. There are a number of possible alternative outcomes worth sketching.

- The consolidation of power by the current clerical government, the elimination of rivals, and the control of the key sectors of the country and bureaucracy.
- Civil war, possibly the disintegration of the country, certainly the dispersal of power in a condition of near-anarchy in which there is no dominant grouping but a continuing competition among several factions (this condition of drift currently prevails).
- The gradual alienation of the populace from the theocratic régime, radicalization, and the emergence of a leftist secular alternative to constitute a coalition government.
- Alienation and violence resulting in popular support for a return to security and away from revolutionary austerity. This outcome could lead to a military-civilian coalition encompassing various ethnic and centrist groups, including liberals, monarchists and nationalists.

What is abundantly clear is that no single grouping is able to run the country and that no specific catalyst capable of unseating the régime is currently visible. From the Soviet viewpoint the first outcome would be unattractive; it is also highly unlikely. The second condition currently prevails and may indeed be the prerequisite for the type of régime the Soviet Union would wish to see installed, notably the third of the outcomes. The final scenario would, given its likely pro-Western orientation, be unacceptable.

Aside from developments within Iran, either direct Soviet military intervention (on a large scale) or subversion is an avenue of influence that the Soviets might consider. The disincentives for a large-scale military intervention range from a probable Western reaction to a threat to Gulf oil to the practical difficulties involved in such an operation[53] (terrain, distances, assets in the South, and the problems of physical or military control without a prior political base—witness the Afghanistan experience). The use of military force for a limited temporary incursion into northern Iran for demonstrative purposes, vis-à-vis the Tehran government or the Western bloc, would run fewer risks (by decoupling from the Gulf), would avoid the problems of control, and could serve as a warning of Soviet concern to both parties. For reasons implicit in this depiction, a large-scale Soviet military intervention in Iran is not the most probable contingency.[54]

Soviet opportunities for covert intervention are plentiful, and the condition of political instability provides Moscow with ample time to build up an adequate political infrastructure to create a reliable basis for intervention.[55] The most obvious Soviet asset—the Tudeh party, now driven underground— can be used either as a pressure group or as a power base for an alternate government. It would be a mistake, however, to see the Soviets' choices as confined solely to the Tudeh party members and its sympathizers. There is sufficient evidence of widespread Soviet activity in Iran to assume that an alliance with other Marxist groupings in the country (including the fedayeen and parts of the Mujahedin and Paykar and other offshoots) is a real and growing possibility. Tudeh activity in the oil fields, factories, and armed forces can also be assumed. Furthermore, some of the figures in the Islamic Republican party are sufficiently shadowy to raise questions about their political inclinations. Soviet and Marxist activities in some of the minority areas including Kurdistan, Azerbaijan, and Baluchistan should also be noted. A Popular Front government comprising these and other elements might well emerge at an appropriate time of confusion.

By virtue of contiguity, the Soviet Union possesses many intrinsic advantages in Iran: in providing communications, arms, training, and a sanctuary (through a porous frontier), for example. Its diplomatic, economic, and cultural presence in the area has grown as that of the Western states has declined. Detailed knowledge of the country, including of its minorities and tribes, has long been a Soviet specialty and there is no reason to assume that this is for purely academic purposes. In addition, the Islamic card is by no means a Western monopoly; there is some evidence of Soviet contacts, through the (government-controlled) Shi'i clergy, with the clerics in Qum[56]—an entrée that the West does not possess.

In the light of Iran's current international isolation, its protracted military confrontation with Iraq, its internal turmoil, and the absence of any countervailing Western presence, the Soviet Union is given a free field of activity. It would be difficult to imagine a condition more suitable for extensive Soviet covert activity, and it would require extraordinary self-restraint by the Soviets to forego it. Under these circumstances the Soviet Union is maneuvering itself into a position to be able to veto the emergence of a government it finds unacceptable and to assist the emergence of its preferred candidate. That this position of de facto predominance can be converted into an acknowledgment of its requirements in Iran and serve as the basis for a negotiated settlement in the wider Middle East–Gulf context appears to be the Soviet hope.[57] Even if it is unrealized, the unchecked growth of Soviet power in Iran will make the defense of the Gulf problematic and present an irresistible impulse for other local states to make some accommodation to it.

The Arab-Israeli Zone

As in the Gulf, Soviet policy in the Arab-Israeli zone is essentially revisionist, encouraging changes in the basically pro-Western status quo. Given the distances involved, the emphasis is more on flexibility and competition than on the Soviets' immediate security needs. Nevertheless, the persistence of regional rivalry, combined with the problems of ensuring order with change, gives the revisionist power ample scope for maneuver. Regional forces opposed to the status quo have found the Soviet Union a convenient ally in their quest to confront their enemies, be they Israel or the West. The Soviet Union is well situated to exploit problems and to thrive on disorder opportunistically, while confronting the West with the need to pursue constructive policies that dampen problems and reduce the prospects of disorder. The Soviet ability to exploit or exacerbate revolutionary tendencies or conflicts in the third world[58] is perhaps nowhere better illustrated than here.

Seen dynamically, this asymmetry in aims favors the USSR because of the regional problems. But the Soviet Union has other advantages. Clearly the continuation of the Arab-Israeli conflict provides an entrée for the Soviet Union into the Arab world, justifying its military assistance (and even access to facilities or bases) and inhibiting criticisms of the latent Soviet threat. Through the medium of the Arab consensus, the Soviets' constructive role on this issue is transmitted into the Gulf region, where the Soviet threat is at least as immediate as that of Israel.[59] To the Arab states of the Near East and Africa, Soviet imperialism appears to have been relatively benign, at least on the issue of Israel and the Arabs. The West's connection with Israel, however, is indefensible, especially to the radical domestic oppositions of these countries.

The Soviet Union's interests in the Middle East only partially coincide with those of the Arab states. Moscow's attitude toward the conflict has been relatively consistent, as have its aims: to increase its strategic flexibility in the region and to acquire an internationally recognized presence there.

Its policies have therefore been instrumental and benefitted from the conflict and regional polarization to enhance its political and military presence while avoiding iron-clad commitments that entangle it in superpower confrontation. In this respect, Soviet policy has sought to benefit from controlled tensions, or conditions that maximize its influence without resultant commitment. As Philip Windsor has argued, the Soviets have not sought to prevent crises but rather to stabilize crises.[60] By the same token the Soviet Union is not opposed to a settlement but to an American settlement of the Palestine question; a settlement that recognizes the Soviet Union as a Middle Eastern power (with a right to a permanent presence) would be quickly supported.

It may be argued that the Soviet Union is playing with a weak hand in the Arab-Israeli conflict, that in the past Soviet unwillingness to confront Israel (and the West) showed its regional rivals that Moscow had no war card to play, and that the peace process, however stalemated, still relies on the West and Israel if it is to achieve fruition. It might also be observed that the Soviets have encountered all the traditional problems of involvement: the evanescent influence attached to arms supplies, the lack of control over their ultimate use, squabbling allies, the weak domestic base of allies, the prospect of unlimited investments when faced with competing demands, and so on.

To be sure, the Soviet involvement in the Middle East crisis has no guarantee of success and is faced with reverses, competing goals, and fractious partners. The Soviet Union's interests are not identical with those of its partners in the Middle East; they never have been. Soviet officials can be quite blasé about this. Leonid Zamyatin blandly responded to a question about Soviet commitments to Iraq under the 1972 friendship treaty in the light of the war with Iran: The "treaty of friendship is a treaty of peace and not war." The Iraqis were not dissatisfied with the Soviet Union's neutrality, he argued.[61]

The Soviet Union nevertheless remains an intrinsic element in any Middle Eastern equation. For its own purposes it is bound to remain committed to an involvement in an issue in which its credibility as a superpower is at stake. This commitment will involve a willingness to make investments in the face of an uncertain future. Like Soviet investments in Syria and Libya, these may not be risk free, but they will assist in generating (or maintaining) tensions that are a prerequisite (in the Arab view) to attention to this issue. In the past, Soviet risk taking has been constrained by the strength of the U.S. commitment and the prevailing military balance in the region. Given a more favorable military balance, whether or not the Soviet Union will be prepared to embark on confrontation with the United States in a Middle East crisis remains to be seen. There is no evidence that in the Lebanon crisis in May 1981 or war of mid-1982 the Soviet Union either encouraged or restrained the Syrians. But the crises achieved one Soviet objective: to focus on the Israeli threat to the region.

In the past, the argument that all the problems of the region stemmed from the Arab-Israeli conflict (and that its settlement would reduce Soviet influence, bring U.S.-Arab amity, and ensure stability in the Gulf) was so oversold that it is now in danger of being completely discarded. In truth, the shifting of strategic interests to the Gulf region has diminished the importance of the conflict in terms of Soviet influence. But it does remain connected in a number of ways. The Soviet Union can and does use the liability of the Western connection with Israel to inhibit the establishment of ties between the United States and the moderate Arab states. The West cannot decouple the Gulf and Israeli conflicts because neither Moscow nor the Arab consensus will allow it. Furthermore, it is on the long-term[62] hope of radicalization and in particular anti-Western sentiment stemming from the Arab-Israeli conflict that the Soviet Union appears to count.

In the meantime, the Soviet Union seeks to woo the Arab countries into a more balanced relationship. The Soviets hope to encourage Jordan and Saudi Arabia to follow Kuwait's example, but they have no excessive expectations. Even Soviet relations with Syria, Libya, Iraq, and the PLO are depicted officially as ordinary, in contrast to those with the "progressive" states of Afghanistan, Ethiopia, and the Peoples' Democratic Republic of Yemen (PDRY). Unable to tangibly exploit Arab dissatisfaction with Camp David, Moscow has periodically renewed its offers of a collective approach to the problem. Crises are a useful means of underscoring the point and of reentering Middle Eastern diplomacy. The Soviet Union is no doubt prepared to match the U.S. commitment to remain involved in the Middle East.

The Soviet Union's dim immediate prospects in the region should not be a source of excessive reassurance to the West. Although Moscow may have no apparent war or peace card, the Western position looks little better. Although it can match the Soviets' military commitment, the West may retain the monopoly on the ability to furnish a peace settlement. But this claim is yet to be tested. Whether Israeli concessions can be delivered is uncertain. The Reagan administration's sporadic and largely ill-conceived ideas about the region certainly give few grounds for optimism in this regard. Proclaiming and then ignoring its own peace initiatives, it shows little interest in the area beyond the oil or superpower dimensions. At the same time changes in the internal structure of Israel make the achievement of peace (and the reversal of West Bank settlements) more difficult with each passing day, and the disillusion in the moderate Arab state grows apace. Perhaps a policy of calculated nonsettlement substituting some movement for a settlement will be adequate to shore up the West's allies and contain its enemies. Clearly, only the continuing threat of the Soviet Union (rather than oil embargoes or abstract notions of justice) will furnish the Arabs with the means to pressure the West into encouraging a settlement. The failure to do so risks not a direct military challenge by the Soviet Union but the exacerbation of local conditions, creating the basis for a much more solid Soviet alliance with the Arab world.

Conclusions: Western Policy

Implicit in the preceding analysis has been the contents of an appropriate Western policy. In the case of Iran the slide from an anti-Western revolution to anarchy is clearly complete; what remains for the future is the shift to predominant Soviet influence. The West's current inattention risks communicating the wrong signal to all interested parties. A future Western response to some unacceptable occurrence in that country will look highly precipitous if it is preceded by a low level of attention. If the West seeks credibility to deter Soviet mischief-making in Iran, its commitment must be visible and appropriate now. Discussions of the military scenarios are useful for sizing up the problem and sensitizing policymakers to its dimensions but have little relevance to the type of creeping Soviet intervention and subversion that defy precise definition and that constitute the present threat in Iran.

The future of Iran is the most pressing problem in Gulf security today. Western policies there will affect Western credibility in the Arab states of the Gulf as a security partner. The growth of Soviet power, doubts about both Western will and capability, and the problems of partnership with the rich, disruptive, and pro-Israeli Americans create a constant need for reassurance on the part of the West's friends in the Middle East. Besides balancing Soviet power (on every level), the West needs to show greater sensitivity to the complex and often competing pressures on the Gulf states, recognizing the constraints under which they operate. A willingness to reaffirm publicly the value of the partnership from time to time, more discretion, and a less commercial attitude toward the Gulf states, in which a truly equitable long-term partnership is sought, would be helpful.

To reduce the Arab-Israeli problem to the issue of the imminence of the threat it poses is to ignore the more profound and incalculable effects of persistent frustration on this issue for regional security. On this issue the argument that the Soviet Union is the cause of the problem (or that the problem would be manageable without it) is at its weakest. Soviet power has been helpful for the Arab cause; without a settlement of the problem it will not be possible to focus attention on the threat posed by that power. American willingness to pressure and reward Israel for compromises requires an equal willingness to reward those Arab states (Egypt, Oman) prepared to take risks for peace. The military balance in this region is bound to remain unstable because of the possibility of domestic changes and realignments within the Arab world. This issue must be dealt with between crises and not merely after them.

Stripped of polemics, it seems clear that the Soviet Union assists groups—sometimes directly[63]—in achieving their goals through the use of force and sometimes terror. No doubt this approach affects the perceptions of régimes that feel themselves exposed to domestic or regional enemies; that it is intended to inhibit them is not in question. The problem is to disentangle local cause from Soviet involvement and to assign the correct degree of responsibilty to Moscow. Although the Soviet Union clearly must be confronted on this issue and made to pay a price for this type of unconventional activity, it is by no means clear how to do this without equivalent covert operations. At the very least in the diplomatic arena it reflects a general truculence, noted by Philip Windsor: "In many respects the Soviet Union seems to be developing a peculiar notion of legitimacy: that superpowers are not as other nations, and that they enjoy special dispensations from the norms and rules of international conduct."[64]

As long as it follows this policy, there seems to be no reason to acknowledge the Soviet Union as an equal state, giving it the legitimacy and formal status it appears to crave. By the same token, the Soviet line that it will be a spoiler unless it is included in the comanagement of international relations and in specific regions should be given short shrift. Although exclusion may entail a spoiler role for Moscow, there is no sign that inclusion guarantees restraint. In my view, Soviet interests should be acknowledged not as facts but as favors, requiring Moscow to show a sense of responsibility as well as a taste for privilege.

The Soviet threat in the Gulf may well derive from a combination of general strategic nervousness and interest in defense of the homeland. Whether it is only regional or part of a larger global thrust is immaterial; in either case, vital Western interests in the Gulf are threatened. The Soviet threat is not just a purposeful pursuit of grand strategy or the "motiveless malignancy" (in Philip Windsor's phrase) of a revisionist power. One need not underestimate the Soviets' overextension elsewhere or their capacity to create for themselves security problems that might otherwise be mere aggravations to see that the Soviet threat derives from the conjunction of three factors: greater military capability, regional volatility, and enhanced interests (whether for border security or for denial). In the face of Soviet persistence and a willingness to use many instruments of power, one sees a Western bloc smug in its appreciations and veering fitfully between defeatism and rhetorical overkill. The danger of seeing the Soviet threat as a short-term issue—a window (or as exclusively military)—is to miss the very real dangers posed at other levels which must be met over a much longer period of competition.[65] It may well require the containment of Soviet power through disciplining it as well as by taming the competition. In either event it seems to me self-evident that one requirement for a Western policy that seeks to communicate clearly and unequivocally which aspects of Soviet behavior it considers intolerable is the capacity to respond in kind. This may mean inflicting reverses on the Soviet Union's allies on occasions when Soviet policy is clearly aimed at doing this to Western allies.[66]

Notes

1. The Soviet strategy of storing up chips to exchange at an appropriate time is generally recognized. For the Soviets' offers linking their actions in Egypt to those of the United States in Iran, see Henry Kissinger, *The White House Years*

(London: Weidenfeld and Nicolson, 1980; Boston: Little, Brown, 1979), pp. 583, 1,288, 1,292.

2. Edward Said quoted a Middle East Institute report on current research written in 1958 as emphasizing the importance of Arabic to oil company executives, technicians, and military personnel: "Russian universities are now producing fluent Arabic speakers. Russia has realized the importance of appealing to men through their minds, by using their own language. The U.S. need wait no longer in developing its foreign language programme" (*Orientalism* [London: Routledge and Kegan Paul, 1980], p. 292.

3. "It seemed in Europe not that the United States was mistaken in its handling of the [Middle East] situation, but that it was incapable of handling it at all" (Michael Howard, "Return to the Cold War?" in "America and the World 1980," *Foreign Affairs* 59, no. 3 [1981], p. 469).

4. Soviet divisions have three degrees of combat readiness: Category I, between three-quarters and full strength, with complete equipment; Category II, between one-half and three-quarters strength, complete with fighting vehicles; Cateogy III, about one-quarter strength, possibly complete with fighting vehicles (some obsolescent).

5. "The traditional Russian tendency to border expansion has found few promising outlets, and except in Asia, little incentive in recent years. It may make itself felt again in the more distant future. For the moment it is not a major component in Soviet motivation. It is, in any case, an impulse which is regional, not universal, in character" (George Kennan, *The Cloud of Danger* [Boston: Little, Brown, 1977]), p. 178). One wonders whether even if true Western policy should be any different as a result of such an appreciation.

6. Even more when it is seen as perpetuating a condition of division in the Arab world.

7. Philip Windsor, "The Soviet Union in the International System of the 1980s," in "Prospects of Soviet Power in the 1980s," Part II, *Adelphi Paper 152* (London: International Institute for Strategic Studies, 1979), p. 3.

8. Henry Rowen, "How the West Should Protect Persian Gulf Oil and Insure against its Loss," draft paper presented to European-American Institute Workshop, June 4–6, 1981.

9. For a concise and useful discussion of the evolution of Soviet policies in the region, including the use of Soviet power for its regional allies, see Francis Fukuyama, "New Directions for Soviet Middle East Policy in the 1980s: Implications for the Atlantic Alliance," P-6446 (Santa Monica, Calif.: The Rand Corporation, February 1980).

10. For a sensitive discussion of one dimension of the problem see Fouad Ajami, *The Arab Predicament* (London: Cambridge University Press, 1981).

11. See G. Kim, "The National Liberation Movement Today," *International Affairs*, 4 (April 1981), pp. 27–37.

12. H. Trofimenko, "America, Russia and the Third World," *Foreign Affairs* 59, no. 5 (summer 1981), p. 1034.

13. See especially Vernon Aspaturian, "Soviet Global Power and the Correlation of Forces," *Problems of Communism* 29 (May-June 1980), pp. 1–18.

14. For a summary of the Soviet view, see *The Times* (London), November 18, 1980. See also Aspaturian's quote from Chervonenko (in "Soviet Global Power").

15. Alvin Z. Rubenstein, "Air Support in the Arab East," in Stephen S. Kaplan, ed., *Diplomacy of Power: Soviet Armed Forces as a Political Instrument* (Washington, D.C.: Brookings Institution, 1981), p. 515.

16. Certainly the Soviets act optimistic. See Leonid Medvedko, "Islam: Two Trends," *New Times* 13 (1980), p. 29. Note also Brezhnev's pragmatic comment at the party congress: "The liberation struggle can develop under the banner of Islam [but it can also be reactionary and counterrevolutionary]. Consequently, what really matters is the actual content of a particular movement."

17. A point consistently ignored by Western analysts is the depth of Soviet expertise in this area. There seems to be no lack of specialized institutes dealing with the culture, history, language, ethnic, and sociological factors in the region. This detailed knowledge of tribal folkways, minority sects, and the like is invaluable in the cultural exchange regularly fostered and gives the USSR a strong base on which to build a long-term policy as well as a presence that can become formidable.

18. Conversations with Hélène Carrière D'Encausse.

19. See for example Ruben Andreasyan, "The 'Vital Interests' of Oil Imperialism," *New Times* 14 (1980), p. 21.

20. For an extended discussion of these see my *The Scope and Conditions of Outside Power Influence in the Persian Gulf* (London: IISS, Gower Press, 1981), and Arnold L. Horelick, "Soviet Strategy in the Persian Gulf," draft paper presented to European-American Institute Workshop, June 4–6, 1981.

21. Both from its large Palestinian community, which it seeks to keep happy by large subventions to the PLO and a supportive stance, and toward the Soviet Union, which it hopes to appease by occasional purchases of arms (1976 and currently under discussion) and by declaratory policy supportive of Soviet initiatives in the region. See its joint communiqué in April 1981. See British Broadcasting Corporation (hereafter cited by broadcast number) SU/6708/A4/1-3, April 27, 1981.

22. Tehran Radio, July 2, 1980 in BBC SWB ME/6462/A/3, July 4, 1980.

23. For instance, that communism, Islam, and monarchy are not incompatible with good working relations. See especially Igor Belyayev, *Literaturnaia Gazeta*, January 31, 1979, and Radio Moscow in Arabic, February 22, 1979.

24. The Saudis have acknowledged the "positive policy adopted by the Soviet Union toward Arab issues" in the words of Prince Saud al-Faisal. See *International Herald Tribune*, March 5, 1979.

25. *Al-Safir* (Beirut), January 9, 1980.

26. These points were prefaced by Foreign Minister Saud al-Faisal's reference to the Soviet Union as a "power which one cannot ignore" (*Riyadh Radio*, July 21, 1980, in ME/6478/A/1, July 23, 1980).

27. See Eugenei Primakov, *Literaturnaia Gazeta*, March 12, 1980; *Izvestiya*, April 27, 1981; and *Tass*, SU/6710/A4/11, April 29, 1981.

28. Report in "Asia and Africa" broadcast August 14, in SU/6194/A4/1, August 15, 1979.

29. Igor Belyayev, "Who is Threatening Saudi Arabia?" *Literaturnaia Gazeta*, in SU/6469/A4/1, July 12, 1980.

30. See Radio Moscow's broadcast on Saudi Arabia's National Day, September 23, in SU/6532/A4/4-5, September 25, 1980.

31. "Sovetskaya Rossiya," *Tass*, April 10, 1981, in SU/6699/A4/1, April 14, 1981.

32. Prince Turki al-Faisal, head of Saudi intelligence, *Fortune*, March 10, 1980, p. 56. Sheikh Yamani, as petroleum minister, often made the same point.

33. Brezhnev's formulation at the party congress put this succinctly: "The revolution in Iran has a special character. It was a major international event of recent years. For all its complications and contradictions, it is fundamentally an anti-imperialist revolution even though internal and foreign reaction is striving to change its nature" (BBC SU/6657/C/8).

34. For illustrative examples, see *Pravda*, July 17, 1980, Moscow SU/6475/A4/ 1, July 19, 1980, and Igor Sheftanov, Moscow, May 29, 1981, in SU/6739/A4/4, March 6, 1981, and *Tass*, March 25, in SU/6381/A4/1-2, March 27, 1981. A constant theme is that Iranians must remember who their real or true friends are. See especially *Tass*, February 10, SU/6647/A4/1, February 12, 1981; *Tass*, January 12, SU/6622/A4/1, January 14, 1981; and "A False Thesis and a Real Threat," *New Times* 8 (1980).

35. Andrei Gromyko offered this view that the treaty was mutually beneficial, *Moscow in Persian*, August 28, in SU/6510/A4/1, August 30, 1980. It is developed more explicitly by Professor Bandarevskiy, in a commentary on the 1921 treaty, *Moscow in Persian*, April 30, 1981.

36. *Moscow in Persian*, August 31, 1980, in SU/6514/A4/1, September 4, 1980.

37. See the interview with its leader Nourredin Kianouri, *Le Monde*, April 18, 1980.

38. See Georgiy Kuvaldins, *Tass*, June 21, in SU/6452/A4/2-3, June 23, 1980.

39. See for example *Pravda*, January 17, 1981. That this policy might prove counterproductive, by stimulating American public opinion to greater determination to resist the Soviet Union and to finance the very force that the Soviets argue threatens their security, appears to have been considered but dismissed. See *The Times* (London), January 23, 1981.

40. *International Herald Tribune*, February 11, 1980.

41. See *Tass*, August 26, in SU/6508/A4/1-2, August 28, 1980. See also *Tass*, June 19, in SU/6450/C2/1, June 20, 1980. For the Communist party's criticism, see National Voice of Iran (*Baku*), August 11, in ME/6498/A/6, August 15, 1980. See also *Le Monde*, August 12, 1980.

42. July 9, in ME/6468/A/8, July 11, 1980.

43. *Moscow in Persian*, March 19, in SU/6682/A4/3, March 25, 1981.

44. "We are in conflict with international communism to the same extent as we are against Western exploiters. . . . You should know that the danger of communist power is not less than that of America" (*Washington Post*, March 22, 1980).

45. *The Economist*, August 2, 1980, p. 13. See also Shahram Chubin, "The Soviet Union and Iran," *Foreign Affairs* (spring 1983).

46. Alexander Bovin (*Izvestiya* correspondent), Moscow *Home News*, June 13, in SU/6749/A4/2, June 15, 1981.

47. It was therefore strongly criticized by the National Voice of Iran (*Baku*), July 29, ME/6790/A/1, August 1, 1981.

48. Trade in 1979 was only half that of 1977, $500 million versus $1 billion. A trade protocol was signed in June 1980 and a transit agreement in December 1980. Moscow did not link agreement on the latter with agreement on a new gas arrangement, which it insisted upon earlier. The volume of Iran's goods transiting Soviet territory in 1980 was 1.7 million tons, and this enabled the régime to continue its trade despite the EEC embargo and the Gulf war. Iran's oil shipments to the Eastern bloc have also increased.

49. President Bani-Sadr's interview, *Le Monde*, July 2, 1980.

50. See *The Sunday Times* (London), July 5, 1981.

51. Personal interviews with diplomats stationed in Tehran.

52. See *International Herald Tribune*, August 27, 1980.

53. See in this volume Dennis Ross, "Considering Soviet Threats to the Persian Gulf," and Bruce Kuniholm, "The Persian Gulf and Southwest Asia: Toward a Viable Political/Military Strategy"; and Joshua M. Epstein, "Soviet Vulnerabilities

in Iran and the RDF Deterrent," *International Security* 6, no. 2 (fall 1981), pp. 126–158.

54. But clearly this depends very much on the outcome of the Afghan adventure and on the West's ability to fashion both a capability and a commitment to make it unattractive.

55. I am indebted to Pierre Morel for his comments on this analysis.

56. Information provided by Hélène Carrière D'Encausse.

57. Yair Hirschfeld has reminded us of the Soviets' longstanding interest in concluding a superpower deal on Iran (in August 1941 and June 1961), as well as their aim to acquire international legitimization through negotiations of their interests in the Middle East. With the turmoil in Iran and Afghanistan, the timing may appear suitable. See Yair P. Hirschfeld, "Moscow and Khomeini: Soviet-Iranian Relations in Historical Perspective," *Orbis* 24, no. 2 (summer 1980), pp. 219–240.

58. Stanley Hoffmann, "Foreign Policy: What's to be Done," *The New York Review of Books*, April 30, 1981, p. 39.

59. Israel's actions in Iraq admittedly do make this harder to argue in the Arab world.

60. Philip Windsor, "The Soviet Union in the International System" p. 10.

61. Zamyatin, a Central Committee member, was interviewed by *As Siyasah*, broadcast by Kuwait News Agency, May 2, in SU/6719/A4/2-3, May 9, 1981.

62. Again, the specter of radicalization sparked by frustration on the Arab-Israeli impasse has been raised so often that there exists the danger that it may be totally discounted.

63. See the admission by a Palestinian of six months' training in the Soviet Union (*International Herald Tribune*, November 2, 1980).

64. Windsor, "The Soviet Union in the International System" p. 9.

65. This point is well made by Dimitri Simes, "Disciplining Soviet Power," *Foreign Policy* 43 (summer 1981), p. 43. Simes referred to "the conservative persistence of the Soviet geopolitical effort" as the important aspect of the Soviet challenge.

66. Several analysts have suggested this, including Simes, "Disciplining Soviet Power," pp. 46–47; William E. Odom, "Whither the Soviet Union," *Washington Quarterly* 4, no. 2 (spring 1981), pp. 30–49; and Joseph Kraft, "A Spoiler Strategy," *Washington Post*, March 26, 1980.

14

American Diplomacy and Arab-Israeli-Palestinian Peace Since 1967

Harold H. Saunders

The Arab-Israeli war of June 5–10, 1967, was the starting point for renewed efforts to establish a peaceful relationship between Israel and its Arab neighbors. Attempts in the 1950s had ended in continuing belligerency and stalemate. Efforts begun after the 1967 war have been on the agenda of the world community almost continuously ever since. The purpose of this chapter is to sharpen perspective on the principal issues in the conflicts between Israel and the Palestinian Arabs and Israel and neighboring Arab states and to analyze the development of thinking about what peace requires in the period since 1967. The chapter is written from the vantage point of the policymaker rather than the historian. It seeks to explore what the peace effort has become rather than to chronicle its progress in detail.

Through developments since 1967, more of the elements of a negotiated resolution of the Arab-Israeli-Palestinian conflicts became available than at any time since 1949, and the definition of the conflicts has been sharpened. By the early 1980s, no questions seemed more acute than these: Could these conflicts be resolved peacefully through political and diplomatic initiative and the assistance of the United States? Could the incentives for a negotiated settlement be increased peacefully? Or could a settlement be achieved only when a new balance of power within the Middle East forced a settlement?

Given the stakes—the security and future of Israel and the Jewish people, the continuing suffering and statelessness of the Palestinian people, the interests of the United States and the Soviet Union—the question of whether political leaders can marshal the courage and skill to achieve a peaceful settlement and avert further tragedy is more than academic. Judgments of the abilities of the United States to function as a world power in the 1990s will be partially shaped by the way American leaders handle these issues in the Middle East in the 1980s.

In the years following the 1967 war, significant Arab leaders moved slowly from a position of refusing to recognize, negotiate with, or make peace with Israel toward readiness to accept Israel as a state within pre-1967 borders. Israelis and Palestinian Arabs have interacted across an open border since Israeli military occupation of the West Bank and Gaza in 1967. Three interim agreements between Israel and neighboring states were signed in 1974 and 1975. Israel's longest frontier (with Jordan) has remained virtually free of violence since 1974, as did the frontier with Syria on the Golan Heights. In 1978–1979, the Camp David accords and the peace treaty between Egypt and Israel were signed, Israel committed itself to full withdrawal from Egyptian territory, a normalization of relations between the Egyptian and Israeli peoples began, and the Palestinian problem came to the top of the negotiating agenda.

Arab leaders and most of the world's governments also came to believe that the Palestinian Arabs, represented by the Palestine Liberation Organization rather than by existing Arab governments, should build the Palestinian homeland in some part of the former mandate of Palestine west of the Jordan River. The institutionalization of Palestinian nationalism in the PLO has focused responsibility for the Palestinians' future. That development has made it more difficult to work out a solution among existing governments, but it has become an irreversible fact that forces redefinition of the problem.

The fundamental question of the 1940s as seen from Washington has resurfaced: How will Jews and Arabs live together in peace in the area of the former Palestine mandate between the Jordan River and the Mediterranean Sea? This is not an idle issue. Many Arabs do not accept that a Jewish homeland should be there. Most Arab governments have not unequivocally and convincingly stated a readiness to recognize and make peace with Israel or even to negotiate without a guarantee that the final outcome will meet Arab terms. Israeli actions in the West Bank have demonstrated that a growing number of Israelis think in terms of one state—Israel—in all of the area west of the Jordan River. Those Israelis have made no provision in their thinking for the Palestinian Arabs except as a subordinated ethnic group or as candidates for expulsion across the Jordan River. Even those Israelis who would still accept partition of the land west of the Jordan would, for the most part, oppose creation of a sovereign Palestinian state alongside the Jewish state and separate from Jordan, which they regard as already predominantly Palestinian.

The issue for the mid-1980s has once again become the question of how to find a solution to the Palestine problem of the 1940s. At that time, two options were considered: (1) one state encompassing both Jews and Arabs and (2) partition of the land into two separate homelands. One of the purposes of this chapter is to bring those options into perspective again and to ask how conditions have changed over time and whether and how much they fall short of the goal of a peaceful settlement that has so far eluded the people of that area.

To pose the issue in these words is in no way to question the fact that Israel is an established fact. It is to continue the search for a formula that will permit Israel, its neighboring Arab states, and the Palestinian people to live together in mutual recognition and acceptance.

The years since 1967 have been a period when Americans have been reexamining the responsibilities of the United States as a world power under conditions of nuclear parity with the Soviet Union. It has also been a time of global readjustment, during which the influence of the great powers has been diminishing relative to the capacity of developing nations to affect the course of events. The American experience with peacemaking in the Middle East during these years and beyond could have a profound effect on how the United States develops its role as a global power in the closing years of the twentieth century.

The Substantive Framework

Although we speak most often of the Arab-Israeli conflict, the issue in an historical perspective is how to resolve the Palestine problem of 1946–1948 as well as the state-to-state conflict that emerged from it. The Palestine problem involved whether a Zionist state would be established and recognized in Palestine and how it would relate to Palestinian Arab inhabitants of the land and neighboring states. It had roots deep in history and dimensions as fresh as the processes of decolonization and growing nationalism that intensified in the postwar world. In American eyes, Israel is an established state, but the issue remains how to win lasting acceptance for its establishment by arranging a just solution for those whom its establishment displaced.

In Washington's eyes the basic problem in the Palestine of the 1940s, which had developed in the 1920s and 1930s, was how a rapidly growing number of Jewish immigrants and the Arab inhabitants already there could live together in peace in the area west of the Jordan River. In Arab eyes, the problem was that the West's attempt to solve problems of Jewish persecution in Europe by creating a Jewish national home in Palestine could only succeed through the Palestinians' loss of part of their land. Among the many aspects of the problem were the rival claims of two peoples to the same land. As one Israeli described the problem in a private conversation in 1981: "Two national movements claim rights in the same land. The land of our fathers is the land of their fathers." That definition of the problem may reflect hindsight because at the time Arab governments accepted neither a Jewish state, nor a separate Palestinian Arab state, nor partition of Palestine between Jews and Arabs. Nevertheless, it seems analytically accurate as a way of focusing on the underlying problem.

In the 1940s two approaches to resolution of the problem were considered: (1) One secular state could be created encompassing all of the area of the mandate of Palestine in which Jews and Arabs would live together with full guarantees for their individual human, religious, and political rights; or (2), the land could be divided between Jews and Arabs with the creation of two separate homelands. The world community, acting in the UN General Assembly in 1947, proposed partition against vociferous opposition from the Arab states.

When Israel declared itself an independent state in May 1948, neighboring Arab states refused to accept partition and attacked Israel. Thus the Palestine problem took the form of conflict between Israel and existing Arab states. This basic conflict became even more complicated by Arab shame over defeat in that war, an urge to win back dignity and self-respect, and fear that the Israelis would continue to expand their territory and power.

The 1949 armistice agreements were signed not only to end that fighting but also "with a view to promoting the return to a permanent peace in Palestine." Whatever hopes there might have been for negotiating a permanent settlement faded by the mid-1950s, and the area settled into prolonged stalemate. Within the armistice lines of 1949, the Zionists were able to develop their state because of international recognition and their own ability to defend it. Some of the Palestinian Arabs continued to live in the area that became Israel; others lived in refugee camps in the neighboring Arab states or as inhabitants of Arab and other states. Jordan governed on the Arab side of the armistice lines in the West Bank area of the former Palestine mandate and Egypt in Gaza. Other Arab governments could not agree among themselves on the framework for peace with Israel, and so the conflict between Israel and the Arab states continued.

The 1967 war changed the situation more dramatically than realized at the time: Israel was put in military control of all the area west of the Jordan River and in occupation of Egyptian and Syrian territory. Although decisions were made in major capitals and at the United Nations to begin new efforts to establish "a just and lasting peace," by this time most of the world had shifted its focus from the Israeli-Palestinian conflict to the conflict between Israel and the Arab states. The language of the state-to-state conflict was used to describe a solution unanimously adopted by the UN Security Council in Resolution 242: Israeli withdrawal from territories occupied in the 1967 conflict in return for peace within secure and recognized borders. The Palestinians were mentioned only as refugees. The central issue was no longer seen as resolution of the Palestine problem—the problem of two peoples claiming national rights in the land west of the Jordan. In 1967 there was little talk by Arabs or anyone else of the reciprocal recognition of a politically separate Palestinian Arab identity. The Arabs still focused on the illegitimacy of Israel, and the demoralized Palestinians had no policy of their own.

One of the most contentious issues since 1967 has been whether the Palestinian problem could continue to be dealt with in the context of a state-to-state settlement or whether it had to be redefined and approached again as the Palestine problem of 1946–1948—a conflict between two peoples with claims in the same land that must be resolved justly before the state-to-state conflict can be resolved.

Obstacles to a Permanent Peace

Even in the mid-1980s, most of the remaining parties to the Arab-Israeli-Palestinian conflict are not committed to accept each other or to negotiate peace with each other. Few even have a vision of the overall shape of a possible solution. They have given lower priority to reaching a settlement than to keeping their full demands intact, partly because they see little possibility of even a limited settlement. Efforts to resolve the problem have been stalemated again. The psychological obstacles are profound. Each side feels itself the victim of history; it has little empathy for the suffering of the other and denies that the other has rights that must be fulfilled. Most Arab leaders, whatever their private feelings, have been afraid openly to step outside the basic Arab consensus that Israel should not be recognized.

Before serious negotiation can take place, the parties to a potential settlement must have decided that they are ready for a settlement that will require compromise, and they must have a sense that they could live with the kinds of compromise that appear likely to be required of them if agreement is to be achieved. Negotiation can bridge the gap between conflicting claims only when the parties cannot force their own solutions and can find incentives for seeking common ground among available compromises. As long as either party insists on an all-or-nothing settlement, the only solution is surrender and not a negotiated resolution. Until there is some understanding on the overall shape of a possible compromise, they cannot determine whether they can enter negotiation and live with the possible outcome.

The problem for more than three decades has remained that some Arabs and some Israelis have not been able to come together on the basic point that Arabs and Jews should live together at peace in Palestine. For much of this period, most Arabs did not accept the existence of a Jewish homeland there, whereas most Israelis accepted the partition that resulted from the 1948 war. In the 1970s, as more Arabs came to accept Israel, an increasing number of Israelis came to believe either that the land of Israel encompasses all of Palestine west of the Jordan River or at least that the establishment of a Palestinian state would jeopardize the security and boundaries of their own state. Nevertheless, some influential Israelis still acknowledge that peace with the Palestinian Arabs is essential to Israel's long-term security and that there will be no peace while the Palestinian Arabs remain displaced persons, subjugated, or under military occupation.

The problem is a deeply human one that needs confirmation of acceptance on both sides.

- After centuries of cruel rejection and pain in re-establishing a Jewish homeland, the Israelis have consistently argued that the heart of the Arab-Israeli conflict is Arab acceptance of Israel as a Jewish state in the Middle East. They believe that a substantial number of Arabs remain committed to the destruction of Israel. Concrete evidence of Arab acceptance has been the essential minimum for Israel. Prime Minister Golda Meir once spoke of

Egypt's closure of the Suez Canal not in terms of harm to Israel's interests, but in terms of her memory of a sign in the Russian town where she lived as a child which warned, "No Jews." What was important to her, as to other Israelis, was the symbol of nonacceptance. What President Sadat provided in his trip to Jerusalem was not a substantive breakthrough in negotiations but a break with the negative Arab consensus. It was convincing evidence that his government was prepared to accept Israel as a neighbor, to make peace with Israel, and to develop normal relations with it. Many elements in the Arab position—including the Palestinian National Charter and Arab governments' reluctance to state unequivocally their acceptance of Israel's right to exist—have been concrete symbols to the Israelis of nonacceptance and rejection.

• The Arabs since the disintegration of the Ottoman Empire have sought the right to work out their own destiny in homelands of their own—the right of self-determination in the full meaning of the term. They have suffered foreign occupation in this area for centuries. Many of them consider the Zionist settlement of Palestine and the establishment of Israel as another form of western colonization in the land they regard as their own. Whatever the tragedies suffered by the Jewish people in Europe, Arabs felt that they were being forced to compensate the Jews at Arab expense. Arab understanding of the Balfour Declaration and other agreements relating to the establishment of a Jewish homeland was that this would be achieved without prejudice to the rights of Arab inhabitants of the land. After 1948, they saw Palestine divided and a Jewish state established. Having rejected partition themselves, they have seen the Arab position in Palestine steadily diminished. Many of the Arabs of Palestine became refugees and displaced persons—accepted as a people by neither Jews nor Arabs. As the Palestinian Arabs became politically more self-confident and outspoken in the late 1960s and 1970s, they sought acceptance as a people with the right of self-determination. As one Palestinian put it in a private conversation in 1981: "We never had our rightful self-determination. All along, the Arabs were determining for us." Only in the 1974 recognition by the Arab League of the Palestine Liberation Organization as the "sole legitimate representative of the Palestinian people" did the Arab governments formally agree that the Palestinian Arabs should represent themselves in working out a solution to the Palestinian problem.[1]

The 1967 Framework

In the diplomacy that followed the 1967 war, a framework emerged for new efforts to deal with the basic issues. The United States played a major role in articulating the principles that would govern these new efforts. They were eventually refined in negotiation and embodied in UN Security Council Resolution 242 of November 22, 1967.

Within the U.S. government, these principles evolved rather than being designed through intensive policy analysis. From the statements made at the beginning of the 1967 war and President Johnson's speech of June 19 through the intense negotiations that produced Resolution 242, a U.S. position emerged that the objective of diplomacy after the Six Day War would be to resolve the Arab-Israeli conflict once and for all. Although the ramifications of this position were significant, the pros and cons or consequences of such a commitment were never formally assessed, and there was no formal moment of decision. The Israelis took the position that they would not accept another armistice. The Johnson administration did not want a repeat of the 1957 Israeli withdrawal without peace and from its first White House statement on June 5 spoke of settling the conflict in all its aspects.

More specifically, the administration came to the position that there would be no change in the basic situation on the ground, other than the cease-fire, until the right of each state—including Israel—to live in peace and security was recognized. Although the United States in the first hours of the war had supported a Security Council resolution calling for a cease-fire and withdrawal, as the hours passed with the Soviet Union blocking such a resolution, the council on June 6 adopted a resolution calling for a simple cease-fire in place. By late June, that had developed into a position calling for a package settlement of the main issues that had divided Israel and its Arab neighbors since 1948.

On June 19, President Johnson laid down "five principles of peace in the region":

- First . . . every nation in the area has a fundamental right to live, and to have this right respected by its neighbors.
- Second . . . is a human requirement: justice for the refugees.
- Third . . . is that maritime rights must be respected. . . .
- Fourth, this last conflict has demonstrated the danger of the Middle Eastern arms race. . . .
- Fifth, the crisis underlines the importance of respect for political independence and territorial integrity of all the states in the area.

President Johnson continued:

These five principles are not new, but we do think they are fundamental. Taken together, they point the way from uncertain armistice to a durable peace. We believe there must be progress toward all of them if there is to be progress toward any. There are some who have urged, as a single, simple solution, an immediate return to the situation as it was on June 4. . . . this is not a prescription for peace, but for renewed hostilities.

Certainly troops must be withdrawn, but there must also be recognized rights of national life, progress in solving the refugee problem, freedom of innocent maritime passage, limitation of the arms race, and respect for political independence and territorial integrity.[2]

Following a summer and autumn of intensive diplomacy at the United Nations as well as in the June meeting between President Johnson and Soviet Premier Alexei Kosygin, this approach was embodied essentially in Security Council Resolution 242. That resolution was so finely balanced that it is considered prejudicial to the interest of one side or another to quote selectively from it. It is fair to say, however, that the American assumption underlying the negotiation of that resolution was that a settlement this time should produce a comprehensive resolution of the Arab-Israeli conflict and a permanent peace in Palestine on the basis of an equation that called for Israeli withdrawal from territories occupied during the conflict in return for "establishment of a just and lasting peace" and "respect for an acknowledgement of the sovereignty, territorial integrity and political independence of every State in the area and their right to live in peace within secure and recognized boundaries free from threats or acts of force."[3]

There was an explicit effort by the United States and other sponsors of Resolution 242 to avoid specifying withdrawal to the prewar lines in order to allow for negotiation of boundaries that would rectify injustices resulting from the 1949 armistice lines and for special arrangements in Jerusalem. In the discussions of 1967, U.S. officials spoke of those border adjustments as "minor." Some of the Arabs felt that they should be reciprocal. Israelis left the question of change open ended, arguing that the boundaries would be negotiated.

This portion of the resolution later became a point of significant disagreement between the United States and Arab governments. Most Arab parties came to argue that Resolution 242 required Israel's withdrawal from all the territories occupied in the 1967 war and that a prerequisite for discussion of a settlement would be for Israel to implement Resolution 242 by withdrawing to the prewar lines. The Arabs did not promise negotiation of peace, even if Israel withdrew completely. Israel, on the other hand, took the position that final boundaries were to be negotiated and that, in any case, no Israeli move was required until Arab governments made clear their recognition of Israel and readiness to live at peace with it. Israel maintained that important evidence of Arab recognition would be Arab readiness to negotiate face to face with Israeli representatives and to sign a peace agreement with Israel.

Despite the fact that the United States supported negotiation of precise borders, it made clear through its promises to King Husayn and statements to Israel that the principle of withdrawal applied to the West Bank and Gaza as well as to other fronts. The United States recognized that Israel would seek changes in the boundaries but understood that Israel accepted the principle of withdrawal in these areas.

Thus with three significant exceptions, Resolution 242 addressed fundamental issues of the conflict. By calling for Israeli withdrawal it tacitly reaffirmed that the land west of the Jordan River should be divided between Jews and Arabs. It called for mutual recognition. It also called for resolution of other important issues—freedom of navigation through international waterways, the refugee problem, and measures to assure security. The resolution did not address fully three important points:

1. It did not acknowledge the Palestinian Arabs as a people with a need for acceptance of their identity and recognition of the injustice they as a people had suffered. It mentioned them only as refugees. At that time their identity as a people with a right to separate political expression as in a state of their own had not yet been formally accepted by either the Arab

or the larger international community. Resolution 242 assumed that Jordan and Egypt would resume the Arab role in the areas of the West Bank and Gaza from which Israel would withdraw. It did not recognize that the West Bank and Gaza had a status different from occupied Syrian and Egyptian territories, which were defined by internationally recognized borders.

2. The resolution also tended to define peace in terms of the end of the state of belligerency between Israel and its neighbors. It did not attempt to define the nature of the relationship that would constitute a state of peace between them.

3. It did not address the status of Jerusalem, which under the 1947 partition plan would have become a separate internationally protected entity. The Israelis widened the city limits, extended their law there, and ultimately formally annexed the city. The Security Council called on them to rescind those measures.

Although Resolution 242 was important because key parties to the conflict accepted it, the ambiguity that made that acceptance possible allowed widely differing interpretations. The resolution did not resolve basic issues; it provided one possible starting point for negotiation. The task of trying to launch those negotiations was placed in the hands of the UN Secretary General's special representative, Ambassador Gunnar Jarring.

Even after administrations changed in Washington in 1969, the Nixon administration demonstrated that its view of a settlement remained consistent with the U.S. position of 1967. Secretary of State William Rogers in a speech on December 9, 1969, summarized the essence of the position that the United States had taken during months of extensive talks with the Soviet Union. Making clear that "implementation of the overall settlement would begin only after complete agreement had been reached on related aspects of the problem," the secretary said of a settlement between Egypt and Israel:

> It would require the U.A.R. to agree to a binding and specific commitment to peace. It would require withdrawal of Israeli armed forces from U.A.R. territory to the international border between Israel [or mandated Palestine] and Egypt which has been in existence for over half a century. It would also require the parties themselves to negotiate the practical security arrangements to safeguard the peace. We believe that this approach is *balanced* and fair.

The secretary also stated the U.S. position on Jerusalem:

> Specifically, we believe Jerusalem should be a unified city within which there would no longer be restrictions on the movement of persons and goods. There should be open access to the unified city for persons of all faiths and nationalities. Arrangements for the administration of the unified city should take into account the interests of all its inhabitants and of the Jewish, Islamic, and Christian communities. And there should be roles for both Israel and Jordan in the civic, economic, and religious life of the city.[4]

The 1973–1975 Framework

Diplomatic efforts from 1967 to 1973 were conducted within the framework of Resolution 242 as each party interpreted it. After the 1973 war, that framework was formally reaffirmed but with little effort to resolve critical ambiguities.

UN Security Council Resolution 338 of October 22, 1973, worked out in Moscow by Secretary Kissinger and Foreign Minister Gromyko, not only called for a cessation of all military activity but also "called upon the parties concerned to start immediately after the cease-fire the implementation of Security Council Resolution 242 (1967) in all of its parts." The resolution ended by stating the council's decision "that, immediately and concurrently with the cease-fire, negotiations shall start between the parties concerned under appropriate auspices aimed at establishing a just and durable peace in the Middle East."[5] This last point alluded to a Gromyko-Kissinger agreement that the Soviet Union and the United States would jointly chair a peace conference in Geneva. That conference was actually convened in December within the framework of Resolution 338, which subsumed Resolution 242.

In the two years that followed, Egypt, Israel, and Syria each formally committed itself to the objectives stated in Resolution 338. In the Disengagement Agreement signed January 18, 1974, Egypt and Israel stated: "This agreement is not regarded by Egypt and Israel as a final peace agreement. It constitutes a first step toward a final, just and durable peace according to the provisions of Security Council Resolution 338 and within the Framework of the Geneva Conference."[6] Similarly, Israel and Syria agreed on May 31, 1974: "This agreement is not a peace agreement. It is a step toward a just and durable peace on the basis of Security Council Resolution 338."[7] Egypt and Israel repeated their position in signing the second Sinai agreement on September 1, 1975.[8]

During this period the United States, on the basis of numerous conversations with Arab leaders and Secretary Kissinger's many trips to the Middle East, began to address the issue of Palestinian Arab identity. The Palestinian movement (in particular the Palestine Liberation Organization) had steadily gained ground since 1967 as a potential participant in the peace process in its own right. The position of the PLO in the Arab world was shown at the Arab summit meeting in Rabat on October 28, 1974, at which the PLO was recognized as "the sole legitimate representative of the Palestinian people."

In August 1975, at the time of the Sinai II agreement, the United States had committed itself in a memorandum of understanding with Israel not to "recognize or negotiate with the Palestine Liberation Organization so long as the Palestine Liberation Organization does not recognize Israel's right to exist and does not accept Security Council Resolutions 242 and 338."[9] The wording of that commitment was carefully revised by the United States during the negotiations so as not to preclude exchanges of views with the PLO, as the Israeli draft proposed to do. In practice, however, the administration did not pursue such contacts. The reasoning within the administration was that discussions with the PLO would arouse a storm of Israeli protest and diminish the U.S. ability to work closely with Israel. It judged that such a step should be taken only when discussions might lead to a breakthrough in the negotiations.

Nevertheless, in November 1975 Secretary Kissinger authorized as part of testimony on behalf of the Ford administration before the Middle East subcommittee of the House Foreign Affairs Committee a full statement on the Palestinian dimension of the Arab-Israeli conflict. The statement submitted in that testimony said in part:

> We have also repeatedly stated that the legitimate interests of the Palestinian Arabs must be taken into account in the negotiation of an Arab-Israeli peace. In many ways, the Palestinian dimension of the Arab-Israeli conflict is the heart of that conflict. Final resolution of the problems arising from the partition of Palestine, the establishment of the state of Israel, and Arab opposition to those events will not be possible until agreement is reached defining a just and permanent status for the Arab peoples who consider themselves Palestinians.
> . . .
> The statement is often made in the Arab world that there will not be peace until the "rights of the Palestinians" are fulfilled, but there is no agreed definition of what is meant and a variety of viewpoints have been expressed on what the legitimate objectives of the Palestinians are. . . .
> What is needed as a first step is a diplomatic process which will help bring forth a reasonable definition of Palestinian interests—a position from which negotiations on a solution of the Palestinian aspects of the problem might begin. The issue is not whether Palestinian interests should be expressed in a final settlement, but how. There will be no peace unless an answer is found.[10]

The Camp David Framework

The Carter administration achieved a breakthrough in bringing about peace between Egypt and Israel. Five developments in 1977 are worth noting as background:

1. President Carter brought to the presidency a renewed commitment on behalf of the United States to basic human rights around the world and a particular sense that establishment of a homeland for the Palestinians would be consistent with that posture. As the president said in response to a question during a town meeting in Clinton, Massachusetts, on March 16, 1977:

> The third ultimate requirement for peace is to deal with the Palestinian problem. The Palestinians claim up 'til this moment that Israel has no right to be there, that the land belongs to the Palestinians, and they've never yet given up their publicly professed commitment to destroy Israel. That has to be overcome. There has to be a homeland provided for the Palestinian refugees who have suffered for many, many years. And the exact way to solve the Palestinian problem is one that first of all addresses itself right now to the

Arab countries and then, secondly, to the Arab countries negotiating with Israel.[11]

Later in the year, the administration let it be known to the PLO that the administration would understand if the PLO were to accept Resolution 242 while stating simultaneously its view that the resolution does not adequately reflect the identity of the Palestinians as a people. On that basis, the United States would be prepared to talk with the PLO.

2. The Carter administration also adopted the normalization of relations as an explicit objective in establishing a state of peace between Israel and its neighbors to provide a continuing demonstration of mutual acceptance. The Israelis had pressed since 1967 for real or genuine peace in contrast to another truce, and President Carter put the normalization of relations specifically on the agenda of objectives.

3. Menachem Begin's election as prime minister of Israel brought to power a coalition, substantial parts of which were committed to Israeli control of all the area of the former Palestine mandate west of the Jordan River. Whereas previous Labor party governments had accepted the principle of withdrawal in the West Bank, albeit with border changes to enhance Israel's security, Prime Minister Begin repeatedly rejected in negotiations any formulation saying that Resolution 242 applies to the West Bank. The Begin government changed the pattern of Israeli settlement in the occupied territories from areas useful for security to Arab-populated areas so as to implant a permanent Israeli presence. Although the government continued to pay lip service to Resolution 242, its actions raised fundamental questions about whether it accepted the principle of withdrawal. It explicitly stated its intention to assert an Israeli claim of sovereignty in the West Bank in the negotiations on the final status of the West Bank and Gaza.

4. There was an abortive attempt by the administration to work together with the Soviet Union on achieving a comprehensive Middle East peace. The joint statement released in September 1977 was thought to be in preparation for renewal of the Geneva Conference, adjourned since December 1973.[12] But other events, especially President Sadat's November initiative in going to Jerusalem, changed this game plan.

5. In November, President Sadat's visit to Jerusalem provided a convincing demonstration that Egypt was prepared to negotiate peace with Israel. However, his substantive message was not what Israelis wanted to hear: withdrawal to 1967 borders, Arab sovereignty in East Jerusalem, and Palestinian self-determination along with a comprehensive peace. What was critical was the demonstration of Egyptian readiness to accept Israel as a state in the Middle East, to make peace with Israel, and to develop normal relations with it.[13] For Israel, it offered an opportunity to take Egypt out of the war and, Israelis hoped, to gain a free hand in the West Bank and Gaza.

What emerged in part from President Sadat's historic visit and Israel's response to it were the two frameworks agreed upon at Camp David on September 17, 1978, and the Egypt-Israel Peace Treaty signed on March 26,

1979. The Camp David accords and the treaty reflected two principal achievements in the eyes of those who supported this approach.

First, a genuine peace between Egypt and Israel and Israeli withdrawal from the Sinai were agreed upon. Both of the framework documents negotiated at Camp David affirmed, as stated in the preamble to "A Framework for Peace in the Middle East Agreed at Camp David," that "the agreed basis for a peaceful settlement of the conflict between Israel and its neighbors is United Nations Security Council Resolution 242, in all its parts."[14] The peace treaty provided for Israeli withdrawal to the pre-1967 border between Egypt and Israel, for detailed demilitarization and security measures in the Sinai Peninsula, and for a process of normalizing relations between the two countries detailed in a protocol to the treaty.[15] Thus on the Egyptian-Israeli front, the fulfillment of Resolution 242 was realized—Israeli withdrawal in return for peace in the full definition that the Carter administration had adopted. As the treaty stated, "The Parties agree that the normal relationship established between them will include full recognition, diplomatic, economic, and cultural relations, termination of economic boycotts and discriminatory barriers to the free movement of people and goods, and will guarantee the mutual enjoyment of citizens of the due process of law" (Article III-3).

A second step at Camp David was the attempt to ensure that the next issue at the top of the agenda in the continuing effort to achieve a comprehensive peace would be an effort to resolve the Palestinian problem. As agreed in the "Framework for Peace":

> The parties are determined to reach a just, comprehensive, and durable settlement of the Middle East conflict through the conclusion of peace treaties based on Security Council Resolutions 242 and 338, in all their parts. Their purpose is to achieve peace and good neighborly relations. They recognize that, for peace to endure, it must involve all those who have been most deeply affected by the conflict. They therefore agree that this framework as appropriate is intended by them to constitute a basis for peace not only between Egypt and Israel, but also between Israel and each of its other neighbors which is prepared to negotiate peace with Israel on this basis. With that objective in mind, they have agreed to proceed as follows:
> A. West Bank and Gaza
>   1. Egypt, Israel, Jordan and the representatives of the Palestinian people should participate in negotiations on the resolution of the Palestinian problem in all its aspects. To achieve that objective, negotiations relating to the West Bank and Gaza should proceed in three stages[16]

The process agreed upon at Camp David for dealing with the West Bank and Gaza was developed around agreement on a five-year transitional period, to begin with establishment of an elected Palestinian Arab self-governing authority from among the inhabitants of the West Bank and Gaza and withdrawal of the Israeli military government and its civilian administration. The Palestinian authority would then exercise full autonomy in those areas with powers and responsibilities defined in the agreement. Next, "as soon as possible, but no later than the third year after the beginning of the transitional period, negotiations will take place to determine the final status of the West Bank and Gaza and its relationship with its neighbors, and to conclude a peace treaty between Israel and Jordan by the end of the transitional period." Elected representatives of the inhabitants of the West Bank and Gaza as well as other Palestinians as mutually agreed would participate in those negotiations. In effect, the decision between the one-state and the two-homeland solutions would be made in those negotiations with full participation of Palestinian Arabs, mainly those in the West Bank and Gaza. The agreement from those negotiations would be submitted to a vote by the elected representatives of the inhabitants of those territories.

Most of the rest of the world regarded the Camp David approach as inadequate. The Arabs rejected it with intense bitterness because they believed that President Sadat and the United States had walked away from the Palestinian cause by not pressing for Israeli agreement to withdraw unconditionally from the West Bank and Gaza. The accords did not, in their view, make clear that the objective of the transitional process was an outcome based on the principles of Israeli withdrawal and Palestinian Arab self-determination. They did not believe the Palestinians would have adequate authority over land and water. They felt that autonomy would only be a cover for perpetuating Israeli occupation. They also feared to be out in front with Sadat.

The feeling within the Carter administration was that the Camp David approach tried to do what no one else had seriously attempted since 1947. Since the decision for partition, only those states that wanted to control parts of Palestine had attempted to define the nature of political authority in the Palestinian Arab homeland. The immediate establishment of the Israeli state had resolved the question on the Jewish side, but who was to exercise authority in a separate Palestinian Arab homeland was not decided. Syria, Jordan, and Egypt all had designs on part of the land. When Jordan annexed the land it controlled in the area of the former Palestine mandate after the 1949 armistice, it met such opposition from Arab governments that it rescinded the annexation measure while continuing to govern in that area. In short, the Arab governments did not agree until 1974 on who should speak for the Palestinian Arabs, and even then there was no effort to present a practical offer of peace between Israel and the Palestinians.

Even if Israel were prepared to withdraw in the spirit of Resolution 242 and turn over territory to a Palestinian Arab authority, it would insist that whoever exercised authority in that land accept Israel as stated in Security Council Resolutions 242 and 338 and be willing to live in peace with Israel. The Camp David framework attempted to define procedures through which a Palestinian authority could first begin to play an autonomous role in administering the territories now occupied, prove its ability to secure borders and to conduct a peaceful relationship with Israel, and then play a role in negotiating a permanent relationship. Unlike any previous efforts, the agreement at Camp David defined a procedure for moving the Palestinian

Arabs into position to speak for themselves in helping to achieve a permanent peace in Palestine. Although the PLO would not have had a seat at the table in its own name, even Israelis acknowledged that Palestinian leaders in the West Bank and Gaza maintained a close relationship with the PLO.

The American strategy was based on belief that autonomy offered a way—the only way politically available at the time—to arrest the steady progress of de facto Israeli annexation by establishing a countervailing Arab authority. Since a clear-cut single move from full Israeli occupation to full Israeli withdrawal was not feasible, beginning a process toward a new Israeli-Palestinian relationship was considered a necessary first step toward an ultimate compromise settlement.

The Carter administration's approach depended on demonstrating that a process could begin that would steadily increase Palestinian participation in real ways. The Arabs and most of the rest of the world quickly judged that the administration could not deliver the Israeli restraint necessary to make this approach more than a cover for a continuing process of de facto Israeli annexation of the West Bank. The Begin government refused to accept a moratorium on Israeli settlements in the West Bank during negotiations on autonomy for the Arabs living there and publicly stated its intent to assert a claim of Israeli sovereignty over these areas in the negotiations on the final status of the West Bank and Gaza. Israeli actions caused most of the world to ask whether Israel intended to submit the critical issues to negotiation or to resolve them by presenting the world with faits accomplis. At the same time, the fact that neither Syria nor the Palestinians had agreed to negotiate peace with Israel made it more difficult for the United States to argue that Israeli restraint could open the door to peace.

Camp David in Perspective

The Camp David framework was the product of negotiators grappling both among themselves and within themselves over conflicting goals. Objectively, the conflict lay between the Arab demand that the Palestinian Arabs be given the homeland in Palestine that they felt is their right and Israeli inability for varying reasons to accept outright partition of Palestine and creation of an equal and sovereign Palestinian state. Subjectively, individuals in the Begin government could not bring themselves to accept a partition that would require Israel to renounce any claim to areas in Judea and Samaria historically important in Jewish tradition. Other Israelis recognized deep inside that control of the entire area west of the Jordan would ultimately corrode the integrity of the Jewish state. Egyptians recognized that they could not speak for the Palestinian Arabs in agreeing that they should accept less than a state in all or part of Palestine. The negotiated compromise was to set aside for an agreed period a decision on long-term relationships in Palestine and to commit the parties to a process for working out the terms of those relationships.

This dilemma led some Israelis to grope for a solution that would preserve Israeli control while giving the Palestinians some sense of identity and self-government. Israeli Foreign Minister Moshe Dayan, in discussion with an Egyptian delegation at Leeds Castle in July 1978, expressed the thought essentially this way: Israelis have not been able to draw a line through the West Bank that would be secure for Israel and politically acceptable to the Arabs. In addition to their security concerns, Israelis cannot give up the right to visit and live in the historic areas of the West Bank. Some way must be found to define a relationship between Jews and Arabs in the West Bank that allows for Arab political expression while not resolving the issue of sovereignty in a way that would permit Arabs to exclude Jews from these areas. Other Israelis since have spoken in terms of a "Benelux" type relationship involving Israel, Jordan, and the Palestinian Arabs. One way or another, Dayan and others in Israel were groping to define a relationship that they could persuade Israelis to accept in the first instance and that would enable Israel to reach agreement with the Palestinian Arabs.

The Carter administration felt that the Camp David accords—apart from agreement on the outlines of an Egyptian-Israeli peace—obtained formal Israeli commitment that resolution of the Palestinian problem in all its aspects is critical to overall peace, that there must be a Palestinian Arab negotiating partner in the peace process, and that the question of sovereignty in the West Bank and Gaza should remain open. However, the Camp David accords failed to provide the Arabs with recognition that the Palestinian Arabs could come to the negotiating table with equal respect as citizens of the world entitled to govern themselves and to determine their own future. The process agreed upon at Camp David was designed in part to permit the evolution of a relationship in the context of which Israelis and Palestinians might convincingly express their readiness to accept each other. But it did not win Arab acceptance.

Subsequent Israeli actions demonstrated a different Israeli interpretation of what was agreed at Camp David. The failure of the United States to follow through by demonstrating that its approach could produce significant results eroded confidence in Washington as a fair mediator. Egypt's alienation from the Arab states weakened the moderate Arab coalition.

Through its last 18 months, the Carter administration pressed negotiations between Egypt and Israel to establish a Palestinian self-governing authority in the West Bank and Gaza as agreed at Camp David. Because events in other areas like the hostage crisis in Iran and the challenge to Carter's reelection overshadowed them, those negotiations were not concluded.

The Reagan Framework

The Reagan administration at its outset chose not to press the negotiations for a Palestinian self-governing authority. Even though Secretary of State Haig briefly raised the question in two trips to the Middle East in early 1982, the administration again decided to let the issue rest until after Israel's final withdrawal from the Sinai in April 1982 under the Egyptian-Israeli peace treaty.

In June 1982, the Israeli invasion of Lebanon and attack on the military elements of the PLO forced the administration's notice. The invasion further involved the United States in the internal problems of Lebanon, but it also focused attention on the larger framework for an Arab-Israeli peace. In part, the invasion was directed at crushing or removing PLO military elements as a threat to the security of Israel's northern towns. In part, it reflected efforts of the Begin government to damage severely the main rallying point of the Palestinian movement so as to break Palestinian resistance in the West Bank and Gaza. As the fighting was slowly brought to an end, President Reagan's new secretary of state, George Shultz, in July and August steadily worked toward a formulation of the Reagan framework for an Arab-Israeli peace.

On September 1, 1982, President Reagan told the nation, "It seemed to me that, with the agreement in Lebanon, we had an opportunity for a more far-reaching peace effort in the region." His position was consistent with the United States position as it had evolved. "When our Administration assumed office in January 1981, I decided that the general framework for our Middle East policy should follow the broad guidelines laid down by my predecessors. . . . We have embraced the Camp David framework as the only way to proceed."[17]

In calling for a fresh start to end the Arab-Israeli conflict, President Reagan based his approach "squarely on the principle that the Arab-Israeli conflict should be resolved through negotiations involving an exchange of territory for peace. This exchange is enshrined in UN Security Council Resolution 242, which is, in turn, incorporated in all its parts in the Camp David agreements. UN Resolution 242 remains wholly valid as the foundation stone of America's Middle East peace effort."

The president endorsed the Camp David framework's proposal for a five-year transitional period of Palestinian autonomy in the West Bank and Gaza. He called on Israel to freeze its program for placing new settlements in the West Bank and Gaza as a step to "create the confidence needed for wider participation in these talks."

Then he stated his administration's position:

> Beyond the transition period, as we look to the future of the West Bank and Gaza, it is clear to me that peace cannot be achieved by the formulation of an independent Palestinian state in those territories. Nor is it achievable on the basis of Israel's sovereignty or permanent control over the West Bank and Gaza.
>
> So the United States will not support the establishment of an independent Palestinian state in the West Bank and Gaza, and we will not support annexation or permanent control by Israel.
>
> There is, however, another way to peace. The final status of these lands must, of course, be reached through the give-and-take of negotiations. But it is the firm view of the United States that self-government by the Palestinians

of the West Bank and Gaza in association with Jordan offers the best chance for a durable, just and lasting peace.

President Reagan's framework in its basic elements was, as he said, squarely in line with the position that the United States had taken since 1967. He was, however, more specific in stating formally a U.S. view on the nature of the political settlement in the West Bank and Gaza after Israeli withdrawal in return for peace, recognition, and security.

As the first Reagan administration drew to a close, three questions remained at the top of the agenda: On what basis would key Arab states in addition to Egypt recognize Israel as a state in the Middle East and make peace with it? What peaceful relationship between Jews and Palestinian Arabs could be developed in the land west of the Jordan River? Through what steps can those relationships of peace be achieved?

It may be that experience since 1967 has made a clear-cut partition of the area of the Palestine mandate between exclusive sovereignties impossible. It may be that the ultimate solution will lie in mutual acceptance by each party of the other's right to live, work, own property, and do business in both territories. It may be that each side for the sake of peace would negotiate a relationship in peace that would go well beyond the conventional relationship between the sovereign states. Defining that relationship remains the work of mediators and negotiators.

Approaches for Achieving a Settlement

Almost as difficult as developing a substantive framework for negotiating resolution of the Israeli-Palestinian problem and peace between Israel and its neighbors has been developing procedures for bringing the parties to the point of decision among realistic choices. Efforts since the mid-1940s to define such procedures have confronted the parties to the conflict and mediators with three persistent issues:

1. How should substantive exchanges be conducted to produce agreement? A continuing part of the problem has been some degree of refusal by the parties to recognize and to deal directly with each other.

2. Should the parties aim for a comprehensive settlement or for a sequence of partial agreements that might serve as building blocks for an overall peace? Many of the Arab parties have refused to negotiate unless they can see the shape of a possible comprehensive agreement in advance, but so many parties as well as complex intra-Israeli, intra-Palestinian, and inter-Arab issues are involved that decisionmaking bodies have found it difficult to deal with them all at one time. Additionally Israel has preferred negotiation with one party at a time.

3. Who should mediate? The Arab-Israeli conflict came to a head as part of the experience of decolonization at the end of World War II and then became an element in the new global strategic contest between the United States and the Soviet Union. Since the interests of powers outside

the region have been affected by conflict within the region, the resolution of the conflict has become partly a global issue.

Negotiation

Negotiation in the Arab-Israeli context has been both a way of trying to reach agreement and a symbol of recognition. It has also at times been a symbol of the alternative to a settlement imposed by the great powers.

In a speech on June 19, 1967, President Lyndon Johnson laid a major share of the responsibility for achieving a settlement on the parties to the conflict themselves: "Clearly the parties to the conflict must be parties to the peace."[18] Although others should be prepared to help those parties, they could not expect any of the great powers to find a solution unless they themselves felt that they had an interest in making it work.

The Israelis insisted on face-to-face or direct negotiation. At first, they pressed for direct exchanges as evidence that Arab governments were prepared to accept Israel and to deal with it in ways common to states that recognize and conduct normal relations with each other. After Secretary Rogers' speech of December 1969, they held up the principle of direct negotiation as a counter to any U.S. or other great-power effort to impose terms not acceptable to Israel. The Israelis felt that their best chance for a settlement would result from the recognition by Arab countries that they could not destroy Israel with their own resources or rely on the great powers to give them what they wanted and would have to take account of Israel's military strength in reaching agreement.

The Arab governments, on the other hand, at a summit meeting in Khartoum issued a communiqué on September 1, 1967, stating "the main principles to which the Arab states adhere, namely: no peace with Israel, no recognition of Israel, no negotiations with it, and adherence to the rights of the Palestinian people in their country."[19] This statement indicated that they were not ready politically to accept Israel. It also reflected their inability to consider negotiation in the wake of a major military humiliation.

Much of the diplomatic effort between 1967 and 1973 was directed at trying without success to establish a basis for bringing the parties together in negotiation. The 1973 war, however, removed the humiliation of the 1967 defeat in Arab minds, especially in Egypt, and progress toward negotiation was achieved on a variety of fronts. Egyptian and Israeli military officers and civilian officials met directly or with UN representatives in a tent at Kilometer 101 between Cairo and Suez. Representatives of Egypt, Israel, and Jordan (with Palestinians in their delegation) met under the sponsorship of the U.S. and the Soviet Union at Geneva in December 1973. Secretary Kissinger's shuttle mediation led to disengagement agreements between Egypt and Israel and Israel and Syria in 1974 and 1975, and each agreement was followed by direct discussions between the parties under UN auspices within the framework of the Geneva Conference to negotiate the details of implementing the agreements. In 1977, President Sadat's visit to Jerusalem not only provided a breakthrough in establishing a pattern of direct negotiation between the two governments but also eventually opened the door to normal relations between the citizens of the two countries. The experience at Camp David and in the subsequent negotiation of the Egypt-Israel Peace Treaty proved the value of the continuing presence of a third party—the "full partner"—in the negotiations. Although many issues were resolved by the two parties themselves, others required persistent American intervention, and still other crucial questions were left unresolved.

Apart from Jordan, which also attended the 1973 Geneva Conference, and Lebanon in 1983, the other Arab governments and the PLO had not by mid-1984 shown themselves unambiguously ready to negotiate a peace agreement. This was partly because they did not believe that Israel would withdraw from occupied territory or treat its neighbors as having equal rights and partly because acceptance of Israel remained politically controversial in the Arab world. The act of negotiation remained in some measure a symbol of recognition, although by mid-1984 it seemed likely that the act of negotiating would not be a stumbling block—except between Israel and the PLO—if it seemed possible to work out an honorable and just settlement.

Comprehensive or Partial Agreements

Running through efforts since 1949 to resolve the Arab-Israeli conflict has been the issue of whether to try for a comprehensive settlement of all important issues or whether to deal with one part of the problem at a time. Most policy statements or agreements attempted to bridge the gap between these two positions.

Arguing for a comprehensive settlement has been the fact that many of the issues are intertwined. For instance, Arab states have not been willing to consider negotiation unless assured that they could expect an honorable settlement, and Israel would not consider withdrawing troops from the West Bank, Gaza, and the Golan Heights unless assured of Arab acceptance and of adequate security arrangements. It was generally accepted that the problem could not be solved unless the problems on all fronts were solved.

Arguing for a series of partial agreements has been the difficulty for any of the governments involved in making the substantial concessions that a comprehensive settlement would require. For instance, before 1967 efforts were made by mediators to achieve agreement on water allocation (Eric Johnston beginning in 1953) and on a refugee settlement (Joseph Johnson beginning in 1961), and after the 1973 war, the three disengagement agreements stated that each agreement was not regarded as a final peace agreement but as "a first step toward a final, just and durable peace." There was an argument for not delaying attainable solutions by waiting for solutions not attainable at the time. It was also argued that an agreement in any area could build confidence that other agreements were possible.

The emphasis after the 1967 war turned toward a comprehensive settlement. All the elements of Resolution 242 were seen as a package deal. In winter 1970-1971, however, the idea of a partial step emerged again in the form of a partial pullback from the Suez Canal. The United States pursued the idea through summer 1971 but eventually was unable to achieve agreement between Egypt and Israel. Nevertheless, a shift in approach from a comprehensive peace to a partial agreement had begun.

After the 1973 war, Secretary Kissinger personally spent a great deal of time in the Middle East pursuing a series of interim agreements with the understanding that they would be considered partial steps on the way to an overall settlement. His purpose was to establish a process of negotiation by dealing with the practical steps of disengaging armies and stabilizing the cease-fire while beginning to build some confidence that agreements could be negotiated and kept. One of the rules in this step-by-step approach was that neither side should try to resolve in an interim agreement issues like final borders, which could only be resolved in a final peace agreement. The three disengagement agreements of 1974 and 1975 resulted: Egypt-Israel in January 1974 and September 1975 and Israel-Syria in May 1974.

After the second Egypt-Israel agreement in 1975, there was a general feeling among those who had participated in negotiation of the second Sinai agreement that perhaps the step-by-step approach and shuttle diplomacy had gone about as far as possible without turning attention again to the broader principles of a comprehensive settlement and seeking a larger forum in which military, legal, and other specialists could more easily be brought into the negotiations.

The Carter administration in 1977 immediately began to discuss with the parties and with the Soviet Union the terms of reference for resumption of the work of the Geneva Conference. Before the Carter approach could be completed, however, President Sadat made his unexpected and historic visit to Jerusalem in November in an effort to break the impasse. In fact, while demonstrating Egypt's acceptance of Israel and readiness to negotiate peace as part of a comprehensive settlement, he opened the door to negotiation of an Egyptian-Israeli peace linked in concept but in no concrete way to a larger peace. When eventually the Egypt-Israel Peace Treaty was signed on March 26, 1979, other Arab states broke relations with Egypt because they judged that Egypt had made a separate peace with Israel. For those who negotiated at Camp David there was no doubt that they committed themselves to negotiating further agreements leading toward a comprehensive peace and inviting other Arabs to join.

The tension remained between the Arab parties and the United States. Many Arabs believed that principles of a settlement are self-evident and awaited only the American will to impose such a settlement. The United States, on the other hand, recognized that the democratic government in Israel can only take decisions on issues of national importance in the context of a negotiation and even then may be able to deal only with one set of issues at a time.

The Great Power Context

The role the United States has played in negotiation of an Arab-Israeli peace has been a function of American domestic politics, of changing

American perceptions of the U.S. role and interests on the world stage, and of the evolution of the United States' relationship with the Soviet Union.

The U.S. role that President Johnson judged practicable in 1967 was heavily influenced by the deep preoccupation with Vietnam, by the unwillingness of the Congress to give the president unqualified support for assuming primary responsibilities in another major international conflict, by a strongly felt obligation to protect the security of Israel, and by the need to avoid confrontation with the Soviet Union. Before the 1967 war, the United States sought to act mainly in concert with the international community. During the war, the hotline was used to establish that both Washington and Moscow intended to stand aside. After the war, it became apparent that the United States did not have the energy to spare from Vietnam to take on a solo mediating role and put that assignment in the hands of a special representative of the Secretary General of the United Nations.

In 1969, both President Nixon and National Security Adviser Henry Kissinger came to Washington believing that the situation was too dangerous to allow to drift further. They also held the view that the most urgent objective on the nation's foreign policy agenda in an age when the Soviet Union was achieving equality of nuclear power was to bring some order to relations among the great powers. U.S. Middle East diplomacy through the first Nixon administration has to be understood in the context of the evolving relationship between the United States and the Soviet Union. The Nixon administration, however, also had an interest in diminishing Soviet influence in the Middle East.

The centerpiece of the Nixon administration's Middle East diplomacy for much of 1969 was an extended series of talks between Assistant Secretary of State Joseph Sisco and Soviet Ambassador Anatoly Dobrynin as well as Soviet officials in Moscow, culminating in meetings between Secretary of State Rogers and Foreign Minister Gromyko at the United Nations in October and November. The theory behind those talks was that if the United States and the Soviet Union could agree on the terms of a fair settlement, they would try to persuade their respective friends in the Middle East to negotiate a settlement along those lines. Much was agreed upon in the talks between the United States and the Soviet Union, but in the end Gromyko backed away, apparently because he concluded that Moscow would not be able to deliver Egyptian agreement to negotiate with Israel. When Secretary Rogers made public in his speech of December 9 the terms the United States had agreed to, the Israelis and their supporters in the United States were furious—both because the substance included Israel's withdrawal to prewar borders between Egypt and Israel and because the secretary, even though he had met with Israeli Foreign Minister Eban shortly before the speech, had given the Israelis no inkling that the U.S. position would be made public.

At the end of 1969, events in the Middle East began to take a turn that was to put the Arab-Israeli conflict even more squarely in the context of American-Soviet relations. From the end of February 1970, through a cease-fire–standstill agreement negotiated by the United States in August, the intensification of the war of attrition across the Suez Canal took on the form in Washington's eyes of a confrontation with Soviet efforts to help a client achieve its objectives with Soviet-supplied military force. The same perspective dominated the Nixon administration's reaction to the Syrian invasion of Jordan in September 1970. As King Husayn's government sought to prevent the Palestine Liberation Organization from establishing the authority of a state within a state, Syrian tanks crossed the border. Coming to this situation from the confrontation by proxy in Egypt, the administration's immediate perception was that Soviet military advisers in Syria must at least have been informed of the Syrian move.

In 1972 and 1973, the administration resumed exchanges with Moscow in conversations between Kissinger and Foreign Minister Gromyko, but the U.S. objective was more to preserve an atmosphere of consultation in the context of the larger U.S.-Soviet relationship than to achieve a result. The Nixon-Brezhnev summits in May 1972 and June 1973 confirmed President Sadat's view that he could not rely on the initiative of the superpowers to change the situation in the Middle East. After the first summit, he ordered Soviet military personnel out of Egypt. In 1973, he decided that the Arabs' only recourse was to go to war to regain enough territory to be able to claim a victory as a starting point for negotiation and to involve the superpowers. He succeeded in both objectives, and the October 1973 war ended with Kissinger, who had become secretary of state on September 22, in Moscow agreeing with Foreign Minister Gromyko on joint sponsorship of a peace conference at Geneva.

Early in 1974, however, the course shifted again when President Sadat in January asked Secretary Kissinger to serve as intermediary to work out an Egyptian-Israeli disengagement agreement. Israel also preferred U.S. mediation to Soviet involvement. As Secretary Kissinger pursued his shuttle diplomacy in 1974 and 1975, he went through the motions of consulting with Foreign Minister Gromyko, but increasingly the deliberate effect of his diplomacy was to put the United States on center stage with the Soviet Union relegated to the wings. With the exception of a period in September and October 1977, the United States continued to be the prime mover of diplomatic efforts through the remainder of the 1970s.

The Reagan administration at its outset concentrated on developing what Secretary of State Haig called a strategic consensus among states that saw the Soviet Union as the main threat to their security. Secretary Haig learned during his April 1981 trip to the Middle East that states in the area regarded perpetuation of the Arab-Israeli conflict as a more immediate threat to their security. The administration gradually widened its focus to give more attention to regional conflict.

By the mid-1980s, the administration's recurrent emphasis on strategic cooperation with Israel, its apparent initial acquiescence in Israel's invasion of Lebanon, and its inability to halt Israeli settlements in the West Bank all contributed to increased doubts about U.S. mediation. Even though progress achieved in the 1970s had been achieved through American mediation, Arabs, Europeans, and Soviets all questioned whether the United States alone—with what they all regarded as a strong bias toward Israel—could reach the objective it had set for itself. On the one hand, only the United States had a reasonable working relationship with Israel; on the other hand, Washington refused to talk with the PLO under current circumstances and, in the world's eyes, seemed unable to make Israel observe the basic guidelines of Resolution 242.

Reflections

The years from 1967 through the 1970s witnessed substantial progress in important respects toward an Arab-Israeli peace; yet resolution of the conflict seems as far away as ever. Several reflections may be warranted.

1. Time, events, and political process can change attitudes and make possible tomorrow what may not be possible today. We do not have to accept a straight-line projection from a dangerous present to a disastrous future. In the mid-1980s, more Arab leaders are prepared to accept and to make peace with Israel than were in 1967. Israel has formally recognized the need for resolution of the Palestinian problem in all its aspects. One peace treaty has been signed. The Arab world has agreed on who will play the Arab role in the area of the former mandate of Palestine. This progress should not be exaggerated, but the point deserves to be made with force and precision because of the tendency to dwell on the obvious intractability of the problem and the obstacles constantly obstructing the path to peace. That tendency provides an inadequate basis for policy.

2. The involvement of the highest political leadership of the United States can make a difference, and vigorously conducted diplomacy can achieve modest results. In a situation so complex that it is sometimes difficult for the parties to the conflict to see the elements of a solution, an outsider with a sense of direction and willingness to lead can help crystallize agreements. It must also be stated that top political leaders in the United States have often waited to be pushed into a leadership role by tragic events rather than taking the initiative to prevent them and to achieve progress toward peace. This statement is made with full recognition that the power balance and attitudes in the Middle East may raise obstacles that on some occasions cannot be moved by any outsider.

3. The breakthroughs on the path to peace in this period have resulted mainly from developments in the Middle East—the 1967 and 1973 wars, the oil embargo, the Sadat visit to Jerusalem—rather than from great power initiative. Sometimes outside powers helped develop the context, but even top leaders in a country like the United States are unable to force peace on unwilling parties to a regional conflict. Opportunities such as Sadat's trip to Jerusalem may generate more pressure for peace on the parties than tragedies such as war or pressure from great powers. Outsiders may help

construct such opportunities, especially when prior developments have provided the ingredients for peace, but active involvement of the regional parties is critical.

4. No peace can be achieved without negotiation. This is a practical matter. The give and take of negotiation can bring out the real concerns of the parties and produce agreements that each party will have a stake in keeping. Only precisely defined negotiated agreements accepted by the necessary political institutions have a reasonable chance of enduring.

5. Readiness for a negotiated solution is now voiced tentatively in key Middle Eastern capitals, but some ingredients essential to a settlement have not crystallized. Two keys to further progress toward peace are judgments by the parties that a negotiated settlement would serve their interests better than the alternatives and related judgments by the parties that the balance of forces would permit a fairly negotiated settlement. Under the Begin and Shamir governments, Israel seemed more determined to tighten its control over all the land west of the Jordan River than to negotiate peace with Jordan or the Palestinians. The Palestinians were divided over making peace with Israel, and most Arabs questioned whether a negotiation could produce a fair outcome given Israel's superior power.

6. Even if the parties can envision a settlement that would serve their interests and believe it could be negotiated, they still face difficult practical questions of how to get started. Psychological obstacles of suspicion and mistrust must be overcome, and enough communication must take place to identify common ground from which to negotiate. In the mid-1980s, despite whatever shortcomings the United States may have as a mediator, it is still the outside power with the greatest potential for communicating with all the parties.

The issue that faces the parties to the Arab-Israeli conflict as well as states affected by the conflict is whether a determined effort to achieve peace will again be mounted or whether the conflict will once more be allowed to drift. The experience since 1967 suggests that progress is possible if political leaders commit themselves to it and that the absence of such commitment and progress leaves no alternative but violence.

Notes

1. *The Search for Peace in the Middle East: Documents and Statements 1967–1979*, report prepared for the Subcommittee on Europe and the Middle East of the Committee on Foreign Affairs, U.S. House of Representatives, by the Foreign Affairs and National Defense Division, Congressional Research Service, Library of Congress, CP-957, U.S. Government Printing Office, Washington, D.C., 1979, p. 273.

2. *Ibid.*, pp. 286–287.

3. *Ibid.*, p. 93.

4. *Ibid.*, pp. 297, 299, 300.

5. *Ibid.*, p. 97.

6. *Ibid.*, p. 1.

7. *Ibid.*, p. 2.

8. *Ibid.*, p. 3

9. *Ibid.*, p. 15.

10. *Ibid.*, pp. 305–306.

11. *Ibid.*, p. 311.

12. *Ibid.*, pp. 159–160.

13. Sadat's speech to the Knesset, *Ibid.*, pp. 224–227.

14. *Ibid.*, pp. 20–23.

15. *Ibid.*, pp. 30–47.

16. *Ibid.*, p. 21.

17. Ronald Reagan, "A New Opportunity for Peace in the Middle East," broadcast from Burbank, California, September 1, 1982, *Weekly Compilation of Presidential Documents*, September 6, 1982, vol. 18, no. 35, p. 1084.

18. See note 2.

19. *The Search for Peace in the Middle East*, p. 269.

15

A Political/Military Strategy
for the Persian Gulf and
Southwest Asia

Bruce R. Kuniholm

The Iranian revolution and the fall of the Shah in January 1979 compelled the United States to restructure its military posture to confront contingencies in the regions of the Gulf and Indian Ocean. Initial changes occurred on the level of U.S. declaratory policy, but in the urgency of shoring up a crumbling military position, both the Carter and the Reagan administrations failed to fully articulate a viable political strategy that related the new military instruments to the broader objectives and purposes of U.S. interests in this complex region. This chapter reviews the premises and emerging outlines of a U.S. military strategy in Southwest Asia and advances some ideas concerning the integration of U.S. military capabilities into a broader political framework.

Oil and Other U.S. Interests

Oil remains the West's primary strategic concern in the Gulf. Despite conservation efforts and research on alternative energy sources, Europe, Japan, and the United States continue to depend on Gulf oil imports (see Chapter 11). The continued stockpiling of oil, together with the U.S. failure to establish a comprehensive energy program, underscores the vulnerability of the United States to embargoes and other political/military measures that could disrupt the flow of oil from the Gulf.

A recent study by the Congressional Research Service (CRS) examined the macroeconomic impacts on the United States and six other Western industrialized economies of two hypothetical, total disruptions of the West's

This chapter is drawn in part from *The Persian Gulf and United States Policy: A Guide to Issues and References* (Claremont, Calif.: Regina Books, 1984). Reprinted by permission.

access to Gulf oil for one year. The disruptions were set in two very different economic contexts: April 1, 1980, a time of economic growth prior to the emergence of significant trends in energy conservation and substitution, and January 1, 1982, a time of economic recession, increased conservation, substitution, and mounting petroleum reserves. Although the 1980 disruption would have produced a dramatic economic decline among the Western industrialized countries, the 1982 disruption would have resulted in markedly less severe but nevertheless significant economic consequences. The Congressional Research Service study asserts that resumption of economic growth in the future will increase the demand for energy and that U.S. dependence on imported oil will grow as domestic oil and gas production declines. The study suggests that, if the Western nations relax their efforts to address their energy problems, the United States (even if it is less dependent than other nations on oil from the Gulf) in the short term would suffer from a Gulf disruption to the same extent as its allies in Western Europe and Japan.[1]

Experts have debated at length the extent of Soviet oil production capacities and needs in the context of their implications for Soviet interest in access to Gulf oil. The CIA adjusted its controversial prediction of Soviet oil production in 1985 from 8 to 10 million barrels of oil per day (mbd) to 12.1 mbd. The Defense Intelligence Agency estimated Soviet oil production in 1985 at 12.2 to 12.9 mbd, whereas estimates by the European Economic Community (EEC) were as high as 14 mbd.[2] The trend in predictions suggests that need for oil as a potential source of Soviet adventurism in the Gulf is a less significant motivation than initially thought. But less urgent needs do not preclude the possibility that the Soviet Union would be interested in increasing access to oil to supply its allies' energy demands or, under extreme circumstances, in damaging the Western economies by denying them Gulf oil.

The Soviet Union would encounter serious economic and military risks by denying the West access to Gulf oil. As domestic Soviet demand for oil increases, probable compensating cutbacks in oil exports (Soviet oil exports to OECD countries were 1.62 mbd in 1984 and fell to 1.36 mbd in 1985) will make Soviet gas an increasingly important hard currency earner. Though European dependence on Soviet natural gas will be relatively small (Soviet gas will provide less than 25 per cent of total gas consumed and, except for Austria, less than 5 per cent of total energy consumed in 1990), Soviet dependence on European consumption for hard currency will be significant.[3] In 1979, for example, the Soviets relied on energy sales to Western Europe for over 50 per cent of their hard currency earnings. By 1982, that figure had risen to 60 per cent, and natural gas, though less significant, was earning an increasing share. In 1982 the Soviets exported 1.1 trillion cubic feet of gas to Western Europe. According to the Soviet magazine Foreign Trade, the Soviet Union has signed contracts for the delivery of an additional 1.1 trillion cubic feet in connection with the 2,759-mile-long Yamal pipeline (completed in January 1983).[4] Since Soviet gas reserves constitute one-third of the known world total, the Soviets will be reluctant to jeopardize the market for this abundant and increasingly important resource by pursuing adventurist policies—particularly in the Middle East.

Regardless of Soviet intentions, the importance of oil to the NATO countries and Japan renders continued access to Gulf oil (on reasonable commercial terms) a primary U.S. interest in the Middle East. This interest is one among several well-defined and generally accepted interests, including containment of Soviet expansion and influence; prevention of arms imbalances, nuclear proliferation and nuclear war; regional stability and peaceful change; the security of Israel; and advancement of the Middle East peace process.[5]

Threats to U.S. Interests

Analysts generally agree upon the broad definition of U.S. interests in the Middle East but differ on the priority assigned to them and on the assessment of threats to these interests. Potential threats to U.S. interests fall into three categories: those from the Soviet Union itself, those from other countries in the region (possibly supported by the Soviet Union), and those from within particular countries (also possibly supported by the Soviet Union and/or other countries in the region).

The Soviets would prevail if they were to conduct limited attacks on areas, such as northwest Iran, that are close to their borders. The political and military occupation costs, however, would be sufficiently high and the marginal benefits (potential air superiority at the head of the Gulf) sufficiently low to render such moves unlikely. Soviet attacks on noncontiguous states would be even more risky and difficult, although the buildup of intervention forces and staging areas in the People's Democratic Republic of Yemen (PDRY) could make it more costly for the United States to combat successfully a Soviet attack.[6]

The two most probable worst-case scenarios for a direct Soviet attack are (1) an overland assault on Iran, possibly coupled with an airborne assault on Khuzestan and a bomber attack on U.S. carriers in the Indian Ocean; and (2) an overland assault from Afghanistan into Pakistani and Iranian Baluchistan, coupled with an airborne assault on Chah Bahar or Gwadar and a bomber attack on U.S. carriers in the Indian Ocean.

Such attacks are highly unlikely, not only because of enormous economic and political costs (often ignored by worst-case analysts), but because the logistical difficulties and military costs of such a move would vastly outweigh the potential benefits:

- Only seven of 24 Soviet divisions in the North Caucasus, Transcaucasus, and Turkestan Military Districts could be utilized without seriously degrading Soviet capabilities in other, more important contingencies (NATO, Poland, Afghanistan, and China).
- These divisions are in a relatively poor state of readiness, would take at least three to four weeks to mobilize, and would encounter enormous

logistical, geographical, and military problems in their movement south, especially if American forces were deployed according to a strategy designed to delay and cause attrition while allied forces were constructing a defensive perimeter in Khuzestan.

- Aside from the problem of available lift capability to send in airborne troops (estimates range from a low of one to a high of four airborne divisions; the consensus is two), the Soviets lack the capacity to provide them with fighter escort (Khuzestan is out of range for all Soviet tactical fighters based in Afghanistan or the Soviet Union, and access to Iraqi bases is unlikely).
- Soviet bombers, limited by possible commitments to more important contingencies and without fighter escorts, would also be vulnerable to U.S. and regional air power once a conflict occurred.[7]

Given the logistics and current disposition of Soviet forces, it is unlikely that a Soviet force could be supported in Khuzestan without penalizing Soviet capacity to handle simultaneous contingencies in more important areas. Joshua Epstein, currently a Research Associate at the Brookings Institution, believes that Soviet forces "would be unlikely to enjoy any meaningful superiority over an RDF assembled under the same strategic constraint." In short, he has found that while there are serious challenges to U.S. force deployment, "the current situation warrants neither the kind of pessimism that has been heaped upon it nor an ill-considered 'drive for bases' which may flow from over-assessments of the Soviet threat."[8]

Dennis Ross observes in Chapter 12 that the Soviet Union's "coalition maintenance" decisionmaking environment tends to generate lowest common denominator policies that discourage bold departures and high-risk actions. A direct attack, he surmises, would be conceivable only in circumstances that the Soviets perceived to be defensive or extreme: If the costs of inaction were high (as in Afghanistan), or if the stakes were high (if the United States were to attempt to recreate the northern tier barrier or reestablish Iran as a strategic barrier to the projection of Soviet power). Short of such high stakes, Ross would agree with Epstein that indirect means of achieving Soviet objectives are much more likely than the direct use of military force.[9]

If, in spite of all calculations to the contrary, the Soviets were to launch a direct attack on Khuzestan, most analysts would probably agree with the staff of the Carnegie Panel on U.S. Security and the Future of Arms Control that, whatever the short-term outcome, in the long run, the Soviets would prevail—if the battle remained conventional and if the Soviets kept pouring in human resources and materiel at the expense of weakening their forces in other theaters. Both of these "ifs" are important assumptions.[10] The uncertain risks of escalation to nuclear war (vertical escalation) or of widening the war to NATO and other countries (horizontal escalation) would weigh heavily on Soviet considerations.

The Soviets might in some circumstances be willing to risk a quick military thrust, particularly in northwest Iran, under the assumption that faced with a confrontation, the United States and its allies (e.g. Turkey) would be unwilling to assume the onus of initiating an attack on Soviet troops. But such a risk would be high and would, at a minimum, result in the immediate development of U.S. bases throughout the Gulf. Given the stakes involved, an expectation of resistance and even confrontation could lead the Soviets to make their first move a surprise attack on U.S. carriers in the Indian Ocean in an effort to undercut U.S. tactical air superiority. Such a course would risk global war, and the Soviets would find it virtually impossible to ensure access to oil in the aftermath of such hostilities.[11] Consequently, options that focus on denial (through support of an attack by a surrogate, a massive air strike, or the use of missiles with conventional warheads) would seem to have greater attraction, even though their provocative nature makes them extremely risky.

Regional conflicts that can threaten U.S. interests are only limited by the imagination. These conflicts pose difficult problems by themselves but become even more problematic to the extent that the Soviets are directly involved. Such problems include the following:

- The historical conflict between Arabs and Israelis, which gave rise most recently to the war between Israel and the Palestinians in Lebanon, and the subsequent confrontation between Israel and Syria, both of which have important implications for the Gulf states.
- Historical differences between Arabs and Persians, exemplified by the Iran-Iraq war, and complicated by differences among Shi'i and Sunni Muslims.
- Iraqi desires for hegemony in the Gulf, evidenced by threatening maneuvers against Kuwait over the last two decades.
- Long-standing tensions between India and Pakistan, which have led to three wars since World War II.
- Attacks on the Yemen Arab Republic (YAR) by the People's Democratic Republic of Yemen (PDRY) and PDRY-supported attacks on Oman.
- YAR-Saudi border differences.
- Border conflicts between Afghanistan and Pakistan.

All these problems derive from historical regional differences. Although they may be influenced by outside powers, they are much less susceptible to outside control. Any of them could develop into a major war, a war that, in the event of superpower involvement (as threatened in the Yemens in 1979), might escalate out of control. With the exception of a war between two important oil-producing states such as Iran and Iraq or a threat to Saudi Arabia (whether from Iran, Iraq, or the PDRY), regional conflicts, though serious, pose much less of a threat to U.S. interests than does a Soviet attack, providing that the Soviets are not or do not become directly involved. If the Soviets are involved, much depends upon the proximity of the area to their borders.[12] If, in the Iran-Iraq war, the Soviets were to use troops in support of either country, they would precipitate a serious contingency with all the trappings of a direct Soviet attack. Soviet intervention in noncontiguous states, as pointed out earlier, would be risky and difficult.[13]

Coups, terrorism, insurgencies and revolutions stem from complex political, economic, and social problems for which military responses are often inappropriate and counterproductive. Given the rapid pace of modernization in the region, historical ethnic and religious differences, and discrepancies between rich and poor that exist among and within countries, challenges to established authority are likely. To the extent that challenges endanger régimes friendly to U.S. interests, such as that of Sultan Qabus's strategically important Oman, American policymakers should favor preventive measures (including the prudent creation of structures for political participation) over reactive ones, which have often proved to be counterproductive or even disastrous.

When threats to established authority endanger continued oil production and when production cutbacks in countries such as Saudi Arabia can drastically affect the Western industrial economies, the United States could consider responding to a régime's invitation to protect its oil fields or, in a worst-case scenario, could contemplate seizing them under hostile conditions.[14] The latter possibility, of course, is precisely the concern of the Gulf states when they seek U.S. assistance, and it dictates their ambivalence toward American offers of protection.[15] Were the United States to attempt the seizure of Saudi Arabia's oil fields under hostile conditions, the oil fields would probably suffer major damage, the risk of inviting a Soviet or Soviet-supported challenge would be high, the military feasibility would be dubious, and the political costs would be so great as to threaten U.S. interests throughout the world.[16] The use of force would also be a long-term proposition since, as the American experience in Lebanon suggests, U.S. troops are unlikely to stabilize a régime otherwise incapable of managing an indigenous challenge to its authority.[17]

If, on the other hand, the Soviets were invited to intervene in a civil war in Iran (to support Kurdish or Azerbaijani separatists or a rump Tudeh faction) or in Pakistan (to support Baluch or Pushtun separatists), the problems discussed earlier concerning a direct Soviet attack would arise. For this reason, military strategists who must plan for such contingencies cannot be too cavalier in dismissing the probability, however small, of a Soviet attack.

Devising appropriate responses to these threat assessments is difficult. The most serious threat (a direct Soviet attack) is the least likely, whereas the more likely threats (those from within the region) are least responsive to military influence. Finally, the threats are not mutually exclusive; one can easily lead to or be part of another.

American preparation to counter the most serious threats may encourage and even precipitate other problems. The United States could look to Jordan, Pakistan, or Turkey as surrogates for American power or attempt to establish a ground presence in the Gulf in order to give real as well as symbolic support to moderate régimes and thereby strike a credible deterrent posture. Such policies, however, could foster the development of a radical, anti-American opposition in those countries or in the region as a whole, undermining rather than supporting regional stability. Depending on the surrounding circumstances, such actions could also result in Soviet pressures on Iraq, Iran, or even Kuwait to establish a countervailing presence in the region, thus bringing great-power rivalry to the head of the Gulf.

If, however, the United States discounts the utility of military force in addressing these problems, downplays the Soviet threat, and maintains a low profile out of sensitivity to the political vulnerability of the Gulf's fragile régimes, it may be leaving the Gulf states open to coercion and attack. Such attitudes could contribute to a perception that U.S. influence is waning and to a belief among the local states that they should reckon with the Soviet Union. In so doing, the United States could encourage regional initiatives that increase a destabilizing Soviet influence to the detriment of American interests.

Finally, in the event of a great power confrontation in the Gulf, it would be infinitely more difficult for the United States or the Soviet Union to ensure access and control over the oil fields than it would be for either to deny the other such access and control. The relative ease that either would have in denying access and control to the other constitutes an important limitation on any military strategy in the Gulf. This constraint underscores the current asymmetry between U.S. and Soviet interests: The United States must ensure access and control; the Soviet Union, which in the short run does not need the oil, has only to deny it to the industrialized nations of the West to have a major impact on their economies.

Developing a Military Strategy

Current U.S. capacity to respond to Soviet threats and to project its forces into the Gulf region is based on naval superiority in the Indian Ocean, substantial tactical air power, and ground forces that are lightly armed but readily deployable. Essential elements include the following:

- One and occasionally two carrier battle groups (with up to 110 fighter and attack aircraft) deployed in or near the Indian Ocean; since 1983, supporting naval forces include a total of three carrier groups.
- Facilities in the region (in Kenya, Somalia, Oman, Diego Garcia, Egypt, Morocco, and Israel, along with potential facilities in other areas depending on the contingency).[18]
- AWACS and associated command, control, and communications equipment currently in Saudi Arabia and occasionally in Egypt.[19]
- B-52 bombers staged in Spain or Guam and capable of operating out of Diego Garcia.
- Prepositioning of a 30-day supply of ammunition, fuel, and spare parts for a marine amphibious brigade aboard seven near-time prepositioning ships (NTPS) capable of putting the brigade ashore in 48 hours at

well-equipped ports (this does not include steaming time); these ships form part of a larger near-time prepositioning force that includes additional stocks, ammunition, fuel, water, two 400-bed Army field hospitals, and one 200-bed combat support hospital aboard 11 additional ships.
- Various elements of the rapid deployment force (as of January 1, 1983, the U.S. Central Command, or CENTCOM), including one marine amphibious force (MAF), five army divisions, and the equivalent of ten tactical air wings (totaling over 200,000 troops and 400 fighter and attack aircraft).[20]

By 1987, the United States will also have completed a number of strategic mobility initiatives currently under way:

- Prepositioning of a 30-day supply of ammunition, fuel, and spare parts for a Marine Corps division aboard 13 maritime prepositioning ships (MPS) in the Indian Ocean.
- Prepositioning of support equipment at Diego Garcia, Masirah (Oman), and Ras Banas (Egypt), as well as overbuilding and overstocking of maintenance sets at selected sites such as Dhahran and King Khalid Military City in Saudi Arabia.
- Acquisition of eight SL-7 fast deployment logistics container ships capable of moving a mechanized division to the Gulf via the Cape of Good Hope from ports in the United States in 15 to 19 days (this does not include loading and off-loading, which take an additional ten days).
- Enhanced strategic airlift, including extension of the service life of the C-5A, an increase in the cargo capacity of the C-141, procurement of 56 additional KC-10 tanker aircraft and 50 C-5B's, modification of commercial aircraft for a military transport role, and possibly, development and production of the costly and controversial strategic transport C-17.

Although estimates vary, it is reasonable to conclude that these initiatives will give the commander of CENTCOM the capability of deploying the equivalent of four to five divisions, or 80,000 to 100,000 combat troops, to the Gulf in 30 days.[21]

In addition to these initiatives, some have proposed prepositioning stocks and development of a regionwide, integrated defense network in Saudi Arabia to support the projection of U.S. tactical air and ground forces in the event of serious contingencies.[22] Development of a similar infrastructure in eastern Turkey will give the United States even greater flexibility in the region and, by its very existence, deter Soviet adventurism in Iran. In principle, these developments are clearly desirable. At the same time, the United States must be sensitive to regional limitations on its policies and be careful not to let design considerations—based in part on a worst-case analysis of the threat to be confronted and in part on interservice rivalries within the Pentagon—confuse the strategy that the United States pursues. At present, in spite of improvement in the U.S. capacity to deal with military contingencies in the Gulf, debate continues over the military strategy that should undergird American military readiness.

Most analysts agree that to deter Soviet adventurism in the Gulf, the United States must at a minimum be capable of beating the Soviets to the region. But disagreement exists about the sufficiency of a preemptive capacity to safeguard U.S. interests.

Some who minimize the Soviet threat believe that, if the United States develops the capability for quick preemptive intervention, it can prevent Soviet adventurism.[23] They argue that the Soviets would back away from any situation in which the United States has established a trip-wire. A corollary to this argument is that a relatively limited, over-the-horizon sea-based force (with land-based air support) is sufficient to establish a trip-wire if necessary. A more elaborate force is not only superfluous and costly; it is also counterproductive. According to this interpretation, the asymmetry of the two countries' interests in the region is sufficient to underscore U.S. determination and dictate Soviet caution.

Critics have pointed out that preemptive intervention is a theory of deterrence, not a strategy, since it fails to address the question of what to do if deterrence fails.[24] If deterrence should fail (and it could, they argue, because most Western nations do not act as if their vital interests are at stake), elaborate conventional forces would be essential to back up the trip-wire force. Without such a backup, the United States would have recourse only to a nuclear threat. This threat would lack credibility unless the United States had previously committed sizable numbers of troops whose lives were jeopardized. Recognizing Western impotence, the Soviets might be prompted to disregard problems posed by a small conflict with the United States, particularly if they could outmaneuver American forces and establish themselves in some trouble spot before the United States could get there. The Soviets could also provoke the United States to move preemptively in response to a Soviet feint and then use U.S. intervention as justification for actions elsewhere.

As a result, most analysts see the need for an American strategy that transcends a preemptive intervention capacity. Some have advocated a direct theater (or regional) defense by the United States designed to entangle Europe either through Turkey or through the requirements of U.S. operations in Southwest Asia, which would be contingent upon allied assistance.[25]

A strategy of direct regional defense relies on quick reaction to Soviet initiatives. A Soviet move into Azerbaijan, for example, would require early American intervention (e.g., the insertion of airborne troops in the Zagros Mountains) to buy time. Simultaneously, this strategy seeks to create a buffer between Soviet forces and the Gulf through more elaborate military operations, with a view to building a coalition of allies that would make it very difficult for the Soviets to succeed in any aggressive action in southwest

Iran. The operating assumption of this strategy is that the Soviets' most significant advantage is not strategic but tactical and that theater linkage (a linkage between the Middle East and Western Europe), with its escalatory risks, is necessary to counter that advantage. A corollary to coalition politics is that a credible deterrent strategy requires a more elaborate regional framework (facilities and prepositioned materiel). How elaborate the regional framework should be depends on the interpretation of the magnitude and likelihood of the Soviet threat. Those seeking the military capacity to counter a sizable Soviet attack generally argue for more elaborate and expanded facilities and discount the political costs in regional stability associated with an increased U.S. presence.

Interservice rivalries and competition within the defense establishment for a larger share of the defense budget continue to fuel debate over the role the United States should play vis-à-vis its allies, the division of labor among the services in responding militarily to developments in the Middle East, and the kind of conventional defense appropriate to the problem. A maritime strategy, articulated by F. J. West before his tenure as assistant secretary of defense for international security affairs and endorsed at least in part by the Reagan administration's defense program (which plans for three new nuclear carrier battle groups), supports a policy of horizontal escalation that links NATO to any U.S.-Soviet conflict in the Gulf.

West argues that a theater defense is not feasible. Sustaining a toehold in the Gulf is nevertheless necessary since Soviet control of the Gulf means Soviet control of Western Europe. Naval operations, unlike ground operations, cannot be limited by geography. As a result, West argues, NATO agreement to reinforce U.S. troops is an agreement to naval combat because the naval threads of NATO forces are too intertwined. In the event of Soviet aggression, he asserts, the Soviets would be confronted by a conjunction of unacceptable threats, including the threat of catastrophic naval losses, a full NATO buildup, mobilization of U.S. and European military might, and a hair-trigger nuclear balance. The uncertain threat of vertical escalation, presumably, is expected to be more credible given the actions already taken. At the root of West's argument is the assumption that command of the sea confers a distinct advantage upon the United States and that superior naval power is a category of military power separate from the capacity to fight a land war in the NATO countries. Articulation and implementation of a policy based on this assumption will, in West's estimation, provide the most credible defense possible for the United States.[26]

Critics of West's argument, led by former Under Secretary of Defense Robert Komer, argue that maritime supremacy is essential but that primary reliance on it to project offensive forces will build the wrong kind of costly navy (Komer estimates that the three carrier battle groups will cost over $50 billion) at the expense of larger U.S. strategic interests. Such a strategy, Komer argues, will not prevent Soviet domination of Europe and the Middle East. As a result, its implications ("at best a form of unilateral American global interventionism and at worst a form of neo-isolationism") will pressure

U.S. allies to consider accommodation with the Soviet Union. America's efforts to rejuvenate the security relationship with its NATO allies, promotion of a more rational and efficient burden sharing, and development of a more balanced force structure offer a better prospect for achieving a conventional deterrence/defense in Western Europe, the Gulf, and northeast Asia.[27]

Those who agree with Komer's criticism of a maritime strategy built around a few supercarriers for projecting power do not always share his enthusiasm for a coalition approach. Former Director of Central Intelligence Stansfield Turner, for example, emphasizes the importance of smaller carriers exercising traditional maritime capabilities (control of the sea lanes and air lanes above them). Turner believes that more small ships, in conjunction with a revised doctrine that includes smaller amphibious assault operations and more mobile follow-on ground and air forces, would give the United States the flexibility it must have to move forces where unexpected contingencies dictate. This could be done without threatening the programs that presently support the defense of Europe and northeast Asia. This strategy would not be as dependent on the NATO alliance as that espoused by Komer and would provide insurance against European failure to cooperate with the United States.[28]

Finally, two members of the Strategic Studies Institute of the U.S. Army War College have criticized the deterrent posture of both schools. In their judgment, the continental/coalition school's reliance on theater nuclear weapons (vertical escalation) and the maritime school's reliance on war-widening options (horizontal escalation) both threaten a fundamental concern: the avoidance of superpower conflict. Their preference is to keep political-military objectives limited; otherwise, their recommendations do not appear that different from Komer's. They advocate a balance of conventional capabilities, seeking to combine a coalitional approach with a policy of force procurement that emphasizes strategic mobility assets. A policy built on these recommendations, they believe, would be flexible enough to allow for nonnuclear deterrence in the Gulf, a region they regard as significant but secondary in importance to Europe.[29]

Since these two analysts regard the Gulf region as more unstable than Europe, they also see it as more likely to require U.S. assistance. They circumvent the question of cost by recommending that the United States shift its defense budget priorities and pursue military operations sequentially rather than simultaneously. Although they acknowledge that shifting budget priorities would be difficult politically, they never confront the crucial importance of the Gulf region to the security of Western Europe and Japan, a factor that created the problem of simultaneous fronts in the first place. As a result, they also ignore the tough question of how successful a publicly declared nonnuclear policy in the Gulf would be in deterring the Soviets. Finally, they do not provide any insight into what the United States should do if nonnuclear deterrence fails and conventional forces, once committed, are on the verge of defeat.

Where Do We Go from Here?

Given the political context within which the United States must operate in the Gulf, the most sensible military strategy for it to pursue is one consistent with current American military capabilities and plans to enhance sea lift and air lift. This strategy should allow for a conventional force sufficient to assist American allies (e.g., Saudi Arabia); help defend them against threats from other regional forces (e.g., Iran, Iraq, or the PDRY); and deter a Soviet attack by means of (1) a capacity to deploy a preemptive force in readiness; (2) a capability to transport (by air and sea) conventional reinforcements that would hinder Soviet aggression in the unlikely event that were to occur; and ultimately, (3) the uncertain threat of vertical and horizontal escalation.

The level of forces required to throw back, rather than impede, a determined Soviet attack on the Gulf would be far in excess of what is required to accomplish these three goals. A sizable ground presence would also be politically counterproductive, and it is not at all clear that sizable forces could prevent the Soviets from destroying the oil fields and terminals or denying the United States access to Gulf oil anyway. As a result, the strategy recommended here eschews a ground presence. Rather, it initially relies on airborne divisions and sizable sea-based capabilities that could react quickly; second, on air-lifted and sea-lifted forces; and ultimately, on the uncertain threat of nuclear weapons and war-widening capabilities (both at sea and on the ground) to deter a Soviet attack. It places its confidence in a force that is quick, no larger than necessary to perform its regional functions, but large enough to require Soviet military intervention to defeat it. A trip-wire force, Kenneth Waltz has observed, must be thick enough so that only a national military force—not a loose band of irregulars—can snap it. "This then gives the United States the target for retaliation and establishes the conditions under which deterrence prevails."[30] Should deterrence fail, a full range of options would still be available to decisionmakers, providing that the options of vertical and horizontal escalation have not been renounced.[31] The United States may never intend to resort to either option, but public declaration of nonintent would weaken the deterrent effect.

There are a number of ways to implement such a strategy. One is articulated by an analyst who advocates "a small, agile, tactically capable intervention force that is based on and supplied from the sea, governed by a single, unified command, and supported by expanded sea power, especially forcible-entry capabilities."[32] Such a force would stress quality over size, prompt responsiveness over the important capacity for delayed augmentation from the United States, sea-based power projection capabilities over land-based tactical air power, and air-transported forces and logistical self-sufficiency over a dependency on facilities ashore. Air-transported forces and facilities ashore, it should be stressed, would be extremely important in the event that the Soviets were involved.

Such a force, operating under the strategy outlined above, would have several virtues:

- Although the proposed strategy recognizes that the United States must improve its capacity to rapidly move tactical air and ground forces, it directs attention to regional and lesser threats, both of which are much more likely than a worst-case Soviet attack.
- A sea-based force, supplemented by a rapidly deployable airborne force and an increasingly developed infrastructure (overbuilding, enlarged airstrips, and prepositioned material in selected locations), would afford the United States the option to intervene but would also allow American decisionmakers the choice of avoiding situations that would engulf a land-based American force in hostilities.
- The Soviets, who currently do not have a capacity equal to that of the United States to project force without bases, would have greater difficulty (politically and militarily) matching the U.S. presence.
- As a result, the proposed strategy, though giving the United States qualified capacity to respond credibly to a Soviet attack, would also be more responsive to the internal problems of countries in the region and to the fact that American forces stationed there would be a serious liability to their interests and those of the United States alike.
- A corollary is that it would allow for greater receptivity to the needs and concerns of the regional states and greater flexibility in American dealings with those states.

Formulating a Political Strategy

A military strategy toward the Gulf region is meaningless unless it is conceived in the context of a political strategy. As Professor Rouhollah Ramazani of the University of Virginia has observed, the United States must share with the region a policy based on a common vision of its priorities and stability; in short, the soldier must remain the servant of the diplomat.[33]

Prerequisites and Operating Assumptions

The imperatives that condition the development of a political strategy deserve some elaboration. Washington officials must acknowledge that relations with the states of the Gulf region are symbiotic and that regional imperatives must have equal footing with mutual concerns about the Soviet threat. They must also recognize that, although there are no reliable substitutes for America's military power, political constraints limit its use and efficacy. Finally, they must accept the uncertainties inherent in the development and maintenance of a flexible political strategy toward a rapidly changing region. Having accepted these premises, American policymakers will be in a position to consider a broader range of viable political options toward the Gulf region and Southwest Asia.

Implicit operating assumptions, which are crucial in a discussion of political options, warrant identification. A potential aggressor (Soviet or other) against certain countries in the region must anticipate a credible conventional response by the United States on behalf of those countries. Since conventional U.S. forces are constrained both in size and in manner of deployment by regional sensitivities, the United States, in confronting a Soviet threat, can rely on conventional forces only to a certain point. Beyond that point, the United States must rely on the uncertain threats posed by horizontal and vertical escalation. This does not imply that the United States would definitely resort to either course; rather, it acknowledges the fact that the Soviet Union cannot ignore U.S. capabilities.

Another important consideration in the Gulf is the balance between Soviet land forces (in the Transcaucasus and Central Asia) and the U.S. rapid deployment force (operating out of the Indian Ocean). This equilibrium, if appropriately nurtured, could foster the gradual creation of what should be the central component of any strategy toward the region: a de facto buffer zone between East and West, a zone for which there is historical precedent.[34] It is reasonable to assume that Iran and Afghanistan would be amenable to an agreement (code of conduct) between the United States and the Soviet Union about their policies in such a zone. Iran has already chosen to follow a nonaligned role, evident in the slogan "neither East nor West," that follows traditional policies and currently characterizes its foreign policy.[35] Afghanistan's traditional policy of *bi-tarafi* (without sides), which seeks to balance external influences,[36] is one of the few policies that most Afghans, should they ever reconstitute themselves as a nation, could agree upon. In the context of a Soviet/American understanding, regional states could be relatively free of great power influence and pursue nonaligned policies to the benefit of all parties.[37]

In the context of an entente, U.S. military capabilities could impede regional adventurism against vital Western interests, and they could also stimulate regional cooperation, if properly deployed. Secure from pressures to accommodate Soviet demands (though still vulnerable to situations that excite great power rivalry), regional states would have a strong incentive to head off troubling situations through regional cooperation.

The military balance would also make it possible for Gulf states to control their own destinies to the extent that their policies do not directly threaten vital U.S. or Soviet interests. Ultimately relying on the balance of power between the United States and the Soviet Union, regional states to varying degrees could and would have to play a primary role in the management of regional conflicts.

This development would make it easier for the United States and the Soviet Union to accommodate political change and to avoid involvement within the region, as long as neither country seeks to change the status quo by drastic measures. Although the United States could support particular states within the broader region, especially Turkey and Saudi Arabia and to a lesser extent Pakistan, it would have to be sensitive to the various regional contexts within which those states operate. Turkey, for example, is a NATO ally, but it is also a rival of another ally, Greece. Its Islamic identity, moreover, may become increasingly significant and its historical role as a buffer between the great powers is still applicable.

Recent governmental changes and attempts to implement Islamic laws in Iran and Pakistan have drastically altered their former pro–United States orientation and membership in CENTO. Accordingly, the United States has to anticipate changes, constantly evaluate the significance of changing circumstances, and develop adjustable policies. To facilitate the evaluation process, policymakers must think in terms of cooperating with and encouraging subregional groupings of states (a nonaligned northern tier, the Gulf Cooperation Council (GCC), or a bloc of states on the subcontinent). These subregional groups would constitute discrete if not always cohesive sources of political, economic, or military strength and could address collective problems and advance common interests.

The role of America's NATO allies and Japan in the Gulf must be carefully thought through and closely coordinated. Operational problems and political concerns associated with joint military responsibilities might lead the United States to rely essentially on its own reaction forces in the Indian Ocean, although it would continue to coordinate with France, Britain, and Australia on naval deployments. The United States could explore a division of labor with its NATO allies and Japan whereby they would increase their defense responsibilities in Europe and in the Pacific, respectively, to balance increased American efforts in the Gulf and Indian Ocean. The United States could also encourage its NATO allies to exercise their influence in particular countries of the region (e.g., Germany in Turkey, France in Iraq, Japan in Iran, Britain in Oman).

As European commercial ties with the Soviet Union improve (a development that the gas pipeline will encourage), the Soviet Union might be more amenable to allowing European influence to serve as a third alternative to that of the two superpowers. The Germans and the Japanese provided Turkey, Iran, and Afghanistan with an alternative to Soviet and British influence earlier in this century, and the French certainly aspire to such a role in the Gulf in the 1980s.[38] Though the rest of the European countries and Japan have been more reserved about playing such a role, they, too, may seek to develop special relationships with individual countries in the region.

Were the United States to encourage a third alternative to U.S. and Soviet influence in the Gulf, the Soviet reaction would be difficult to predict. Implementation of the strategy could result in the creation of a buffer zone there between East and West and would encourage the developing and nonaligned countries in the region to use their collective influence to restrain the Soviet Union and the United States from taking risks. This would lessen the chances of confrontation between the United States and the Soviet Union. It would encourage regional stability, would reassure the Soviet Union of American interest in amicable relations if the Soviets desire them, and might facilitate a resolution of the Afghan problem.

These positive effects would be far more persuasive if presented along with other initiatives in the context of a thaw or at least a tough-minded détente in U.S.-Soviet relations. If the Soviets reacted cooperatively, Moscow and Washington might agree to take advantage of this opportunity to reach a modus vivendi and go back to some of the rules of the "Great Game" that the great powers have played in the region since the eighteenth century.[39] This, in a much more restricted way, could be the consequence of the so-called "tanker war" in the Persian Gulf. Since the battle at sea began in 1984, over 230 vessels (97 in 1986 alone) have been attacked by Iran and Iraq. Iraq has sought to prevent Iran's relentless pursuit of victory by cutting off its oil exports. In the process, and apparently accidentally, one of Iraq's Mirage F1 fighter bombers attacked the USS Stark on May 17, 1987, killing 37 Americans. Iran, too, has attacked ships servicing the Arab Gulf states (particularly those of Kuwait, which has been an important supporter of Iraqi war efforts), and apparently without official sanction has inadvertently attacked two Soviet ships. Kuwaiti concern for protection, meanwhile, has led it to turn for assistance first to the United States and then, when the United States did not respond, to the Soviet Union—with the result that both countries have accepted the risk of providing Kuwaiti ships with protection under their respective flags. This development raises the possibility that the two superpowers may seek basing rights in the region in order to provide air cover over the Gulf. While each may see such policies as necessary to protect its interests and maintain its credibility as a superpower, the commitments that they entail give the Iranian government an unprecedented opportunity: to provoke a conflict that escalates the war to a superpower level and provide Iranians with an explanation of why they have not yet won the war. Meanwhile, the two superpowers are working together rather than at cross-purposes. Both support freedom of nevigation in the Gulf and agree on the need to bring the war to an end. On March 17, 1987, Soviet Foreign Minister Eduard Shevardnadze and U.S. Undersecretary of State Michael Armacost, meeting in Moscow, agreed to avoid open rivalry in the Gulf.

If the Soviets believed U.S. initiatives concerning a modus vivendi were a guise for recreating a pro-U.S. northern tier barrier, Moscow would probably attempt to subvert the strategy. The strategy's success would then depend on the extent to which countries of the region believed U.S. policy to be in their best interests and the degree to which they could be convinced of the strategy's efficacy, U.S. determination, and U.S. staying power.

A strategy that builds on such assumptions and follows the lines suggested in the following sections would provide convincing evidence of American support for the sovereignty and territorial integrity of existing states and would best safeguard U.S. interests in the region. The policy would address realistically the regional constraints on American policies. It would be consistent with American ideals, would be more acceptable to states of the region, and would provide for a potentially significant and politically effective voice against aggression from any front (especially the Soviet Union). At the same time, the strategy would avoid repetition of the American experience with other formerly conservative régimes (in Libya, Iraq, Ethiopia, and Iran)—all of which established close military cooperation with the United States, all of which were overthrown, and all of whose successors are among the most rabidly anti-U.S. régimes in the world. Oman may one day experience a similar fate, and the Soviet Union's experience in Egypt should also be instructive.

Strength Through Respect: A General Political Strategy

The strategy proposed here could be characterized as one of strength through respect, for it acknowledges that pluralism has come of age and that support for regionalism is in the security interests of all countries.[40] It could signal the beginning of a constructive and fruitful U.S. policy toward the third world.

To safeguard the interests of the industrialized countries while respecting the flux in the Gulf region, the United States could develop a general three-pronged strategy of strength through respect with the following components.

- A regional coalition of Arab Gulf states such as the Gulf Cooperation Council, under Saudi leadership, whose defense systems the United States could help to integrate.
- A de facto regional coalition of former CENTO countries (an aligned Turkey, a nonaligned Iran, and a quasi-aligned Pakistan), which would constitute a buffer zone between the Soviet Union and the Gulf states.
- Quiet support for the Islamic Conference (IC). The IC is the best forum for subsuming the interests of the two groupings of states. It makes the Soviets uncomfortable because of its religious focus and its possible effect on the Soviet-Muslim population. It would also keep Afghanistan in the public eye and undercut the influence of secular radical coalitions.[41]

To complement this three-pronged strategy, the United States might also wish to support a concept designed to support Egyptian,[42] Jordanian,[43] Pakistani,[44] or possibly Turkish[45] troops with U.S. airlift capabilities and build closer ties between those Muslim countries and the Gulf states. To the extent that it relies on Islamic states to protect mutual interests, this concept would be more acceptable than the introduction of American forces into the region or closer strategic cooperation with Israel. It would also facilitate a mutually beneficial arrangement between countries rich in human resources but poor in oil and those that have small populations but are oil rich.

Such a scheme could, however, commit the United States to greater involvement in the Gulf or cause it to incur more far-reaching responsibilities in the region (especially to Pakistan) than presently envisioned. These are all desirable options only to the extent that some regional power, perhaps

Iran, poses a serious threat to regional security or gravitates toward the Soviet Union. Such a shift would change the political and strategic contexts within which U.S. forces operate and would create the opportunity to change policies in response to regional shocks.[46] In the absence of such an opening, these options must be developed cautiously because of the consequences that a heavy-handed American influence could have on the often tenuous power bases of leaders in the region. The extent of Gulf cooperation would hinge on a number of variables, including perceptions of the Soviet threat, Soviet relations with Iran, progress on the Palestinian question, the role of Israel in America's strategic posture, the relationship at the time between Iran and Iraq, and the climate of opinion within the Gulf.

In the event of serious differences between the United States and Saudi Arabia, the United States might be limited to reliance on Turkey, Israel, and Egypt as its only important allies in the region, with Oman being America's primary Gulf partner. American options would be extremely grim with this scenario. The limitation of options indicates the importance of precluding the deterioration of U.S.-Saudi relations and the desirability of operating within the framework of the strategy previously outlined. Before examining the components of a political strategy toward the region, however, the crucial connection between the Palestinian problem and the Gulf region deserves brief attention.

The Palestinian/Arab-Israeli Problem and the Gulf

For many writers, the Arab-Israeli problem is not the key issue in the Gulf. The problem is so tenuously related that its resolution would neither remove nor affect the main sources of conflict and instability in the region.[47] Others have insisted that, although not the sole issue nor the solution to all American problems in the region, the Palestinian problem is regarded by Arab leaders of the Gulf as the prime political issue. It is a concern which, as long as it exists, will continue to impede American efforts to elicit closer security cooperation from the Gulf states.[48]

Whether or not the Palestinian question is resolved, serious problems will continue to develop in the Gulf; the Iran-Iraq war has made that clear. What seems equally clear, particularly in the aftermath of the Israeli invasion of Lebanon, is that if there were progress toward a resolution of the Palestinian question, Gulf problems might not develop in the context of a situation that threatens so completely to counter U.S. interests in the region. Until there is progress, American efforts at security cooperation with the Gulf states will be at best impeded and at worst fundamentally challenged.[49] As a result, although this is not the place for further elaboration, a determined effort should be made to resuscitate the discussions initiated by President Reagan's statement of September 1, 1982. Once discussions are revived, an equally determined effort should be made to nurture and sustain them.

The Gulf Region

The major question of any political strategy toward the Gulf region is how to think about the Gulf's littoral states. Safeguarding U.S. interests in the Gulf is complicated by three separate sets of problems: the historical animosity between Iran and some of the Arab states (now exacerbated by Sunni-Shi'i differences); the possible disintegration of either Iran or Iraq, which could make the regional role of one or the other particularly significant; and ideological differences exemplified by those between Iraq and Saudi Arabia. These threats to regional stability suggest the practicability of a policy whose essential thrust is to prevent domination of the Gulf by any single power (Iraq or Iran) and to foster a sense of cohesion among Saudi Arabia and the states of the northern Arabian Peninsula littoral.

Iran and Iraq

Formulating a policy toward Iran and Iraq has been difficult since, following the 1967 Arab-Israeli war and the 1979–1981 hostage crisis, the United States did not maintain formal diplomatic relations with either country (the United States and Iraq resumed formal diplomatic relations on November 26, 1984). Long-term U.S. interests also preclude total support of, or opposition to, either country and dictate the desirability of better relations with both.

The war between Iran and Iraq shows no sign of ending. According to Gulf officials, the most probable catalyst for a solution will be the death of Ayatollah Khomeini, the overthrow or death of Saddam Husayn, or some other event that allows a face-saving truce to replace the current stalemate. Face-saving mediation is possible, but first there must be the desire. At present, there is little in Iran.[50] In the meantime, according to knowledgeable observers, the key to Saddam's survival is the strength, discipline, and loyalty of the Baath party workers, the loyalty of the army (whose lower ranks are dominated by Shia), and financial aid from the Gulf.[51]

Future U.S. relations with Iran and Iraq will be determined to a great extent by the interplay between internal and external factors: between Iranian politics and the capacity of the clergy to maintain its revolutionary dynamism in the wake of Khomeini's demise, the ability of the Baath régime in Iraq to survive the war, and traditional geopolitical realities that will continue to operate in the region long after the Iran-Iraq war winds down.

The United States can do relatively little to modify relations with Iran until the Iran-Iraq war ends or the two countries reach a modus vivendi. Should the war end and Iranian animosity toward the United States begin to abate,[52] the United States could seek to establish relations with Iran at a joint commission office established in Europe. The United States has little choice but to maintain a low profile and gradually work to restore Iranian confidence in American intentions. Such confidence will be restored only when Iranian religious leaders who enjoy wide popular support feel sufficiently secure in their leadership and convinced of the economic and geopolitical desirability of better relations with the United States to marshal public opinion along these lines.

In the interim, the United States should encourage European and Japanese economic relations with Iran in order to strengthen those elements and groups wishing to rebuild Iran's relations with the West. On the political level, American leaders could gradually encourage (through Turkey and Pakistan) Iran's informal cooperation with its former CENTO allies. Their aim should be to support independence from Soviet pressure and influence, without suggesting that the Iranians should participate in a defensive military association aimed at Moscow. Recent trends suggest that Iran is receptive to playing the role of not only an anti-American bulwark but an anti-Communist bulwark as well. This dual role explains Iran's attempts to improve ties and trade relations with Pakistan and Turkey, much to Moscow's annoyance.[53] These trends, one should note, are not so much pro-Western as they are traditionally Iranian. Historically the Iranians have rejected the influence of the great powers, using one as a counterweight against the others when necessary and seeking aid from third parties when possible to extricate Iran from its geopolitical predicament. A traditional response to geopolitical pressure is also evident in the slogan, "neither East nor West," which currently governs Iranian policy toward the two superpowers.

Encouraging cooperation between Europe, Japan, and Iran avoids an overactive U.S. posture during a period of political turbulence. This strategy reduces the likelihood that Americans will be made scapegoats for internal Iranian problems and the target of Shi'i rhetoric. At the same time, it encourages pro-Western influence as a counter to Soviet influence in Iran in a manner (e.g., Turkish and Pakistani initiatives) acceptable to the Iranians. It facilitates Iran's gradual cooperation with other regional states in security areas of concern to Iran, and it minimizes conflict as much as can be expected in the short run with other U.S. security interests in the Gulf.

Were the Iran-Iraq war to end, the Iranian government to change, and an opportunity to arise, the United States might be inspired to move quickly to build its relations with the government in power. It might be tempted to reestablish diplomatic relations at the embassy level (although with a small presence), to respond to spare parts and limited arms requests, and to support Iran's economic development requirements, with an eye to reviving the Iranian economy and reconstituting Iran, along with Turkey and Pakistan, as an anti-Soviet buffer between East and West. This course, although it could under certain conditions be a logical extension of the strategy outlined, is unlikely to be viable in the short run. If pursued without inhibition, it could precipitate a destabilizing Soviet response. Since the main interest of the United States is not to acquire influence but to prevent undue Soviet influence in a country commonly recognized as the region's strategic prize, policymakers would be wise to move with caution and to avoid a policy that legitimates precisely what they should be trying to prevent.

Supporting certain groups in Iran that oppose the present government with the objective of creating a government more favorably disposed to

U.S. interests is a course sometimes advocated for the United States.[54] Exile groups that are divided into monarchist and republican leftist movements and that are hopelessly dispersed will prove relatively useless for such purposes. Others in Iran may appear more attractive: factions within the military, *bazaaris*, selected political and religious moderates, and various tribes.

The impracticality of such suggestions should be clear. It was evidenced in November 1986 and more recently in 1987 during the Iran-Contra Congressional hearings by revelations of the fiasco regarding U.S. arms shipments to Iran as part of a deal to improve U.S. relations with Iranian "moderates" and effect the release of American hostages in Lebanon. It is virtually impossible to stay attuned to the shifting attitudes and splits within the government. Rivalry between the technocrats and the free-market advocates or between the ultraconservative fundamentalists and the social reformers is illustrative of the problem and suggests the difficulty of manipulating the amorphous groups that could one day vie for power in Iran. Analysts believe that if Khomeini were to die tomorrow, no group in the army or the Revolutionary Guard would be able to overthrow the régime. No opposition group, moreover, has the necessary popular support. The concept of *velayat-e faqih* (the governance of the jurisprudent), considered by many to be the hallmark of the new order, maintains legitimacy, and until this changes, debate will center around whether Khomeini will be succeeded as supreme jurisprudent by a single individual (such as Ayatollah Montazeri) or a small group of three to five clerics elected by the 83-person Council of Experts.[55] Although a government favorably disposed to the United States would be desirable in the abstract, the process of effecting it would be fraught with difficulties. An activist U.S. policy, meanwhile, could result in undesirable consequences such as the partition of Iran, which would be extensively destabilizing for the region, or Soviet intervention, which would be catastrophic. Although the Iranians themselves have renounced the Soviet-Iranian treaty of 1921, the Soviets have not, and they have declared that any foreign intervention in Iran would be considered a threat to Soviet security (i.e., cause for invoking the treaty).[56]

An activist U.S. policy toward Iran, in addition to working against U.S. interests in the region, would also be contrary to the notions of territorial integrity and sovereignty essential to U.S. policies toward other states in the region. The United States, therefore, should reject an activist posture unless Soviet policies, such as massive support for the Tudeh party in the struggle for power that will follow Khomeini's demise, result in a situation in which the United States has few other options. The Tudeh was the object of three major purges in 1982, and it was again the object of a major purge in 1983,[57] when posters that served as backdrop to the purge trials ranked its members as second in their devilry only to the United States. Since the Iranians have always regarded the Tudeh as a Soviet puppet organization, U.S. policymakers should be cautious lest they exaggerate the Tudeh party's influence and overreact to inflated reports about its activities.[58]

To the extent that the Iraqis are severely threatened by an Iranian offensive and/or the Soviets move closer to Iran, the United States could, and perhaps should, move closer to Iraq. President François Mitterrand of France, asserting that France has friends but no enemies in the Gulf, did precisely that in late 1983 by warning that France would not allow Iraq to collapse because such a development would destabilize the entire region.[59] In conjunction with its NATO allies, the United States could play a more supportive role in helping the Iraqis to resist continued Iranian attacks. It could also play a quiet but important role in protecting maritime commerce and consolidating local resistance to possible Iranian aggression in the Gulf. In the unlikely event of Soviet aggression in Iran, such a role would also allow consideration of U.S. support for anti-Soviet forces in southwest Iran—a Khuzestan option—based on a pre-1957 defense line at the Zagros Mountains that protects the oil fields.

Better U.S. relations with Iraq, if handled with care, are not necessarily harmful to or incompatible with an improvement in U.S.-Iranian relations, particularly if U.S. support for Iraq is solely defensive.[60] If Saddam Husayn survives and can reach a modus vivendi with a post-Khomeini Iran, better relations with both Iran and Iraq would be consistent with American support for nonalignment—a policy position to which both states subscribe. Overzealous pursuit of U.S.-Iraqi relations, of course, would jeopardize American interests in Iran. Support for an Iraqi resistance effort such as both the Soviets and U.S. NATO allies are currently undertaking, however, is less dangerous. The normalization of U.S.-Iraqi relations is helpful to U.S. regional interests and welcomed by the Gulf states, who remain concerned about Saddam's aspirations to play an important regional role but are more concerned at present about his survival.[61]

Developments in progress in Saudi Arabia and the Arab Gulf, meanwhile, should enhance Gulf security and allow those states, with some assistance, to serve as a countervailing force to Iranian and Iraqi desires for hegemony within the region. The most significant of these developments is that Saddam Husayn's difficulties with Iran have encouraged an alliance among Iraq, Jordan, and Saudi Arabia. Formed in response to regional developments such as the Iranian revolution, Soviet activities in the PDRY, Ethiopia, and Afghanistan, and Iraqi difficulties in the Iran-Iraq war, this alliance has fostered a gradual rapprochement between Egypt and Saudi Arabia. The alliance may help bring Egypt back into the Arab system, as suggested by the Islamic Conference organization's decision in early 1984 to invite Egypt to join its ranks. The alliance may even provide a balance to the threat that Iran now poses to the Arab Gulf states.

Saudi Arabia and the Gulf States

An examination of U.S. policy options toward Saudi Arabia and the Arab Gulf states requires not only a keen sense of the Gulf's regional dynamics but careful attention to the priorities that shape the foreign policies of the states themselves. This is particularly true of Saudi Arabia, which has emerged as the cornerstone of U.S. policy in the Gulf.

With the loss of Iran, the demise of America's two pillar policy, and the problems posed by the Iran-Iraq war, a closer relationship with Saudi Arabia and the smaller Gulf states is the only real option left open to the United States. The Carter doctrine, to which President Reagan has added his corollary (the United States will not permit Saudi Arabia "to be an Iran"), provides a general framework for the continuing special relationship between the United States and Saudi Arabia. In spite of longstanding historical quarrels among the Arab Gulf states, a natural alliance among them,[62] which transcends some extremely bitter territorial and boundary disputes, is based on a belief in common ancestry and reinforced by external threats. Events during the last decade have contributed to a common concern that collective security requires some form of political/military integration[63] in addition to economic integration.[64]

Recent events have heightened concern for political and military integration: the Israeli bombing of Iraq's nuclear reactor; Iran's bombing on three different occasions of Kuwaiti oil installations; the tripartite agreement signed in August 1981 by Libya, the PDRY, and Ethiopia that formalized their rivalry with Iraq, Saudi Arabia, and Jordan; Iranian support for the December 1981 coup attempt in Bahrain and a subsequent coup attempt in Qatar; the Iranian counteroffensive against Iraq; the bombing of the U.S. embassy in Kuwait in December 1983; and the "tanker war" since 1984. These events in progression have helped to bridge differences among Gulf states. In May 1981, Saudi Arabia, Kuwait, the United Arab Emirates, Bahrain, Qatar, and Oman were able to form the Gulf Cooperation Council (GCC). Because of the war between them, Iran and Iraq were conveniently excluded from the council. The GCC states were able to agree on basic principles of collective security and to take concrete steps to implement those principles.[65] In October 1983, the GCC conducted its first joint military exercises in the United Arab Emirates' western desert—a development whose importance was underscored by Iranian threats to close the Strait of Hormuz. Although joint military exercises were more symbolic than functional, the United States should encourage this trend and support it in every way possible.[66]

The Saudis, apparently, have also been giving serious attention to an Omani proposal for a united defense strategy in which member states would group their naval vessels under a joint command and integrate, as well as strengthen, their existing defense systems.[67] To the extent that these developments enhance Gulf security and allow the Gulf states, with outside assistance, to serve as a countervailing force within the region, and to the extent that concerns about regional threats and great power intrusion in the Gulf cement the GCC's increased cohesion, the United States can play a less obtrusive role in Gulf security affairs. This would benefit both Saudi and regional security.

The Arab Gulf states are growing more confident of their influence in international fora, at least in economic matters, and are beginning to establish closer economic, political, and military ties with each other. The key for the United States is to ensure Gulf security by maintaining a balance among the region's three centers of power, to restrain Oman's dangerous enthusiasm for American involvement in the region, and to respect the Saudis' survival instinct. To push the Saudis beyond what that instinct tells them is acceptable can only result in damage to the interests shared by the United States and Saudi Arabia.[68] Dramatically increasing the U.S. presence in the region beyond that necessary for the prepositioning of project stocks and development of the Saudi infrastructure, and raising the profile of U.S. forces in the Gulf, would make the Saudis vulnerable to internal criticism and could have serious repercussions once the conflict between Iran and Iraq subsides.

The Northern Tier

The countries along the northern tier of the Middle East and Southwest Asia play an important role in regional and great power politics. Their relationships with the Gulf states consequently represent an important consideration in any U.S. strategy toward the region. Although Turkey, Iran, Afghanistan, and Pakistan may be perceived as a strategic buffer zone that historically has been a bone of contention between East and West, each of these states has a role to play in other regional groupings as well. Iran, which is a Gulf state, has been examined in the context of Gulf politics. But Iran has a religious and geopolitical importance that transcends its position on the Gulf littoral. As a result, one should be wary of the arbitrary geographical categories required for analysis and keep firmly in mind Iran's roles as a fount of revolution within the Islamic community and a buffer between East and West.

This section examines the nature of the relations between two areas that are not normally associated with the Gulf region but that nevertheless are crucial to U.S. policy in the region. First it explores Turkey's emerging economic interests in the Middle East and its increasingly important potential role in the security of the Gulf and Southwest Asia; it also attempts to address questions raised about the priority of its European and Middle Eastern roles. Finally this section examines U.S. policy toward Southwest Asia. Against the background of the relationships between East and West that shape the politics of the subcontinent, discussion of U.S. options will focus on regional imperatives that in turn constrain the influence of the great powers and will suggest how one might think about the interplay between regional and geopolitical forces.

Although Turkey's role in the defense of Europe and Asia Minor continues to be the focal point of its security concerns, its potential role in the security of the Gulf and Southwest Asia has become increasingly significant to the broader security interests of its Western allies. If one were to rank the strategic importance of the Middle East and Southwest Asia's northern tier countries, such factors as geography, political cohesion, military capability, and sheer numbers would give Turkey priority. This was true in the early 1950s when Turkey joined NATO, and it is even more true now that the Iranian revolution has removed Iran from the ranks of U.S. allies and the Soviets have occupied Afghanistan.

Turkey's economic relations with the Middle East, meanwhile, have become increasingly significant. Since 1980 the percentage of Turkish exports to the Middle East has increased from 22.3 per cent to over 40 per cent of total exports. Turkey's construction contracts in the Middle East amount to over $15 billion, including $5.1 billion in Saudi Arabia and $1.15 billion in Iraq. There are also approximately 250,000 Turkish workers in the Middle East, including 54,000 in Saudi Arabia.

Turkey's economic relations with the Gulf states are especially important. In early 1982, Iran and Turkey signed a major barter arrangement in which they exchanged agricultural products and manufactured goods for crude oil. By the end of 1982, Iran was Turkey's major export market. The volume of trade between them was over $2.3 billion in 1983, and in 1984 Turkey may have doubled its exports to Iran. Turkey's relations with Iraq are also significant, particularly for Iraq. The 1,000-kilometer pipeline through Turkey, in operation since 1977, is Iraq's only means of exporting oil while the Shatt al-Arab and the pipeline through Syria are both closed. In October 1983, Iraq and Turkey also agreed to build a pipeline to transport three million tons of liquid petroleum gas annually through Turkish territory to Yamurtalik on the Mediterranean. In addition to oil and gas, trade also plays an important part in Turkey's relations with Iran and Iraq. One analyst estimated that in 1982 approximately six million tons of goods crossed over from Turkey into Iran and Iraq, approximately three million tons to each country. Since 1982 the goods crossing Turkish soil have increased.

The October 1982 U.S.-Turkish co-located operating-base agreement highlighted Turkey's role in deterring Soviet adventurism in Iran and protecting the West's access to Gulf oil.[69] This agreement will result in the modernization of ten Turkish airfields and the building of one or two new ones at Mus and Batman in eastern Turkey. With a length and width sufficient to accommodate long-range bombers and cargo planes, these airfields would enhance Turkey's deterrent role and perhaps dissuade aggressive Soviet intentions in the area. They would put modern NATO fighter bombers within striking distance of the Transcaucasus and the Rapid Deployment Force (RDF) within 700 miles of Abadan. These facilities would be far closer to the head of the Gulf than any of those to which the U.S. Central Command (CENTCOM) now has access. Although these bases are designed primarily for NATO contingencies and their use is subject to Turkish approval, they have potential value in the event of a serious crisis. Whether or not they are actually used, they will serve as an important deterrent both to Soviet adventurism in Iran and to Soviet ambitions in the Gulf.

Speculation about Turkey's role in the defense of the Gulf raises questions about its European and Middle Eastern roles and the implications of these roles for U.S. policies in the Gulf. Presently, the Turks do not view alternatives to their Western alliance and their special relationship with the United States as promising, at least as long as the Soviet Union remains a potential threat. The Nonaligned movement is too fragmented. Because of the Cyprus question, raised once again on November 15, 1983, when the Turkish Cypriots declared their independence, the Nonaligned movement is anti-Turkish. It is also unable to provide Turkey with the security or the technical and military assistance that the Turks require.[70]

Thus, though Turkey has an extremely important strategic as well as economic role to play in the Middle East, it sees the best guarantee of its security not in any unstable coalition of weak Middle Eastern or third world states but in its alliance with the West. Its Middle East role may well become even more important in the next decade, particularly in view of its capacity to deter Soviet adventurism along the northern tier and to help ensure Western access to Gulf oil. But this role is likely to develop only in the context of Turkey's relationship with the West. At present, Turkey's ability to become involved in contingency planning is impeded by NATO's failure to remove the artificial barriers between its borders and the Middle East.

The extent to which U.S.-Turkish interests in the Gulf and Southwest Asia are compatible remains to be seen. Some U.S. officials would like a clearer commitment on the use of bases in eastern Turkey in the event of a contingency in the Gulf. In return, they are interested in, but because of congressional constraints not necessarily capable of, supplying the Turks with extensive military assistance as a quid pro quo. The Turks are extremely eager to obtain such assistance but are understandably reluctant to be more forthcoming on the question of access in non-NATO contingencies. To do so would give the United States, in the event of a contingency involving such adversaries as Iran and Iraq, the capacity to damage Turkey's good diplomatic and economic relations with both. Even worse, it could increase the risk of Soviet intervention in Turkey in a non-NATO crisis that would not automatically trigger NATO obligations to protect Turkey. Turks still remember President Johnson's letter to their Prime Minister Inonu in June 1964, warning him not to use U.S.-supplied military equipment to invade Cyprus and informing Turkey that, if it took a step that resulted in Soviet intervention, its NATO allies might have to reconsider their obligations to Turkey. The arms embargo from 1975 to 1978 reinforced Turkish doubts about the reliability of the United States as an ally, and differences over Cyprus will continue to pose problems.

As a result, Turkey has attempted to respond as cautiously and con-structively as possible to the complex political, economic, and social forces evolving in the region. If the Turks have accommodated themselves to new realities, however, there are limits to this accommodation. Just as the Turks are reluctant to do the bidding of the West when it involves a non-NATO contingency, so they are determined not to be intimidated by the threat of greatly increased Soviet capabilities in the region.

Turkey's distrust of the Soviet Union and, consequently, its commitment to an alliance with the West are influenced by history. Russia, whether Christian or Communist, has consistently followed a policy toward Turkey that is grounded in self-interest and geopolitics. As 12 wars between the two countries would indicate, Russian policies have rarely been in Turkey's best interests. Western nations have based their policies on the same self-serving considerations as the Russians, but with less damage to Turkey's interests. Since the 1960s, Turkey's alliance with the West has been troubled, but it has also ensured the country's survival. Given the predispositions of the states that play a dominant role in the international balance of power and Turkey's historical vulnerability to both East and West, the Turks have tried to walk a delicate line between the competing power blocs.

Were a Soviet threat to diminish markedly, the notion of a neutral nonaligned buffer zone across the northern tier states of the Middle East and southwest Asia would be increasingly attractive for the Turks. This was true, to some extent, during the period of détente; it could be true again if U.S.-Soviet relations took a turn for the better and U.S.-Turkish relations a turn for the worse. Such a development, though unlikely, is nevertheless possible. It would require a continuation of Soviet leader Mikhail Gorbachev's strategy of modernization through democratization and glasnost, a far more neighborly Soviet policy toward the states on its southern flank, and a decision to withdraw Soviet troops from Afghanistan. Serious Turkish-NATO differences over both Cyprus and human rights, meanwhile, could encourage the process. Until such changes occur, however, the threat posed by the Soviet Union means that the NATO countries need Turkey and Turkey needs them. As a result, though the Turks may never formally commit themselves to assist the United States in a contingency in the Gulf region, their assistance can never be ruled out.

This state of affairs may well be in the interests of both parties. To pursue a greater commitment could be extremely costly for the United States and extremely risky for Turkey because it would make Turkey a prime target in any contingency; nor would such a course, given the caution that the Turks would inevitably exercise, provide much greater deterrence. To discount Turkey's deterrent role, on the other hand, would be to ignore the geopolitical realities of the region and forsake an important component of U.S. and Turkish security interests. As a result, the United States should support Turkey's helpful but ambiguous role in the Gulf region while attempting to improve good relations in the context of NATO.

Southwest Asia

Any political strategy toward the Gulf region is intricately tied to the question of U.S. policies toward Southwest Asia, where intractable regional conflicts are shaped and influenced by the broader U.S.-Soviet and Sino-Soviet conflicts. Before addressing that connection, however, it is necessary to take a look at the region as a whole, keeping in mind that the interaction in Southwest Asia between regional and geopolitical forces—which India and Pakistan sometimes invite and the great powers sometimes impose—invariably has disappointed all parties. The result has been a web of relationships that, far more than those between the United States and Turkey, are riddled with ambivalence, ambiguities, and apprehensions. These developments have led one analyst to conclude that however necessary it may be for the United States to involve itself in the subcontinent's political disagreements and security concerns, "the most promising way to attempt to deal with the subcontinent in the long-run is indirectly—by helping to build better societies. This is emotionally less satisfying than taking a 'tough' line—particularly when other countries irritate us at times—but it is more likely to achieve long-term success."[71]

A Regional Policy

The notion of building a better society suggests that, instead of emphasizing security relationships with either India or Pakistan, U.S. policy should attempt where possible to separate cold war issues from regional tensions and encourage local initiatives that promote regionalism in the context of nonalignment. Regional receptivity to such ideas, of course, is crucial. According to Jagat Mehta, former foreign secretary of India, lessons of the last decade are beginning to register: "The leadership of the erstwhile Hindu Party (Jan Sangh), which for three decades has remained unreconciled to partition, now urges good relations with Pakistan. A growing body of non-official opinion in Pakistan feels that, ultimately, national security and progress for Pakistan hinges more on good relations with India than on American arms or exclusively Islamic connections."[72]

Under a regionally based policy, the United States would avoid pressing any of the countries in the area for special security access rights. The United States would use its own resources whenever possible to promote programs that could have regional impact and enhance regional cooperation and would urge the World Bank and other donors to follow a similar course. It would also try to maintain current projected levels of assistance for India, Bangladesh, Nepal, and Sri Lanka and continue to expand the economic, as opposed to the military, aspects of the new assistance program for Pakistan. Though 40 F-16s from the United States will greatly improve Pakistan's ability to reach and attack Indian oil facilities and nuclear power plants, they will not significantly alter India's marked advantage (at least three to one and probably greater) in advanced aircraft. MIG-25s, 27s, and 31s from the Soviet Union, Jaguars from Britain, and Mirage 2000s from France, moreover, eventually will increase India's advantage in a competition the Pakistanis cannot hope to win.[73]

The five-year $3.2 billion U.S. assistance program for FY 1983-1987 to Pakistan, on the other hand, because it was evenly divided between economic assistance and foreign military sales credit guarantees and because it began to balance India's large-scale arms purchases from the Soviet Union over the last four years, helped delay Pakistan's desire to acquire a nuclear weapons capability. Now that such a capability has been acquired, at the very least, the threat of the next assistance program's cancellation will impede a decision to conduct a so-called peaceful nuclear explosion.

Meanwhile, taking advantage of India's interest in mutual understanding, evidenced by the late Prime Minister Indira Gandhi's visit to the United States in July 1982 and that of her son Rajiv Gandhi in June 1985, American officials have been responsive to some of India's concerns. The Reagan administration in 1982 agreed to France's providing nuclear fuel for the American-built Tarapur nuclear reactor near Bombay and in 1983 guaranteed that the reactor would be supplied spare parts by U.S. companies in third countries. In 1985, the Reagan administration decided, conditional on Indian acceptance of strict safeguards, to provide India with advanced military technology and weaponry.[74] One policy option suggested by these developments is for the United States to work even more closely with India to encourage India's cooperation as the keystone to subcontinental regionalism. Such a role is dictated by India's predominate position in South Asia and was given concrete recognition in March 1983 by India's leadership of the Nonaligned movement. Economic and security factors will continue to give India's relationship with the Soviet Union a higher priority than that with the United States, as was evidenced in summer 1983 by an apparent $5 billion Indo-Soviet arms deal.[75] Nevertheless, the United States could build on the gradual but steady improvement in its relations with India by encouraging India's desires not only to expand relations with China and the West but also to reduce its dependence on Moscow and to establish greater balance in its relations between the United States and the USSR.[76]

To encourage India in this direction, the United States could support a cooperative grouping of South Asian states which, while working more actively together in the interest of their own security, would be resistant to outside pressures and willing to work with the United States on broad foreign policy issues. This probably would not include any agreement on issues of military access, however, with the possible and limited exception of Pakistan. This approach would build on the concerns of each state in the area that international tensions and military competition in the region will lead to great power confrontation. It would also dictate an even-handed role in restraining nuclear competition between India and Pakistan.

Pakistan's acquisition of American F-16s, meanwhile, though fostering a sense of mutual vulnerability, could also encourage a sense of mutual restraint between India and Pakistan. Under the right circumstances, this development could further political rapprochement between India, China, and Pakistan.[77] It could also promote optimal long-term use of resources on the subcontinent through coordinated and cooperative development efforts by aid consortia and the World Bank, and it would be consistent with support for the more general strategy of a nonaligned buffer zone across the Middle East and Southwest Asia's northern tier of states.[78]

This approach is constrained by a number of factors: the present impasse in U.S.-Soviet relations; persistent and deeply held antagonisms between the states of the area; Indian and Pakistani nuclear policies, which may seriously compromise American relations with both countries;[79] the risk of Indian resentment at outside efforts to equate India with its smaller neighbors; Indian suspicions of China and of Chinese relations with the United States, Pakistan, and Nepal; and Pakistani fears (reinforced by the Soviet occupation of Afghanistan) of an Indo-Soviet pincer.[80] Such a policy may overestimate India's capacity and will to play a key role in deterring Soviet hegemony in Afghanistan and could, if poorly managed, lead Pakistan to accelerate rather than delay its acquisition of nuclear weapons. A conjunction of adverse events involving these constraints could undermine the ability of the United States to influence either Pakistan or India and chill American relations with the smaller states of the region to the detriment of U.S. security interests. As a result, implementation of the described approach would depend on an improved dialogue with India and Pakistan and on a willingness by all parties to take the initiatives necessary for their long-term interests.[81]

The Pakistan Option

In the interim, recognizing that the Soviet-Indian relationship is a long-term proposition that will be difficult to alter to any significant degree,[82] the United States could continue its current policy of placing more emphasis on Pakistan. The Pakistan option makes a certain amount of sense within the context of America's Islamic-oriented Gulf interests. Pakistan, like Turkey, has reasonably cordial relations with Iran. Together with Pakistan's willingness to send troops to Saudi Arabia and the Saudis' largess toward Pakistan (approximately $1 billion a year), these relationships lend credence to the notion that U.S. support for Pakistan helps to protect common interests in the Gulf. According to one reliable report there were at least 20,000 Pakistani military personnel in Saudi Arabia in October 1983, including pilots, advisers, instructors, antiterrorist squads, and intelligence experts. Another contingent of 7,000 reportedly was on its way. Proposals still being examined in Washington and Islamabad include the upgrading of port facilities at Karachi and the development of a new naval facility at Gwadar on the coast of Baluchistan, less than 50 miles from Pakistan's border with Iran and only 300 miles across the Gulf of Oman from Muscat.[83]

Emphasis on Pakistan, which at a minimum requires a credible economic and military commitment such as the recent $3.2 billion commitment, or the $4 billion commitment programmed for FY 1988-1993, responds to Pakistani as well as regional fears of steadily increasing Indian military power and Indian domination of the subcontinent. Such assistance provides the foundation for a more balanced relationship between India and Pakistan. It also complements the U.S. relationship with Turkey and, because Turkey and Pakistan both have reasonably good relations with Iran, makes it more likely that Iran will be encouraged by its neighbors to remain outside the Soviet orbit. Because of its military orientation, however, an increasingly strong U.S. commitment to Pakistan has a number of liabilities.

To the extent that General Zia ul-Haq postpones a return to democratic rule, excessive U.S. support for Pakistan risks identifying the United States with his policies, alienating those who oppose his military régime, and jeopardizing good relations with future Pakistani governments. Excessive support for Pakistan also risks undermining long-term U.S. interests by antagonizing India, whose government continues to be concerned by the fact that over 80 per cent of Pakistan's troops are deployed on the Indian border.[84] Insofar as U.S. support for Pakistan is accompanied by significant aid to Afghanistan, it will also antagonize the Soviet Union. India could compensate by moving closer to the Soviet Union, calling a halt to its gradual rapprochement with China, and beefing up its forces along Pakistan's border. Depending upon the threats that India perceives, a number of worrisome scenarios are imaginable: a preemptive strike against Pakistan's nuclear facilities, a military move against the territories of Azad Kashmir, or, in conjunction with the Soviet Union and in support of Pushtun, Baluch, and Sindi separatist movements, an attempt to dismember Pakistan. As a result, a strong American commitment to Pakistan should be pursued with caution.

The Afghan Connection

If a strong U.S. commitment to Pakistan poses problems, however, so does a weak one. The dilemma for the United States in dealing with Pakistan is that without a significant American commitment, Zia, who rejected President Carter's 1980 offer of $400 million as "peanuts," would be unwilling to jeopardize his relations with the Soviet Union. This he now does by allowing his country to serve as a supply line to Afghanistan—a prerequisite for any meaningful assistance to the resistance in Afghanistan.[85] If the United States cuts back on its assistance to Pakistan, the opportunity to aid Afghanistan is not the only policy option that would be foreclosed. Responding to a combination of Soviet influence and intimidation, Zia might well be tempted to accommodate Soviet desires that Pakistan assume a neutral, nonaligned status, without a Soviet withdrawal from Afghanistan, leaving the Soviet Union as the dominant force in regional politics.[86] Although American and Western intelligence sources agree that Moscow has not improved its logistical capabilities in Afghanistan for offensive action in the Gulf region, the potential for such improvement is ever present. The all-weather airbase at Shindand, for example, is only 600 miles from the Strait of Hormuz, and Soviet reconnaissance planes flying from Shindand currently monitor U.S. naval ships in the Indian Ocean.[87] Over time, the implications for a continued Soviet occupation of Afganistan could be serious, not only for Afghanistan but for Pakistan, the Gulf states, and the United States as well.

The Interplay Between Problems and Options

Although the solution to the Afghan problem ultimately rests in Moscow, the context within which such a solution might take place can be affected by the regional orientation of U.S. policies. Nancy and Richard Newell have suggested, for example that "[by] offering to supply military and medical equipment at the *request* of the Islamic Conference or some other agency that might be established to conduct collective regional defense, the United States could act as a counterforce against Soviet encroachment without directly deploying its own military forces in the region."[88] Such a policy would be compatible with U.S. support for the Islamic Conference. For this particular policy to be truly effective, the United States would have to establish a credible deterrent to Soviet intimidation of Pakistan and make a real effort to remove Islamic concerns by addressing the Palestinian problem.

In the final analysis, a Soviet departure from Afghanistan will require more than U.S. support of the resistance, which the United States can express in conjunction with its commitment to Pakistan. Political pressure on the Soviet Union from India will also be necessary and can occur only in a regional context in which India feels secure. For this reason, it is important that the relationship between the two primary policy options in the region—the first an attempt to foster regional cooperation, the second a commitment to bolster Pakistan's standing in the region—be constantly kept in mind. Neither option by itself can address all U.S. concerns in the region. Flexible application of both options, on the other hand, may create an environment conducive to safeguarding many of the interests that the U.S. shares with the states of the region.

Conclusion

The political and military strategies outlined herein, though only suggestive and requiring both greater precision and further elaboration, nevertheless provide a framework within which to view American security policy in the Gulf region. In the absence of such a framework, which officials in the White House have conceded the administration lacks,[89] and without agreement within the government about what the framework ought to be, the United States will continue to risk operating on the basis of inadequate assumptions and will engage in short-term tactical maneuvers to extricate itself from situations that have not been foreseen in the development of current policies. Without a framework that bounds U.S. options, events themselves will determine administrative actions, and policy initiatives will be left to others.

Development of a political-military strategy for the Gulf and Southwest Asia is among the Reagan administration's more pressing tasks. Once developed, such a strategy in conjunction with similar strategies for other regions would form the global framework needed by the government to plan and coordinate policy initiatives. Outside the government, critics of particular decisions would be forced to address the limitations and inconsistencies inherent in their own perspectives and to consider the broader contexts within which difficult choices are made. Public articulation of a comprehensive framework, at once both flexible enough to accommodate change but rigorous enough to ensure that the relationship among various interests has been carefully considered, would set the terms of a public debate. Such a debate, in turn, would generate a more responsible discussion of how to balance conflicting interests in the face of the various threats to which they are vulnerable; it would establish a clearer sense of priorities; and it would allow for a more informed analysis of proposed increases in the defense budget.[90] Finally, because discussion would underscore the West's long-term dependence on vulnerable supplies of Gulf oil (the current oil glut notwithstanding) it could help to marshall broader support for a meaningful domestic energy program.[91]

Notes

1. *Western Vulnerability to a Disruption of Persian Gulf Oil Supplies: U.S. Interests and Options: An Analysis of the Economic Impact of an Hypothetical Disruption of Persian Gulf Oil Supplies and Policy Implications for the Future*, Congressional Research Service, Report 83-24F (Washington, D.C.: Library of Congress, March 24, 1983).

2. *Washington Post*, May 19 and 20, June 15 and 20, 1981; *New York Times*, May 19 and September 3, 1981; *International Herald Tribune*, June 22, 1983.

3. "Soviet Foreign Trade and Payments in 1985," *Wharton Centrally Planned Economies Service, Analysis of Current Issues* 6, no. 16 (April 24, 1986), p. 6.

4. Jeanne Robertson, *Christian Science Monitor*, November 1, 1983; David Willis, *Christian Science Monitor*, July 18, 1983. A quantity of 1.1 trillion cubic feet of natural gas translates into approximately 3 billion cubic feet per day, or the equivalent in energy terms of about 500,000 barrels of oil per day.

5. See Harold Saunders, *The Middle East Problem in the 1980s* (Washington, D.C.: American Enterprise Institute for Public Policy Research, 1981), pp. 12–73.

6. *Challenges for U.S. National Security. Assessing the Balance: Defense Spending and Conventional Forces. A Preliminary Report, Part II* (Washington, D.C.: Carnegie Endowment for International Peace, 1981), pp. 172–181.

7. *Ibid*, and Thomas McNaugher, "Balancing Soviet Power in the Persian Gulf," *Brookings Review* 1, no. 4 (1983), pp. 20–24.

8. See Joshua Epstein, "Soviet Vulnerabilities in Iran and the RDF Deterrent," *International Security* 6, no. 2 (1981), pp. 126–158.

9. See also Dennis Ross, "Considering Soviet Threats to the Persian Gulf," *International Security* 6, no. 2 (1981), pp. 159–180.

10. *Challenges for U.S. National Security*, p. 175.

11. See *Oil Fields as Military Objectives: A Feasibility Study*, prepared for the Special Subcommittee on Investigations of the Committee on International Relations, House of Representatives, U.S. Congress, by the Congressional Research Service, Library of Congress (Washington, D.C.: Government Printing Office (GPO), 1975).

12. *Challenges for U.S. National Security*, pp. 172–181. See also Keith Dunn, "Constraints on the USSR in Southwest Asia: A Military Analysis," *Orbis* 25, no. 3 (1981), pp. 607–629.

13. *Ibid*. The Carnegie Study concluded that, in a U.S.-Soviet conflict, Soviet land and air forces would dominate near the country's border with Iran, U.S. air power would prevail in the southern part of the Gulf area, and there would be a

stand-off at the head of the Gulf, with the immediate outcome uncertain, although the Soviets would probably prevail (p. 191).

14. See Robert Tucker, "Oil: The Issue of American Intervention," *Commentary* 59, no. 1 (1975), pp. 21–31; Miles Ignotus (Edward Luttwak), "Seizing Arab Oil," *Harper's* 250 (March 1975), pp. 45–62; subsequent articles by Tucker, "Further Reflections on Oil & Force," *Commentary* 59, no. 3 (1975), pp. 45–56; "Oil and American Power—Three Years Later," *Commentary* 63, no. 1 (1977), pp. 29–36; and "Oil and American Power—Six Years Later," *Commentary* 68, no. 3 (1979), pp. 35–42; and J. B. Kelly's discussion of the issue in *Arabia, The Gulf and the West: A Critical View of the Arabs and their Oil Policy* (New York: Basic Books, 1980), pp. 494–504. Aside from failing to acknowledge (other than rhetorically) the magnitude of the difficulties that would attend an opposed intervention, these critics dismiss too easily problems associated with Russian involvement.

15. See, for example, Abdul Kasim Mansur (Anthony Cordesman), "The American Threat to Saudi Arabia," *Armed Forces Journal International* 118, no. 1 (1980), pp. 47–60; and "The Military Balance in the Persian Gulf: Who Will Guard the Gulf States from the Guardians?" *Armed Forces Journal International* 118, no. 3 (1980), pp. 44–86.

16. John M. Collins, *U.S.-Soviet Military Balance: Concepts and Capabilities, 1960–1980* (New York: McGraw-Hill, 1980), pp. 391–392.

17. Jeffrey Record, *The Rapid Deployment Force and U.S. Military Intervention in the Persian Gulf* (Cambridge, Mass.: Institute for Foreign Policy Analysis, 1980), p. 17.

18. For elaboration of the role and function of these facilities, see James Wooten, *Regional Support Facilities for the Rapid Deployment Force*, Report No. 82-53F, Congressional Research Service, Library of Congress Service, Washington, D.C., March 25, 1982.

19. For the role and function of the AWACS, see U.S. Congress, Senate, *Arms Sales Package to Saudi Arabia*, Parts 1 and 2, Hearings before the Committee on Foreign Relations (Washington, D.C.: GPO, October 1981); *Military and Technical Implications of the Proposed Sale of Air Defense Enhancements to Saudi Arabia*, Report of the Hearings before the Committee on Armed Services (Washington, D.C.: GPO, 1981).

20. CENTCOM generally refers to the planning headquarters, the RDF to the forces that are available to CENTCOM. For discussion and elaboration of the mission, organization, training, logistical support facilities, and tactical doctrine of the RDF, see Maxwell Johnson, *The Military as an Instrument of U.S. Policy in Southwest Asia: The Rapid Deployment Joint Task Force, 1979–1982* (Boulder, Colo.: Westview Press, 1982). For further details, the policy implications of alternative RDF levels, and the budgetary implications of such levels, see *Rapid Deployment Forces: Policy and Budgetary Implications* (Washington, D.C.: Congressional Budget Office, February 1983).

21. The Reagan administration intends to double the size of the 220,000-person RDF to 440,000 by the end of the decade (*Rapid Deployment Forces*, pp. 11–15).

22. Interviews with officials in the Department of Defense.

23. Christopher Van Hollen, "Don't Engulf the Gulf," *Foreign Affairs* 59, no. 5 (1981), pp. 1064–1078; Stanley Hoffman, "Security in an Age of Turbulence: Means of Response," *Third-World Conflict and International Security (Part II)*, Adelphi Paper 167, September 1980.

24. F. J. West, "NATO II: Common Boundaries for Common Interests," *Naval War College Review* 34, no. 1 (1981), pp. 59–67.

25. Interviews with officials in the Department of Defense; see also John Hackett, "Protecting Oil Supplies: The Military Requirements," in *Third-World Conflict and International Security (Part I), Adelphi Paper 166,* September 1980, pp. 41–51; Albert Wohlstetter, "Meeting the Threat in the Persian Gulf," *Survey* 24, no. 2 (1980), pp. 128–188; W. Scott Thompson, "The Persian Gulf and the Correlation of Forces," *International Security* 7, no. 1 (1982), pp. 157–180.

26. F. J. West, "NATO II: Common Boundaries for Common Interests," pp. 59–67. See also Secretary of the Navy John Lehman's letter to the editor, *Foreign Affairs* 61, no. 2 (1982-1983), pp. 455–456.

27. Robert Komer, "Maritime Strategy vs. Coalition Defense," *Foreign Affairs* 60, no. 5 (1982), pp. 1124–1144; and "Security Challenges of the 80's," *Armed Forces Journal International* 119, no. 3 (1981), pp. 64–77. See also Komer's letters to the editor, *Foreign Affairs* 61, no. 2 (1982-1983), pp. 453–454 and 456.

28. Stansfield Turner and George Thibault, "Preparing for the Unexpected: The Need for a New Military Strategy," *Foreign Affairs* 61, no. 1 (1982), pp. 122–135. See also Turner's letters to the editor, *Foreign Affairs* 61, no. 2 (1982-1983), pp. 454–457.

29. Keith Dunn and William O. Staudenmaier, "Strategy for Survival," *Foreign Policy* 52 (fall 1983), pp. 22–41; see also the exchange of letters between the authors and Robert Komer, *Foreign Policy* 53 (winter 1983-1984), pp. 176–178.

30. Kenneth Waltz, "A Strategy for the Rapid Deployment Force," *International Security* 5, no. 4 (1981), pp. 49–73. The emphasis on rapid is crucial because rapid deployment of even a small force makes counterintervention by the Soviet Union extremely risky. Given the difficulties discussed earlier of seizing oil fields under hostile conditions, a reasonable interpretation of what should constitute "an asset-seizing, deterrent force" is that which would allow the United States to respond rapidly and effectively to a régime's invitation to protect its oil fields. To move without an invitation or to conduct a preemptive operation without regional support would probably not work and would be extremely risky.

31. For discussion of this issue, see "A Conversation with Zbigniew Brzezinski," *Bill Moyer's Journal,* PBS no. 702, November 14, 1980, p. 9.

32. Record, *The Rapid Deployment Force,* p. 69. See Robert Hanks, "Rapid Deployment in Perspective," *Strategic Review* 9, no. 2 (1981), pp. 17–23, and Albert Wohlstetter, "Meeting the Threat in the Persian Gulf," pp. 128–188. Providing that the U.S. force is sea based, its capacity to meet a threat at its own level makes the threat of escalation more credible and remains politically tolerable to the regional states.

33. Rouhollah Ramazani, "Weapons Can't Replace Words," *Newsweek* (International) (September 1980), p. 23.

34. For discussion of this issue, see Bruce Kuniholm, *The Origins of the Cold War in the Near East: Great Power Conflict and Diplomacy in Iran, Turkey, and Greece* (Princeton, N.J.: Princeton University Press, 1980).

35. For tradititional Iranian policies see Rouhollah Ramazani, *The Foreign Policy of Iran: A Developing Nation in World Affairs* (Charlottesville: University of Virginia Press, 1966), pp. 53, 68, 70–71, 91.

36. Alvin Rubinstein, *Soviet Policy Toward Turkey, Iran, and Afghanistan: The Dynamics of Influence* (New York: Praeger, 1982), pp. 131, 141, 147.

37. Greece and Turkey also recognize the limitations of U.S. commitments and, because of internal pressures, have periodically gravitated at least partially back to a traditional posture in which they carefully balance their relations with the great powers.

38. Foreign Minister Jean-Francois Poncet, in a press conference in the UAE in December 1978, referred to France as the "third alternative."

39. The Balkan problem, the Eastern Question, the Persian Problem, and the Great Game all refer to different geographical foci of the rivalry between East and West (initially between Russia and Great Britain and later between the Soviet Union and the United States) that began in the area stretching from the Balkans to India as long ago as the eighteenth century. The term "Great Game" was used by Rudyard Kipling to describe what he saw as Britain's attempts to contain Russia's expansion southwards into Southwest Asia. J. B. Kelly, "Great Game or Grand Illusion," *Survey* 24, no. 2 (1980), p. 118, argued that "over the past decade, through inattention rather than design, the West has failed to abide by the rules of the Great Game as it is played in Persia, thereby inadvertently paving the way for the Soviet Union, in their turn, to break them in Afghanistan."

40. An essential component of this strategy, which should be underscored, is a comprehensive energy program. Such a program is necessary if the United States is to reduce its vulnerability to OPEC and convince the countries of the Middle East that the strategy is more than a ruse to trick them out of their oil. For the desirability of such a program, see the conclusion of the CRS study, *Western Vulnerabilities to a Disruption of Persian Gulf Oil Supplies*, cited in note 1.

41. Hermann Eilts, "Security in the Persian Gulf," *International Security* 5, no. 2 (1980), p. 112, has urged that the United States avoid misguided efforts to harness the Islamic world, as represented by the Islamic Conference, to the American policy bandwagon. He has underscored the United States' poor understanding of it and emphasized that tying it to superpower policies taints the limited, moral effectiveness it may have. The argument here is not to tie the IC to U.S. policies but to make it possible for the IC to support them.

42. For a report of 12,000 Egyptian volunteers already serving with Iraqi troops, see *Christian Science Monitor*, July 5, 1983. In October 1983, President Mubarak warned that if Iran blocked oil shipments through the Gulf, Egypt would take military action against Iran: "Egypt's army is Arab and will intervene to help its brothers" (*International Herald Tribune*, October 20, 1983).

43. For discussion of U.S. involvement in the training of a two-brigade, 8,000-person Jordan strike force (conceived after the takeover of the Great Mosque in Mecca in 1979) for use in military emergencies in the Gulf, see the *Washington Post*, October 22; and the *New York Times*, October 24, 1983.

44. For discussion of the Pakistani connection with the Gulf states (President Zia ul-Haq also took part in the Jordanian civil war in 1970-1971), see Claudia Wright, "India and Pakistan Join in the Gulf Game," *Middle East*, June 1981, pp. 31–34; Shirin Tahir-Kheli and William O. Staudenmaier, "The Saudi-Pakistani Military Relationship: Implications for U.S. Policy," *Orbis* 26, no. 1 (1982), pp. 155–171; David O. Smith, "Pakistan and the Middle East Connection," *Military Review* 62, no. 10 (1982), pp. 42–49; and Mary Anne Weaver, *Christian Science Monitor*, October 3, 1983. Reports of Pakistani air and army units in Saudi Arabia have estimated their number to be over 20,000. (President Zia ul-Haq has acknowledged 1,500–2,000.)

45. Although more problematic than relations with other countries, the rapprochement between Turkey and the Gulf states nevertheless makes an arrangement between them a possibility. The Turks, for example, have recently intervened in northern Iraq to deal with a common Kurdish problem. See the *International Herald Tribune*, May 28–29, 1983.

46. This is what economists call the displacement effect. Examples of past shocks are the fall of the shah and the Soviet invasion of Afghanistan. Future shock would

be an Iranian victory over Iraq, or an Iranian decision to mine the Strait of Hormuz, or, less likely, a Soviet decision to send troops (invited or otherwise) into northwest Iran. The latter decision clearly would affect the magnitude of the U.S. relationship with Turkey as well as Gulf state attitudes toward U.S. bases in the Gulf and would open up an entirely different set of options for the United States in the region.

47. See Robert Tucker, "American Power and the Persian Gulf," *Commentary* 70, no. 5 (1980), pp. 25–41; "The Middle East: Carterism Without Carter?" *Commentary* 70, no. 3 (1981), pp. 27–36; and J. B. Kelly, "A Response to Hermann Eilts' 'Security Considerations in the Persian Gulf,'" *International Security* 5, no. 4 (1981), pp. 186–195.

48. See Hermann Eilts, "Security Considerations in the Persian Gulf," *International Security* 5, no. 2 (1980), pp. 79–113; "A Rejoinder to J. B. Kelly," *International Security* 5, no. 4 (1981), pp. 195–203; David Newsom, "Miracle or Mirage: Reflections on U.S. Diplomacy and the Arabs," *Middle East Journal* 35, no. 3 (1981), pp. 299–313.

49. If, for example, the United States fails to address the Palestinian question, Israel continues its annexation of the West Bank and symbolic incidents (the April 1982 slaying of Arabs in Al Aqsa mosque by an American-born Israeli, the so-called strategic cooperation agreement between Israel and the United States in 1983, the movement in the U.S. Congress in 1984 to move the U.S. embassy in Israel from Tel-Aviv to Jerusalem) continue to inflame the Arab world, it becomes much more difficult for the Saudis to cooperate with the United States. Criticism of the House of Saud's irresponsible use of the national patrimony (oil) to subsidize indirectly (through the United States) Zionist aspirations in the West Bank and Jerusalem is likely to challenge the royal family's Islamic and Arab credentials and directly affect its legitimacy. Recognizing these threats to its legitimacy, the House of Saud might well consider reducing its ties with the United States.

Constructive mediation that addresses the Israeli search for security and the Palestinian quest for self-determination, on the other hand, could allow for a modus vivendi that satisfies the aspirations of both Palestinians and Israelis and is compatible, both politically and militarily, with the policies advocated in this chapter. (For elaboration of this issue, see Chapter 10.)

50. A story making the rounds of the Arab Gulf states in early 1983 was that one of Khomeini's siblings had recently died, and his parents were very upset. The point of course is that if one is waiting for Khomeini's death to resolve the Iran-Iraq war, one may have to wait a long time. (Khomeini apparently does have a brother 15 years older than he.)

51. Phebe Mar, *New York Times*, July 27, 1982; Stephen Grummon, *The Iran-Iraq War: Islam Embattled* (Washington, D.C.: Praeger, 1982), p. 38.

52. The United States should not underestimate Iranian hostility toward the United States.

53. For the Soviet attitude toward Turkish and Pakistani relations with Iran, see Muriel Atkin, "The Islamic Republic and the Soviet Union," Nikki Keddi and Eric Hooglund, eds., in *The Iranian Revolution and the Islamic Republic* (Washington, D.C.: Middle East Institute and the Woodrow Wilson International Center for Scholars, 1982), pp. 143 and 149, no. 15.

54. For rumors of a strategy along these lines, see Leslie Gelb, *New York Times*, March 7, 1982, whose report was subsequently discounted by Marvine Howe, *New York Times*, April 5, 1982. For the Reagan administration's secret overtures to Iran, see numerous articles in the *Washington Post*, November 1986.

55. See "Khomeini & the Opposition," *MERIP Reports* 104 (1982), entire issue; and "Iran Since the Revolution," *MERIP Reports* 13, no. 3 (1983); Amir Taheri,

International Herald Tribune, May 12, 1982; Elaine Sciolino, "Iran's Durable Revolution," *Foreign Affairs* 61, no. 4 (1983), pp. 913–915; Shahram Chubin, "The Soviet Union and Iran," *Foreign Affairs* 61, no. 4 (1982), pp. 942–943; Shahrough Akhavi, "Clerical Politics in Iran Since 1979," and W. G. Millward, "The Principles of Foreign Policy and the Vision of the World Expounded by Imam Khomeini and the Islamic Republic of Iran," *The Iranian Revolution and the Islamic Republic,* pp. 17–28, and 189–204 (see also the remarks by Ervand Abrahamian, p. 210); Liz Thurgood, *Washington Post,* August 6, 1983; and Claude Van England, *International Herald Tribune,* August 16, 1983.

56. Article VI of the treaty states in part: "If a third party should attempt to carry out a policy of usurpation by means of armed intervention in Persia, or if such power should desire to use Persian territory as a base of operations against Russia, or if a foreign power should threaten the frontiers of federal Russia or those of its allies, and if the Persian Government should not be able to put a stop to such a menace after having once been called upon to do so by Russia, Russia shall have the right to advance her troops into the Persian interior for the purpose of carrying out the military operations necessary for its defense."

Premier Brezhnev's implicit reference to the treaty on November 19, 1979, when he declared that any foreign intervention in Iran would be considered a threat to Soviet security was underscored by Soviet use of its 1978 treaty with Afghanistan as a source of legitimacy for intervention in Afghanistan later in December 1979.

57. See Claude Van England, *Christian Science Monitor,* July 22, 1983.

58. The issue of Tudeh strength is constantly debated in the government and among academics. See, for example, the discussion in Keddi et al., *The Iranian Revolution and the Islamic Republic,* pp. 157–158; Shahram Chubin, "The Soviet Union and Iran," pp. 930–931, 943.

59. *International Herald Tribune,* October 29–30, 1983. For indications that the United States has made moves to prevent an Iraqi loss, see the *Washington Post,* January 1, 1984.

60. Nameer Ali Jawdat observed that "it is an article of faith in Teheran that Saddam Husayn would never have dared attack without specific instructions from America." He implied that, since the United States is already credited with the worst motives, it would not have much to lose by tilting a little bit toward Iraq (Nameer Ali Jawdat, "Reflections on the Gulf War," *American Arab Affairs,* no. 5 [1983], p. 97).

61. Eilts, "Security Considerations in the Persian Gulf," p. 105, correctly observed that any U.S.-Iraqi axis aimed at Iran would only miscarry.

62. For elaboration of this issue, see Bruce R. Kuniholm, *The Persian Gulf and U.S. Policy* (Claremont, Calif.: Regina Press, 1984).

63. See "Gulf Security Document," *The Middle East,* January 1981, pp. 16–17; and John Duke Anthony, "The Gulf Cooperation Council," a paper presented to the Annual Convention of the Middle East Studies Association of North America, Seattle, Washington, November 5, 1981.

64. See Roger Nye, "Political and Economic Integration in the Arab States of the Gulf," *Journal of South Asian and Middle Eastern Studies* 2, no. 1 (1978), pp. 3–21.

65. The failure to form a formal defense alliance has been due in part to resistance from Kuwait, which for obvious reasons wants to retain its nonaligned position.

66. *International Herald Tribune,* September 24–25 and November 7, 1983. Although the symbolic role should not be discounted, the functional role cannot

be totally ignored either. As one American official in the Gulf put it, "until recently, the GCC RDF consisted of 27 Rolls Royces filled with bedu."

67. John Yemma, *Christian Science Monitor*, October 26, 1982.

68. As several ambassadors in the Gulf states indicated to me in spring 1983, the United States must be careful not to push the Gulf states too far, too fast. Although the forces for stability appear to be able to cope with the centrifugal forces of instability, a coalescence of external forces, and particularly U.S.-Saudi relations, could shake the foundations of the House of Saud. See John Shaw and David Long, *Saudi Arabian Modernization: The Impact of Change on Stability* (Washington, D.C.: Georgetown University Press, 1982).

69. Conversations with officials in the Departments of State and Defense, *Washington Post*, October 16 and November 1, 1982.

70. Conversations with Turkish academics and officials in the military and foreign ministry, Istanbul and Ankara, Turkey. For discussion of these issues see also Duygu Sezer, "Turkey's Security Policies," *Adelphi Paper 164*, spring 1981, p. 38. Sezer observed that even though association with the U.S. entails risks, eliminating that association will not eliminate other risks and could increase them. The difficult choices confronting Turkey arise because, like most countries, it is neither totally secure nor totally threatened. See also, Harris, "The View from Ankara," *Wilson Quarterly* 6, no. 5 (1982), p. 132.

71. William Barnds, *India, Pakistan, and the Great Powers* (New York: Praeger, 1972), p. 347.

72. Jagat Singh Mehta, "The Origin of the Cold Wars: Myopia and Misperceptions in the Great Powers and the Subcontinent," Colloquium Paper, Woodrow Wilson International Center for Scholars, Washington, D.C., April 19, 1982.

73. See "Shared Security Concerns: U.S. Cooperation with Pakistan," *Current Policy no. 347*, Bureau of Public Affairs (Washington, D.C.: U.S. Department of State, November 12, 1982); *The Military Balance: 1982-1983* (London: International Institute for Strategic Studies, autumn 1982); and the *International Herald Tribune*, May 21-22, June 5, and July 2-3, 1983.

74. Bernard Weinraub, *International Herald Tribune*, May 21-22, 1983; "Shultz Tries to Keep U.S.-Indian Ties Durable—But Vague," *Christian Science Monitor*, July 5, 1983; and Michael Weisskopf and Don Oberdorfer, *Washington Post*, June 13, 1985.

75. See Don Oberdorfer and William Claiborne, *International Herald Tribune* July 2-3, 1983.

76. For indication of India's desire to move in this direction, see Walter Andersen, "India in 1982: Domestic Challenges and Foreign Policy Successes," *Asian Survey* 23, no. 2 (1983), pp. 111-122 and note 74.

77. The best summary of the nuclear problem in South Asia is Richard C. Cronin, "Prospects for Nuclear Proliferation in South Asia," *Middle East Journal* 37, no. 4 (1983), pp. 594-616. Cronin stresses the limited influence available to supplier countries and argues that the prospects of proliferation are primarily dependent on the dynamics of India-Pakistan relations. The best hope for containing the problems, he believes, lies in the normalization of India-Pakistan relations. The prospects for normalization, of course, depend on internal as well as on external security. Christopher Van Hollen, "Leaning on Pakistan," *Foreign Policy* 38 (1980), pp. 35-50, correctly observes that "if Pakistan is to become genuinely secure, it must be encouraged to liberalize its internal political system and move toward rapprochement with India" (p. 50). For a corroboration of the liberalization argument with respect to the Baluch issue, see Selig Harrison, *In Afghanistan's Shadow: Baluch*

Nationalism and Soviet Temptations (Washington, D.C.: Carnegie Endowment for International Peace, 1981).

78. For discussion of the merits and problems of a Swedenized South and Southwest Asia and a Finlandized Afghanistan, see Jagat Mehta, "Afghanistan: A Neutral Solution," *Foreign Policy* 47 (summer 1982), pp. 139–153, and the letters to the editor, *Foreign Policy* 49 (winter 1982–1983), pp. 186–190.

79. For indications of India's intentions to conduct a second underground test in the Rajasthan desert (the first was conducted in 1974), see *International Herald Tribune* June 24 and July 16–17, 1983; for one of the many discussions of Pakistan's desire to acquire a nuclear potential, see *Christian Science Monitor*, December 1, 1981.

80. For a discussion of Pakistani fears, see Imroze Sagar, "Indo-Soviet Strategic Interests and Collaboration," *Naval War College Review* 34, no. 1 (1981), pp. 13–33; and Parvaiz Iqbal Cheema, "The Afghanistan Crisis and Pakistan's Security Dilemma," *Asian Survey* 33, no. 3 (1983), pp. 227–243.

81. For recent arguments along these lines that suggest the virtues of detaching India from its virtual alliance with the Soviet Union and steering it toward a true neutrality and reconciliation with Pakistan, see Lawrence Ziring, "Indo-Pakistani Relations: Time for A Fresh Start," *Asian Affairs* 8, no. 4 (1981), pp. 199–215; the references in note 74; and Amaury de Riencourt, "India and Pakistan in the Shadow of Afghanistan," *Foreign Affairs* 61, no. 2 (1982–1983), pp. 416–437. For the difficulty of this endeavor, see S. Nihal Singh, "Can the U.S. and India Be Real Friends?" *Asian Survey* 23, no. 9 (1983), pp. 1011–1024.

82. In addition to the sources cited, see Robert L. Horn, "Afghanistan and the Soviet-Indian Influence Relationship," *Asian Survey* 23, no. 3 (1983), pp. 244–260.

83. For discussion of the Saudi-Pakistani relationship, see the sources cited in note 44.

84. During the Carter administration, the Pakistanis rejected a U.S. proposal that they redeploy their forces from the Indian to the Afghan fronts because of their belief that India was a more serious threat. Raju G.C. Thomas, "The Afghanistan Crisis and South Asian Security," *Journal of Strategic Studies* 4, no. 4 (1981), p. 428.

85. President Zia ul-Haq apparently felt that the $400 million offer was enough to provoke hostility without ensuring security (*New York Times*, July 16, 1980).

86. A number of individuals have noted the popularity in Pakistan—even among the military—of closer ties with the Soviet Union. The real debate developing within Pakistan, Ghulam Mustafa Khar has asserted, "is about whether to accept the Soviet or Indian alternatives" (Khar, "Four Choices Facing Front-Line Pakistan," *The Economist* 281 [October 31, 1981], p. 27. See also Ali Mehrunnisa, "Soviet-Pakistan Ties Since the Afghan Crisis," *Asian Survey* 23, no. 9 (1983), pp. 1025–1042; and Javad Ansari, "Pakistan Revisited," who notes the Pakistan army's need for political rapprochement with the Soviet Union and the People's party's desire to abandon the Afghan *jihad*. One observer has suggested that the United States leaked news of its aid to Afghanistan to prevent Pakistan from being more receptive to Soviet overtures over the Afghan problem. The leverage held by the United States is that Pakistan could lose U.S. assistance if it is too soft. See Mary Anne Weaver, *Christian Science Monitor*, May 10, and Louis Wiznitzer, *Christian Science Monitor*, June 14, 1983.

87. Selig Harrison, "A Breakthrough in Afghanistan?" *Foreign Policy* 51 (summer 1983), pp. 8–9; Dmitri Simes, *Christian Science Monitor*, June 13, 1983; Yossef Bodansky, cited in Drew Middleton, *International Herald Tribune*, November 8, 1983; and de Riencourt, "India and China in the Shadow of Afghanistan," p. 432.

88. Nancy Newell and Richard Newell, *The Struggle for Afghanistan* (Ithaca, N.Y.: Cornell University Press, 1981), p. 211.

89. See the editorial page, *Christian Science Monitor*, December 14, 1983.

90. For a discussion of attacks by conservatives and liberals on the strategy—or absence of strategy—that provides a rationale for the administration's military spending plans, see Richard Halloran in the *New York Times*, March 22, 1982. For a discussion of the administration's response to this criticism and the FY 1984-1988 Defense Guidance, see the *New York Times*, May 25 and 30, 1982; and the *Washington Post*, May 27 and June 2, 1982. See also Brad Knickerbocker, *Christian Science Monitor*, June 15 and July 28, 1983.

91. In spite of a complacency regarding energy use, the International Energy Agency in October 1982 concluded that unless nations did more to reduce their dependence on imported oil, the world could face shortages of up to 4 mbd of oil by 1990 (*Christian Science Monitor*, October 18, 1982). See also the concerns about a third oil shock expressed in Daniel Yergin and Martin Hillenbrand, eds., *Global Insecurity: A Strategy for Energy and Economic Renewal* (Boston: Houghton Mifflin, 1982); and Daniel Yergin, "Third Oil Shock Might be Manageable After All," *International Herald Tribune*, October 17, 1983, who notes that what kept the Iran-Iraq war from having any effect on the world oil market was a large cushion of unused capacity resulting from conservation, recession, fuel switching, and new oil production. His concern is that escalation of hostilities in the Gulf could raise the question of yet another oil shock and that complacency, coupled with a return to dependence on the Gulf, could make the consequences of instability in that region even more dangerous for the world economy. See also note 1.

Selected Bibliography

Ajami, Fouad, *The Vanished Iman: Musa al Sadr and the Shia of Lebanon*, Ithaca, New York: Cornell University Press, 1986

Bakhash, Shaul, *The Politics of Oil and the Revolution in Iran*, Washington, D.C.: Brookings Institution, 1982

————, *Reign of the Ayatollahs: Iran and Islamic Revolution*, New York: Basic Books, 1986

Batatu, Hanna, *The Old Social Classes and the Revolutionary Movements of Iraq: A Study of Iraq's Old Landed and Commercial Classes and of its Communists, Ba'athists and Free Officers*, Princeton, N.J.: Princeton University Press, 1979

Benard, Cheryl, and Zalmay Khalilzad, *The Government of God: Iran's Islamic Republic*, New York: Columbia University Press, 1984

Brown, L. Carl, *International Politics and the Middle East: Old Rules, Dangerous Game*, Princeton, N.J.: Princeton University Press, 1984

Chubin, Shahram, *The Scope and Conditions of Outside Power Influences in the Persian Gulf*, London: IISS, Gower Press, 1981

————, *The Foreign Policy of the Islamic Republic of Iran*, Geneva: Graduate Institute of International Studies, 1984

Cole, Juan, and Nikki Keddi, eds., *Shi'ism and Social Protest*, New Haven, Conn.: Yale University Press, 1985

Congressional Quarterly, *The Middle East*, sixth edition, Washington, D.C., 1986

Congressional Research Service, *The Search for Peace in the Middle East: Documents and Statements 1967-1979*, report prepared for the Subcommittee on Europe and the Middle East of the Committee on Foreign Affairs, U.S. House of Representatives, Washington, D.C., Government Printing Office, 1979

Cordesman, Anthony H., *The Gulf and the Search for Strategic Stability: Saudi Arabia, the Military Balance in the Gulf, and Trends in the Arab-Israeli Military Balance*, Boulder, Colo.: Westview Press, 1984

Dawisha, Adeed, *Islam in Foreign Policy*, New York: Cambridge University Press, 1986

Dawisha, Adeed, and Karen Dawisha, eds., *The Soviet Union and the Middle East*, London: Heinemann Educational Books, 1982

Day, Arthur R., *East Bank/West Bank: Jordan and the Prospects for Peace*, New York: Council on Foreign Relations, 1986

Deeb, Marius, *The Lebanese Civil War*, New York: Praeger, 1980

Dessouki, Ali E. Hillal, *Egypt and the Great Powers 1973-1981*, Tokyo: Institute for Developing Economies, 1983

Devlin, John F., *The Ba'ath Party: A History From Its Origins to 1966*, Stanford, Calif.: Hoover Institution Press, 1976

————, *Syria: Modern State in an Ancient Land*, Boulder, Colo.: Westview, 1982

Fahmy, Ismail, *Negotiating for Peace in the Middle East: An Arab View*, Baltimore, Md.: Johns Hopkins University Press, 1983

Freedman, Robert O., *Soviet Policy Toward the Middle East since 1970*, third edition, New York: Praeger, 1982

_____ , *Israel in the Begin Era*, New York: Praeger, 1982

Heller, Mark A., *A Palestinian State: The Implications for Israel*, Cambridge, Mass.: Harvard University Press, 1983

_____ , *The Iran-Iraq War: Implications for Third Parties*, Tel Aviv: Jaffee Center for Strategic Studies of Tel Aviv University, 1984

Helms, Christine, *The Cohesion of Saudi Arabia: Evolution of Political Identity*, Baltimore, Md.: Johns Hopkins University Press, 1981

_____ , *Iraq: Eastern Flank of the Arab World*, Washington, D.C.: Brookings Institution, 1984

Jansen, Michael, *The Battle of Beirut: Why Israel Invaded Lebanon*, Boston: South End Press, 1982

Kerr, Malcolm H., and El Sayed Yassin, eds., *Rich and Poor States in the Middle East: Egypt and the New Arab Order*, Boulder, Colo.: Westview Press, 1982

Khalek, Gouda Abdel, and Robert Tigonor, eds., *The Political Economy of Income Distribution in Egypt*, New York: Holmes and Meier, 1982

Khalidi, Rashid, *Under Siege: PLO Decisionmaking during the 1982 War*, New York: Columbia University Press, 1986

Khalidi, Walid, *Conflict and Violence in Lebanon: Confrontation in the Middle East*, Cambridge: Center for International Affairs, Harvard University, 1979

Kolodziej, Edward A., and Robert E. Harkavy, eds., *Security Policies of Developing Countries*, Lexington, Mass., and Toronto: Lexington Books, Heath, 1982

Korany, Baghat, and Ali E. Hillal Dessouki, *The Foreign Policies of the Arab States*, Boulder, Colo.: Westview Press, 1984

Kuniholm, Bruce R., *The Origins of the Cold War in the Near East: Great Power Conflict and Diplomacy in Iran, Turkey, and Greece*, Princeton, N.J.: Princeton University Press, 1980

_____ , *The Persian Gulf and US Policy*, Claremont, Calif.: Regina Press, 1984

Lenczowski, George, *The Middle East in World Affairs*, New York: Cornell University Press, 1980

Lieber, Robert J., *The Oil Decade: Conflict and Cooperation in the West*, New York, Praeger, 1983, and Lanham, Md.: University Press of America, 1986

Litwak, Robert S., *Security in the Persian Gulf, Vol. II: Sources of Interstate Conflict*, London: IISS Gower Press, 1981

Mansfield, Peter, *The Middle East: A Political and Economic Survey*, fifth edition, New York: Oxford University Press, 1980

Ma'oz, Moshe, *Palestinian Leadership on the West Bank: The Changing Role of Mayors under Jordan and Israel*, London: Cass, 1984

Ma'oz, Moshe, and Avner Yanov, eds., *Syria under Assad: Domestic Constraints and Regional Crises*, New York: St. Martin's Press, 1986

Marantz, Paul, ed., *Superpower Involvement in the Middle East: The Dynamics of Foreign Policy*, Boulder, Colo.: Westview Press, 1985

Mortimer, Edward, *Faith and Power: The Politics of Islam*, New York: Random House, 1982

Polk, William R., *The Arab World*, Cambridge, Mass.: Harvard University Press, 1980

Quandt, William B., *Decade of Decision: American Policy Toward the Arab-Israeli Conflict, 1967–1976*, Berkeley, Calif.: University of California Press, 1977

_____ , *Saudi Arabia: Foreign Policy, Security, and Oil*, Washington, D.C.: Brookings Institution, 1981

————, *Camp David: Peacemaking and Politics*, Washington, D.C.: Brookings Institution, 1986

Rabinovich, I., and H. Shaked, eds., *From June to October: The Middle East between 1967–1973*, New Brunswick, N.J.: Transaction Books, 1977

Rafael, Gideon, *Destination Peace: Three Decades of Israeli Foreign Policy*, New York: Stein and Day, 1981

Reich, Bernard, *The United States and Israel: Influence in the Special Relationship*, New York: Praeger, 1984

Rubin, Barry, *Paved with Good Intentions: The American Experience and Iran*, New York: Oxford University Press, 1980

————, *The Arab States and the Palestine Conflict*, New York: Syracuse University Press, 1981

Rubinstein, Alvin, *Soviet Policy Toward Turkey, Iran and Afghanistan: The Dynamics of Influence*, New York: Praeger, 1982

Salibi, Kamal S., *Crossroads to Civil War: Lebanon 1959–1976*, Delmar, N.Y.: Caravan, 1976

Saunders, Harold H., *The Middle East Problem in the 1980s*, Washington, D.C.: American Enterprise Institute, 1981

————, *The Other Walls: The Politics of the Arab-Israeli Peace Process*, Washington, D.C.: American Enterprise Institute, 1985

Schiff, Ze'ev, and Ehud Ya'ari, *Israel's Lebanon War*, New York: Simon and Schuster, 1984

Sick, Gary, *All Fall Down: America's Tragic Encounter with Iran*, New York: Random House, 1985

Speigel, Steven L., ed., *The Middle East and the Western Alliance*, London: Allen and Unwin, 1982

Tillman, Seth P., *The United States in the Middle East: Interests and Obstacles*, Bloomington, Ind.: Indiana University Press, 1982

van Dam, Nikolas, *The Struggle for Power in Syria*, second edition, London: Croom Helm, 1981

Vatikiotis, P. J., *Arab and Regional Politics in the Middle East*, New York: St. Martin's Press, 1984

About the Editors and Contributors

Samuel F. Wells, Jr., is associate director of the Woodrow Wilson International Center for Scholars in Washington, D.C., and chairman of its European Institute. He was educated at the University of North Carolina at Chapel Hill and at Harvard University and has taught history and defense studies at the University of North Carolina at Chapel Hill, where he directed the Richardson Fellows Program (an experimental leadership program for undergraduates) and was a member of the directing committee for the Curriculum in Peace, War, and Defense.

He is the author of numerous articles on defense and foreign policy and the co-author of *The Ordeal of World Power: American Diplomacy Since 1900* (1975). He was a contributor to and co-editor of *Economics and World Power: An Assessment of American Diplomacy Since 1789* (1984) and co-editor of *Limiting Nuclear Proliferation* (1985) and of *Strategic Defenses and Soviet-American Relations* (1987).

During 1974–76 Wells participated in an extensive study of the Soviet-American strategic arms competition sponsored by the Department of Defense. He had earlier served as an artillery officer in the U.S. Marine Corps, rising to the rank of captain. He has held fellowship appointments at the Hoover Institution, Woodrow Wilson International Center for Scholars, and the Institut Français des Relations Internationales and was the recipient of a three-year Ford Foundation grant for research in international security.

Mark A. Bruzonsky is a journalist, political consultant, and lawyer specializing in Middle East and international affairs. He has been the associate editor of *Worldview Magazine*, interview editor of *The Middle East Magazine*, Washington associate of the World Jewish Congress, adviser to Philip M. Klutznick, and consultant on Middle East affairs to the Wilson Center, the National Geographic Society, and Congressional Quarterly. He has previously edited *The Middle East: U.S. Policy, Israel, Oil, and the Arabs* (Congressional Quarterly, 3rd edition) and is now completing *Peace Between Arab and Jew*, a book of readings from Jewish leaders from the 1920s to the present. In November 1977 Bruzonsky interviewed Egyptian President Anwar Sadat five days before his historic visit to Jerusalem and arranged for the first telegram ever sent from an Arab leader to Israel. In July 1982 he authored "The Paris Declaration" in which three of the world's most prominent Jewish personalities—Nahum Goldmann, Philip Klutznick, and Pierre Mendès-

France—jointly called for an immediate end to Israel's invasion of Lebanon, direct negotiations between Israel and the PLO, and creation of a Palestinian homeland. As a journalist his articles and analyses have appeared widely throughout the Middle East, the United States and Great Britain. Bruzonsky received his B.A. in economics and government from Lawrence University, his M.P.A. in international affairs from Princeton's Woodrow Wilson School, and his J.D. from New York University Law School where he was a Root Tilden Scholar. From 1971 to 1973 he served as chief representative to the United Nations for the International Students movement for the United Nations (ISMUN).

Shahram Chubin is director of research in the Programme for Strategic and International Studies at the Graduate Institute of International Studies in Geneva. He has taught at the Fletcher School of Law and Diplomacy, has directed the Regional Security Programme at the International Institute for Strategic Studies in London (1977–1981), and has been a research fellow at the Institute for Political and Economic Studies in Tehran (1974–1976). During a guest scholarship at the Wilson Center in 1984 he worked on a comparative study of regional conflicts in the third world. His publications on the Middle East include *The Role of the Outside Powers in the Persian Gulf* (London: IISS, 1981), "The USSR and Iran" (*Foreign Affairs*, spring 1983), and "Reflections on the Gulf War" (*Survival*, July/August 1986).

Adeed I. Dawisha is professor of government and politics at George Mason University. Born in Iraq and educated in Britain, Dawisha is a specialist on the Middle East. During a fellowship at the Wilson Center in 1985–86 he completed a project on Arab politics and the lessons and implications for the United States. He is the author of numerous books, the latest of which is *The Arab Radicals* (New York: Council on Foreign Relations, 1986).

Ali E. Hillal Dessouki is professor in the Faculty of Economics and Political Science and director of the Center for Political Studies at Cairo University. Dessouki has also been an adviser to the Minister of Information, Egypt (1975-1976), a visiting professor at UCLA (1979-1980), and a fellow at the Center of International Studies, Princeton University (1980-1981). His book *Politics and Government in Egypt* (in Arabic, 1978) was awarded Egypt's state prize for best book in political analysis.

John F. Devlin is an independent consultant. He held several posts in the Middle East (1953-1959) while in the U.S. Foreign Service. In 1960 he joined the Central Intelligence Agency; from the mid-1960s to 1973 he directed the Near East Staff in the Office of National Estimates and later became deputy director of its Office of Political Research (1974-1977). His publications on the Middle East include *The Ba'ath Party: A History from its Origins to 1966* (Stanford, Calif.: Hoover Institution Press, 1976) and *Syria: Modern State in an Ancient Land* (Boulder, Colo.: Westview, 1982).

Simha Flapan, in Palestine since 1930, lived in a kibbutz until 1972. He was director of the Arab Department of Mapam (1954–1965) and founder and editor of *New Outlook* (1957–1982). He is the author of *Zionism and the Palestinians* (1979) and many essays. In 1982 he received the Kreisky Foundation Human Rights Award for his work for Israeli-Palestinian peace.

Christine Moss Helms is program analyst for the directorate of international activities at the Smithsonian Institution. Prior to assuming this position, she was a research associate in foreign policy studies at the Brookings Institution. She hs been a consultant for numerous organizations including the National Geographic Society. Her works on the Middle East include *The Cohesion of Saudi Arabia: Evolution of Political Identity* (1981) and *Iraq: Eastern Flank of the Arab World* (1984). She is currently researching a work to be entitled *Islamic Paradigm: A Graceless World Refined*.

Herbert C. Kelman is Cabot Professor of Social Ethics at Harvard University and associated with the Harvard Center for International Affairs, whose Middle East Seminar he has chaired since 1977. Kelman did his doctoral research in psychology (with emphasis on social psychology) at Yale University and has strong interest in the social-psychological dimensions of international relations. He helped lay the groundwork for the development of the peace research movement and was a cofounder of the *Journal of Conflict Resolution*. His publications on international relations include *International Behavior: A Social-Psychological Analysis* (1965). Kelman was a Wilson Center fellow in 1980-1981.

Bruce R. Kuniholm is associate professor of history and public policy and director of undergraduate studies at the Institute of Policy Studies and Public Affairs, Duke University. He has been a Council on Foreign Relations International Affairs fellow, has served on the Department of State's Policy Planning Staff, and was a fellow at the Wilson Center in 1986-1987. His publications include *The Origins of the Cold War in the Near East: Great Power Conflict and Diplomacy in Iran, Turkey and Greece* (Princeton, N.J.: Princeton University Press, 1980), which won the Stuart L. Bernath prize in 1981, and *The Persian Gulf and United States Policy* (Claremont, Calif.: Regina Press, 1984). He is currently working on a book on U.S.-Turkish relations from World War II to the present.

Robert J. Lieber is professor of government at Georgetown University. His most recent book is *The Oil Decade* (1983, 1986). He is also co-editor (with Kenneth Oye and Donald Rothchild) of and contributing author to *Eagle Resurgent? The Reagan Era in American Foreign Policy* (1987). Lieber was a fellow at the Wilson Center in 1980-1981, during which time he completed a study on European-American relations and the international energy crisis.

Robert S. Litwak is senior program associate in the International Security Studies Program at the Woodrow Wilson International Center for Scholars. He is the author of *Détente and the Nixon Doctrine* (Cambridge, England: Cambridge University Press, 1984) and *Security in the Persian Gulf, Vol. II: Sources of Interstate Conflict* (London: IISS, 1981). Litwak is currently working on a study of Soviet foreign and military policies in the third world.

Augustus Richard Norton is permanent associate professor of comparative politics in the Social Science Department at the U.S. Military Academy at West Point, New York. His articles on Lebanon have appeared in a number of well-known publications including the *New York Times*, the *Los Angeles Times*, *Wall Street Journal*, *Middle East Journal*, and *Middle East Insights*, and he is the author of *Amal and the Shi'a: Struggle for the Soul of Lebanon* (Austin: University of Texas Press, 1987).

Bernard Reich is professor of political science and international affairs and former chairman of the Department of Political Science at George Washington University in Washington, D.C. He also serves as a consultant on Middle Eastern affairs to various U.S. government agencies. He is the author of numerous books and articles on the Middle East including *Quest for Peace: United States-Israel Relations and the Arab-Israeli Conflict* (1977), *The United States and Israel: Influence in the Special Relationship* (1984), and *Israel: Land of Tradition and Conflict* (Boulder, Colo.: Westview, 1985). He is co-editor of *The Government and Politics of the Middle East and North Africa* (Boulder, Colo.: Westview, 1980 and 1986) and *Israel Faces the Future* (1986).

Dennis Ross is director of Near East and South Asia affairs on the National Security Council staff. Prior to becoming director of this office, he served as special assistant to the president for national security affairs and senior director of Near East and South Asia affairs on the NSC staff. Before joining the NSC, Ross was executive director of the Berkeley-Stanford Program on Soviet International Behavior, deputy director of the Office of Net Assessment in the Office of the Secretary of Defense (1982–1984), and senior staff member responsible for Middle East Affairs on the Policy Planning Staff in the State Department. He has published extensively on Soviet and Middle East issues, with a special emphasis on Soviet behavior in the Middle East.

Harold H. Saunders became visiting fellow at the Brookings Institution in 1987. He was previously resident fellow at the American Enterprise Institute for Public Policy Research in Washington, D.C., from 1981 through 1986. He served on the National Security Council staff, 1961-1974. In the State Department he has held positions as deputy assistant secretary (1974-1975), assistant secretary for Near Eastern and South Asian affairs (1978-1981), and director of the Bureau of Intelligence Research (1975-1978). He flew on the Kissinger shuttles and participated in the Camp David negotiations. His publications on the Middle East include *The Middle East Problem in the 1980s* (Washington, D.C.: American Enterprise Institute, 1981) and *The Other Walls: The Politics of the Arab-Israeli Peace Process* (Washington, D.C.: American Enterprise Institute, 1985).

Index